A History of Political Trials

The Past in the Present

Editor in Chief

Francis Robinson, Royal Holloway, University of London

Editorial Board

John Laughland

A History of Political Trials

From Charles I to Saddam Hussein

Peter Lang Oxford

Cover design: Dan Mogford

First published in 2008 by Peter Lang Ltd
International Academic Publishers, Evenlode Court, Main Road,
Long Hanborough, Witney, Oxfordshire OX29 8SZ, England
© Peter Lang Ltd 2008
www.thepastinthepresent.com, www.peterlang.com

British Library and Library of Congress Cataloguing-in Publication Data:
A catalogue record for this book is available from the British Library,
UK, and the Library of Congress, USA.

ISBN 978-1-906165-00-0 (Paperback)
ISBN 978-1-906165-05-5 (Hardback)

Printed in Hong Kong

To Emily, for Lydia, with love

Can one save a king who is on trial? He is dead as soon as he appears in front of his judges.
(Peut-on sauver un roi mis en jugement? Il est mort quand il paraît devant ses juges)

Danton, remark to Théodore de Lameth, November 1792
(Théodore de Lameth, *Mémoires*, p. 243)

We mean [by the rule of law], in the first place, that no man is punishable or can be made to suffer in body or goods except for a distinct breach of law established in the ordinary legal manner before the ordinary courts of the land.

A. V. Dicey, *Introduction to the Study of the Law of the Constitution*, ch. 4

Contents

Acknowledgements   11

Introduction   13
1   The Trial of Charles I and the Last Judgement   21
2   The Trial of Louis XVI and the Terror   35
3   War Guilt after World War I   51
4   Defeat in the Dock: the Riom Trial   63
5   Justice as Purge: Marshal Pétain Faces his Accusers   77
6   Treachery on Trial: the Case of Vidkun Quisling   91
7   Nuremberg: Making War Illegal   103
8   Creating Legitimacy: the Trial of Marshal Antonescu   119
9   Ethnic Cleansing and National Cleansing in
     Czechoslovakia, 1945–1947   129
10   People's Justice in Liberated Hungary   143
11   From Mass Execution to Amnesty and Pardon: Postwar
     Trials in Bulgaria, Finland, and Greece   153
12   Politics as Conspiracy: the Tokyo Trials   163
13   The Greek Colonels, Emperor Bokassa, and the Argentine
     Generals: Transitional Justice, 1975–2007   175
14   Revolution Returns: the Trial of Nicolae Ceauşescu   185
15   A State on Trial: Erich Honecker in Moabit   195
16   Jean Kambanda, Convicted without Trial   207
17   Kosovo and the New World Order: the Trial of Slobodan
     Milošević   221
18   Regime Change and the Trial of Saddam Hussein   237
     Conclusion   251

Notes   259
Bibliography and Further Reading   285
Index   295

Acknowledgements

In writing this book, I have contacted many people out of the blue, asking them for help. I have been immensely touched by the generosity with which they have responded, spent time on my requests, and imparted their knowledge. I am in debt to the following for their kindness:

Chris Black, David Brewer, Richard Crampton, István Deák, Vesselin Dimitrov, Penelope Evans, James Felak, Aaron Fichtelberg, Ivaylo Gatev, Milan Grba, David Jacobs, László Karsai, Lasse Lehtinen, Radomír Malý, Takis Nitis, Hannu Rautkallio, Filip Reyntjens, Urmi Shah, Phil Taylor, Kjetil Tronvoll, Ilya Vlassov, James Ward.

Introduction

Whenever heads of state go on trial these days – and the phenomenon is becoming increasingly common – you can usually rely on someone to say that the event is unprecedented. In October 2007 a leading human rights organization said that the extradition of the former Peruvian president, Alberto Fujimori, to his native country from Chile was 'the first time that a court has ordered the extradition of a former head of state to be tried for gross human rights violations in his home country.' The same organization had previously said that the conviction for genocide of Jean Kambanda, the former prime minister of Rwanda, in 1998, was 'historic'; that the trial of Slobodan Milošević, the former president of Yugoslavia, from 2001 to 2006, was 'ground-breaking'; and that the trial of Charles Taylor, former president of Liberia, which started in late 2007, was 'a break with the past'.[1]

The reason why such trials are greeted as marking new events is that they are indeed part of a new trend towards military and judicial interventionism, and towards rule by supranational political and judicial institutions. In most cases, recent trials of heads of state have been conducted before those international or partly international tribunals which have proliferated since the end of the Cold War: the International Criminal Tribunal for the former Yugoslavia (ICTY, created in 1993); the International Criminal Tribunal for Rwanda (ICTR, created in 1994); the Special Court for Sierra Leone (created in 1996, which organized the trial of Charles Taylor, the former president of Liberia, in The Hague); the International Criminal Court (ICC, created in 2002); and the Iraqi Special Tribunal (created by the American-run Coalition Provisional Authority in Iraq in 2003). In other cases, recent trials or attempted trials of heads of state have had an important international component: General Pinochet, the former president of Chile, was arrested in London on an warrant issued by a judge in Spain who invoked universal laws against torture. (The attempted extradition was rejected on medical grounds and Pinochet eventually returned to Chile, where he faced further legal procedures but died before ever coming to trial.) Meanwhile, former president Fujimori was extradited from Chile to Peru on a similar legal basis.

In tandem with this development, the post-Cold War period has also been marked by a rise in the view that international law should be coercive (instead of consensual, as in the past) and that, if necessary, war should be waged against states for failing to observe it or to protect universal human rights. The new coercive nature of international law was born when the United Nations Security Council authorized a coalition of states under United States leadership to repel Iraqi forces from Kuwait following the invasion of that country in August 1990: on that occasion, the then American president, George H. W. Bush, proclaimed 'a new world order'[2], by which he meant that international law would henceforth be enforced by means of military violence. The same sentiment was expressed at the end of the decade by the chief prosecutor of the ICTY, Louise Arbour, who said, 'We have passed from an era of co-operation between states into an era in which states can be constrained.'[3]

The key point about this new development is that states, and the political decisions of their leaders, are henceforth subject to a body of law which is tailor-made for the purpose of controlling them and generally applied by external (international) bodies or by other states calling themselves 'the international community'. As a leading proponent of this trend has eloquently argued, 'The movement for global justice has been a struggle against sovereignty.'[4] This is because human rights law is specifically law directed to deal with state acts, not with the acts of private individuals: 'What sets a crime against humanity apart both in wickedness and in the need for special measures of deterrence is the simple fact that it is an act of real brutality ordained by government – or at least by an organisation exercising or asserting political power. It is not the mind of the torturer but the fact that this individual is part of the apparatus of a state which makes the crime so horrific.'[5] Human rights law is not interested in torture if it is practised by a drug-dealer to extort money from his clients, but only if it is practised by an officer of a state.

The doctrine of universal human rights has therefore quickly become a basis for overriding national sovereignty, which until then had been the bedrock of the international system. While the doctrine of human rights appears to be incontestably moral and above politics, it is in fact the basis for a highly ambitious political project involving the creation of a new supranational jurisdiction and new law – a new right to rule. This development has inevitably led to the wielding of new political power through war. Whereas non-interference in the internal affairs of states had been a key principle of international law – for the simple reason that states were not considered to have legal jurisdiction outside their own borders, and because there was no supranational organization which had such jurisdiction either – the proclamation of 'no-fly zones' over the North and South of Iraq in 1991, on the basis that human rights were being abused in Iraq, heralded a new departure in international law. On the basis of it, Iraq was bombed, more or less continuously, until the invasion of 2003. This new philosophy of international relations also led to the 1999 attack on Yugoslavia by NATO, a war not authorised by the UN Security Council but justified on the purely moral (not really legal) claim that it was being waged against a state which was abusing its own people and violating their human rights. As the president of Yugoslavia was indicted by the ICTY at the height of the bombing – on the basis of exactly the same allegations as those being made by NATO – the twin principles of military and judicial interventionism became so completely intertwined with one another that they were effectively indistinguishable.

Whereas international affairs (including war) and domestic policing and judicial policy had previously been regarded as separate domains – the international system being based on the principle that all states are both sovereign and equal – they were soon blended together in the anti-egalitarian concept of 'rogue states' (some states are better than others) and in the interesting oxymoron, 'the war on terror' (which presents international war as being akin to internal policing). And because the policies of interventionism and regime change became so quickly entrenched, it seemed almost natural that the occupying forces in Iraq in 2003 should abrogate the country's constitution and sack most of its judges, even though the existing international law on the rights of occupying authorities prohibits this, and that the former president, Saddam Hussein, should be put on trial for human rights abuses, as duly occurred in 2005.

By the same token, few expressed surprise when, in February 2007, the ICC adopted the interventionist practices of the ICTY and issued an indictment against a Sudanese minister, even though Sudan is not a signatory state of the ICC treaty and therefore does not come under its jurisdiction. This new interventionism stands in stark contrast to what the American judges said at Nuremberg in 1947, when they specifically ruled it out: 'Within the territorial boundaries of a state having a recognised, functioning government presently in the exercise of sovereign power throughout its territory, a violator of the rules of international law could be punished only by the authority of the officials of that state.' The power 'to establish judicial machinery for the punishment of those who have violated the rules of the common international law,' they went on, could never be assumed or exercised 'by an international authority without consent ... within a state having a national government presently in the exercise of sovereign powers.'[6]

Human rights activists hail this brave new world in which the judicial system is used to enforce political change, and to bring dictators to heel, the fashionable name for which is 'transitional justice'. They foresee a new regime in which they will say who has the right to rule and who does not. But the general principle of subjecting heads of state (and therefore acts of state) to the criminal law is in fact neither new nor brave. On the contrary, it has a rich and fascinating history which it is the goal of this book to examine. What follows, indeed, is a chronological account of the development of that specific phenomenon, the organization of criminal trials of heads of state (and heads of government) for acts of state. The story begins with the trial of Charles I in 1649, and a very large number of such trials were conducted in the aftermath of World War II, but the political ideology behind these trials is generally the same: that the law should be the same for everyone, including sovereigns, and that there should be no impunity for political crimes.

This idea that powerful politicians should be called to account has a very deep appeal. Most people take it for granted that bloody tyrants should not be allowed to kill and steal with impunity, and they welcome the fact that they are put on trial. There is, after all, something especially repugnant about the power of the state being used to commit atrocities against conquered peoples or – perhaps even worse – against the state's own citizens. Such acts seem to break the very contract which is at the heart of all societies, namely the overriding duty of the state to protect its citizens, not to persecute them. Rather like treason in wartime, such acts are often considered to make their perpetrators enemies of the people, and perhaps even of humanity itself, putting them firmly outside the normal ambit of the law. It seems obvious that particularly atrocious acts which seem to put the perpetrators beyond the pale of normal human behaviour should be subject to sanction.

However, the desire for vengeance is seldom, on its own, a spur to justice, especially in the case of trials of head of state or government for state acts. There is a danger that too naive a reaction to the welcome spectacle of seeing a tyrant fall can allow new injustices to be committed. It is important, therefore, to look more closely at the historical record of these trials, especially at a time when new political and judicial institutions are being set up on the basis that they are desirable, because the prosecution of political sovereigns as criminals raises the most fundamental questions of political philosophy. Who has the right to conduct criminal prosecutions? Who has the right to adjudicate the acts of another state? What accountability is there for the decisions taken by international tribunals? To what extent is the trial of a defeated enemy an example of victors' justice? Why are his crimes on trial and not those of the people bringing the prosecution? What are the rights and motives of the prosecution itself? How can the demand that the law should be the same for all be reconciled with the widespread practice (common throughout history, as we shall see) of creating 'special tribunals' to try sovereigns? If the new regime has the power retroactively to declare acts criminal when they were not criminal at the time when they were committed (a common phenomenon, as we shall also see), then what controls are there on the new regime's own power?

And can acts of state really be compared to private crimes? Acts of state are precisely public acts, not private ones. Politicians govern because they have been legally empowered to do so (or at least so they claim) and officers of the state are distinguished from ordinary citizens because the state has the power to take life or to deprive people of their liberty, in war or after a conviction, without being subject to criminal prosecution. Yet can the processes of history, or political careers spanning many years and decades, really be subjected to adjudication by procedures which have been designed for common murderers? What happens to the criminal law when vast events are subject to its adjudication? Does it rise to the occasion and offer truth and reconciliation, or does it simply break down under the burden? Does it represent a welcome full stop after a period of conflict, or does it merely represent a final stage in the cycle of vengeance, perhaps even distorting historical truth in the process?

The expression 'political trials' in the title of this book is therefore not used, as it commonly is, to denote prosecutions brought against political opponents in general for the purpose of eliminating them. The focus here is on the prosecution of true acts of state. Trials of heads of state or government will therefore not be discussed if the crimes alleged were matters of private corruption, as was the case, for instance, in the trials of General Noriega of Panama (accused of drug-trafficking) or Deputy Prime Minister Anwar Ibrahim of Malaysia (accused of homosexuality). The same is true of Pol Pot, tried by a 'people's court' of the Khmer Rouge itself not for that regime's judicial murder of millions of Cambodians in the late 1970s, but instead for the killing of one man, his deputy Son Sen, in 1997. I have also not dealt with trials from which the chief defendant was absent for all or most of the proceedings: examples include Pol Pot himself (earlier sentenced to death *in absentia* for genocide by a people's revolutionary tribunal in 1979) and the 'Red Terror trials' of Colonel

Mengistu Hailemariam of Ethiopia and his Derg regime, which ended in the death sentence passed, also *in absentia*, on Mengistu in January 2007, after a trial which had started in 1994 and in which there are over five thousand defendants.[7]

Trials will also not be discussed of holders of high office if the acts for which they were prosecuted were allegedly committed after they had fallen from power, as for instance happened to St Thomas More and Mary Queen of Scots. I have also glossed over trials of co-sovereigns or deputies, like Marie-Antoinette or Pierre Laval, when the primary sovereign is discussed instead. The book will not deal with acts of impeachment brought against heads of state – one thinks of American president Andrew Johnson in 1868, of Bill Clinton in 2000, or of President Rolandas Paksas of Lithuania in 2004 – because impeachment is a political, not a criminal, procedure and the sanction is usually political: Henry the Lion, the duke of Saxony and Bavaria, may have been tried (*in absentia*) by Emperor Frederick Barbarossa in 1180 but his punishment was destitution (i.e. removal from office), not imprisonment or death.

Finally, trials of heads of state and government will not be included if the defendants were not, in fact, sovereigns. In 587 BC, Zedekiah, the last king of Judah, was captured by Nebuchadnezzar's troops after the fall of Jerusalem and 'they gave judgement upon him' (2 Kings 25:6). The Babylonians killed his sons in front of him and then put his eyes out, while the Jews were carted off to their Babylonian captivity. But Zedekiah was not really a sovereign, Judah having fallen under Babylon's suzerainty a few years previously; he was tried for breaking his oath of fealty. His fate therefore resembles that of another head of government, Count Lajos Batthyány, the first prime minister of Hungary, convicted of high treason and executed in 1849 by firing squad for his support for the rebels in the 1848 revolution, and whose crime was therefore to have shown disloyalty to the emperor. (He is revered in Hungary as a patriot.)

The reader will immediately notice two things about the following account: the chronological treatment and the voice given to the Defence. The purpose of the chronological treatment of the subject matter is threefold. The first is to show that, despite modern claims to the contrary, contemporary trials of heads of state do have precedents and these are usually overlooked. By seeing the historical context of such modern trials, we can perhaps avoid the dangers associated with the intoxicating and hubristic belief that one is breaking new ground. The second aim is to show the historical context of certain specific trials. Nuremberg, for instance, which is the great reference point for today's trials, was in fact only one of a very large number of such trials which occurred after World War II, and which were of very questionable regularity. The third goal is to show how similar such trials are across history, with many of the same themes recurring: war, conspiracy, treason and revolution.

I have tried to give voice to the Defence for similar reasons of historical interest: generally speaking, we know more about the reasons why ex-sovereigns were prosecuted than about what they said in reply. The purpose of the book is to encourage people to reflect on the true nature and motives of the Prosecution, and of course on the procedural shortcomings of these trials; there is a danger of too naively believing that because evil men were punished, the Prosecution must have been flawless. But where I have criticized those prosecutions, or drawn attention to the irregularities of the trials, the goal is not necessarily to exonerate the defendants, at least not morally. It is instead to show the intractable difficulty associated with all such political trials: their distinguishing characteristic is that the Prosecution is invariably as political as the Defence. The overriding goal of this book, therefore, is to look at the *constitutional* issues raised by political trials, and by the creation of international tribunals. It is not to discuss the guilt or innocence of individual defendants.

Victors both administer justice and also write the history. Perhaps this is why past trials of heads of state are very often presented as examples of what Oscar Wilde ridiculed as the very definition of fiction: the good ends well and the bad ends badly. I shall argue that the historical account is in fact not kind to the claims made by today's international humanitarian law activists. It is often said that we must understand the past in order to understand the present, but the opposite is also true: it is by observing events in our own day that we can better comprehend historical events (otherwise so distant, often so horrifying). Past and present then interpenetrate one another and the comparison shines back onto our own day, hopefully illuminating the fact that our naively enthusiastic endeavours today have questionable antecedents.

1 The Trial of Charles I and the Last Judgement

The first trial of a head of state for acts committed in his official capacity while in power was that of King Charles I of England in January 1649. His entry as a prisoner into the Palace of Westminster in front of a specially constituted High Court of Justice on a freezing cold morning was both the culmination of a century of religious and political turmoil in England, and also the beginning of the distinctly modern attitude to kingship, sovereignty, and the state.

Ever since Henry VIII had broken with Rome in 1534, England had been engulfed in political and religious upheaval. But the English Civil War (1642–51) mirrored the similar religious wars which ravaged Central Europe from 1618 to 1648. It is generally believed that, when an end was put to that war by the Treaties of Westphalia in 1648, the modern international system was born in which states were considered sovereign, not subject to any superior religious authority. This date, 1648, is generally taken to mark the rise of modern secularism, and the establishment of the key principle of modern politics that there is no religious authority above that of the state. Indeed, the execution of Charles I, and the destruction thereby of belief in the 'divine right of kings', itself occurred in that year according to the way the calendar then worked, since the new year did not begin until March.

It seems wrong, however, to say that that the events in England and the continent were a consequence of the rise of secularism. On the contrary, it was religion that had been the cause of both the English Civil War and the Thirty Years war in Germany. Both conflicts were between two competing theologies: they were not conflicts between a religious and secular outlook. While the war in Europe was essentially between Protestants and Catholics, the English Civil War was, at bottom, a battle over control of the English Church. The Puritans who had seized control of the army were determined to prevent any backsliding by future monarchs towards Rome, and their suspicions that such a rapprochement might occur had been aroused when King Charles married Henriette of France, the daughter of the French king Henri IV and the sister of Louis XIII.

Puritan radicals wanted the wholesale dismantling of the ecclesiastical structure of the Anglican Church which had remained broadly intact even after the Protestant revolution. They rejected the very notion of any Church structure other than that of the faithful gathered together in worship. The English revolutionaries argued that eternal truths were best perceived by 'the saints', i.e. themselves.[1] The problem was not that King Charles believed in the divine right of kings, but that the revolutionaries believed in their own divine right instead. The Puritans' determination to control the Church and Parliament was therefore not a consequence of democratic views. On the contrary, many of the more extreme Puritans specifically disagreed with the notion of the sovereignty of the people, regarding it as a potential impediment to the sovereignty of Christ – administered of course through them.

It was around these fundamental religious differences that the more prosaic battles over the rights of Parliament and the financing of the state crystallized. Charles had summoned Parliament in 1628, when he had accepted its Petition of Right – a statement of Parliament's rights – in order to obtain the funding he needed. But no Parliament was summoned again for a decade. During this period, Charles appointed William Laud as archbishop of Canterbury. Laud was attached to High Anglicanism, a relatively ceremonial form of Protestantism which keeps one or two of the exterior forms of the old Catholic faith without actually abandoning Anglicanism's key Protestant tenets. Laud introduced some superficial reforms such as putting stone altars back in place of the wooden communion tables which had been introduced at the Reformation. This was enough to convince the Puritans that their king was at the head of a Popish conspiracy, for their religious fundamentalism ran very deep: when the future Prosecutor of King Charles, John Cooke, was born, his parents deliberately travelled for many miles outside their village to have him baptized not by an Anglican priest but instead by a Puritan minister, the difference being that the latter would not even make the sign of the cross over the infant, a gesture rejected by the Puritans as an impure form of worship.[2] It is no doubt for this reason that that great historian of seventeenth-century England, Christopher Hill, emphasized in 1969 that one should not ignore the role of the 'lunatic fringe' in history, i.e. the English revolutionaries.[3]

Violent skirmishes between Scottish opponents of episcopacy and the forces of the Crown broke out in 1639 and 1640, and Charles needed money from Parliament to suppress these rebellions. A newly elected Parliament was summoned in 1640, but its members used the occasion to attack the Crown and its prerogatives. Parliament was dissolved after two weeks but recalled again in November as the king needed money urgently. In May 1641, following the execution by Charles's enemies of Thomas Wentworth, the earl of Strafford, former governor of Ireland, rebellion erupted in Ireland, where Catholics rightly feared the resurgence of vicious Protestantism, and soon that kingdom had descended into anarchy. England quickly followed, and the country polarized into civil war in 1642. Battles raged for three years and the Puritan New Model Army was created in 1645, with Oliver Cromwell second in command. The army was known for its fundamentalist religious ideology and for its modernist doctrine of 'the new man': the army's rule book was called *The Souldiers Catechisme*, and discipline was maintained through regular prayer sessions and the frequent singing of Psalms.

The so-called First Civil War ended in 1646, but the Second Civil War erupted two years later. In the spring of 1648, a group of senior officers from the New Model Army resolved to put Charles on trial in the event of their victory, which duly ensued at the end of that year. The already Manichaean views of the Puritans were only further radicalized when, on 5 December 1648, Parliament voted to come to negotiate a peace agreement with the king; this was furiously denounced as appeasement by the radicals who controlled the army. They were convinced that the king had broken the implicit contract with his people, that he had violated the rights of Parliament, and that his armies had committed war crimes during the civil conflict.

In order to prevent any accommodation between Parliament and the king, therefore, soldiers under the command of Thomas Pride marched on Parliament in December 1648, expelled 180 Members of Parliament from it and arrested forty-five others. These latter were thrown into a cellar nicknamed 'Hell'. The euphemistically named 'Pride's Purge' was, in other words, a simple *coup d'état*. Only one third of the House of Commons was left after this, the first great purge in modern political history, and it was the remaining pro-putsch army collaborators who were then instructed to create the High Court of Justice with the express purpose of trying and convicting the king. The House of Lords was excluded from the process, leaving the truncated House of Commons ('the Rump Parliament') to declare itself the holder of supreme power in the nation.

In spite of the parliamentary and regicide rhetoric claiming that even the king had to be subject to the law, the Act of 6 January 1649 which created the High Court a month after the purge was in fact a Bill of Attainder, i.e. a legislative act providing for the prosecution of a specific individual. The law was specific to the king, not the same for all. Bills of Attainder are among the most notorious abuses of government power, and for this reason they have been illegal ever since: laws are precisely general statements and not particular commands addressed to or concerning specific individuals.

The eighty 'Commissioners' appointed by the Army to sit in judgement over the King were pre-selected from among his enemies. They were either soldiers from the New Model Army or members of the pro-army Rump Parliament: none of them was an ordinary judge. All the leading lawyers of England, including the Lord Chancellor, the Chief Justice, and the Attorney General, had fled London precisely to escape being pressganged into participating in what they regarded as a judicial farce, being without precedent and in contradiction to the laws of the kingdom as they then existed. For them, the trial of the legally immune sovereign was itself a violation of the law. Only John Bradshaw – according to A. L. Rowse 'a second-rate lawyer who was hyped up to as much dignity as possible'[4] – was prepared to front the show, and so he was appointed 'Lord President' of the court. This is why historians have been nearly unanimous in denouncing the court, which people already called 'England's Black Tribunal' or 'Cromwell's Slaughter House' after the Restoration.[5]

The strong men who controlled the army and what was left of Parliament had resolved in advance of the trial that Charles should die. Paradoxically, this put Charles on strong moral and legal ground when he entered the Great Hall at Westminster on the morning of Saturday 20 January 1649 (1648 according to the then calendar). Proceedings began when Lord President Bradshaw entered the hall. He was preceded by a mace and a sword, the insignia of the new revolutionary authority, and followed by a retinue of some eighty members of his court. He took his seat on a crimson velvet chair. In front of him there was a desk with a cushion on it, while the other members of the court sat on benches on either side of him, wearing scarlet. Silence was called and the great gate of the hall of Westminster was flung open (according to the contemporary account by the Earl of Clarendon) 'to the end that all persons, without Exception, desirous to see and hear, might come into it'.[6] The new revolutionary authorities wanted to give their proceedings a democratic feel. When the hall was filled, silence was called again. A Colonel Tomlinson had charge of 'the prisoner', and he was commanded to bring him in. Charles was conducted to a seat, and he made his way there without taking off his hat or showing any form of respect to the judges or the court. He stood up to have a good look at the guards and at the people in the hall. Silence was called once again, and the Act of Parliament which provided for his trial was read out by the clerk of the court.

Never before had a king been put on criminal trial for acts committed in his public capacity. Edward II and Richard II had both been overthrown by Parliament and then killed, but far from carrying this out in a public procedure, the usurpers disowned the assassins. Having inherited the crown, they did not want the principle of monarchy itself to be called into question. In more recent memory, Charles's own grandmother, Mary Queen of Scots, had been tried and executed. Royalists were deeply shocked at this treatment of an anointed queen, and at its implications for royalty as a whole – and rightly so, since her execution was the result of a conspiracy to frame her for her role in a non-existent plot – but the trial was not conducted by her own people and the charges did not concern acts committed while she was queen.

Oliver Cromwell had famously said, 'We will cut off his [i.e. Charles's] head with the crown on it,' and by this he meant that the trial was to be a public attack upon monarchy itself, not just a furtive assassination committed in private. The trial was to be the founding act of the new regime, and therefore the very prototype for revolutionary trials to come: Trotsky, indeed, was to call Lenin 'the proletarian twentieth-century Cromwell'.[7] Charles was accused of not having governed with that 'limited power' with which he had been entrusted, and of having conceived 'a wicked design to erect and uphold in himself an unlimited and tyrannical power to rule according to his Will, and to overthrow the rights and liberties of his people'. With this goal in view, he had 'traitorously and maliciously levied war against the present Parliament and the people therein represented' and his forces had committed atrocities in so doing. He was said to bear what we would today call command responsibility for 'all the treasons, murders, rapines, burnings, spoils, desolations, damages and mischiefs to this Nation acted and committed in the said Wars, or occasioned thereby'.

The Act of Indictment took only about ten minutes to read out and, after having done so, the judge, Bradshaw, spoke as if he himself were the prosecutor.

> Charles Stuart, King of England, the Commons of England assembled in Parliament being deeply sensible of the Calamities that have been brought upon this Nation (which is fixed upon you as the principal author of it) have resolved to make Inquisition for Blood; and according to that Debt and Duty they owe to Justice, to God, the Kingdom and themselves, and according to the Fundamental Power that rests in themselves, they have resolved to bring you to Trial and Judgement; and for that purpose have constituted this High Court of Justice, before which you are brought.

Charles's defence strategy was very simple: it was to deny the legitimacy of the court. This approach was to be copied by numerous other sovereigns in future centuries, but always in vain; as we shall see, in three hundred years of trials of former sovereigns, not one has ever been acquitted. As the Indictment was being read out, he had listened sternly, his only visible reaction being to laugh when he was accused of being a tyrant and a traitor. When Bradshaw asked the king how he pleaded, Charles replied,

> I would know by what power I am called hither. . . . by what Authority, I mean, lawful; there are many unlawful Authorities in the world, Thieves and Robbers by the highways: but I would know by what Authority I was brought from thence, and carried from place to place, (and I know not what), and when I know what lawful Authority, I shall answer: Remember, I am your King, your lawful King, and what sins you bring upon your heads, and the Judgment of God upon this Land, think well upon it, I say, think well upon it, before you go further from one sin to a greater; therefore let me know by what lawful Authority I am seated here, and I shall not be unwilling to answer, in the meantime I shall not betray my Trust: I have a Trust committed to me by God, by old and lawful descent, I will not betray it to answer a new unlawful Authority, therefore resolve me that, and you shall hear more of me.

This was to remain Charles's position throughout the trial, and the proceedings did not progress beyond this stalemate. 'Let me see a legal Authority warranted by the Word of God, the Scriptures, or warranted by the Constitutions of the Kingdom, and I will answer,' he said. He insisted that any citizen had the right to know by what authority he was being tried but that he, as king, had a special duty not to submit to illegitimate power. 'For I do avow that it is as great a sin to withstand lawful Authority, as it is to submit to a tyrannical, or any other ways unlawful authority.'

Bradshaw merely replied that he was not prepared to debate the court's authority, occasionally making vague invocations of natural law, Scripture, and, on one occasion, an unrealistic claim that Charles had been 'elected' king and that he had broken the terms of his election. Bradshaw said, 'You were told over and over again, *That the court did affirm their own Jurisdiction*, that it was not for you, nor any other Man, to dispute the Jurisdiction of the supreme and highest Authority of England, *from which there is no Appeal, and touching which there must be no Dispute.*'

Charles's arguments in court, therefore, had nothing to do with the concept known as the 'divine right of kings', with which his name is usually associated. On the contrary, his stated position throughout the trial was one of respect for the law as it then existed, including for the rights of the English people and the parliamentary institutions of the state. No law in the kingdom provided for the criminal trial of the king: on the contrary, the existing laws of treason provided for precisely the opposite, namely that any attack on the person of the king was a criminal act. Moreover, he was surely right to say that the king had a special duty not to act under constraint by an illegitimate authority: numerous heads of state were to be tried for collaboration after World War II for doing precisely this. Inasmuch as Charles invoked God, it was to show that he was charged with a divine *duty* not to betray the sacred trust which he had been given – not that he enjoyed divine *right*. Charles's stated attachment to lawfulness was therefore quite compatible with modern constitutionalism.

The argument between Charles and Bradshaw therefore illuminated the very nub of the matter in all such disputes about political legitimacy. That nub has been well discussed by the jurist H. L. A. Hart, who in turn draws on the theories of the constitutionalist John Austin. All political systems repose, in the last instance, on something which is outside law, and this is as true of dictatorships and tyrannies as it is of constitutional democracies. 'There are,' writes Hart, 'no legal limits on [the sovereign's] law-making power,'[8] and the emphasis here is on 'legal': the claim is not that there can be no limits on the sovereign's power, merely that such limits are not legal. If there were legal limits on a sovereign's power, then he would not be a sovereign. This is not to say, of course, that a government cannot be subject to the law as laid down in the courts. On the contrary, a state may well have such mechanisms as part of its constitution, and no doubt this is a desirable thing. But sovereignty is not an attribute of one body within a state but instead of the state as a whole. The theory of sovereignty does not state at what level – national or international – nor in what form – dictatorial or democratic – it is desirable to embody sovereignty: it simply states that the buck always stops somewhere.

If measures are taken to subject a state to a superior body (an international tribunal, for instance) by means other than its own consent (i.e. not when a state freely joins a treaty organization which contains an arbitration mechanism), then that body will be sovereign and therefore legally unimpeachable instead. As Hart goes on, the theory of sovereignty asserts that 'there could only be legal limits on legislative power if the legislator were under the orders of another legislator ... and in that case he would no longer be sovereign.' The question of who has ultimate political authority to make laws and prosecute criminals lies outside the law in the sense that it is a political and not just a legal question. It was precisely this question, which in the last instance is usually resolved only by violence when there is disagreement over it, that divided Bradshaw from Charles.

In pre-modern times, the arresting paradox that the law is sustained by a sovereign who is himself above the (civil) law, and that the sovereign therefore had a particularly heavy and almost sacred duty to perform – that of upholding the basic social contract, the natural law, and God's commands – was emphasized by the elaborate quasi-religious veneration accorded to sovereigns.[9] Royalty was precisely something set aside, and above, the ordinary weal. This pre-modern attitude expressed an eternal truth: the fact that state power is indeed something awesome and potentially terrifying, bound only by a supra-legal obligation on the state to protect citizens. The specifically religious symbolism of coronation ceremonies emphasized that the king was allowed to rule only because he was equally required to obey his very special duties to God and to his subjects. In the early modern period, displays of monarchical power in the age of so-called absolutism became even more ostentatious and of course less religious. In modern democratic states, by contrast, where the invisible 'people' are sovereign, the mystery of state power cannot be venerated or shown off in the same way. But something of the old sense of that mystery remains in modern courtrooms, where judges continue to wear robes – the symbol of spiritual power – even though priests and kings have largely abandoned them.

The trial of King Charles was therefore the paradigm for all future trials of heads of state. The revolutionaries claimed to believe that the law must be the same for everyone, i.e. including the king. But Bradshaw repeatedly said there was no appeal against the power of the new revolutionary authority of Parliament. The creation of the revolutionary court had therefore not removed the principle of sovereign immunity at all: it had simply displaced it from the king to Parliament. When international tribunals were set up in the late twentieth and early twenty-first centuries, they too were based on the claim that an end had to be put to immunity, but like the High Court of Justice meeting in Westminster Hall, those courts and their judges were similarly protected by explicit clauses guaranteeing their immunity and indeed sovereignty. This is inevitable: all political systems repose, in the last instance, on such unimpeachable authority, and in spite of all the rhetoric about overcoming the logic of sovereignty, it is in fact impossible to escape it.[10] Anyone who tries to do so is simply like a dog chasing its own tail.

When the second session was held on 22 January 1649, John Cooke, the Prosecutor, requested that King Charles be made to enter a formal plea. Cooke wanted to have his own day in court and to present the case for the Prosecution. The Commissioners also wanted to call Prosecution witnesses to demonstrate the king's guilt to the public, but they could not do this without a plea. Charles refused. He again insisted that it would be treasonable if as king he answered to an illegal power. Charles uttered a memorable and unanswerable line: 'For if Power without Law may make Laws, may alter the fundamental Laws of the kingdom, I do not know what subject he is in England that can be sure of his life, or any thing that he calls his own.' He added, 'For the charge, I value it not a rush. It is the liberty of the people of England I stand for.'

The king's refusal to plead threw the Commissioners into disarray. They argued over whether to consider it the equivalent of a guilty plea, as the law on treason provided. But this would have meant that there was no need to call any witnesses, as they wanted to do. They therefore resolved to hear the witnesses in committee, in the absence of the defendant and outside the procedures of the trial itself. Thirty-three prosecution witnesses were heard on 24 January and their depositions were read out at a public session of the High Court on 25 January, albeit still without the king there to hear them. The evidence offered concerned principally war crimes which royalist soldiers were accused of committing under the command of the king himself.

The Commissioners reassembled on 26 January to draw up the sentence, in discussions from which (in contrast to the ostentatious display at the opening of the trial) the public had been excluded. The death sentence was agreed, and the king was brought to Westminster for the fourth session, which took place on Saturday, 27 January 1648. Judge Bradshaw made a long peroration about the ancient contract and natural law; it was heavily influenced by the speech which the Prosecutor, John Cooke, had wanted to deliver – and to whom, indeed, Bradshaw seemed often to glance for guidance during the trial itself. The king tried to interrupt but Bradshaw refused: he said that Scripture enjoined the conviction of the guilty. His appeal was directly to the natural law and not to the civil. The king tried to speak again but was once again silenced before being led out to his execution.

On the way, Charles was mocked and spat upon. Led to the point of his execution, Charles denied trying to infringe the rights of Parliament or that he had started the war. He said he forgave everyone and claimed that he had defended the liberty and freedom of the people. 'I am the Martyr of the People,' he said, and then, 'I go from a corruptible to an incorruptible Crown, where no Disturbance can be, no Disturbance in the world.' Charles asked the executioner to make sure that the block was fast, and when the king gave the sign, the axe fell and killed Charles with one blow. The executioner held up the severed head and proclaimed, 'Behold the head of a Traitor.' According to a contemporary account, 'There was a dismal universal Groan among the People.'[11]

* * *

In view of the fact that Charles's trial was unprecedented in world history, it is surprising that it is relatively neglected by historians. Moreover, the few accounts of the trial which do exist do not ask where it was that the novel idea of holding a trial came from. There were plenty of reasons for wanting the King dead – the Puritans wanted to dash royalist hopes in Ireland, where new anti-parliamentary forces were being raised – but monarchs had been deposed before, and even murdered, without being subjected to a criminal trial.

The emergence of the idea of a trial is additionally remarkable because, at the beginning of the English Civil War, the Parliamentarians had fought on the basis that the king had been led astray by evil advisers. They did not attack the king himself. None of the initial parliamentary propaganda even suggested that the king would be deposed, still less treated as a criminal. On the contrary, even the radically Puritan Solemn League and Covenant, proclaimed in 1643 between the Scots and the English Parliamentarians to fight the king and to establish a Puritan church, undertook 'to preserve and defend the King's majesty, person and authority'.

This all changed in 1648. Following the outbreak of the Second Civil War, Parliamentary opinion turned against the king's own person. But even then not all the anti-royalists wanted an actual trial. The decision to opt for a trial was actually reached by senior army officers at a prayer meeting held at Windsor Castle on 29 April 1648.[12] According to William Allen, who attended the meeting and published an account of it ten years later,[13] the army was 'in a low, weak, divided, perplext condition in all respects', the Second Civil War having just broken out, and the soldiers spent the night in prayer, enquiring into the cause of their calamities. 'The then Lieutenant-General Cromwell did press very earnestly, on all there present, to a thorough consideration of our actions as an Army, as well as our waies particularly, as private Christians, to see if any iniquity could be found in them; and what it was, that if possible we might find out, and so remove the cause of such sad rebukes, as were upon us by reason of our iniquities, as we judged at that time.'

The men came to the conclusion that the renewed outbreak of war was divine retribution for their own sins. They concluded that the Lord had departed from them because their own lack of religious faith had prompted them to try to negotiate a peace agreement with the king. Instead, they should have fought his evil tooth and nail. They concluded that, 'It was our duty, if ever the Lord brought us back again in peace, to call *Charles Stewart*, that man of bloud, to an account for that bloud he had shed, and mischief he had done, to his utmost, against the Lords cause and people in these poor Nations.' The men's depression instantly lifted and their emotion was so great 'that none was able hardly to speak a word to each other for bitter weeping.' It was as a result of this meeting that the army issued its Remonstrance of 20 November 1648, a document which reproached the Parliament for trying to negotiate with the king and called for Charles to be 'brought to justice'.

So the idea of putting the king on trial arose not because of secular liberal sentiments, but instead as a result of the anthropological phenomenon known as the mechanism of the scapegoat. The soldiers met to reflect on evil and they came to the conclusion that Charles embodied it. Because they agreed to destroy him in an open ceremony, a trial, their mood changed and their depression vanished. It was an emotional moment, whose unifying power Allen was precisely trying to reactivate by recalling it ten years later.

René Girard has written at length on this deep-seated human reflex. I shall argue, as this account of the history of political trials unfolds, that it often plays a decisive role. A community can purchase unity by projecting evils (often its own evils) onto an external victim and then destroying that victim. It thus appears to purge itself of those evils, although in fact the unity thus obtained is only ever temporary.[14] The sacrificial victim is very often an outsider to society – a foreigner, a cripple, a leper, or a king. Kings, indeed, being set outside society in order to sustain it, are venerated precisely because of their power to unite; but precisely in this respect, they resemble (and sometimes become) sacrificial victims. The inheritance of Christianity, in which a supremely innocent victim was sacrificed, has caused us to forget that, in pre- and un-Christian societies, victims are destroyed *because they are believed to be guilty*.[15] Collective acts of violence committed in pogroms or by lynch mobs should remind us that acts of violence against a victim are perpetrated when a society or a crowd becomes convinced that a dark conspiracy is being mounted against it by outsiders.

In addition to these anthropological explanations for the idea of a trial, it is also clear that the soldiers' motivation for trying the king was explicitly theological. It is amusing, indeed, to see modern-day commentators regard the execution of King Charles as the beginning of secular liberalism, for in reality it was inspired instead by religious fundamentalism. The officers reasoned that the shedding of innocent blood had to be formally avenged through a judicial trial and a solemn public condemnation of the king. A negotiated settlement with evil was itself a form of evil which required expiation before God through an act of sacrifice.

Such reflections may seem far-fetched today but the obsession with the concept of 'blood guilt' was very real for the soldiers who took that decision at Windsor Castle. They were convinced that the impurity caused by the shedding of innocent blood had to be cleansed. Many Puritans were deeply impressed by the injunction in the Old Testament book of Numbers (35:33) that 'Blood … defileth the land: and the land cannot be cleansed of the blood that is shed therein, but by the blood of him that shed it,' and they often quoted this passage. *The Souldiers Catechisme* (the title itself is revealing) of 1644 had stated that 'God now calls upon us to avenge the blood of his Saints that hath been shed in the Land.' The blood-thirsty 'fast sermons' preached by religious radicals, both in Parliament and around the country on days when fasting was encouraged for the atonement of sins, typically called for 'innocent blood' to be avenged, and for the land to be thereby cleansed of the associated guilt. (The very fact that such sermons were preached in Parliament again emphasizes the role fundamentalist religion played in the Civil War.) One of the preachers of such sermons, Henry Scudder, said, 'It cannot go well with a Kingdom where the guilt of innocent blood is not put away by the hand of the Magistrate [Deuteronomy 19:13]. God will not pardon a Land polluted with innocent blood: he will sooner or later be avenged of it [2 Kings 24:4].'[16] The same sentiment was often repeated by other preachers.

The Puritans therefore wanted Charles to be sacrificed, in the full theological and anthropological sense of the term: their sacrifice of him was to be a propitiatory offering made to God to placate His wrath for their own earlier attempts to compromise with evil instead of combating it. By quoting the Book of Numbers, they were saying that God's wrath would destroy them if they did not counter Charles's guilt and cleanse the land with a purificatory act – his execution – which closely resembled the original wrong and thereby cancelled it out. Because they believed that God's wrath would take the form of a terrible judgement, their sacrificial act had to resemble God's own judgement.

The Puritans, indeed, were obsessed with the religious idea of the Last Judgement. Many of them believed that the end of the world was nigh. 'Fifth Monarchy' fanatics believed that the Second Coming was due in 1666 and that it would usher in a fifth monarchy to succeed the four discussed in the books of Daniel and Revelation (the Assyrian, Persian, Greek, and Roman empires). They were fascinated by the apocalyptic passages in the Old and New Testaments, and Oliver Cromwell himself was one of the principal apocalypticists. One of the main reasons why he permitted the return of Jews to England, indeed, was to prepare the country for their conversion at the end of time.

Like all millenarians, the Puritans did not believe in the notion of a peaceful cosmos.[17] Their universe was not the orderly result of a loving and free decision by God to create it; instead, it was the battlefield of a great clash between the forces of good and evil. The world was not a divinely inspired order, of which kingship and hierarchy were a partial reflection, but instead the battleground of destiny, a dangerous chaos in which constant struggle is needed to ensure the victory of the good. Obsessed by the notions of good and evil, judgement and damnation, millenarians hated the notion of neutrality. Stephen Marshall, who preached his famous sermon, *Meroz Cursed*, on sixty-seven occasions all over the country, including in the House of Commons itself, railed against those who refused to take sides. 'The Lord acknowledges no neuters,' he said, 'Cursed is everyone that withholds the shedding of blood.' In a similar vein, in *Sions Memento, and God's Alarum,* a fast sermon preached on 31 May 1643, Francis Cheynell urged that 'A just war is better than an unjust peace … our peace with idolaters has caused this war.'

Puritans and other millenarians loved using military imagery for religious purposes. Just as Calvin (1509–64) had written in his *Commentaries on the Last Four Books of Moses* that God was 'armed in military attire' and ready to 'contend with all the forces of His foes', so Stephen Marshall wrote in 1644, 'There was never any sword drawn on earth till it be first drawn in heaven.'[18] For the Puritans, therefore, there was a direct congruence between the sword unleashed in war and the sword used to administer justice. War, indeed, was itself a means by which justice was done: it was 'the great court of appeal', (Thomas Case[19]), 'the solemn instrument of justice' (Thomas Manton[20]). Fighting in a just war became a means by which to achieve salvation, a redemptive act, and the battlefield was the ground of spiritual transformation. As a result, the propaganda of the radical Parliamentarians was extremely bloodthirsty, and that propaganda in turn incited the regicides as their Bible mania drove them to heights of moralistic fervour. Stephen Marshall was one of the worst:[21] in one of his sermons, he made a bloodthirsty appeal justifying bashing children's brains out 'if this work be to revenge God's Church against Babylon.'[22]

The most important holder of such beliefs was Oliver Cromwell himself. A scion of a family which had grown rich on the spoils of the Reformation, when the lands of the Church were stolen and pocketed by powerful families, Cromwell drew heavily on his readings of Holy Scripture when making political and military decisions; it has been said of him that never doubted that he understood perfectly the mind and the plans of God.[23] Cromwell combined a curious pretence at being the instrument of a higher power with a love of arbitrary decisionism: he is said to have leant over the body of the dead king, whose head had been surgically reattached to his body, and muttered, 'Cruel necessity!' Later in his career, he said of the atrocities he organized in Ireland that there were moments 'in which some men are called to great service in the doing of which they are excused from the common rule of morality'.[24]

The intertwining between war, judgement, and punishment in the thought of Calvin and other Puritans led directly to their deep attachment to the role of the magistrate. No doubt the Puritans harked back to the days of Israel's rule by judges. The Puritans followed Calvin in believing that war was a form of police action to punish criminals and in holding that the magistrate was semi-divine: 'All those who hold the office of magistrate are called gods,' Calvin had written. '[Magistrates] have a commission from God, they are endowed with divine authority and they in fact represent His person.'[25] More generally, the Puritans' belief in the imminence of Christ's reign on earth, and in their own sainthood, made them want to imitate that most divine of activities, judgement, in their own tribunals. This is why the Prosecutor at King Charles's trial, John Cooke, made the theological motives behind the trial absolutely explicit when he said, 'The High Court of Justice is a resemblance and representation of the great day of judgement when the saints shall judge all earthly powers and where this judgement will be confirmed and admired.'[26]

2 The Trial of Louis XVI and the Terror

The role of theology in politics, indeed, is often overlooked. This is in spite of the fact that all political systems draw their legitimacy from a claim to uphold certain absolute values. In modern societies, these are typically expressed in written constitutions; in pre-modern societies, those values were more overtly theological. The contemporary move towards the creation of international tribunals for prosecuting extreme acts which shock the very moral conscience of mankind is also an example of how new political regimes are founded on such appeals to universal values. The controversial German jurist Carl Schmitt wrote that all modern political concepts are in fact secularized theological ones,[1] and even that distinctly un-theological novelist, Albert Camus – who is widely associated with the atheistic view that human life is meaningless – emphasized the religious significance of the French Revolution in his writings. 'The condemnation of the King is at the crux of our contemporary history,' he wrote in his great political tract, *The Rebel*. It symbolizes the secularization of our history and the disincarnation of the Christian God.'[2] That great opponent of the French Revolution, Edmund Burke, also stressed the religious aspect of the French Revolution, referring to it specifically as a sacrilegious event.[3]

Europe may have shuddered when Louis XVI was led to the guillotine but in fact the French revolutionaries were only imitating what their English neighbours had done a century and a half previously. Indeed, it was precisely in England and France that the theological aspects of kingship had been most heavily emphasized: the monarchies of both countries were were overtly sacred, the kings (and queens, in the case of England) being anointed and not just crowned.[4] Rebellion against them, especially public rebellion in the form of a secular trial, was therefore as much a theological as a political act. Moreover, like the English revolutionaries, the French revolutionaries wanted what they called 'a republic of laws', not personal rule by God's vicar on earth; they associated such personal rule with tyranny and, like all rebels, it was in the name of a demand for the realization of universal values that they overthrew the existing legal structures of the day (in this case, the monarchy itself) which, they said, violated them. It was this legal and political conflict about what constituted lawfulness, and what the source of that lawfulness was, which caused the French revolutionaries to be interested in the judicial process as an instrument of political change.

Louis's trial was shorter than that of Charles I: there were only two hearings, on 11 and 26 December 1792. (The death sentence was pronounced on 17 January 1793, confirmed on 19 January 1793, and the king was executed in Place de la Concorde on the morning of 21 January 1793.) But the prior debates in the National Assembly (later Convention) about how to conduct the trial went on for four months, from August to December 1792. At them, some of the deepest constitutional questions raised by political trials were discussed. Although Louis' trial took place in what was then the French parliament, just as Charles's had taken place in the Palace of Westminster, the French National Convention met in full parliamentary session whereas the specially constituted High Court of Justice was itself only a subset or committee of the already purged House of Commons. The judgement in Paris was therefore more overtly political than the one handed down in London against Charles I.

Louis was no longer king of France at the time of the trial (or even 'king of the French' as the 1791 constitution had styled him). He had been imprisoned in the Temple since 10 August 1792, following the uprising of that date in which revolutionary crowds, enraged by the ultimatum issued by the duke of Brunswick on 25 July 1792 declaring his intent to restore the French king to his full power, had attacked the Tuileries palace and massacred some 500 soldiers of the king's Swiss guard. Although royalist troops later joined forces with republican volunteers to repulse the invading Prussian army at Valmy on 20 September 1792, the king's overthrow was legally formalized when the newly constituted National Convention proclaimed the Republic on 22 September. Charles, by contrast, had still been styled 'king of England' at the moment when the axe fell on his neck.

France had been in a state of chronic ebullition ever since the storming of the Bastille on 14 July 1789. Louis XVI had encouraged hopes that France would adopt a parliamentary system on the English model when he summoned the Estates General for the first time since 1614 on 4 May 1789. The three estates (clergy, nobility, and the Third Estate) turned out to be unable to agree with each other, despite Louis's best efforts to force them to do so; each estate either camped on its acquired privileges or struggled to gain new ones. The Third Estate decided to proclaim itself a 'National Assembly' on 17 June 1789. Its members claimed to represent the people and therefore to have the right, solemnly affirmed in the Tennis Court Oath of 20 June, to assemble when they wished and not only when the king commanded them to. It was the rumour that the king would not accept the authority of the new National Assembly, and that he would sack its reforming ministers, which led to the famous disturbances of July and the storming of the Bastille. Subsequent to these, on 20 August 1789, the Declaration of the Rights of Man and the Citizen was adopted by the National Assembly. Just as he had accepted the existence of the new National Assembly, so the king accepted the Declaration too. Indeed, that famous document therefore bears only one signature – his.

When he first summoned the Estates General, Louis had been hailed as the restorer of French liberties. In October 1789, however, things started to get ugly for the reforming monarch. A great crowd set out from Paris to Versailles in October 1789 and brought the king back to Paris. Two years later, as tension rose between the king and the National Assembly, the situation took a sharp turn for the worse with the flight to Varennes in June 1791, when the king, queen, and immediate family were caught travelling incognito, allegedly in order to lead royalist and foreign troops to march on Paris to crush the revolution. The royals were taken captive and returned forcibly to Paris. The National Assembly voted to depose the king until such time as he accepted a new constitution, which he did on 3 September 1791. When the king next appeared before the National Assembly later that month, the deputies sat with their hats on (instead of standing and removing their hats when he entered), while in October, the forms of address 'Sire' and 'Your Majesty' were abolished (albeit only for a day). Yet even that constitution declared the person of the king to be 'sacred and inviolable', a fact which caused much soul-searching and debate when Louis was overthrown and put on trial the following year.

Although the constitution was essentially parliamentary, it contained a number of 'presidential' elements (having no doubt been modelled on the recently drafted American constitution) and these included certain powers of veto which were reserved for the king. It was the king's use of these powers, against the background of scepticism and hostility towards him as an enemy of the revolution, which caused the 1791 political settlement to break down almost immediately. In particular, the king refused to accept the revolutionaries' anti-Catholic laws, especially the law requiring priests to swear an oath of allegiance to the new constitution. This requirement flowed from the introduction in July 1790 of the 'Civil Constitution of the clergy', a new law which radically restructured the French Church along Presbyterian lines, providing for the election of vicars and bishops. The link between the king's opposition to this policy and his eventual overthrow and execution only underlines the specifically anti-religious politics of the French Revolution.

After the overthrow of the king on 10 August 1792, the idea of putting Louis XVI on trial gained currency. The atmosphere was inflamed by the revolutionaries' conviction that the king was conspiring with the kings of Spain and Prussia, and with his brother-in-law the emperor of Austria, to invade France and crush the revolution. The duke of Brunswick's ultimatum had seemed proof of this conspiracy, but the accusations had been flying around before then. When the Girondin politician, Pierre Vergniaud, for instance, had made an impassioned speech on 3 July 1792 claiming that the king was conspiring against the revolution, he received nearly unanimous support in the Assembly. When the king was suspended from his royal functions, and when it was decreed that he would be placed 'under the guard of citizens and the law', this idea became more explicit, as it did when French forces clashed with German at Valmy in September. Pierre Manuel, Chief Prosecutor of the Paris commune, told the Assembly, 'Legislators, France is free because the King is finally subject to the law … all that remains is Louis XVI's right to justify himself before the sovereign.'[5]

In reality, Louis was detained without charge for four months and the preparations for the trial were anything but lawful. A parliamentary report published on 16 September 1792 made numerous references to Louis's alleged conspiracy against the revolution and it was uncritically accepted by the Assembly.[6] As a propaganda campaign was launched against him, and as accusations accumulated without the charges being subject to any control or procedure, the Assembly actually intervened in the judicial process to prevent the arrest of the instigators of the massacre of 10 August. Instead of trying those who attacked the soldiers, special courts martial were set up to try the Swiss guards defending the King. The Assembly's own Surveillance Committee was re-named Committee of Police and General Security, and it soon obtained the right to arrest whomever it liked. On 12 August, the commune requested the right to send two commissioners from the courts martial to execute 'the judgement which the Assembly passed on these criminals when it issued the decree of accusation'.[7]

In other words, the grim apparatus of a police state, based on terror and direct political control of the police and judiciary, was being put in place at the very time when the king's trial was being prepared. Maximilien Robespierre – 'the Incorruptible' – called for the members of the Committee of Police and General Security themselves to have the right to convict people, claiming that otherwise 'the vengeance of the people would be too greatly restricted'.[8] This proposition was accepted in the Assembly, one deputy explaining that it would 'accelerate the judgement of the guilty' by 'suppressing any appeal'.[9] Thus were born tribunals with powers of summary arrest and execution – true Bolshevik-style 'people's tribunals' *avant la lettre*. Louis's trial was itself followed by the Terror which began formally with the establishment of the Revolutionary Tribunal on 10 March 1793, less than two months after his execution; within a year, until Robespierre's own arrest in July 1794, between 17,000 and 50,000 people were judicially murdered by it.

Soon after Robespierre's proposal was accepted, a guillotine was erected on Place du Carrousel (in front of where the glass pyramid now stands outside the Louvre) and people were executed for 'preaching moderation' and for other forms of alleged involvement on the royalist side in the events of 10 August.[10] The Intendant of the Civil List, Arnaud de Laporte, the man whose signature was required for all financial transactions from the royal budget, was arrested and executed on 24 August 1792, even though (or perhaps because) he had made available to the Assembly, on the evening of 10 August, a large number of documents from his office. His death meant that an important potential witness to the king's innocence on the charges of conspiracy was silenced.

The work of these tribunals was an evident travesty of justice. Defendants acquitted by them were, on occasions, re-imprisoned and re-tried if people present in the courtroom protested loudly enough. The tribunals also condemned to death a number of petty criminals, accusing them too of being accomplices of the king. Between 2 and 5 September 1792, indeed, at least 1200 prisoners were killed by over 200 paid agents of the Ministry of the Interior and the Ministry of Justice. The victims included priests who refused to swear the oath, Swiss guards who had not been killed on 10 August, prostitutes and other petty criminals, and even about thirty children aged between twelve and seventeen who had been imprisoned for distributing newspapers. Among those executed in this way were several other people who could have been defence witnesses for the king, including a former minister of foreign affairs, the commandant of the national gendarmerie, a general of the southern army, the king's valet, the remaining Swiss guards who could have testified about the orders they received on 10 August, and, most famously of all, the queen's confidante, the Princesse de Lamballe, whose severed head was paraded through the streets of Paris on a stake.[11]

In these, the so-called September massacres, priests and senior prelates were rounded up and taken to the Abbaye de Saint-Germain, where they were executed after brief trials in which they were asked whether or not they had sworn the oath to the new civil constitution. The papal nuncio, Mgr de Salamon tells the grisly tale how Stanislas-Marie Maillard, the

so-called 'grand judge of the Abbey' (Saint-Germain), who has entered
history as 'the chief massacrer', would despatch his victims:

> His interrogation was short. 'Have you sworn the oath?' The curé replied
> with the calm of a conscience at peace, 'No, I have not sworn it.' Immediately
> a blow of the guard's sabre was aimed at his head ... Blow followed blow
> to head and to body, and soon the victim lay on the floor, a corpse. The
> assailants dragged him by the feet out of the room and returned shouting,
> 'Vive la nation!'[12]

Some 300 priests were killed in this way. In this murderous atmosphere,
concepts of justice melted away. Accusation was equivalent to conviction
which was equivalent to death, as the revolutionaries were gripped by
mass hysteria about conspiracies. Their behaviour was the very opposite
of the rationalism and lawfulness they claimed to admire.

On 21 September 1792, while the elections to the Convention were
still in progress, 371 out of the 745 deputies met and voted to abolish the
monarchy. Many of the deputies who were later to sit in judgement over
the king already at this stage made speeches attacking him for his 'crimes',
i.e. pronouncing him guilty. On 30 September, a special committee of
twenty-four members was appointed to examine those alleged crimes:
until this date, indeed, all papers had been gathered by the Surveillance
Committee of the Paris Commune, not subject to any control by the national legislature, and it was only when a representative of the commune
appeared at the tribune of the Convention to say that the names of some
deputies figured among those who had received money from the Civil
List (the implication being that some deputies had been bribed by the
king) that angry deputies protested and demanded that the Convention
take charge of the documentation. The members of this new Committee
of Twenty-Four were also given powers of subpoena and arrest.

On 4 October, the new committee's *rapporteur*, Charles Éléonor Dufriche-Valazé, gave an account of the number of boxes of documents which
the commune had handed over, but indicated that the committee had not
had time to read them. He said that he needed three or four months to
draw up a proper report. In spite of this, he produced a preliminary report by 6 November and claimed in it that he had unearthed an immense
conspiracy which went way beyond that which was documented. This
paradoxical claim was unfortunately to reappear at future trials of heads of
state, many of which were similarly based on unsubstantiated claims about
conspiracies; often, indeed, the lack of evidence is itself taken as proof of
the deviousness of the conspirators. Documentary research now shows
that Valazé was simply lying.[13] One of the main sources of these docu-

ments was a safe (the famous *armoire de fer*) allegedly found in Louis's study, and the discovery of this caused a sensation at the time because it inflamed the belief that Louis had been hatching a secret master plan. But there is no proof that the safe was particularly secret (indeed, it may even not have been a safe, since the keys matched other drawers in the same study) nor even that the documents allegedly found in it had actually ever been there at all. On the contrary, they may well have been planted.

As part of the ongoing debate in the Convention about whether the 1791 constitution allowed a trial at all, the deputy Jean Mailhe addressed the assembly on 7 November, and argued that the constitution's clause providing for the inviolability of the king was not binding.[14] The nation was absolutely sovereign, Mailhe argued, and so it could do what it liked. The Convention debated Mailhe's report on 13 November and the debate lasted a month. Numerous deputies came to the tribune to proclaim the king guilty. Many called for the death penalty. Many (especially Jacobins) said they thought that a trial was unnecessary given the monstrous nature of the king's crimes. Not a single voice was raised to question the veracity of the allegations themselves, and accusations about conspiracies simply mounted. Meanwhile the imprisoned king himself was kept in ignorance of these developments.

One of the most famous and brilliant speeches was made by the then unknown twenty-five-year-old Louis Antoine Léon de Saint-Just, on 13 November. This young man was to emerge as one of the greatest orators of the Revolution, and his rhetoric earned him the soubriquet 'the angel of the Terror'. Like Robespierre and the other Jacobins, Saint-Just insisted that there should be no trial but instead a political decision to kill the king.

> Citizens, if we grant him the right to be judged civilly, that is to say according to the law, then as a citizen, he will judge us, he will judge the people itself ... As for me, I see no middle way. This man must either reign or die ... A law is a relationship of justice: but what relationship of justice is there between humanity and kings? ... With whatever illusion, with whatever conventions royalty envelops itself, it is an eternal crime against which every man has the right to rise up and arm himself ... It is impossible to reign innocently. Every king is a rebel and a usurper.[15]

Saint-Just therefore expressed the same sense of radical exclusion of the defendant which was to lie at the heart of so many trials of heads of state in the future. His rhetorical question, 'What relationship of justice is there between humanity and kings?' is, paradoxically, a confirmation of the pre-modern view that kings are somehow super-human beings. His argument, though, is of course not that they should be venerated, but that instead they should be treated as outcasts and outlaws and that their very existence is itself a 'crime against humanity'. Under such circumstances, it is not appropriate to deal with kings through the normal channels of law – which require calm mutuality, balance, and respect for the rights of the defendant, for these presuppose that the defendant is in some way a normal part of the community – but that instead the normal legal proce-dures must be cast aside to deal with the extreme and exceptional demand for moral condemnation which such people are said to represent.

It is often said that the first legal formulation of this concept of an enemy of humanity came when pirates were declared such: piracy, indeed, in the history of international law in the modern period, was the first 'uni-versal crime', proclaimed as such in the seventeenth century.[16] The same sentiment of outlawry and social exclusion is expressed in our own day by the concept of 'rogue states' and 'crimes against humanity', just as com-munists excoriated 'enemies of the people'. One of Saint-Just's colleagues on the Convention made a similar point. Merlin de Thionville told the Chamber,

> It is time, having decreed the abolition of the monarchy, that the Convention finally demonstrate that *a de-throned king is not even a citizen* and that he must fall under the national sword, and that all those who conspired with him follow him to the scaffold ... I ask that the monster [*l'infâme*] who wanted to shed the people's blood in floods be judged by you, for the Convention must be, for him, both accuser and judge [*juré d'accusation et juré de jugement*].[17]

Robespierre argued similarly on 3 December that it was absurd to hold a criminal trial since the whole issue was political. 'Louis is not an accused, you are not judges. You are, you can only be, statesmen and rep-resentatives of the nation. You do not have a sentence to pass for or against a man but instead a measure of public safety to take, an act of national providence to exercise.' Robespierre emphasized, with unimpeachable logic, that Louis had already been overthrown for conspiring with foreign princes, and that the Republic owed its very existence to this act; any trial now would put the revolution of 10 August under litigation and suppose the guilt of the revolutionaries by presuming the innocence of the ac-cused. 'The constitution forbade everything that you have already done,' Robespierre told his fellow deputies, sarcastically saying that those who wanted a trial should fall at Louis's feet and demand clemency.

But when he concluded, 'Louis must die because *la patrie* must live,'[18] Robespierre seemed to have left the domain of rigorous consti-tutional logic and entered instead upon a more anthropological line of reasoning: he seemed to be demanding a ritual murder of the former king as the founding act of the new regime, rather as the murder of Remus by Romulus was (in mythology) the act which founded Rome. Robespierre, as it happens, was also aware of the danger of following the English precedent. He remained an implacable enemy of the trial even after it had taken place, writing in December 1792 that it was 'just as ridiculous as the trial of Charles I'.[19] After ferocious shouting and much anger, the Convention voted in favour of the Girondin proposal to have a trial, rather than a summary execution. But the fact that the Convention voted to try the king itself, and not to constitute a court of law to do so, meant that key elements of the Jacobin position were retained: the eventual decision to kill the king was overtly political, not judicial.

On 6 December, the Convention decided that a committee of twenty-one members would draw up the definitive accusation document on 10 December, and that Louis would be heard on the following day. The former king was to be given two days to prepare his defence before being heard again. A lone voice, that of a Jacobin deputy, was raised to say that the Convention could not commit a murder. Otherwise the already bloodthirsty atmosphere was thickened yet further when the prominent Jacobin, Jean-Paul Marat, called for each deputy to vote publicly on the king's death and for the voting lists to be made public (as opposed to holding a secret ballot) 'in order that we know the name of any traitors, of which there are some in this Assembly'.[20]

In the event, neither the indictment itself nor the questions to be put to Louis were finalized by the evening of 10 December. Only a preface to both had been drawn up 'in a simple style which all citizens would be able to understand'.[21] In other words, the document was essentially addressed to the outside world: it was not a legal text. In terms which surprised even the most radical deputies – but whose basic sentiment was to be repeated against Germany after World War I in the 'war guilt' clause of the Treaty of Versailles[22] – it accused the king of all-encompassing criminal responsibility for everything:

> Louis is guilty of all these attacks, whose design he conceived since the beginning of the Revolution and which he has tried to execute on several occasions. The coalition of foreign powers, the foreign war, the sparks of civil war, the devastation of the colonies, the troubles at home, which he caused, maintained and fomented, are the means he used either to re-establish his throne or to bury himself under its debris.[23]

Before the king was finally brought in to the Chamber, there was further argument about how the assembly should conduct itself during the hearing: the president made a pompous speech about how absolute silence must be observed in order to set an example to the other nations of Europe, and one deputy said that silence was necessary 'in order to frighten the guilty man'.[24] Finally, the king was brought in. He had not been told of the charges against him and he had no lawyer.

When he entered the febrile National Convention on that cold morning, the King was only thirty-eight years old. But he looked fifty.[25] His captors in the Temple had recently taken away his razor blade, on the pretext that he might use it to commit suicide, and he had four days' worth of beard. His complexion was grey and his clothes were dirty. He had been in prison for four months, held without the right to receive any correspondence. Even pen and paper had been taken away from him in September. His guards had been especially chosen for their 'civic virtues', i.e. they were committed revolutionaries, and they had prevented him from hearing anything about what was going on in the world outside. He did not even know of the 'discovery' of the famous safe in the Louvre. He was ignorant of the propaganda campaign being mounted against him. John Moore, an English journalist based in Paris, wrote at the time that the purpose of keeping the king totally in the dark in this way was deliberately to confuse him and to ensure that his answers to their questions would be incoherent and self-incriminating.

This is exactly what happened. At the best of times, Louis was a bad speaker: he stammered and was often lost for words. (This was not true of his writing style, which was fluent.) A man of excessive emollience and gentleness, Louis did not adopt the proud defiance of King Charles; instead, Louis tried to answer the charges against him. The president of the Convention opened the trial by causing the indictment to be read out. He said, 'Louis, the French people accuses you of having committed a multitude of crimes to establish your tyranny and destroying its liberty.' Louis was then asked for his response to the various parts of the indictment, which were themselves often rambling and unclear. There were thirty-two parts to the original indictment and the president added ten more.[26]

Historians have been unkind to the way that Louis answered these questions, claiming that he hid behind the inviolability he enjoyed under the 1791 constitution, or that he tried to blame his ministers, but a close reading of the transcript shows that Louis referred to the impossibility of prosecuting him for things which happened before 1791 on only one occasion. On seven occasions, he said that the matter was the responsibility of his ministers, but each time he defended their actions and did not try to shift blame onto others. In any case, it was true that the constitution did provide for ministerial responsibility, as it was an essentially parliamentary constitution based on the English model. Louis replied on eleven occasions with a straightforward denial, for instance 'There is not a single true word in that accusation.' On seven occasions, he denied all knowledge of the facts alleged. Twenty-one of the fifty-one documents shown to him were genuinely unknown to him, since they were letters written by his brothers to third parties. On fourteen occasions, he replied to his accusers with exculpatory arguments, whether taken from articles of the constitution or from documentary sources.

The accusations and supporting proof were in any case exaggerated for effect. For example, the fact that the king had supported those priests who had refused to swear the Civil Constitution oath was transformed first into a conspiracy to re-establish 'the Catholic religion', then into a conspiracy 'to regain his former power', and then again into a plot 'to agitate fanatics within the state'. Yet the king answered each accusation patiently, so much so that even Marat was amazed: 'Had he been innocent, how great he would have been to my eyes in such humiliation!'[27]

The reports of this hearing were falsified by the revolutionary press. So, for instance, when the King was accused of fomenting counter-revolution in the colonies via his 'agents' there, Louis replied, 'If there are persons in the colonies who say they are my agents, they have not spoken the truth.' This was reported in *Le Moniteur* as 'If there are some of my agents in the colonies, they have not spoken the truth': the reported version thus implied that Louis had admitted that he had such agents.[28] On other occasions, the press falsified the question. When the king was asked why he had doubled the Swiss guards on 10 August, he replied that he was the constituted authority and that he had the right to defend himself. But the *Moniteur* reported the question as, 'Why did you gather troops in the palace?' and the *Journal Universel* as, 'Why did you give orders to fire onto the people?' which naturally cast a totally different light on the king's reply.[29] The media distortion was so bad, indeed, that on 13 December 1792, a member of the Convention proposed that the transcript of the hearing of 11 December be published precisely because 'the newspapers have disfigured the cross-examination of the former king.'[30]

When the interrogation was over, the president asked Louis whether he had anything to add. The king replied, 'I request a copy of the act of accusation and that the documents which support it be communicated to me. I also request counsel to follow my case.'[31] These simple requests threw the Convention into a new tumult of debate, reopening the pre-trial divisions. The Girondins were in favour of Louis's right to have a defence counsel, the Jacobins against. One deputy said, 'We must not expose ourselves, as did the tribunal in England, to the condemnation of posterity.

We must not cover ourselves with opprobrium by a passionate and atrocious judgement.'[32] Eventually, Louis's request was granted.

Louis's initial choice for defence counsel refused the brief, no doubt because he feared for his life. Louis therefore chose instead François-Denis Tronchet, by then seventy-six years of age and with a weak voice, who accepted with a grudging and cowardly letter which almost implied that he thought the former king was guilty as charged.[33] The circumstances in which the lawyers were initially given access to their client were atrocious: they were subjected to intimate body searches and required to change into special clothes under the supervision of the king's guards.

In addition to Tronchet, Louis also selected Chrétien-Guillaume Lamoignon de Malesherbes, a distinguished lawyer who had served in royal governments. Malesherbes went to visit the former king in the Temple on 14 December and Louis told him, 'Your sacrifice is all the greater, for you are putting your life at risk and yet you will not save mine.'[34] Tronchet also saw Louis that day and he suggested that Raymond de Sèze do the actual pleading. They sent for de Sèze in the middle of the night. Told what they wanted, he roused his sleeping wife to ask her advice. She gave her approval and de Sèze accepted.[35]

The Prosecution inundated the Defence with documents, the majority of which Louis had indeed never seen before since they were things like denunciations made to the police, letters between other people, and minor documents from the office of the Civil List. Delegates for the Prosecution brought the king over a hundred documents in the afternoon of 15 December and stayed with him until two o'clock in the morning as he went through them. Faced with this mass of material, Louis's lawyers asked for more time to prepare the defence but the request was turned down. On 20 December, the same delegates brought a new set of fifty-nine documents, of which Louis denied all knowledge. In total, out of 234 allegedly incriminating documents, 137 were completely unknown to Louis. It was only on 20 December, moreover, that Louis had in his possession the totality of the accusation case against him.

The second hearing was held on 26 December (the revolutionary authorities took no notice of the Christian calendar and even held a session on Christmas Day itself) and the session opened at nine o'clock. The king was asked to come in, which he did, and he said simply, 'My counsel will read you my defence.' Raymond de Sèze rose to his feet.[36]

The lawyer opened by saying that his purpose was to prove the king's innocence and that Louis regretted the fact that he had been unable to respond adequately to the charges levelled against him on 11 December. He complained that he had not had time to prepare the defence fully, since the Prosecution had produced more material than they could process in the time available. Louis did not wish to hide behind the inviolability provided for by the constitution but wanted instead to refute the substantial allegations against him.

In fact, though, de Sèze did devote considerable time to discussing the king's constitutional inviolability. He argued that all nations were sovereign and that they had the right to decide what kind of government they should live under; in the first phase of the French Revolution, France had opted to live under a monarchy and the principle of the inviolability of the sovereign – essential for public order, as even the English had realized – was enunciated on the very first page of the new French constitution of 1791. The nation had to respect the terms of its own contract. The constitution provided for the impeachment and removal from office of the king if he refused to swear the oath, waged war against the nation, or tolerated a revolt. Article 8 specifically said that in such cases, the king would be considered to have abdicated, and that, having abdicated, he could then be judged like any other citizen for acts committed after his abdication. Louis, by contrast, was now being tried for acts allegedly committed while he was still king.

De Sèze then addressed other questions of legality. To the claim, made by the Jacobins, that in the absence of any positive law providing for the condemnation of Louis, he should be judged politically or in the light of the natural law, de Sèze said, first, that the positive law was in place, since the constitution provided for precisely the accusations which were now being made; and, second, that natural law also provided that Louis should have the same rights as any other citizen and that these rights included the right to a fair trial. To the claim, which had also been made during the Assembly's speeches, that the insurrection of 10 August was itself 'a judgement', by the people, the sentence for which the people's representatives now had to carry out, de Sèze simply said that an insurrection was too violent an act to be categorized as the thoughtful reflection of a court ruling.

De Sèze in any case turned the arguments about inviolability on their head when he pointed out that the same inviolability which had previously been accorded to the king was now accorded to the new holders of sovereign power, the deputies of the National Convention. This of course had become evident in King Charles's argument with Bradshaw. De Sèze said that if they denied the rule of the law to the king, then the people would in due course also have the right to deny the rule of law to them; subsequent events were to prove him horribly right. In addition, the principle of the separation of powers, forcefully enshrined by Article

16 of the Declaration of the Rights of Man, was also not being respected: the Convention, the national legislature, was sitting both as judge and jury in the trial of Louis. There was also no two-thirds majority rule for the death penalty, as was normal in criminal courts. De Sèze then rehearsed well-known arguments about how, since his overthrow, Louis had been deprived of the basic rights accorded all citizens and enunciated in the Declaration of the Rights of Man. In a dramatic crescendo, de Sèze pronounced the words which Théodore de Lameth said he had suggested in a note to Malesherbes: 'Citizens, I seek among you judges, and yet I see only accusers.'

The lawyer then tried to address the substantive issues, the charges themselves about tyranny and conspiracy. He began by recalling that it was Louis himself who had summoned the Estates General for the first time in 150 years. He recalled that on 4 August 1789 the nation had proclaimed Louis 'the restorer of French liberty'. He said that the documentation which had been produced as part of the prosecution case could have been tampered with, and that without formal procedures for the seizure of such documents, no citizen could be sure of the protection of the law. De Sèze denied that there had been any conspiracy with foreign princes, usually adding that the documentation provided did not prove anything. De Sèze finished his peroration with a rhetorical flourish: 'Know that history will judge your judgement, and that hers will be that of centuries.'

He sat down, exhausted, having been on his feet for two and a half hours. Louis spoke very briefly after this and seemed resigned to his fate. 'Speaking to you for what is perhaps the last time,' the former King said, 'I declare to you that there is nothing on my conscience and that my defenders have told the truth.' He said that all his actions had been inspired by his love of the people, and that, among all the accusations, his heart was especially torn by the claim that he had wanted to shed innocent blood on 10 August.

Louis was taken back to the Temple at 5 p.m. and the Convention started to debate his defence on 27 December. Jean-Denis Lanjuinais said, 'We would rather die than condemn the most abominable tyrant by violating due process.'[37] But most deputies simply repeated the accusations against Louis without really taking the defence on board at all. The deputies proceeded to debate three issues: whether Louis was guilty, whether the final sentence should be ratified by the people in a referendum, and what the sentence should be. Deputies also availed themselves of the right to vote for a suspended death sentence. The divisions between the Girondins and the Jacobins opened up again, with Robespierre and Saint-Just arguing strenuously against any popular consultation – on the basis that the Convention was itself the embodiment of the nation – and the Girondins arguing in favour of it – on the basis that otherwise the people's famous sovereignty would be alienated. There were also ancillary arguments about the order in which the various votes should be held, and also on whether the votes should be cast openly or in secret.

The final debate on all these issues was held on 14 January. The deputies voted on the three main issues until 9.30 p.m., when the session was adjourned until the following morning. Votes took so long because each deputy took the floor to give his vote. The first vote was on the verdict. On 15 January, guilt was voted unanimously but with twenty-seven abstentions. The second vote was held on whether the decision should be submitted to the people for popular referendum, and the decision was that there should be no further ratification. The third was on the sentence, which was death. When Philippe Égalité – the duke of Orléans, the king's cousin, and a pretender to the throne who evidently hoped that he could become a Girondin monarch himself – voted for death, a groan went up; even the revolutionaries were shocked by this betrayal of his own cousin.

History is not a matter of ineluctable forces, and it is possible that Louis could have lived if these votes had been taken in a different order. If the vote on a referendum had been held after the vote on the sentence, then there might have been a majority in favour of a referendum among deputies keen to spare the king's life.[38] Indeed, there were claims after the Restoration that the voting record had in fact been falsified, and that there had not been a majority in favour of the death sentence for Louis.[39] Certainly the result was close: if one excludes the deputies who voted for a suspended death sentence, then the majority in favour of the death penalty was precisely one vote.

Somewhat belatedly, de Sèze pleaded for the Convention to reconsider, especially on its vote rejecting ratification of the judgement by popular referendum. But it was too late. It was finally decided that the votes, which were taken very slowly and with speeches from 16 to 17 January, would be confirmed by roll call, and this was done on 18 January. A legislative assembly elected by 10 per cent of the voters, and in which foreign citizens like Thomas Paine were allowed to sit and vote, arrogated to itself alone the right to express the popular will. It confirmed the death penalty on the former king. The last session on the king's case was held on 19 January and, in the morning of 21 January 1793, the king was taken to Place de la Concorde, just where the square meets the Rue de Rivoli, where the guillotine's blade duly fell on his neck.

Revolutionary propaganda claimed at the time Louis had struggled as he was led to the scaffold and that a pistol had to be held to his head. But the executioner, Charles-Henri Sanson, wrote a letter to the paper which published this account on 20 February 1793, in order to give instead 'the exact version of what happened'. The letter was never published, but it turned up for sale at Christie's in London in April 2006, 213 years later. 'He behaved with a calmness and a firmness which astonished us all,' wrote the executioner. Far from behaving like a coward, Louis Capet had taken off his own coat and offered his own hands to be bound. 'I remain convinced,' Sanson concluded, 'that he drew on the principles of his religion by which no one seems more penetrated or persuaded than he.'[40]

3   War Guilt after World War I

The empire which grew out of the French Revolution ended in defeat at the Battle of Waterloo. But the universalist principles it enunciated lived on and European politics were never the same again. Throughout the nineteenth century, as European states extended their empires overseas, a universalist concept of law gained ground according to which law was not the prudential balance between competing claims of citizens within a given and clearly delineated territory, as it had previously been understood to be, but instead the application in civil life of absolute moral principles.[1] The worldwide reach of empires encouraged the development of the worldwide reach of the law. The French Revolution had destroyed for ever the principle that the king embodied the rule of God on earth – rule restricted to a particular territory – and so the future now seemed to belong to disembodied and abstract universal moral principles instead. In keeping with this universalist spirit, there was a growth in international law. New international laws of war, supposedly valid at all times and in all places, were formulated in Geneva, the city of Calvin and Rousseau – the philosophers of the English and French revolutions respectively. The founding conference of the Red Cross was held in 1863 and laws of war were to be promulgated there in 1864, 1906, 1929, 1949, and 1977. Geneva was also the city in which the ephemeral League of Nations was to be situated in the inter-war years.

But neither these laws, nor the laws of war and conventions agreed at The Hague in 1899 and 1907, criminalized war as such. Instead, war was regarded, broadly speaking, as an inevitable if unfortunate form of relations between states which needed to be regulated. It was precisely in order to enable such regulation that the enemy was considered to have the legal right to fight: he was *iustus hostis*, a justified enemy, and it was from this that certain key rights flowed, such as those accorded to prisoners of war. The enemy was not regarded as a criminal, and war was not regarded as a variant of police action.

This all changed during World War I, which paradoxically saw a return to a more moralistic and even theological understanding of the enemy. War was no longer seen as akin to a duel, a relatively equal combat conducted according to preordained rules in which both sides had equal rights, but instead as a Manichaean struggle between forces which embodied ultimate values of good and evil. Indeed, it was only on the basis of an appeal to such absolute values that the seemingly limitless killing of the Great War could be justified; a understanding of the conflict as being one between rival (and ultimately legitimate) national interests could never have justified such a terrible blood price.

As a result, although none of the twenty-five international conventions on the conduct of war which had been drawn up and ratified in the fifteen years before the outbreak of World War I had even suggested the criminal prosecution of state leaders, demands for the prosecution of the German emperor and the leaders of Ottoman Turkey – on the basis that their war was itself criminal – started at the beginning of hostilities and only grew louder as the war went on. Public opinion had been radicalized at the outbreak of war by now notorious pieces of war propaganda such as the famous claim that the Germans tossed Belgian babies on their bayonets, but real events like the sinking of the *Lusitania*, the massacre in 1915 of the Armenians in Turkey, and the execution of the British nurse Edith Cavell were also instrumentalized to present the Germans and Turks as beasts to whom it was only right to be beastly in return.

Early on in the war, the Allies proclaimed that the leaders of Ottoman Turkey should be prosecuted for the Armenian massacres of 1915, events which they termed 'crimes against humanity and civilization' in a communiqué issued simultaneously in London, Paris, and St Petersburg on 24 May 1915. After the war, and under massive pressure exercised by the British on the defeated sultan, several leading Turkish ministers (a justice minister, a foreign minister, an interior minister, and even Said Halim Pasha, the grand vizier himself from 1913 to 1917) were put on trial in April 1919 for war crimes. (The total number of people arrested was 107.[2]) Later that month, the death sentence was handed down to a provincial governor, Kemal Bey, for his command responsibility for the Armenian massacres of 1915; his execution caused a storm of protest, as nationalist Turks saw in the tribunal an instrument of repression forced on them by the victorious allies.

On 27 April 1919 the trial of Said Halim Pasha and other wartime leaders began in Constantinople, principally for the Armenian massacres. In May the special court martial acquitted twenty-six of its other defendants and the British, who still retained a military presence in Turkey, reacted instantly, taking Said Halim Pasha and other senior ministers into their own custody and transferring them to Malta. Turkish justice could evidently not be trusted to do what the British demanded of it. The British had in the meantime helped the Greeks occupy Smyrna, which only inflamed Turkish public opinion even more, since stories began to seep out of atrocities committed by Christians against Turks. The British denounced the procedures before the courts martial in Turkey as 'a farce', but they had deprived these very courts, whose creation they had demanded, of their main defendants. The sultan's government, meanwhile, used the courts martial to prosecute its own domestic political enemies. In July 1919 the court martial handed down the death sentence on Enver Pasha and Talaat Pasha, two members of the triumvirate that had governed Turkey during the war. However, they had escaped to Berlin in 1918 and their trial had taken place *in absentia*.

The British, meanwhile, could not work out what to do with their august detainees in Malta. Nationalism was on the rise in Turkey as Kemal Atatürk grew ever more powerful. The Sublime Porte was tottering. As the situation spiralled out of control, and as the empire collapsed, in October 1920, Atatürk's men took a group of British soldiers prisoner and demanded they be exchanged for the ministers still in custody on Malta. The British squirmed. Their legalism seemed to make all outcomes impossible. Even though the call for the persecutors of the Armenians to be tried by an international tribunal had been inserted into the Treaty of Sèvres (Article 230), the British realized that it would be impossible now to obtain evidence from a hostile government in Turkey for events committed five years previously. In November 1921 Said Halim and the others were returned to Turkey and the British captives to Britain. The Treaty of Sèvres was a dead letter, since Turkey had refused to sign it, and instead a triumphant Atatürk signed the Treaty of Lausanne in 1923. International justice had run into the sands of political expediency. But it was the Armenian desire for vengeance which had the last word: a dispossessed Armenian gunned down Talaat Pasha in the streets of Berlin on 14 March 1921, while a Dashnak cell assassinated Said Halim Pasha in Rome in December that year, just one month after his release by the British.

The British demand that Germans be prosecuted was just as energetic. Not coincidentally, in view of the importance of the sea as the birthplace of universal international law – the first universal 'crime against humanity' was piracy – the demands for the criminal prosecution of the Kaiser arose as a result of Germany's sea war against Britain. The British quickly realized that German U-boats were a threat to their navy and world empire, and Winston Churchill, the First Sea Lord, instructed that German U-boat sailors who attacked British merchant navy vessels should be interned as criminals, not as normal prisoners of war, even though those supposedly merchant ships were in fact armed and trying to sink U-boats.

The situation escalated when, in 1916, the Germans responded in kind and executed the captain of a cross-channel ferry whom they had captured. They had discovered that he had tried to ram a U-boat the previous year.[3] Captain Fryatt's execution was intended to deter the commanders of merchant vessels from doing the same, but it only raised the British to new heights of fury. There were calls for the Kaiser to be held criminally responsible for his death. On 31 July 1916 Prime Minister Herbert Asquith called the execution an act of 'terrorism' and vowed that the Germans responsible would be put on trial, especially those in command.[4]

For the rest of the war, the British government issued threats to pursue criminal prosecution of Germans allegedly responsible for various atrocities. The function of these calls was largely propagandistic. The Germans played the same game: when, on 19 August 1915, the British ship, *Baralong*, sank a U-boat and then shot the surviving members of its crew in the water, and when Britain violated Greece's neutrality in 1915 by landing troops at Salonika, just as the Germans had violated Belgian neutrality in 1914,[5] the Germans made much of these violations of the laws of war. The Americans, however, were less keen than their British allies on war crimes prosecutions. This was because President Woodrow Wilson, although he portrayed the war in starkly ideological terms as a struggle between democracy and autocracy, in fact reserved his true hatred for the allegedly autocratic Catholic empire whose capital was Vienna, and whose break-up became American policy at the end of the war, rather than for the Protestant regime based in Berlin.[6]

The German monarchy was overthrown in November 1918 and the Kaiser fled to the Netherlands. Victory, however, did not quench the thirst for vengeance. Parades in American streets strung up effigies of the German emperor, while the British general election of 1918 was marked by demagogic pledges to 'hang the Kaiser'. On 7 November, just a few days before the armistice, Britain announced that it had created a Committee of Enquiry to look into war crimes and war guilt, whose members were appointed by the attorney general. Shortly after the armistice, the committee's remit was expanded to include examining whether the Kaiser could be tried for starting the war in the first place, in addition to looking into more prosaic cases of war crimes.[7]

Prime Minister Lloyd George was especially enthusiastic about the idea of a trial of the Kaiser but others in the Imperial War Cabinet were less so. The Australian prime minister was particularly hostile to the idea:

'You cannot indict a man for making war,' he said. A state had a right to wage war and the victors, he argued, had the same right to kill the Kaiser now outright. There was also debate about the true nature of German guilt: Churchill, for instance, argued that Russia had put the Serbs up to assassinating Archduke Franz-Ferdinand in Sarajevo in 1914 and that it therefore bore guilt for starting the war in the first place.[8] In spite of these disagreements, the war cabinet approved the idea of trying the Kaiser on 28 November 1918. The attorney general, F. E. Smith, made it clear that no Allied war crimes should be allowed to come under unwelcome scrutiny by any neutral judges.[9]

At an Inter-Allied Conference held in London on 2 December, Lloyd George sought and obtained the support of the French for the idea of trying the Kaiser. Together with Georges Clemenceau, the French prime minister who needed no convincing that the Germans had to be punished, Lloyd George succeeded in making war crimes the first item on the agenda at Versailles when the peace conference opened on 18 January 1919. A Committee on the Responsibility of the Authors of the War was created to establish responsibility for starting the war and to set up a tribunal to try those accused. But within the committee, Robert Lansing, the United States secretary of state, was a vehement opponent of the Franco-British plan, and relations between the Americans and the Europeans were strained to breaking point. The committee concluded that positive international law at the time of the conflict made no provision for the prosecution of heads of state for starting wars but it did recommend penal sanctions for war crimes in the future.

President Wilson was eventually persuaded to accept the idea of a trial. Lloyd George convinced him that his pet project, the creation of the League of Nations to prevent war in the future, would be a dead letter if there was no trial. In an act unprecedented in the modern history of international relations, therefore, Germany was not only proclaimed guilty of starting the war but also of all the resulting damage. Article 231 of the Treaty of Versailles said, 'Germany accepts the responsibility of Germany and her allies for causing *all the loss and damage* to which the Allied and Associated Governments and their nationals have been subjected as a consequence of the war imposed upon them by the aggression of Germany and her allies.'[10] Meanwhile, Article 227 stated,

> The Allied and Associated Powers publicly arraign William II of Hohenzollern, formerly German Emperor, for a supreme offence against international morality and the sanctity of treaties.
>
> A special tribunal will be constituted to try the accused, thereby assuring him the guarantees essential to the right of defence. It will be composed of

five judges, one appointed by each of the following Powers: namely, the United States of America, Great Britain, France, Italy and Japan.

In its decision the tribunal will be guided by the highest motives of international policy, with a view to vindicating the solemn obligations of international undertakings and the validity of international morality. It will be its duty to fix the punishment which it considers should be imposed.

The Allied and Associated Powers will address a request to the Government of the Netherlands for the surrender to them of the ex-Emperor in order that he may be put on trial.

This article violated three key legal principles. First, the indictment was brought on the basis of retroactive legislation and in the absence of pre-existing law: the Kaiser was to be tried by an Allied tribunal for crimes which were not crimes on any statute book anywhere in the world. On the contrary, it was quite common for peace treaties to contain agreements on a general amnesty for the defeated party. Second, the indictment was a Bill of Attainder, a government act directed against a specific person, even though such instruments are illegal and unconstitutional in many jurisdictions. Third, the Kaiser's guilt was proclaimed in advance, in virtue of Article 231, the purpose of the 'trial' being only to decide on a suitable sentence.

The Hague Conventions and the other international agreements on the laws of war flowed from the classical understanding of international law, which is that the subjects of it are states. Any violations of international law are therefore penalized, if at all, by actions taken against the signatory states. The criminal indictment of a head of state, by contrast, eradicated the difference between international law and domestic penal law and made the head of state criminally responsible for acts of state. The fact that existing international law did not allow for the indictment was the reason why the Dutch government, proud of its tradition of offering political asylum and of its respect for international law, resolutely refused to extradite the Kaiser when he sought asylum there on the day after his overthrow. In view of the Dutch refusal, and as politics was overtaken by other events, the British eventually let the issue drop and the Kaiser died of natural causes in his Dutch residence at Doorn in 1941.

But the effect of the indictment did not go away. As the great French historian and academician Jacques Bainville accurately predicted in *Les conséquences politiques de la paix* ('The political consequences of the peace'), published in 1920, the criminalization of Germany as a state in fact did more to unify Germany than Bismarck had ever done. It created a sense of collective national resentment and this quickly supplanted the previously disparate identities of the old German states which had remained strong even under the Empire. The reparations imposed on Germany were bad enough, as of course was the defeat itself, but the Germans found collective national humiliation by means of war crimes accusations even more intolerable. Major Otto von Stülpnagel published *Die Wahrheit über die deutschen Kriegsverbrechen* ('The truth about German war crimes') in 1920, refuting these allegations, and the book was a huge success.[11] With ruthless attention to detail, it claimed to rebut, point by point, the allegations made against Germany, usually either justifying individual acts or saying that the Allies had done the same or worse (*tu quoque*).

The Allies continued to demand the trial of other war criminals, and at the London conference in February 1920 they called for 800 Germans to be put on trial, including the wartime chancellor, Bethmann-Hollweg, Admiral von Tirpitz, Field Marshal Hindenburg, and General Ludendorff. This demand eventually led to the Leipzig trials of German soldiers, albeit of a tiny fraction of the number of defendants first mooted, and only relatively junior perpetrators: there were only forty-five names on the list the Allies eventually handed to the Germans on 7 May 1920, and none of them was famous. It required two laws, both of them retroactive, and both passed under intense Allied pressure, for the trials eventually to begin before the Leipzig Reichsgericht on 10 January 1921. The core legal prohibition against trying a defendant twice for the same crime (known as 'double jeopardy' or *non bis in idem*) was retroactively lifted in order to permit the re-trial of some defendants, a measure which aroused huge criticism because it flew in the face of that well-known legal principle. Seventeen trials were held of low-level soldiers for a variety of minor crimes including theft, creating great resentment in Germany, until the last trial petered out in November 1922. It was largely on the back of the outrage at these humiliations that Hitler and his fledgling Nazi party mounted their 'Beer Hall Putsch' the following year.

* * *

The attempt to criminalize Germany and the Kaiser, through trials and punitive reparations, was, in short, a catastrophe. So was Woodrow Wilson's attempt to create a new world order of international law through the League of Nations. Wilson tried to convince isolationists at home by larding his speeches with rich doses of messianic hyperbole which recalled the millenarianism of the Puritans who had executed Charles I: on a tour of the United States to promote ratification, he said, 'I wish that they [opponents of ratification] could feel the moral obligation that rests upon us …

to see things through, to see it through to the end and make good *their redemption of the world*. For nothing less depends on this decision, *nothing less than the liberation and salvation of the world*.[12] But it was to no avail: the League of Nations was set up, to be sure, but the United States Senate refused to ratify the treaty and the Americans never joined it.

On the other side of the world, meanwhile, an intense new political movement had been born which also drew its strength from the same combination of messianism and Manichaeism which inspired Wilson, and to which Wilsonism was in some senses a reply:[13] Bolshevik Communism under Lenin. Like other Manichaeans – indeed, like the English Puritans and the French revolutionaries – the Leninists believed in a great struggle between good and evil and in a final triumph leading to world unity.[14] They believed that politics was itself the field in which human salvation was decided. Lenin was convinced that the enemy must be destroyed and not just defeated, and struggle became a core Communist concept, the very prerequisite for progress itself and the crucible in which the 'new man' would be formed.[15]

Communism's love of conflict and its intense moralism combined in a potent brew to give Communists a deep attachment to the concept and practice of the criminal trial, both as an expression of struggle and as instrument of political repression. Trotsky dreamed of being the prosecutor at a trial of 'Nicholas Romanov' before a revolutionary tribunal, in the manner of the trials of Louis XVI and Charles I. He wrote in his diary many years after the event (in 1935):

> During one of my brief visits to Moscow – I believe it was a few weeks before the execution of the Romanovs – I remarked in passing to the Politburo that, considering the bad situation in the Urals, one should speed up the Tsar's trial. I proposed an open court that would unfold a picture of the entire reign (peasant policy, labour, nationalities, culture, the two wars etc.). The proceedings of the trial would be broadcast nationwide by radio; in the *volosti*, accounts of the proceedings would be read and commented upon daily. Lenin replied to the effect that this would be very good if it were feasible.[16]

In the event, the decision was taken to murder the tsar without judicial ceremony for fear of the White forces advancing on Ekaterinburg where the imperial family was being held. Failing a real trial of the tsar, however, the Bolsheviks quickly discovered the usefulness of political justice in the broader sense. Mock trials were staged all over the Soviet Union from 1920 onwards as means for conducting 'agitation' (political propaganda exercises) for the edification of the proletariat.[17] Trials of all kinds of things were staged: trials of Charles I, trials of Lenin (he was acquitted), trials of poetry, trials of religion. In some cases, real 'show' trials were held in the same public hall as mock agitation trials; it must have been difficult for the casual observer to know the difference.

Soon the concept of such trials became the hallmark of Stalinism and its gruesome excesses, although it was Lenin who originally expressed the nub of the matter with his customary cruel realism: 'The court is an organ of power,' he wrote. 'The liberals sometimes forget this but is a sin for a Marxist to do so.'[18] However, the Soviets did not stage only the trial of internal traitors to Bolshevism. They and their allies across Europe were to play a decisive role in setting up all the major war crimes trials across Europe after 1945, including not only the Nuremberg trials themselves but also those of Nazi collaborators and other political enemies, especially in Eastern Europe.

* * *

In the end, however, it was neither the British nor the Bolsheviks who organized the third trial of a head of a regime in history, but Greece. Following the Greek campaign in Anatolia and its subsequent rout in 1922, Greece was seized by revolution. King Constantine was forced to abdicate by a Revolutionary Committee composed of anti-monarchist naval and army officers loyal to the liberal politician, Eleftherios Venizelos. Revolutionary troops marched into Athens on 28 September 1922, and the leading members of the royalist coalition which had planned the disastrous Anatolian campaign were arrested: Petros Protopapadakis, the prime minister; Dimitrios Gounaris, the former prime minister who had been Protopapadakis's minister of justice (Protopapadakis had been his finance minister); Georgios Baltatzis, the foreign minister; Nikolaios Stratos, the minister of the interior (who had been prime minister for ten days in May 1922 after Gounaris and before Protopapadakis); Nikolaios Theotokis, the minister for war; General Hatzianestis, the commander in chief of the Greek armies during the Greek–Turkish war. The trial is known as the Trial of the Six, because these six men were sentenced to death and executed, but there were in fact eight defendants: General Xenophon Stratigos and Admiral Michalis Goudas were sentenced to life imprisonment. Meanwhile one and a half million Greek refugees streamed into Greece from their ancient homelands in Anatolia, as the Hellenic presence in Anatolia drew to a gruesome close.

The Revolutionary Committee had initially been expected to execute the leaders of the Constantinist government summarily and then proclaim a general amnesty. But the Committee announced on 17 October that those responsible for the national disaster would be put on trial. This was not the result of a sudden desire to respect due process, however, but instead the result of an understanding that a trial would help the revolution. 'The Revolution cannot rest with the resignation of Constantine,' the Revolutionary Committee argued, 'because the political and military Constantinist clique must be neutralised. The Revolution proclaims unity, but unity would be immoral if it signified the forgetting or putting aside of responsibilities and the confusion of innocent and guilty. The exemplary punishment of the enemies of the country is therefore necessary.'[19]

The ministers were accused of treason, on the basis that their lost war had allowed enemy troops to enter Greek territory. It was obvious that this was merely a device for diverting attention from the humiliation of defeat and destroying the royalist politicians into the bargain. The charges closely anticipated those of the Riom trial of 1942 (the subject of the next chapter) because the Constantinist leaders were accused of being criminally responsible for military failure, and for having led the country into war unprepared. The charges were explicitly political in nature: the men were accused of failures of decision-making, causing defeat, wasting money, betraying national interests, ignoring warnings from abroad, making the wrong military appointments. A special court martial was convened and the proceedings started on 13 November 1922. The prosecution witnesses included George Rallis, son of the five times prime minister, Dimitrios Rallis (1844–1921) and brother of the wartime prime minister, Ioannis Rallis (1878–1946), who was himself to face trial for collaboration in 1946. (Ioannis Rallis's son, also George, was prime minister from 1980 to 1981.)

The trial was effectively a wide-ranging discussion about politics. The actual criminal charge of treason was hardly broached: no doubt the prosecutors felt it was a difficult charge to sustain. The second most important defendant, Gounaris, the main leader of the opposition to Venizelos, went down with typhus during the trial and was absent for most of it; the proceedings carried on regardless, in violation of the principle that defendants must be present at their own trial. When it came for the defendants to make their final submissions, Gounaris sent a pencilled note written from his prison hospital bed which was read out in court. At 6.30 a.m. on Tuesday 28 November 1922, the court was hurriedly convened. The sentence – death for the six, life imprisonment for the admiral and the general – was read out to a near-empty room and one must assume that the early hour was chosen deliberately as a way of burying bad news; the defendants had already been taken to their place of execution the previous night.

There, a hundred soldiers accompanied Gounaris, Stratos, Proto-papadakis, Theotokis, Baltatzis, and Hatzianestis as they were lined up in front of their respective graves. There were five soldiers in the firing squad. Baltatzis cleaned his monocle with his handkerchief and put it on; General Hatzianestis stood to attention. As a soldier approached him to carry out the sentence of military degradation, the general stripped off his own epaulettes, refusing to allow anyone to touch him. All six men stared their executioners silently in the eye as the shots rang out shortly after 11 o'clock that morning.[20]

4   Defeat in the Dock: the Riom Trial

The trial of political leaders for leading a country into national disaster was to be repeated twenty years after the Trial of the Six in Greece. The fame of the great Nuremberg trials has obscured historical memory of what was, in fact, the first major war crimes trial of World War II: the Riom trial of the leaders of the democratic Third Republic in France. Edouard Daladier and Léon Blum, both former prime ministers, General Gamelin, the former chief of staff, Guy La Chambre, the former minister of air, and Robert Jacomet, the former controller-general for the administration of the armed forces, were put on trial by Vichy France in 1942 for leading France into war and then losing it.

The regime known as Vichy France was born out of the ruins of France's staggering defeat in May to June 1940, and it blamed the leaders of the Third Republic for that catastrophe. Like the Revolutionary Committee in Athens, Vichy needed a trial to bolster the legitimacy of its own 'national revolution' proclaimed by Marshal Pétain, a programme of national renewal based on the conservative and authoritarian principles of 'work, family, country' (*travail, famille, patrie*). The defeat had inflicted a terrible psychological blow on France, and an urgent need was felt for the re-establishment of solid reactionary principles after the parliamentary chaos of the inter-war years. Stunned by the suddenness of the Germans' victory and the huge cost in lives – which had followed repeated reassurances given by military and political leaders that France was militarily prepared for war – the French therefore threw themselves at the feet of the most revered and popular man in the country, Philippe Pétain, the peasant's son who had become *Maréchal de France* and who, as one of the men who had won World War I, was nicknamed 'the victor of Verdun'. He seemed to be France's providential saviour in her hour of need, and indeed he employed theologically resonant vocabulary when he said that he would make 'a sacrifice of [his] own person' by assuming power just when the country had suffered its worst defeat: Pétain did indeed exchange his glorious historical reputation as the man who had delivered victory in the Great War for the very opposite, and his name has now entered historical vocabulary as a byword for the ignominy of defeat and even treason.

The initial rationale for the decision to sign an armistice with the invading Germans was to stop the fighting which was killing people in their tens of thousands, causing over a million to be taken as prisoners of war and countless numbers to flee as refugees. An armistice which preserved the French government legally intact was, it was reasoned, better than direct rule by the Germans, such as they were to impose on Belgium and the Netherlands. But the defeat produced such a deep shock that there was also a widely held conviction that the very institutions of the state were at fault, and that they needed to be discarded and replaced by new ones. The armistice having been signed on 17 June 1940, on 10 July 1940 the French parliament, meeting in Vichy, voted by an overwhelming majority to dissolve itself and the Third Republic with it. Only eighty deputies and senators voted against handing *les pleins pouvoirs* (including power to legislate and to change the constitution) to the then president of the council (prime minister), Marshal Pétain. The parliamentary regime was abolished (at least provisionally) and a sort of personal dictatorship established. Gaullist constitutionalists immediately attacked the parliament for its vote, saying that it had no right to alienate national sovereignty in this way. Indeed, it was largely because of the experience of 1940 that de Gaulle became a sworn enemy of what he called 'the regime of political parties', which he successfully stemmed when he created his presidential Fifth Republic in 1958.

Pétain's own analysis of the weakness of the parliamentary system was not dissimilar to de Gaulle's. Both were military men – and former close friends. Pétain was godfather to de Gaulle's first son, Philippe, named after the marshal. They had disagreed over military strategy: Pétain believed that the infantry and a war of attrition were the key to military success, while de Gaulle saw the potential of mechanized warfare, especially tanks. But both men inhabited a hierarchical world in which it was natural to give and obey orders. Neither of them was a fan of the impersonal political logic of parliamentarianism, still less of its Machiavellianism and corruption.

But whereas de Gaulle, the young rebel brigadier, acted with dashing audacity, Pétain brought a lugubrious and sombre mood to France. On the day of the armistice, he told the French people, 'I was with you in the glorious days. I stay with you in the dark days. Remain at my side.' He spent the rest of the war playing grandfather to a brutalized and disoriented nation. In his address of 11 October 1940, when he set out the main lines of his national policy shortly before the famous meeting with Hitler at Montoire (on 24 October), Pétain said, 'If all avenues are closed to us, then we know how to wait and suffer.' The political regime which he instigated was thus heavily impregnated with masochism and self-reproach. The marshal of France let it be known that, on rising every morning, like a sinner practising mortification, he repeated to himself, 'We have been defeated.'

The air was also thick with the thirst for revenge. Pétain's very first broadcast to the nation, on 17 June 1940, effectively laid out the case for what was to become the Riom trial. 'The armistice has been inevitable since 13 June,' he said.

> This failure has surprised you. Remembering 1914 and 1918, you are seeking the reasons for it. I will give them to you. On 1 May 1917, we still had 3,280,000 men in our armed forces, in spite of three years of bloody combats. On the eve of the present battle, there were 500,000 fewer. In May 1918, we had 85 British divisions; in May 1940, there were only 10. In 1918, we had with us 58 Italian divisions and 42 American divisions.

He went on: 'Too few sons, too few weapons, too few allies. There is our defeat.'

The desire to blame the previous regime for the defeat therefore formed the very ideological core of the Pétainist project. The Third Republic had to be ritually destroyed in order for Vichy France to live, just as Louis had had to die for the Republic. The Riom trial was therefore a paradigm of what is today called (favourably) 'transitional justice': it was a trial staged to ceremonialize the destruction of an old political system and its replacement by a new one. The minister of justice in 1940 was Raphael Alibert, a member of the extreme right-wing group, *La Cagoule* and the man whose name is forever associated with the anti-Semitic legislation he authored, by which Jews were excluded from public office and retrospectively stripped of their French citizenship. It was he who made the political goals of the trial explicit: 'For a long time, we have been denouncing the defects of the Republic. If it were well done, a grand trial would establish the proof of it. Such a trial would be the touchstone of the new regime and of the new order.'[1]

On 11 July 1940, the day after he was invested with *les pleins pouvoirs*, Pétain promulgated three constitutional acts which were to form the basis of the Riom trial. They established the principle that ministers were henceforth responsible to him as head of state, and not to parliament which in any case had been dissolved. On 30 July 1940, i.e. within a fortnight, a fifth Constitutional Act was decreed which created the 'Supreme Court of Justice', whose role was to put the former ministers on trial. This Constitutional

Act abrogated two articles in two previous laws (Article 9 of the law of 24 February 1875 and Article 12 of the law of 16 July 1875) which had provided that the Senate had the right to constitute itself as a court of justice to try the president of the Republic or government ministers; the new Supreme Court of Justice was henceforth to have this function instead. The Supreme Court of Justice was therefore a special tribunal, created in violation of the key principle of the rule of law that people should be tried only by ordinary courts. It was also based on retroactive legislation. Marshal Pétain, having determined that ministers were responsible to him alone as head of the French state, ruled that a new political crime henceforth existed, that of having 'betrayed the duties of office', and that it could be applied to ministers for acts committed before he had changed the law.

The new Supreme Court was by no means the only special jurisdiction Vichy created. There was a new court martial, special tribunals in each court of appeal, and a tribunal of state in Paris and Lyons. These courts could hand down various punishments including the death penalty. Vichy also had a policy of administrative internments under which people were imprisoned without their cases ever being referred to a judge at all,[2] i.e. *habeas corpus* was suspended and retroactive legislation liberally introduced including for capital offences. The context in which the Riom trial operated was therefore effectively that of a police state and emergency powers. Military leadership and unquestioning deference to power were the order of the day.

There was a widespread view in the aftermath of the defeat that the Third Republic leaders were indeed guilty men. But there was disagreement as to what exactly the charges against them should be. Pierre Laval, Pétain's more overtly pro-German prime minister, wanted the defendants at Riom to be tried for declaring war (the crime for which the Nazi leaders were eventually prosecuted at Nuremberg). Laval presumably thought that such a prosecution would please the Germans: France had, in fact, declared war against Germany, and the Germans insisted they had been forced into a war they had not sought.

Others warned against this, reasoning that if France convicted her own ministers of having started the war, then Germany would demand territorial concessions after it. Germany had already placed Alsace and Lorraine under direct German rule, and the fear was that she would formally annex them again, as she had done in 1871. The military men who were so powerful in the Vichy regime therefore said that the politicians' crime was not that they had declared the war, but instead that they had lost it.

The defendants themselves did think that they were being tried on the orders of the Germans. But just as the anti-Semitic legislation introduced by Vichy was in fact enacted with no encouragement by the Germans, [3] so Hitler did not press for the Riom trial to occur. To the extent that there was any German influence at all, it came from Otto Abetz, the powerful German ambassador in Paris.[4] Abetz quickly understood the value of having the French blame each other for their misfortunes, just at the time when any nascent national unity against the occupying forces needed to be destroyed.

On 1 August 1940 Pétain issued a decree appointing the members of the newly created Supreme Court of Justice. Although the judges were appointed for life, and therefore not subject to the threat of being sacked for political reasons, and although they were all qualified jurists, the decree left no doubt about the political nature of the trial for which the court was summoned on 8 August:

> To seek out and to try ministers, former ministers or their immediate civilian and military subordinates, accused of crimes or delicts in the exercise or on the occasion of their functions, or of having betrayed the duties of their office in acts which led to the passage from peace to war on 4 September 1939 and which subsequently aggravated the consequences of the situation which had been caused thereby.[5]

The phrasing about 'the passage from peace to war' was as close as the Prosecution came to blaming France for actually starting the war, while the actual trial in fact concentrated mainly on the military defeat for which the defendants were held responsible. From his exile in London, General de Gaulle lost no time in denouncing the procedure. That very day, he broadcast, 'Those unfortunate men who have handed France over by capitulating, are now trying to deceive public opinion about their crime. They are hastening instead to prosecute others.'[6] By 1943, i.e. one year after the trial had ended, de Gaulle wrote the preface to a book published in French in London by Pierre Tissier, in which the future president lambasted the trial as 'one of the worst abuses committed by Vichy' and as 'a parody of justice'.[7]

The key crime alleged, that of 'having betrayed the duties of their office' (*d'avoir trahi les devoirs de leur charge*), was completely undefined. It corresponded to no existing law. Although *trahir* implies treason itself, the defendants were not tried for treason, on which there was ample existing law. A further law, passed on 3 September 1940, provided for internment on the orders of the minister of the interior. It was on the basis of this law that the main defendants at Riom were imprisoned at the château de Chazeron: Daladier, Blum, Gamelin, La Chambre and Jacomet.

Paul Reynaud, Pétain's predecessor as prime minister, and Georges Mandel, Reynaud's minister of the interior, were also interned in the same château de Chazeron but they were not tried at Riom. Although the Germans hated both Reynaud, who had been prime minister when France declared war on Germany, and Mandel, because he was Jewish and fiercely anti-Nazi, it would have been politically impossible to put Reynaud on trial because it was he who had appointed Marshal Pétain to the government in the first place. His patriotic and even pro-war credentials were never in doubt.[8] The selection of Léon Blum as a defendant, meanwhile, was clearly a piece of pure political persecution: he had not even been in government at the time of the outbreak of war. Camille Chautemps, who had been prime minister between Blum and Daladier, and who was deputy prime minister (vice-president of the council) under both Daladier and Reynaud, was never even mentioned in the indictment and was left quite alone by the Vichy authorities. We shall see in a moment how the question of Reynaud and Mandel was resolved.

Armed with these two decrees, the new Supreme Court of Justice set about preparing the case. It did so by violating one of the key principles of French judicial procedure, which is that there should be a clear distinction between the magistrate who examines a case for prosecution (*le juge d'instruction*) and the judge who adjudicates it. In contravention of this ancient French legal principle, which in any case reflects the principles of natural justice, the judges of the Riom bench themselves carried out the investigation, collecting documents and interviewing witnesses. They also gave interviews to journalists before the trial started, thereby additionally violating the principle than a judicial investigation remains secret until the allegations have been brought to court.[9]

The Riom judges worked slowly and methodically – too slowly, in fact, for the imperatives of politics. On 27 January 1941, therefore, Pétain promulgated Constitutional Act No. 7; authored by the Minister of Justice, Raphael Alibert, and recalling that ministers (including former ministers) were responsible to the head of state, it ruled that ministers could, on the say-so of the head of the French state, be convicted of 'betraying the duties of their office' and subject to various punishments including destitution (removal from office) and imprisonment.[10] The powers laid out in this new Act were applied retroactively, as the Act's reference, in its Article 5, to 'former ministers' explicitly admitted.

Even this measure, however, did not speed up matters quickly enough and things continued to drag on in Riom. On 12 August 1941, in an extraordinary broadcast read out during the interval of a performance of *Boris Godunov* at the opera house in Vichy, Marshal Pétain expressed his dismay that his regime was having difficulty enforcing its will. An 'ill wind' was blowing in the country, he said, and the authority of his government was being questioned. To combat this, a range of new measures would be introduced: the suspension of the activities of political parties, the suppression of parliamentary immunity, sanctions against Freemasons, reinforcement of the police force, and the creation of a new body, a 'Council of Political Justice' whose purpose was 'to judge those responsible for our disaster'.[11]

The announcement was a bombshell. Pétain referred to Constitutional Act No. 7 of January 1941, in contradiction of the fact that the Supreme Court of Justice had already been constituted by decrees signed in 1940. He made this announcement without consulting the new justice minister, Joseph Barthélemy, who wrote in his diary that day of his shock at the judicial chaos which the new Council of Political Justice would create. The new Supreme Court of Justice was nearly ready to stage the trial, and yet Pétain had suddenly and unexpectedly brought into being a new jurisdiction to try the same defendants for the same alleged crimes. Worse, the Council of Political Justice was to report to the head of state: it represented nothing less than a personal system of justice.

A further decree the following month appointed eight members to this new Council, which was headed by Ambassador Peretti della Rocca, an old friend of the marshal. (Pétain had himself been French ambassador to Spain.) Only two of the members of the Council were jurists. Pétain gave the new Council a month to prepare its judgement on the Riom defendants, plus Georges Mandel and Paul Reynaud. None of the members of this Council went to Riom to examine the documents which the Supreme Court had been collecting for a year; instead, the Council members read only the half-finished indictment, which had not even been given to the defendants themselves by that stage. When in due course the Council submitted its verdict to Marshal Pétain, who duly announced it as his own to the French nation on 16 October 1941, it did so even though none of its members had met any of the defendants, and on the basis of charges of which the defendants themselves were unaware.

Of course the Supreme Court judges and Barthélemy himself should have protested at this point, perhaps by resigning. Instead, these senior jurists covered for the aged marshal and, by staying in their posts, lent a veneer of respectability to this gross act of political interference in the judicial process. But Barthélemy, who had initially welcomed the Riom trial, on the basis that it would be 'the grand trial of a defunct regime',[12] soon began to realize that all possible outcomes were going to be negative. It would prove impossible to separate the new regime from the old, since Pétain himself had been minister of defence in 1934; it was politically costly to exonerate the defendants, because that would imply a judicial condemnation of Germany; and conviction of the defendants would damage relations with Britain.

Pétain went on air on 16 October 1941,[13] the day after the Council of Political Justice had reported back to him, to announce that *he* had found all five Riom defendants guilty. He eulogized the members of the Council, saying that they were 'distinguished servants of the state' who had provided a 'clear and well-founded opinion'. After having thus convicted the defendants, Pétain announced their various prison sentences (life imprisonment in a fortress for Blum, Daladier, and Gamelin, lesser forms of imprisonment for Guy la Chambre and Jacomet, continued detention for Reynaud and Mandel) and then drifted into complete incoherence, saying that French law required separation between the executive and the judicial branches and that therefore the Riom court would now try the men … whom he had just proclaimed to be guilty and sentenced! He made matters worse by adding that the court had to act quickly, since the gravity of the men's crimes meant that sanctions he had announced against them (various forms of imprisonment) would be quite inadequate.

Pétain concluded his message by leaving no one in any doubt that the trial was the trial of the Third Republic as a regime. The sentence, he said, 'will condemn individuals but also the methods, the morals, the regime. The decision will be final; it will not be open for further discussion. It will mark the final point in one of the saddest periods in the life of France.' He also said that the trial was intended to provide a definitive historical account of what had allegedly gone wrong in 1940: the French, he said, had been 'betrayed' but now they would no longer be deceived.[14]

The Council for Political Justice performed one extra political act during its short and ignominious existence. As a result of pressure from the Nazis, and in spite of the fact that two of its members resigned in protest at this blatant political interference, the rump Council reached new heights of hypocrisy when it convicted Paul Reynaud and Georges Mandel – two men whom the Germans hated as warmongers but whom the Supreme Court of Justice saw no reason to prosecute – for conspiring to place France under the control of a foreign power, namely England.[15]

Although the interference of the Germans in the conviction of Reynaud and Mandel was egregious (there was no trial), they tried to interfere with the running of the Riom trial as well. As preparations got under way, the Germans demanded that all the files be sent to them, and that they be allowed to search the lawyers crossing the demarcation line between the occupied zone and the free zone in the south, where Riom was situated.

The Vichy authorities protested, and eventually the matter was settled in negotiations with Abetz, who concluded that the Germans had an interest in allowing the trial to go ahead unimpeded.

The trial eventually opened on 19 February 1942. The indictment was 169 pages long and included such vague allegations as that the defendants had encouraged the illusion that victory would be easy.[16] The Prosecution made overtly political allegations, alleging that the policies of the *Front populaire* were the direct cause of the country's lack of preparation for war, for instance because the introduction of the forty-hour week, a social measure introduced by the left-wing government, had reduced industrial production. The other alleged crimes of the ministers ('betrayal of the duties of office') were nowhere formulated in law, and so the proceedings of the trial involved a lengthy, detailed, and largely technical discussion about the minutiae of France's defence policy in the latter half of the 1930s. The discussions were conducted with no reference to the context in which governmental decisions were taken, in this case the economic crisis into which the whole of Europe was plunged after the Wall Street crash of 1929 and the collapse of the gold standard after 1933. That crisis had caused huge political upheavals in France, most notably the right-wing riots of 6 February 1934 and the election of the socialist *Front populaire* government in 1936. More importantly, the very premise, namely that the outcome of the war was the result of mechanistic determinism – the simple product of a balance-sheet of military force – did not, in fact, correspond to military reality; in the summer of 1940, after the initial decision to hold the trial, the Royal Air Force had defeated the Luftwaffe in the Battle of Britain, even though the Germans vastly outnumbered the British in terms of aircraft.

The authorities issued detailed instructions to the press on 18 February 1942, shortly before the trial commenced, on what journalists were allowed to report and what points they were supposed to emphasize. Reporters were told 'not to forget that the trial is limited to the lack of preparation for the war, in France, between 1936 and 1940', and the censor worked hard to ensure that party line was followed. But these measures quickly backfired. André Le Troquer, who had been Léon Blum's minister of defence, appeared at Riom as Blum's defence counsel. (He went on to become a staunch Gaullist but his political career ended in ignominy when in 1960, aged seventy-six, he was convicted of organizing and attending erotic dances involving underage girls, an accusation he denounced as politically motivated.) Le Troquer caused a sensation when he revealed that he was in possession of these censorship instructions. He read them out in court, stupefying and embarrassing the judges.[17] His revelation made a nonsense of Pétain's claim that the trial would ensure that henceforth the

French people would no longer be deceived. Observers were also shocked when the presiding judge, Pierre Caous, decided to hold certain sessions *in camera*.[18] Such shock is unfortunately not expressed in our own day when international criminal tribunals do exactly the same thing, as we shall see in chapters 16 and 17 dealing with the International Criminal Tribunals for Rwanda and the former Yugoslavia: both these tribunals make widespread use of such secret *in camera* sessions.

But Vichy could not censor the foreign press, who were present. The BBC received regular transcripts from the trial, which it was happy to read out on the radio. The collaborationist press in Paris was critical too; the anti-Vichy fascist leader, Marcel Déat, demanded in various articles that the Riom defendants be simply taken out and shot, and he regarded the trial as proof of Vichy's pusillanimity.[19] On Goebbels's instructions, the German press also attacked the perfidious French for trying to put the blame for the war on a few men, when in fact the whole nation was guilty.

In this context of political control over the whole of the French national press – whether by the Vichy censors or by Otto Abetz's deep pockets in Paris – the Riom trial paradoxically created a little island of relatively free speech. As soon as the trial opened, General Gamelin announced that he would refuse to say anything during the proceedings. (The same strategy was to be adopted by Marshal Pétain himself when he ended up in the dock three years later.) Gamelin's decision infuriated the other defendants, especially Léon Blum, who told the judges that it rendered the whole trial absurd. 'What is this trial about if not a military defeat?' asked Blum.[20] Le Troquer, Blum's counsel, then argued that the court itself did not have a legal foundation since the constitutional order on which the whole of the Vichy government was based had not been ratified by the Assemblies, as the original law of 10 July 1940 required that it should be. He argued that the 1875 constitution provided for the Senate to try ministers, and that it remained in force; he said that that it was morally wrong to conduct such a trial while France was occupied by enemy forces, since the country was clearly not at liberty; he berated Vichy for its attack on civil liberties; and he drew attention to the retroactive effect of the law of 10 July 1940.

Daladier's lawyer, Maurice Ribet (whose presence in court must have been impressive if he spoke as well as he wrote), argued similarly that the trial was illegal because the Constitutional Act No. 5 of 30 July 1940, which created the court, had invented a new crime, that of betraying the duties of one's office, and that it had then applied sanction for this crime retroactively. He attacked the judges for both conducting the investigation and adjudicating the case. Ribet then attacked the Prosecution for fixing the beginning of the period under consideration at 1936 for political reasons.

The Prosecution maintained that this was the year of the reoccupation of the Rhineland, and that it was then that it became obvious that Hitler was intending to overthrow the Versailles settlement and rearm Germany, but Ribet retorted passionately, as did Léon Blum after him, that there were plenty of other dates one could have chosen: the Nazis were elected in 1933; Germany left the League of Nations in 1933; conscription was introduced in Germany in 1935, and so on. Blum said that a proper court of law would have fixed the date using the legal statute of limitations, not on the basis of a political or even a historical assessment.[21] The date 1936 had instead been chosen, he said, to incriminate the socialist *Front populaire* government, elected that year, [22] and to obscure the fact that Marshal Pétain had himself been minister of war in 1934.

However, the main defendants, especially Daladier and Blum, had no desire to hide behind technical arguments about legal legitimacy. These were seasoned parliamentarians who wanted to address the wider public outside the courtroom – a reflex which was to motivate many subsequent former heads of state and government on trial, from Vidkun Quisling to Slobodan Milošević. Ribet wrote later, 'We had to take advantage of the hearings – if they had the courage to commence them – to transform the witness box into a political tribune.'[23] Unlike the strategy adopted by Louis XVI, therefore, the Riom Defence consisted in refusing to accept the terms laid down against the defendants by the Prosecution, and in trying dramatically to turn the tables on their accusers instead. Blum and Daladier were therefore both on their feet during the very first hearing, on 19 February, eager to speak in public after seventeen months of captivity. Daladier protested vehemently at the fact that he and the other defendants had already been proclaimed guilty by Marshal Pétain and the press, and he protested that he was a patriot who had rearmed France.[24] Blum gave a magnificent speech, alleging that the trial had been rigged to target specifically political enemies but to exonerate the army. 'The trial which is opening,' Blum declared, 'is a political trial, a trial of reprisal against the government of the *Front populaire*.' He also insisted that the purpose of the trial was to discredit the Republic and the democratic system of government.

While many of the hearings were taken up with technical discussions about how many aircraft had been ordered, the only purportedly legal part of the indictment was the charge that the defendants had declared war without the consent of the two houses of parliament, as the constitution required. This accusation was a halfway house between the Vichyite position that the defendants had not prepared France sufficiently for war, and the German position that they had been guilty of starting the war in the first place. However, the accusation was ill grounded, since the defendants' position – that the declaration of war had in fact been triggered automatically when Germany invaded Poland, and in virtue of the undertaking given to Poland on 31 March 1939, which the French parliament had supported – had been argued persuasively in a learned law journal by none other than Joseph Barthélemy himself, by now Vichy's minister of justice.

The trial struggled to come to terms with the vast questions of world politics and military strategy at stake in 1940. By ignoring the true context, the indictment seemed to accept the Vichyite analysis of the war as a Franco-German conflict and not a world one. Ironically, moreover, the trial emphasized that the defendants shared the same defensive attitude to warfare as Marshal Pétain had done: huge sums had been built constructing the ultimately useless Maginot line on the Franco-German border, which the Germans had simply bypassed by invading through the Low Countries instead. And what about events beyond France's control, especially the attitude of Belgium? Belgian neutrality presented France with an intractable problem: to build a defensive barrier on the border with Belgium as well as the Maginot line would have implied that France would never ally with Belgium, or help her in case of attack, but Belgium's neutrality also made it impossible for France pre-emptively to move her forces into Belgian territory. Such a move would have been precisely what Germany had done in 1914. The result was that the land was left unprotected, and over it the Germans eventually drove their tanks into France.

There are grounds for saying that France and Britain should have attacked Germany when she invaded Poland in September 1939: Hitler had sent nearly the entire German army east, leaving Germany effectively undefended in the west. German senior staff regarded with horror the prospect that France might detect this weakness and take advantage of it, but she never did. But such a charge could never have been included in the prosecution because the Germans would not have allowed it. In any case, such huge questions of state policy simply cannot be subsumed within the framework of the criminal law.

In fact, the hearings demonstrated that the indictments were unfounded and that the various Third Republic administrations had, in fact, rearmed France: France did have plenty of tanks, and German superiority lay instead in communications, guns, and training.[25] The defendants succeeded in their strategy of exploiting their time in the dock to attack their accusers. Already imprisoned and convicted on Pétain's say-so, they had nothing to lose by deriding him and other pillars of the Vichyite order, whose reputations as irreproachable men suffered concomitantly.

If anyone in Vichy had thought the trial would improve relations with the Germans, they were proved wrong. The Germans wanted what the Allies were to obtain at Nuremberg, a condemnation of the opposing side (in this case, France) for starting the war; Vichy France, by contrast, wanted a condemnation of the defeat. Otto Abetz had persuaded his masters that the trial would help lever France into joining the new European order, but leading Germans started to fear that the trial would lead to an acquittal, and many regarded Abetz as an untrustworthy Francophile.

Worse still, from the German point of view, was that anti-German feeling ran very high in the courtroom, as the defendants put up their robust show. One witness (the exquisitely named Marquis de Moustiers) shouted out at the German journalists in the courtroom, 'I killed a Kraut!' (*J'ai tué un Boche!*). Far from silencing him, the presiding judge said that it was comforting to know that there were still Frenchmen like him around.[26] Daladier and the other defendants called openly in court for an Allied victory. Léon Blum's speeches, reported by the foreign press, earned him a telegram on his birthday in 1942 (9 April) from Eleanor Roosevelt. The German military commander in France even reported that a rise in Resistance actions against Vichy was due to the Riom trial.[27] The war in the east was beginning to turn against Nazi Germany at this stage, and the German generals resented the implication contained in the indictment that their victory against France had been anything less than a brilliant military achievement; they did not want the court to show that France had been hopelessly unprepared, or that the fall of France was therefore a foregone conclusion.

Matters came to a head when Hitler attacked Vichy and the Riom trial explicitly in a speech in Berlin on 15 March 1942. He said,

> A trial is taking place these days in France, whose main characteristic is that not a word is spoken about the guilt of those responsible for this war. Only a lack of preparation for war is being discussed. We are here looking at a mentality which is incomprehensible to us but which is perhaps better suited than any other to reveal the causes of this new war.

The French authorities were shocked by this public attack. Pétain ordered the trial to be suspended on the pretext that all responsibilities should be examined and not just those currently being debated. The pretence was that the trial would reopen once the indictment had been reformulated, but this was just a diplomatic euphemism to hide the fact that the political desires of the Germans and the French were fatally opposed. The press was told to publish the indictments again, which it did, and the impression was given that the facts alleged in them had been proved. They had not.

The defendants were deported to Germany where they were imprisoned until the end of the war. As Maurice Ribet harshly put it, the old marshal had capitulated once again. Vichy had both lost face in public and irritated the Germans. A trial of politicians which had started for reasons of pure political expediency was closed for precisely the same reason. It was, as Henri Michel says, a combination of opera buffa and tragedy – rather like the Vichy experiment itself.

5   Justice as Purge: Marshal Pétain Faces his Accusers

Just over two years after the Riom trial collapsed under the weight of its own contradictions, the tables were turned. Allied troops landed in France on 6 June 1944, and by 25 August, Paris had been liberated. The old marshal had been warmly acclaimed by crowds when he visited the capital in April, but the public mood swung dramatically against him when the Gaullists took power. There were two million French people in Germany – forced labourers, deportees, or prisoners of war – and the huge emotions (especially the desire for revenge) which had been bottled up exploded when they returned. They had that peculiar venom which only civil conflicts generate. At the same time, there were also millions of ordinary French people for whom it was incredible that their wartime government had been composed of traitors. Many had believed that Pétain in Vichy and de Gaulle in London were both fighting the Germans, the one as the shield, the other as the sword. Thus began the mini civil war in France known as *l'épuration*, the purge in which between thirty and forty thousand people were summarily shot.[1]

Taken captive by the Germans (his German minder was the pro-European Nazi thinker and former plenipotentiary in Denmark, Cecile von Renthe-Fink[2]) and sent to Germany in August 1944, Pétain wrote to Hitler demanding that he be allowed to return to France. This eventually occurred in April 1945. He was greeted by crowds shouting for his death. The Communist Party was powerful; it controlled the press and had a million members. The Gaullists, the Communists' allies, had proclaimed Pétain guilty of treason. Pétain's reputation had soared to the heights in 1918; now it plumbed the depths. Like a sacrificial victim in a primitive society, he had been first venerated before being cast down and cast out.

Pétain's trial was the first in what was to be a series of immensely high-profile trials of wartime leaders across liberated Europe, from France to Bulgaria and from Finland to Greece. The judicial origins of the trial lie in a declaration made on 3 September 1943 by the French Committee for National Liberation and signed by generals Giraud and de Gaulle in Algiers.[3] This stated that Pétain and his ministers were 'guilty of treason' for having signed the armistice on 22 June 1940 'against the will of the people'. The Declaration said that, as a result of their guilt, they would be 'handed over to justice' at the liberation. Pétain had proclaimed the defendants at Riom guilty before their trial; now he was getting a taste of his own medicine.[4]

Pétain's trial was just the apex of a vast judicial purge. A government order (*ordonnance*) issued by the provisional government in Algiers on 21 April 1944 dealt with 'the organization of public institutions after the liberation' and provided for Vichy officials (Vichy is referred to throughout as 'the usurper') to be removed from office and debarred from election once regular elections had been re-established (Article 18); departmental liberation committees, composed of *résistants*, were to be set up to 'assist' the prefects in each part of France in this task (Article 19). This was the legal beginning of the *épuration*. On 27 June 1944 de Gaulle having set up his headquarters in Bayeux, a further order was published creating the relevant purge committees (*commissions d'épuration*).

Vichy had interned 70,000 people, and of course contributed to the deportation of over 75,000 Jews – albeit under conditions of terrible constraint by the Germans, who habitually wrought barbaric vengeance by executing innocent civilian hostages if their demands for deportations were not met.[5] The Resistance took its revenge. In addition to extra-judicial killings, the military and civil tribunals examined some 150,000 prosecutions and over 7,000 people were condemned to death, 767 of whom were in fact executed.[6] The purges put many of the most famous figures in French collaboration in the dock: Fernand de Brinon, Charles Maurras, Robert Brasillach. Today, however, the *ordonnance* of 21 April 1944 is remembered only for the fact that it gave women the vote.

In an order dated 26 June 1944, the provisional government proclaimed that acts committed would be adjudicated 'notwithstanding all legislation in force'. This meant that people could be prosecuted and convicted for obeying the law of their country at the time (the laws of the Vichy government), a principle later to be adopted at Nuremberg. Its first article proclaimed that special courts would be created 'to judge acts committed between 16 June 1940 and the date of the liberation' on the basis of pre-Vichy laws 'wherever they reveal the intention of their authors to favour any kind of enemy enterprise'.

A further official instruction to prosecute Pétain and others was issued on 13 September 1944, and the High Court of Justice itself was instituted on 18 November 1944. It was composed of twenty-four jurors – twelve parliamentarians and twelve *résistants* – and three judges. Although the jurisdiction created was a special jurisdiction, trying offences prior to its creation and thereby infringing the principle of non-retroactivity, the allegations themselves against Pétain (intelligence with the enemy and conspiracy against the security of the state) had been on the penal code before the outbreak of war, as Articles 75 and 87.

A government order issued in Paris on 28 November 1944 further modified the competence of the newly created tribunals, allowing them to take into consideration acts committed before 16 June 1940 if they were deemed to have been directed towards helping the enemy. This reflected the view, contained in the original Pétain indictment but (as we shall see) withdrawn by the Prosecution nine days into the trial, that the marshal had somehow actually conspired with Franco and Hitler to overthrow the French Republic.

The harshness of the original condemnation issued in 1943 reflects the political imperatives of the Resistance's battle for legitimacy: de Gaulle and his allies had to prove that they were the legitimate government of France, and that Vichy was legally null and void. The Pétain trial was intended to show this. A government order dated 9 August 1944 and entitled 'On the re-establishment of Republican legality' had proclaimed the legal nullity of Vichy (although this would presumably have obviated the need for special tribunals, since if Vichy had really been legally null and void it could have been prosecuted by restored Third Republic laws and courts). The Gaullists wanted the trial to provide legal confirmation of their view that Vichy had been illegitimate from the moment it signed the armistice (de Gaulle's own 'appeal' having been broadcast on the BBC the following day).

Pétain's trial was preceded by that of Admiral Esteva, the French representative in Tunisia who was tried and convicted in March 1945 for treason, having opposed the Allied landings in North Africa. It was also preceded by Communist-backed executions of Vichy officials, notably that of the Vichy interior minister, Pierre Pucheu, sentenced to death by a military court in Algeria in March 1944. This execution was carried out after a strong campaign in the Communist press against him. Speaking at the Esteva trial, Prosecutor André Mornet (who had prosecuted Mata Hari as a German spy in 1917, and who was later to prosecute Pétain himself) said specifically that, 'With his trial it is the trial of Pétain and Laval which commences today.' Georges Chresteil, Esteva's counsel, was quick off the mark when he advanced the *tu quoque* argument with respect to the Prosecutor himself. 'What did you do in 1940, Mr Prosecutor?' he asked. 'You came out of retirement to associate yourself with the judicial measures taken by the Vichy government. For four years, you were vice-president of the Commission which dealt with the withdrawal of naturalizations, a commission whose president is now in prison.' Mornet, in other words, had himself collaborated, working on the revocation of citizenship which was the legal prerequisite for the deportation of Jews.[7] In the Pétain trial, the marshal's lawyer, Jacques Isorni, was to take a leaf out of Chresteil's book when he revealed to an astonished court that Mornet had even been approached to sit as a judge on the Riom bench.

The main pressure for revolutionary justice of the liberation came from the powerful Communist Party, with whom the Gaullists had concluded an alliance in 1943. The Communist-controlled press called unanimously for Pétain to be put to death. Jacques Isorni, Pétain's counsel, argued that the June 1943 agreement between de Gaulle and the Communists to create the French Committee for National Liberation included an agreement that the party's behaviour in the period 1939 to 1941, when the Soviet Union was an ally of Nazi Germany, would never be mentioned in court.[8] The complicity between de Gaulle and the Communists also became clear when, in the autumn of 1944, de Gaulle amnestied Maurice Thorez, the Communist leader, who had been convicted of desertion at the outbreak of war in 1939.

The structure of the specially constituted High Court of Justice left little room for error. Composed of jurors and parliamentarians, the members of both groups were pre-selected on the basis of their political affiliation as *résistants*, i.e. enemies of Vichy and Pétain. The parliamentarians, for instance, were barred from sitting on the jury if they had voted *les pleins pouvoirs* for Pétain on 10 July 1940, as indeed the great majority of parliamentarians had. (Only eighty had voted against.)

The Pétain trial opened on Monday 23 July 1945, Pétain having returned to France from German captivity on 26 April 1945. The Prosecution had therefore had only three months to prepare its case. The trial lasted a mere three weeks, and the verdict and sentence were read out after all-night deliberations at 4 a.m. on 15 August. Many of the most important documents of Vichy France, including Pétain's own personal files, were never consulted, while the original indictment was largely devoted to a charge of conspiracy to overthrow the Republic, allegedly on the basis of an affidavit which turned out not to exist. The fact that the indictment was based on a conspiracy charge emphasizes how determined the Gaullist prosecutors were to prove that the armistice itself had been an act of treason and that, as a result of it, theirs was the only legitimate government of France.

Photographs of the proceedings that day show a cramped courtroom; contemporary reports emphasize how hot and stuffy it was. Many of the major political and military players of France's wartime tragedy assembled here for the final dénouement; Albert Lebrun, the president of the Republic overthrown when Pétain became head of the French state, testified, as did Paul Reynaud, his prime minister, who had declared war on Germany in September 1939 and who had then been imprisoned in Germany until 1945. Reynaud stood so close to Pétain during his testimony that he could have shaken his hand. Louis Marin, one of Reynaud's ministers and one of the eighty parliamentarians who had refused to vote for Pétain on 10 July 1940 testified, as did Michel Clemenceau, son of Georges Clemenceau, 'The Tiger' who had led France to victory in World War I. Jean-Jules Jeanneney, former president of the Senate, and Edouard Herriot, three times president of the council in the Third Republic and president of the National Assembly at the time of the vote of *les pleins pouvoirs*, were there. General Weygand testified, the man who had replaced Gamelin as chief of staff and who had been in that post when the armistice was signed. The trial was also attended by a future leader of France: photographs show a young François Mitterrand sitting on the press benches. Having worked for the Vichy government until 1942, and having been given Vichy's highest honour, the *Francisque gallique*, Mitterrand was president of the Republic from 1981 to 1995.

The trial was conducted in a very French manner, without the formalism and structure one associates with English legal proceedings. Witnesses were allowed to make long statements with minimal prompting from the presiding judge, who would usually tell them to start speaking with a neutral invitation like 'Tell us what you know.' Witnesses were not always cross-examined afterwards. People would come to testify at very short notice, and sometimes on the basis of their own request as a result of something they had read about themselves in the papers. Jurors were allowed to intervene and ask witnesses questions, which they frequently did when the witnesses were appearing for the Defence. The speakers were often eloquent, especially Pétain's counsel, the young Jacques Isorni, whose brilliance and dedication impressed many. But there were also heated exchanges, in spite of the fact that the presiding judge, Paul Mongibeaux, opened the first session with a reference to the love and hatred felt for Pétain at different times and by different people, calling for all passions to be extinguished and recalling that the court's only concerns were truth and justice.

During the pre-trial interrogations, which had started in May 1945, Pétain had given contradictory answers which suggested that he was going senile. When he eventually appointed defence lawyers, they disagreed about which strategy to follow. Defence counsel Fernand Payen wanted simply to plead for clemency and to save the marshal's life: he wanted to argue that he was too old to die and that Vichy's excesses were the fault of his ministers, his advisers, and the Germans. Isorni, by contrast, who had defended Communists during the occupation, wanted to save the marshal's reputation. He became an active admirer of Pétain, even saying to him before the trial, 'Marshal, I make to you the gift of my own person,' – the very words Pétain had used of himself in 1940. He told Pétain to remember the trials of Joan of Arc, Napoleon's exile in St. Helena, and the trial of Louis XVI.[9] The two were joined by Jean-Marie Lemaire, but it was Isorni's strategy which was adopted. Pétain himself resolved that only history and God could be his judge: he therefore decided to remain silent in the courtroom, after having read out a declaration which was to be his final testament to the French people.

Before he did so, however, and as soon as the proceedings had been opened by the presiding judge, Fernand Payen contested the right of the High Court to judge the marshal. The constitution of 1875, he said, was still in force and, according to it, only the Senate, constituted as a High Court, could judge the head of state or ministers. This was the same argument the Defence had made at Riom. The judges withdrew to deliberate and found in their own favour; although this same ruling was made when the International Criminal Tribunal for the former Yugoslavia adjudicated its own legitimacy during the first case it heard in 1995, it violates a key principle of law that no one may be a judge in his own cause.

The indictment was then read out by the registrar: the bulk of it concerned Pétain's alleged plot to overthrow the Republic, a plot which the prosecutor said the marshal had hatched years previously. He claimed that Pétain and other anti-democratic forces in France had conspired to destroy democracy and introduce a monarchical system along the lines of the political philosophy of Charles Maurras, the leader of the *Action française* who had notoriously said that the proclamation of the national revolution was 'a divine surprise'. The prosecutor marshalled a series of innuendoes that Pétain was 'in contact with' or 'had relations with' various pro-fascist or pro-German personalities, including Fernand de Brinon, the collaborationist theoretician, or with *La Cagoule,* the secretive right-wing paramilitary movement which campaigned for the overthrow of the Republic and which had heavily infiltrated the army. In the course of his opening speech, prosecutor Mornet cited an allegedly 'decisive document', containing evidence given by Raphael Alibert, the *cagoulard* former minister of justice, which, he said, proved the conspiracy and that the marshal was himself a *cagoulard* together with Laval, Darlan, Huntziger, and Déat.[10] The genuine existence of this movement, and the view held by many other sections of the French population besides that the Republic was irredeemably corrupt, led many to believe that Pétain had deliberately conspired to engineer events in order to perpetrate what they saw as his *coup d'état*.

In support of the conspiracy theory, Pétain was accused of the three Constitutional Acts which abrogated the election of the president of the Republic; of relations with the *Cagoule* and other anti-Republican groups; of a treasonable policy in the face of defeat (the decision to meet Hitler at Montoire in October 1940 and to collaborate with Germany); of creating legislation in France similar to that of Germany; of handing over political refugees to the Reich; of providing assistance to Germany by supplying labour and *matériel*; of abandoning Indochina; and of instructing troops to resist the Allies and the Gaullists. These alleged crimes corresponded to conspiracy against the internal security of the state and intelligence with the enemy for personal gain, proscribed by Articles 87 and 75 of the existing penal code respectively.

After the indictment had been read out, Pétain was asked to speak. The court fell silent. 'The French people, through its representatives meeting in a national assembly, entrusted me with power on 10 July 1940,' said the old marshal. 'It is to the French people that I have come to give an account of myself.' Pétain denied that the High Court represented the French people and maintained that he was addressing the nation, not it. He said he would make no further statement or answer any questions but that he would leave his defence to his lawyers. He recalled his great age and his past military glory. His life, he said, had been devoted to France. France had turned to him in its hour of need and 'begged' him to serve again. 'I became thereby the inheritor of a catastrophe for which I was not responsible; those who are really responsible are hiding behind me to avoid the anger of the people,' he said. He said that armistice had been 'a necessary and saving act' and that it had contributed to the victory of the Allies by ensuring a free Mediterranean and the integrity of the French empire. Power had been conferred on him legitimately and his government had been recognized by 'all the states in the world from the Holy See to the Soviet Union'. 'I used this power as a shield to protect the French people. For it, I sacrificed my prestige. I remained at the head of an occupied country.'

'Does anyone understand the difficulty of governing under such conditions?' Pétain asked. 'Every day, a knife at my throat, I struggled against the demands of the enemy. History will tell all that I protected you from, while my enemies think only of reproaching me for the inevitable.' He said he had been obliged to treat with the enemy but that he did this only to prepare France for the liberation. The occupation had also obliged him to say things he did not mean. He had abandoned nothing which was essential for the country's existence but had protected the French people. He referred to de Gaulle as 'continuing the struggle beyond our borders' and said that he had 'prepared a way for the liberation by preserving a France which was sad but alive'. 'What would have been the point of liberating ruins and cemeteries?' he asked.

Pétain defended his government's social policies and the change to the constitution. He said that he had worked only for the union and the reconciliation of the French, and that the Germans had taken him prisoner precisely because they accused him 'of never ceasing to combat them and of ruining their efforts'. He said he had been supported by many French people not for his person but because he represented 'a tradition which is that of the French and Christian civilization, against the excesses of all tyrannies'. He said the condemnation of him would be a condemnation of those who had put their hope in him, and that it would aggravate and prolong the discord of France. He concluded:

> But my life matters little. I have made the gift of my person to France. At this supreme moment, my sacrifice should no longer be called into doubt. If you are to condemn me, let this be the last condemnation and let no French person be detained or convicted for having obeyed the orders of his legitimate leader. But, I say it to you in front of the world, you would be condemning an innocent man while believing you speak in the name of justice, and it is an innocent man who will bear the burden, for a marshal of France asks for grace from no one. Your judgement will be subject to that of God and to that of posterity. They are sufficient for my conscience and for my memory. I confide myself in France's hands![11]

Pétain sat down and said almost nothing for the rest of the trial. He generally refused to answer questions, although he did intervene on a few occasions, for instance to say that Winston Churchill had released France from her obligation not to sign a separate peace with Germany. (Weygand did not agree with his former boss on this crucial point, but de Gaulle recalls in his memoirs that the question of a separate peace was openly raised at a meeting between Churchill and the French government, held at the prefecture in Tours on 13 June 1940, and that the British prime minister – to de Gaulle's shock and annoyance – did release France from her obligation, on the sole condition that she not allow the French navy to fall into German hands.[12]) Generally it was clear that Pétain could not hear what was going on but on one occasion he signalled a clear 'No' with his hand when Léon Blum suggested that he had plotted for years to take power.[13]

In spite of the fact that roughly half of the indictment had dealt with Pétain's alleged anti-Republican links and his conspiracies with Hitler, Franco, and others, on 1 August 1945, the ninth day of the trial, after the Prosecution had produced no evidence to support this crucial charge, Defence counsel Payen asked pointedly whether the conspiracy theory still formed part of the indictment. If so, he said, he wanted to call witnesses to refute it. Prosecutor Mornet dissembled and tried to claim that he had meant not so much actual conspiracy but instead 'pre-meditation'. It was clear that the charge of an actual conspiracy against the Republic was unsustainable, and that the Prosecution had reluctantly realized that it had to abandon it.

The remaining charges concerned whether or not France had broken her promise to Britain not to deal separately with Germany, and whether Vichy had committed a *coup d'état* against the Republic by going beyond the terms of the vote of 10 July 1940. Many Prosecution witnesses, especially Blum, tried to argue that the armistice was itself an act of treason but such an allegation was difficult to sustain: an armistice is a perfectly legitimate form of state action. Instead, the way in which Vichy progressively sold out to the Germans, in spite of claims that it had practised resistance against them – the very thing for which Vichy is now notorious – was hardly dealt with by the trial.

There were some thirty witnesses for the Prosecution and forty for the Defence. The most aggressive towards Pétain were the former prime ministers, Léon Blum and Paul Reynaud. Reynaud's position was compromised by the fact that it was he who had brought Pétain into the government in May 1940 and that, as the Defence was happy to reveal, he had written an ingratiating letter to the marshal on 10 July 1940, saying that he remembered fondly the time when they had worked together.[14] Edouard Daladier took a different position from that of his old rival, Reynaud: he argued that the armistice had been inevitable and situated Pétain's treachery not in 1940 but in 1942 when he had bowed to the German occupation of the southern ('free') zone of France. But Daladier was forced to admit that he did not know whether Pétain had actively colluded with the enemy, nor whether there had been any conspiracy to take power before 1940.

The Defence countered that France had lost the Battle of France, as a matter of fact, and that an armistice, which kept the French government in place and preserved North Africa and the rest of the empire from the Germans, was therefore a better and less dishonourable solution than capitulation, a government in exile, and full occupation by the Nazis.

Isorni deftly exploited the hypocrisy underlying the Pétain trial. During Daladier's testimony, he read out a letter from François Billoux, a Communist who was at that time minister of health in the government of General de Gaulle and who, during the occupation, had written to Marshal Pétain asking for permission to give evidence against Daladier at Riom; Daladier was the Communists' *bête noire*, since he had banned the Communist Party in 1939 and had had many of its members arrested, including Billoux himself. Isorni received 'laughter, murmurs, and protestations' in the courtroom, according to the transcript, when he asked Daladier with savage irony, 'Does this not strike you as odd? Here are three men whose names appear on the same piece of paper. You, Monsieur Daladier, you put M. Billoux in prison. Marshal Pétain then put you in prison. Today M. Billoux is in power and the government of which he is a member has put Marshal Pétain in prison. Doesn't this all make you a little sceptical about the role of justice in political matters?'[15]

The Defence witnesses, who were cleverly chosen, made various points. Charles Tronchu, a former president of the municipal council of Paris under the occupation but a member of a Gaullist network, testified that Pétain was playing a double game, making positive declarations only to trick the Germans. A member of the Resistance who had been imprisoned in the town of Vichy by the French police, and who had then been sent to a German concentration camp, testified that Vichy had prevented things from being worse than they would have otherwise been. Pétain's lawyer reminded the court that, when the Germans had said they would murder a hundred hostages in reprisal for the killing of two soldiers, Pétain wrote to Hitler and said he would present himself at the demarcation line as the first hostage; the plan was abandoned. More generally, the number of workers and matériel transported to Germany was far lower from France than from other occupied countries, as of course was the number of Jews deported, which was one of the lowest in occupied Europe.

General Weygand's testimony was particularly dramatic. Himself now in prison, and in poor health, Weygand claimed that Paul Reynaud, the prime minister, had told him to capitulate on 14 June, saying that he intended to follow the example of the queen of the Netherlands and leave the country.[16] Weygand replied that he would never dishonour himself or France by capitulating, and that capitulation in mid-battle was in any case a capital offence according to the French military code. The courtroom positively crackled with the hatred which Reynaud and Weygand felt for each other. Reynaud replied that he had called for a ceasefire, not a capitulation. Like all Vichy officials, Weygand protested his patriotism and told the court that of course the armistice had been a deep humiliation (he himself had read out the terms of the armistice to the Germans in the railway carriage at Rethondes in November 1918) but that it had been dictated by military necessity.[17] He also argued that the claim that the government should have withdrawn to North Africa was absurd, because France's military presence there was so weak that it would have been captured quickly, especially if Italy and Spain had intervened with Germany to snatch French North Africa. This was to say nothing of the 400,000 Jews who lived in French North Africa and who were essentially unmolested there as a result.

Weygand argued that the armistice prevented the Germans from gaining control of the Mediterranean and that they ended up regretting ever having signed it. It is indeed claimed by Vichy apologists that Goering said that the armistice was Hitler's greatest error. (Gaullists retort that, on the contrary, the armistice enabled Hitler to neutralize France and that, with diabolical political genius, he knew not to push the French too far into a resistance which would have jeopardized his control over western Europe.) General George testified during the trial that Churchill told him precisely this on 4 January 1944 in Marrakesh: the general read out a note he had taken shortly after speaking to Churchill, who had said to him, 'In June 1940, after the Battle of France (*la Bataille du Nord*) Britain was left without weapons. We had not made sufficient preparations in terms of tanks and aircraft. Ultimately, the armistice helped us. Hitler committed an error by agreeing to it. He should have gone into North Africa, he should have taken it and carried on to Egypt. Then our task would have been very difficult.'[18] This was precisely Vichy's defence.

In many respects, the Pétain trial was a mirror image of the Riom trial. Many of the same people were present at both trials, only with their roles reversed. Former accused became witnesses for the Prosecution, especially Edouard Daladier and Léon Blum, both of whom had until only two months previously been prisoners in Germany. Blum raged against the way Pétain had duped the French, at their weakest moment, into believing in him: 'This monstrous abuse of trust, that is treason,' he said. The eerie impression of an inverted re-run of Riom was reinforced when the presiding judge of that trial, Pierre Caous, unexpectedly appeared at the Pétain trial to defend his own name. Caous wanted to testify that the judges on his bench in Riom had not sworn an oath of fidelity to Marshal Pétain, because the oath had been introduced subsequent to their appointments. (Caous himself, as it happened, had sworn the oath, because he had been a judge in the Cour de Cassation when it was introduced, but he still insisted that it had not compromised his professional integrity.) The issue arose because the judges in the Pétain trial were forced to admit that they too had sworn the oath of fidelity to Pétain themselves, having been judges throughout the Vichy period. Caous also testified that Pétain had said to him personally, after the Riom trial had been suspended, that it would be mad to want a judicial condemnation of France for having started the war.[19] Riom surfaced a third time when Jacques Isorni confronted Prosecutor Mornet with the stunning allegation that he had asked to sit on the Riom bench. Mornet reacted furiously, denouncing the claim as 'an infamy'. But Caous' testimony forced Mornet to admit that he had indeed *accepted* an offer to sit on the Riom bench (even if he had not actively sought the post) but that, for other reasons, he had not done so.[20] Such was the close interlinking between collaboration and resistance.

Perhaps the most dramatic moment was when Pierre Laval entered the room. Laval was the most reviled man in France, hated even by the marshal under whom he had crowned his political career. He embodied all the guilt of Vichy, more so than the marshal himself who had many defenders and even whose enemies admitted that he had been unanimously admired in 1940. Joseph Kessel, a reporter at the trial, dwelt on Laval's slitty eyes, reptilian appearance, and bad breath. Laval seemed more convinced than ever that everything he had done was right: he blamed Pétain for what he said were the worst acts, for instance meeting Hitler at Montoire. Pétain broke his silence during the testimony to say that he had never approved Laval's notorious declaration on the radio on 22 June 1944, 'I desire the victory of Germany for, without it, Communism will be installed all over Europe.' Laval came as a witness, of course, but his main goal was to prepare public opinion for his own trial by the same High Court. He spoke for four hours, over two successive sessions: he was funny and eloquent, he cried and raged.[21] It was to no avail. Laval was later to be convicted of treason by the same High Court, and, dragged from his prison cell while writhing in agony from the poison he had taken in a failed attempt to commit suicide, executed by firing squad on 15 October 1945.

One issue was almost completely absent from the trial: the Jewish question. As in the original preparatory reports for the later Nuremberg trials, from which the fate of the Jews was also absent, the deportation of more than 75,000 Jews from France, who eventually died in German concentration camps, was not mentioned in the indictment against Pétain. No Jewish witnesses were called, even though the prosecutor had received representations from Jews, and even though there had been letters in Jewish newspapers on the issue. Instead, the fate of *résistants*, soldiers, deportees, and prisoners of war dominated the public consciousness. The main mention of the persecution of Jews came in Pétain's defence when the president of the French Protestant Federation, Marc Boegner, testified that he was convinced that Pétain had been powerless 'to prevent great evils which, in his inner self, he called by their name and condemned them without limit'. Vichy France had actually obstructed some of the German demands in this regard, for instance by refusing to impose, in the free zone Vichy governed, the German requirement that Jews wear yellow stars.

On 14 August 1945, the trial ended and the judges withdrew. One of the jurors, Pétrus Faure, a left-wing but anti-Communist deputy, was a parliamentary member of the jury. An opponent of Pétain's domestic policies which he called 'reactionary and conservative', Faure however denounced the Pétain trial as 'the very archetype of a political trial of doubtful legitimacy'.[22] Later neutral commentators have shared Faure's condemnation of the trial.[23] Faure came to the conclusion that Pétain had not betrayed France; that the conditions did not exist for a fair trial; that the High Court was an *ad hoc* court stuffed with his political enemies; that purges were raging in France; and that the press was controlled and completely against Pétain. But it would be an understatement to say that this is a minority view.

Faure has described what happened after the judges and jurors withdrew: the presiding judge opened by saying that the evidence tendered had not justified the allegations contained in the indictment, and he suggested a sentence of five years' exile. He was massively outvoted by the Resistance jurors, all of whom save one voted for the death penalty. By contrast, all the parliamentary jurors, including a Jewish deputy who had himself been the victim of racial persecution, were against the death penalty, save three. The matter went to a secret ballot and there were fourteen votes for the death penalty and thirteen against.[24] There was then a vote on whether to suspend the death penalty, in view of the defendant's great age. The vote for suspension was carried seventeen votes to ten; there is some speculation that the Gaullist members voted this way in order to be helpful to de Gaulle, who might have paid a high political price if Pétain had been executed. When the judges returned to the courtroom at 4.30 a.m. on the morning of 15 August and read out the sentence, Pétain looked confused as he was led outside. The old marshal was put in the back of a van and sent to the Ile d'Yeu, a small island off the Atlantic coast of France, where he eventually died on 23 July 1951, aged ninety-seven.

6 Treachery on Trial: the Case of Vidkun Quisling

Marshal Pétain's trial finished on 15 August 1945. Five days later, on 20 August 1945, in the Freemasons' Hall in Oslo, the wartime leader of Norway, Vidkun Quisling, who had been minister-president of Norway from February 1942 to May 1945 and therefore, following the destitution of the king by the Nazis, *de facto* head of state, stood in the dock to face his own accusers on charges of treason.

Quisling's surname has passed into many languages as a synonym for 'traitor'. The coinage was invented by *The Times* within days of the German invasion of Norway and Quisling's assumption of power on 9 April 1940, perhaps because he was the first Western European politician to propose governing in collaboration with the Nazis; France, the Netherlands, and Belgium were not to fall until a month after Norway. But Quisling's life is more interesting than the simple concept to which he gave his name. An extremely talented mathematician, with many other intellectual skills including that of a formidable memory, Quisling was born in rural Norway, the son of a pastor. As a young man, he travelled to Russia with the great Norwegian explorer and philanthropist, Fridtjof Nansen, who won the Nobel Peace Prize in 1922 for his work in famine-stricken Russia where Quisling had been his adjutant. This was the beginning of a fascination with Russia which determined the course of Quisling's life. He married a Russian woman (his enemies said he married two) but he came to detest the Bolsheviks and anti-Communism became the animating principle of his politics. Following the mission to Russia with Nansen, Quisling returned to Moscow in the late 1920s as a diplomat and also served as British chargé d'affaires when London broke off diplomatic relations with the Soviet Union, for which he was awarded the CBE.

On his return to Norway, Quisling entered politics. He became minister of defence from 1931 to 1933, when he founded his crypto-Nazi party, Nasjonal Samling (National Unity). He appointed himself 'Fører' (leader) of the party in apparent imitation of Hitler and its main policy was anti-Communism. Communism had become a significant political issue in Norway; the country had a border with the Soviet Union and the Norwegian socialists joined the Third International when it was founded in 1919. Quisling was convinced they were being financed by Moscow. and he was proved right by a parliamentary inquiry in 1932. In 1936 the social-ist government smuggled the fugitive Trotsky into the country under an assumed name, from where he continued his fight against Stalin, just as the Spanish civil war was flaring up. Quisling argued that the Communist International wanted to catch Europe in a pincer movement between Spain and Scandinavia. Quisling was attracted to Hitler both for his anti-Bolshevism and for his anti-Semitism. Throughout the 1930s, Quisling argued vehemently in favour of Norwegian armed neutrality. He realized the strategic and geopolitical importance of his country which was so close to Britain, Germany, and the Soviet Union.

Quisling proclaimed himself head of the Norwegian government in the evening of 9 April 1940, the day of the German invasion. The events of this day formed the basis of the charges against him in 1945. The speed with which he seized power led many people to believe that he had en-tered into a conspiracy with Hitler, whom he had met in December 1939 in Berlin. When Quisling proclaimed himself leader, the existing govern-ment and the Norwegian parliament, the Storting, were still meeting in a provincial town.

However, subsequent events suggest that there was in fact no prior conspiracy. The Germans were themselves were in disarray about how Norway should be governed under their occupation, and Quisling had numerous enemies within the Nazi hierarchy, especially in Joachim von Ribbentrop's Foreign Office. When the government of Johan Nygaards-vold refused to capitulate, the Germans adopted a twin-track approach of trying both to negotiate with it and also to kill the king by bombing the towns to which he and the government had fled. But the German ambas-sador to Norway, Kurt Bräuer, like Foreign Minister Ribbentrop, had no time for Quisling. He may have been the Nazis' ideological ally but his party commanded negligible support in the country and had failed to win a single seat in the 1936 elections. So the Germans struggled to find some-one else to govern in Quisling's place. Within days of the invasion, the Storting did send a delegation to negotiate with the Germans but, at the same time, the president of the Supreme Court, Paal Berg, proposed that his court appoint an administrative council which would govern the coun-try. Quisling's own self-proclaimed 'government', meanwhile, collapsed almost as quickly as it had been created, as two of the men he appointed had not even been consulted and refused angrily and publicly.

By 15 April, Berg's Administrative Council had been set up. A ceremony was organized in the main hall of the Academy of Sciences to announce the formal transfer of power from Quisling to the new council, and at it, Berg thanked Quisling for stepping into the breach in Norway's hour of need. But on 17 April, the king announced from Sweden that he did not give his consent for the new Administrative Council either, and that only the now exiled government was legitimate. That government, moreover, had received full legislative powers from the Norwegian Parliament in an extraordinary meeting held at Elverum on the day of the invasion.

This renewed failure to establish a clear government caused Hitler to send a Reichskommissar to Norway. The Gauleiter of Essen, Josef Terboven, was given the job and he arrived in Norway on 21 April. But he too disapproved of Quisling. Thus began another five-month struggle for power. On 17 June, a presidential board of the Storting agreed to appoint a State Council, which revoked the special powers granted to the Nygaardsvold government on 9 April, and called on the king to renounce his constitutional prerogatives for the period of the occupation. In spite of orders from Hitler that Quisling himself should be asked to form a government, Terboven announced on 25 September that a commissarial government composed of Nasjonal Samling members had taken over the powers of the Administrative Council, which had been wound up. The king was declared deposed and all political parties were dissolved except the NS. Quisling did control this new government as party leader, but he was not a member of it himself.[1]

He did not become head of government until a year later. By September 1941, with the power struggle between Quisling and Terboven as sharp as ever, it became clear that the transitional commissarial government commanded no authority, and so on 23 January 1942, Terboven finally gave in and asked Quisling to form a government himself. On 1 February 1942 Quisling moved into the Akershus fortress where he was formally installed as minister-president (head of government) by the representatives of the German authority. But Terboven remained Reichskommissar with his powers intact, and Quisling could not initiate policy without his old rival's consent. Quisling obtained approval from the now supine Supreme Court for his government on 31 January 1942, and he and his ministers then proceeded to declare that they had royal and parliamentary authority to govern, i.e. that he was head of state as well.

However, even this 1942 victory was short-lived. By September 1942 a report commissioned by Reinhard Heydrich's RSHA (*Reichssicherheits-*

hauptamt, the head security office of the Reich) concluded that 95 per cent of Norwegians were anti-Quisling and anti-Nasjonal Samling, and that popular resistance to Quisling and the German occupation was on the rise. On 21 September there was a bomb attack on a police station, and Terboven concluded that the situation was spiralling out of control. From then on, Norway was effectively governed out of Berlin by Terboven and General von Falkenhorst, the German commander in Norway, with Quisling making few interventions. In November 1943, for instance, when there were student riots in Oslo university, it was the Gestapo and not the Norwegian police who went in to restore order and to arrest the rebels.

It was against this background that in August 1943 Quisling committed an act which was to form one of the principal charges against him at his trial. A policeman named Gunnar Eilifsen refused to arrest two women accused of violating the Quisling government's labour laws. On 9 August, Eilifsen was himself arrested and Terboven demanded his execution, threatening that his troops would carry out the execution if the Norwegian courts did not. Quisling duly passed a decree (dated 14 August 1943) which provided for the retroactive extension of the military code of 1902 to cover the police, who had hitherto not been governed by its provisions on mutiny, thereby extending the death penalty to them. This was the 'legal' basis on which Eilifsen was then tried by a 'people's court' and shot. The decree was a disaster for Quisling, since the illegality of Eilifsen's murder profoundly shocked Norwegian opinion. But the event also showed to what extent the collaborator Quisling was in fact under the Germans' thumb.

For the last years of the war, the largely powerless Quisling withdrew into increasingly esoteric and mystical reflection. He dreamed of returning to his home village and becoming a pastor. He continued to believe (or claimed to believe) in Nazi Germany's victory – on the basis that the Germans were about to develop and deploy a *Wunderwaffen* which would turn the tables in Germany's favour. An advocate for a lost cause long after many others had deserted it, Quisling sent Hitler a telegram assuring Norway's support for Germany as Allied troops rolled through France in the summer of 1944; he even travelled once again to Berlin to see Hitler on 28 January 1945. On 8 May 1945 Quisling negotiated an agreement with the Norwegian resistance for the peaceful handover of power but, in contravention of its terms, and to his own astonishment, he was arrested on 9 May and imprisoned.

On 26 May, Quisling was brought before a pre-trial hearing and remanded for three months pending the beginning of the proceedings themselves[2.] There were four counts. He was charged with seizing power illegally on 9 April 1940, conspiring to do so prior to the invasion, and issuing an order for the army to demobilize (these charges were brought under the 1902 military and civilian penal codes on treason); with assisting the enemy during wartime (Paragraph 86 of the penal code which states, 'Whoever supports the enemy during wartime in a traitor'); with suspending the constitution illegally, thereby violating Paragraph 98 of the penal code ('Overthrowing the state order is revolution'); and with the illegal execution of Eilifsen.

He spent the next four weeks writing a sixty-page rebuttal of these charges. He argued that he had known nothing of the German invasion and that he was innocent of any conspiracy; that he had issued his demobilization order only in the interests of neutrality and peace; that he had not tried to bring Norway under German control but instead only to preserve her freedom; and that he had himself resisted the demands for resources (both human, industrial, and natural) made by the Germans.[3] He also argued that his government had been legitimate since the government in exile had been out of the country for more than six months, while the Norwegian parliament had rescinded the authority of the commissarial government.[4]

The charges were extended in July, after Quisling had written his rebuttal, because the Prosecution discovered that Quisling had met Hitler in Berlin in 1939 and a German intelligence officer in the Hotel d'Angleterre in Copenhagen on the afternoon of 3 April 1940. At that meeting, it is almost certain that he communicated military secrets to the German, and these may well have been decisive in influencing the decision to invade. If so, it was direct proof of treason. Testimony was also coming in from the interrogators at the Nuremberg trials, which were to start that November. During Quisling's trial, indeed, information gleaned from the interrogations of Alfred Rosenberg (Quisling's main patron in Berlin), Joachim von Ribbentrop, Hermann Goering, Wilhelm Keitel, and Alfred Jodl was produced as evidence for the Prosecution. Quisling produced a new rebuttal of these charges, writing another sixty pages even though he had no access to any of his own papers.

Because Quisling was so heavily compromised with the Nazis, his position seemed hopeless. However, the moral and even legal difference between the defendant and his accusers was less clear than it first seemed. The court was bringing charges under laws which had been passed by the Nygaardsvold government in exile: on the day of the invasion, the Norwegian parliament had voted at Elverum to transfer all its powers to the government, including the power to make laws. There has been considerable debate on this, 'the Elverum authorization', in Norway in recent years, because the constitution made no provision for the parliament to dissolve itself in this way. The identical vote in France, granting Pétain full legislative (and constitutional) powers, was never recognized as valid by the Gaullist Resistance, and indeed it was precisely this alienation of national sovereignty by a parliament which had no right to do so which, Gaullists said, was the reason why Vichy France was illegitimate in its very essence.[5]

Second, the laws themselves were applied retroactively. The death penalty had been abolished in Norway in the penal code of 1902, and it had not been carried out since the 1870s. Many Norwegians were therefore troubled when the Nygaardsvold government reintroduced it retrospectively, and by decree, in a Provisional Statute passed on 3 October 1941, with Quisling explicitly in mind. It is true that the military law of Norway did retain the death penalty, and that Quisling's acts in April 1940 came under the terms of it, but its terms required that any death sentences be carried out before the end of hostilities. The law, in other words, provided for swift military justice in the heat of battle. The government in exile waived these terms, but this itself was an example of retroactive legislation, which was expressly forbidden by Section 97 of the Norwegian constitution.[6] Moreover, it reintroduced the death penalty with little pretence at legality, justifying the change by saying that it was 'the wish of every loyal citizen' and 'a sound and healthy wish at that'.[7]

This decision was shocking because Quisling had done precisely the same thing when he had agreed to execute Eilifsen. However, it was not the only retroactive legislation under which Quisling and his comrades were prosecuted. A further Provisional Statute was passed by the government in exile on 22 January 1942, which retroactively proclaimed the Nasjonal Samling an illegal organization (a decree which anticipated the similar proclamation at Nuremberg that certain Nazi organisms were criminal organizations, comparable to a criminal conspiracy) even though the party had in fact been legal. Statutes were also passed on 26 February 1943 on the purging of the civil service, on 15 December 1944 on treason; and on 16 February 1945 on the organization and procedure of the postwar trials. (These provisions were subsequently gathered together and turned into a general law on treason, duly voted by the Storting on 3 August 1947.[8])

Of these, it is especially the treason ordinance (*Landssvikanordningen*) passed voted on 15 December 1944, which has been the subject of recent controversy in Norway. That decree was explicitly retroactive, introducing new penalties for treason 'even if the illegal act has been committed before the promulgation of this law'.[9] The laws on treason, moreover, were formulated specifically to begin on 9 April 1940, i.e. they were tailor-made for specific events. But Quisling was not the only person targeted: the treason ordinance was to form the basis of a huge purge in which over 28,000 people were arrested and twenty-five executed. Indeed, although the number of executions in Norway was low relative to other occupied countries, the number of prosecutions carried out was enormous: 1400 per 100,000 inhabitants, compared to 300 per 100,000 in Denmark and 309 per 100,000 in France.

Finally, the criminalization of collaboration was itself questionable. The international legal situation of Norway was clear: it was an occupied country and its situation was therefore governed by Section III of the IVth Hague Conventions on 'Military Authority over the Territory of the Hostile State'. Nowhere in this convention does it say that collaboration with an occupying force is a crime; on the contrary, the occupying power is precisely required to co-operate, as far as possible, with the state administration and according to the existing laws of the land, which presupposes that national state officials will collaborate with it.

More generally, when Eric Scavenius, the wartime prime minister of Denmark, acted on the basis of exactly the same reasoning as Pétain and Quisling – namely that it was better that Denmark retain its own political institutions under German occupation, and that the country would thereby be able to mitigate the effects of the occupation – public opinion approved the decision and history has been kind to it since. De Gaulle called on resistance-minded state officials to remain in their posts under Vichy, and several of his most faithful postwar allies had been senior officials under Marshal Pétain, including two of his prime Ministers, the arch-Gaullist Michel Debré and Maurice Couve de Murville. Indeed, so much was the principle of collaboration as a cover for internal resistance approved that one man who had remained a judge in a Nazi-occupied country went on to become a judge in an Allied war crimes tribunal: Bert Röling had been a judge in Utrecht during the Nazi occupation of the Netherlands, yet he joined the bench of the International Military Tribunal for the Far East in Tokyo. He was later praised by Antonio Cassese, a leading authority on modern international humanitarian law who later became the first president of the International Criminal Tribunal for the former Yugoslavia, for 'showing his resolve [during the occupation] in small, but meaningful ways'.[10]

The legal position of Norway as an occupied state was itself more nuanced than the Quisling trial or the later ruling by the Nuremberg tribunal in September 1946 allowed. The Germans were convicted at Nuremberg of waging aggressive war against Norway, but even the prosecutors there knew that their case was not watertight. There were grounds for saying that the Germans had acted pre-emptively to forestall a British invasion.[11] Documents did exist – and were withheld both from Nuremberg and from the Quisling trial – which showed that the British were themselves attempting to move against Norway.[12] In direct violation of Norway's neutrality, the British had started to mine Norway's territorial waters (the Norwegian Leads) on 8 April (in what was known as 'Operation Wilfred') and the Germans moved in that night. International law has long recognized the validity of pre-emptive action when it is literally imperative from a military point of view and, on the law alone, there are grounds for saying that the German invasion fell into this category.[13] Maurice Hankey, a minister in Churchill's government until 1942, wrote eloquently after the war about how in fact the British had triggered the German invasion of Norway by violating her neutrality first.[14]

Quisling's trial started on 20 August 1945. During the intervening period, the harsh prison regime had born down heavily on his health and it was a sick and weak man who rose to face the court. The bench was composed of five lay judges and four professionals, chaired by Erik Solem, a member of the underground resistance and a political enemy of Quisling's. Solem had published three articles about the special laws which were being used to prosecute Quisling, and they had been phrased in such a way that they seemed to condemn Quisling in advance.[15] Objections were raised that Solem was *parti pris* and they went to the Supreme Court, which rejected them. But few denied that Solem was indeed biased and aggressive towards Quisling, or that his constant interruptions of the defendant made it impossible for him to give a coherent account of his actions. Outside, the media railed in frenzy against Quisling, accusing him of vices such as debauchery and luxury – charges which, as even his enemies admitted who knew about his famous asceticism, were a pure invention.

Ironically from today's perspective, the Prosecution's extensive allegations of treason included the charge that Quisling had conspired to bring Norway into a European confederation with a common currency, common security and foreign policies, a common market, and reciprocal rights of work and residence.[16] It is true that Quisling was one of the first wartime politicians to call for European union: he wrote to the British prime minister, Neville Chamberlain, on 11 October 1939, urging him that the only way to achieve peace in Europe was 'to fuse British, French and German interests into a European Confederation'. 'I deferentially appeal to your immense authority,' Quisling wrote (signing himself 'Quisling CBE') 'to suggest that the British government – in accordance with the method of federalisation in America, South Africa and Australia – invite every European State to choose ten representatives to a congress charged with the task of preparing a constitution for an empire of European nations, to be submitted to a plebiscite in each country for acceptance or rejection.'[17] In 1944 Quisling had returned to the European theme, proposing a 'European Community of Peoples' organized along federal lines (and with the German Führer as federal president).[18]

The trial was a strange affair, with Quisling giving long disquisitions to the court about his personal history and philosophy. Quisling was a remorseless man: famously unsociable, he was capable of sitting throughout an entire dinner without saying a word. Perhaps his misanthropy derived from his sense of his own intellectual superiority, or perhaps from his grim Protestant upbringing and his love of remote countryside. (His family's log cabin could be reached only after five hours' walk from his already isolated village, and Quisling often disappeared there for days on end.) But he thought it appropriate to open the trial by baring his soul and telling his life story.

> I grew up among Viking graves, between Bible history and old Saga tales. I belong to an ancient family and I was always injected with the ideas of family pride and family saga as well as with the sense of responsibility towards our people. Bjørnson and Ibsen were of the same family as I: so it was not dishwater in my veins. The name Quisling is not of foreign origin: it is an ancient Nordic name and indicates one who is a side branch of the royal family. The letter Q indicates an ancient protective rune. I have grown up under these conditions and imbibed a most intense love for my country.[19]

Much of the trial consisted of Judge Solem reading out incriminating documents which had not been given to Quisling or his lawyers in advance, and as if he were himself the Prosecutor. Interrogation reports of the defendants at Nuremberg were introduced as Prosecution evidence, even though such third-hand information is not normally admissible in court since the defendant has no ability to cross-examine the original sources of the information, and even though the Nuremberg defendants were on trial for their lives with every motive to blame others. By contrast, Germans who might have appeared as defence witnesses were never called. Terboven and his two police chiefs had in any case committed suicide in May. Meanwhile, documents were withheld which showed that the Allies were preparing an invasion of Norway, which would have partly exonerated Quisling and incriminated Prime Minister Nygaardsvold (whom Quisling accused of complicity in this violation of Norway's neutrality).

Quisling did not acquit himself brilliantly. He insisted that he had fought against others who wanted to bring Norway under foreign control and that all his efforts had been devoted to maintaining the country's independence, including from the Germans. But when he explained that he

had proclaimed himself head of the government because the existing government was 'away', and that he did not realize that it and the parliament
were still in session because he had not listened to the radio that morning,
he made a fool of himself. Quisling was often evasive and dishonest, for
instance when he pretended not to remember much about the meeting
with the German intelligence officer in Copenhagen. He even seemed to
believe that Hitler was his tool, not the other way around. But his physi-
cal exhaustion and weak health sapped both his powers of speech and his
critical faculties. He deluded himself that the trial was going well when in
fact many of his answers only incriminated him further.[20]

Quisling did receive surprisingly positive testimony from General
Otto Ruge, the commander in chief of the Norwegian armed forces who
had fought the Germans in 1940 and who was held in high esteem by Norwegian public opinion. He told the court that he thought Quisling was
talented, intelligent, and honest; this was courageous in view of the fact
that hostility to Quisling was so intense at this time that his own guards
had sworn to murder him if the death sentence was not handed down.[21]
Good character witnesses were also given by General Halvor Hansson of
the Norwegian General Staff and his childhood friend, Vilhelm Ullmann,
whose testimony moved Quisling to tears. They testified of the highest
esteem in which they had held Quisling in his earlier life.

Indeed, it was partly because of these glowing references about Quisling's pre-war character that some wondered whether Quisling had gone
mad in the meantime. He was ordered to undergo excruciatingly painful
neurological tests in the middle of the trial, which lasted three days and
nearly killed him. Compressed air was blown into his spinal marrow and
thence into the brain cavity. No anaesthetic was administered. In another
test, large quantities of iodine were injected into his neck so that X-rays
could be taken of the frontal lobe of the brain. Such tests normally required
patients to be carried on a stretcher afterwards, but Quisling was forced to
walk back up the stairs to his cell at the top of the tower in the fortress. The
trial was suspended for a week since he was too weak to appear.[22]

Following concluding statements by the Prosecution and the Defence, Quisling himself rose to make a final statement. He could hardly
stand as he was on the point of exhaustion. He managed to speak for an
hour before the session was suspended until the next day to give him time
to recover. He then gave what all commentators describe as an excellent
speech, covering his entire life including the early days in Russia and of
course the wartime years. Dahl says it was 'a very convincing speech';[23] an
apologist, Ralph Hewins, calls it 'a tour de force';[24] Paul Hayes, his critic,
says that it was 'an impressive effort'.[25] Quisling ended thus, 'If my work

has really been treasonable, then I would pray to God for Norway's sake that a good many of Norway's sons would also become traitors like me, only that they be not thrown into prison!'[26]

When the verdict and death sentence were announced on 10 September 1945, only three days after the conclusion of the short trial, it was clear that almost none of his defence arguments had been accepted. He was acquitted only on minor charges. He was found guilty of treason, conspiracy, a *coup d'état*, murder, and embezzlement. In fact, the court convicted Quisling of things which had not even been mentioned in the indictment – of going further than the Germans had wanted in handling internal crises, of setting up networks of informers – and it made no mention of any attenuating circumstances, such as his clemency system or his interventions to obtain the release of prisoners and hostages from German prisons.[27]

Quisling announced that he would appeal. He and his lawyer appeared before the Supreme Court on 9 October 1945, where the presiding judge was none other than Paal Berg, whom he had not seen since 15 June 1940 when Berg had announced the formation of the collaborationist Administrative Council and thanked Quisling publicly for stepping into the breach. Berg's Council had governed Norway from 15 April to 21 September 1940, and he had therefore been just as much a party to the destitution of the Nygaardsvold government and of the king as Quisling had. Berg had in the meantime become chairman of the Home Front, the main resistance organization, and so his honour had been retrospectively saved. But it also meant that he was doubly a political enemy of Quisling and therefore not impartial. Berg in any case was himself a politician: a prominent member of the Liberal Party (*Venstre*), he had been minister of social affairs from 1919 to 1920, minister of justice from 1924 to 1926, and founder and chairman of the Norwegian state wine monopoly, Vinmonopolet, from 1922 to 1926. In other words, Berg was not a judge in the British or American sense of the term, but instead a member of the Norwegian political establishment, for whom a job on the Supreme Court bench was just one aspect of his many-faceted career. The same was true of Emil Stang, also on the bench, and who succeeded Berg as chief justice in 1946: Stang was a Communist politician who had attended the founding Congress of the Communist International in March 1919, together with Lenin, Trotsky, and Stalin, where he represented the Norwegian Social Democratic Party. As a Communist, Stang was one of Quisling's bitterest political opponents.

Quisling addressed the Supreme Court himself, and again used this session to make a number of extraordinary personal statements, even though the appeal was based on legal technicalities alone. He said, 'There are many free men here in Oslo and in other cities who have done me political harm, but I have never harmed any of them. Revenge is not a political motive, and I believe in leaving it to others. This case, then, is not just another judicial matter, but a question of politics.'[28]

Quisling concluded his statement with his personal esoteric philosophy, Universism, according to which faith and reason were reconciled and the divine plan was operating directly in historical events on earth. He proclaimed,

> I am clear that there exists in the Universe a divine power connected with the inhabited planets; that what is now happening in these great times on earth is a great change, when the Kingdom of God is beginning to take form here on this earth, in the real sense of the term ... Formerly, it was supposed that the Beyond was the real Kingdom of God. I am of the opinion that we are more and more coming to realise that the Kingdom of God is here in earth ... I have recognised and worked for this new Kingdom of God. It is only this which has motivated me, together with my patriotism and my sense of duty ... Sentence can be passed on me, if so willed, but in doing so a blood-guilt will be brought upon the whole Norwegian people. I have done nothing myself which deserves death or imprisonment. Not that I fear death itself. I regret it for my near relations. I fear it for the whole Norwegian people.[29]

He concluded by saying that he had been judged 'objectively under law' but that 'the facts have not been sufficiently elucidated in my case'. He sat down. On 13 October, his appeal was dismissed. In prison, he wrote a summary of his work, Universism, and spent his last days reading the Bible. He meditated on the life of Christ and seemed to imply that his own death was a martyrdom and a sacrifice. He appeared in court on 17 and 18 October to give evidence in the trials of his former colleagues. He wrote to the king to protest that he had not been lawfully convicted and he was informed on 23 October that there would be no royal pardon. The prison pastor came to him at 7 o'clock that evening and told him that the execution would be carried out at midnight. He asked to see his wife one last time but this request was rejected. In fact, the execution was delayed until 2 a.m. because the Danish chief of police had asked to attend and his plane was delayed. The pastor read him verses from the gospel of St John and he was eventually led out into the courtyard of the Akershus fortress. He asked not to be blindfolded but his lawyer told him it was obligatory. At 2.40 a.m. on the morning of 24 October 1945, the firing squad took up position. Quisling protested his innocence and was shot dead.

7   Nuremberg: Making War Illegal

The Nuremberg trial is the central reference point for late twentieth- and early twenty-first-century political trials. It has been elevated by historical memory to the status of supreme paradigm of how the universal laws of humanity can and should prevail over the arbitrary commands of a tyrannical head of state. Indeed, Nuremberg is probably the most famous criminal trial in history. The moral Manichaeism which is never far below the surface in political trials erupts in all its sharpness in the case of Nuremberg, as the victorious Allies cemented their victory – and confirmed their moral superiority – with the trial and execution of the leading Nazis.

However, Nuremberg was in fact only the most famous of a whole swathe of trials of heads of state and government conducted in Europe and the Far East in the immediate aftermath of World War II. A large number of the chapters in this book is devoted to those trials, partly because the account is chronological and so many of the trials of heads of state in history did take place after World War II, but partly too because the historical account shows that Nuremberg cannot be dissociated from them. The context may force us to reassess that great trial. While Nuremberg's reputation as a moral reference point persists, other trials in postwar Europe, especially those conducted almost simultaneously by the incoming Communists in Eastern Europe, were deeply intertwined with it. Yet even though those trials were conducted on the basis of the same or similar accusations, and in some cases used evidence gleaned from the very same defendants, they are usually dismissed as grotesque illustrations of how the judicial process can be bastardized for political ends.

Nuremberg was a classic 'regime' trial, because the defendants were chosen specifically to represent a cross-section of the Nazi regime as whole. Although of course Hitler himself was not in the dock (he had committed suicide in May 1945), his successor, Admiral Doenitz was, who had been head of state for the twenty-three days between Hitler's death and the German capitulation. The trial was conducted by the four Allied powers who had assumed power following the unconditional surrender demanded and obtained from Germany: the United States, the United Kingdom, France, and the Soviet Union. It lasted from 20 November 1945 to 30 September 1946. In addition, other trials were conducted in occupied Germany by individual Allied powers of others associated with the Nazi regime: the British authorities put the concentration camp commanders from Belsen on trial from September to November 1945, while the Americans continued with trials until 1948, also held in the city of Nuremberg, which were stopped when the new imperatives of the Cold War caused Germany to be courted as an ally. The fact that these trials were stopped because of new foreign policy imperatives underlines the political nature of the prosecutions in the first place.

For the main Nuremberg trial conducted by the International Military Tribunal, twenty-four defendants were selected to represent the key elements in the Nazi power structure: Hermann Goering, the most senior surviving Nazi; Rudolf Hess, Hitler's by now partly insane former deputy; Joachim von Ribbentrop, the foreign minister; Robert Ley, the head of the German Labour Front; Field Marshal Wilhelm Keitel, head of the supreme command of the Wehrmacht; SS *Obergruppenführer* Ernst Kaltenbrunner; Alfred Rosenberg, the racial theorist; Hans Frank, the governor of occupied Poland; Wilhelm Frick, minister of the interior and the author of the Nuremberg race laws; Julius Streicher, the editor of the anti-Semitic newspaper, *Der Stürmer*; Walther Funk, the Nazi economics minister and president of the Reichsbank; Hjalmar Schacht, Funk's predecessor who had been president of the Reichsbank in the 1920s; Gustav Krupp, the industrialist; Karl Doenitz, the head of the German navy and Hitler's successor as head of state; Admiral Erich Raeder; Baldur von Schirach, head of the Hitler Youth and governor of Vienna; Fritz Sauckel, Reich director of labour; Alfred Jodl, head of the Wehrmacht staff; Martin Bormann, Hitler's private secretary; Franz von Papen, Hitler's predecessor as chancellor; Arthur Seyss-Inquart, *Reichskommissar* in the Netherlands; Albert Speer, Hitler's architect and minister of armaments and munitions; Konstantin von Neurath, governor of Bohemia and Moravia; and Hans Fritzsche, one of Goebbels's deputies and head of German radio.

The process of selecting the defendants was chaotic and politicized. The Allies were arguing over the list of indictees almost up to the moment the trial opened. Gustav Krupp was indicted by mistake (the Allies meant to indict his son, Alfried), and when the mistake was realized it was too late, and the elder and senile Krupp was declared unfit to stand trial. (Ley committed suicide in his cell and Bormann was never caught, so there were in fact twenty-one defendants in the box.) All of the Nuremberg defendants were indicted for their alleged participation in the conspiracy to commit crimes against peace, even though Julius Streicher, who was also accused of stirring up hatred against Jews, had nothing to do with planning the war at all. Actual perpetrators were not prosecuted: the commandant of Auschwitz, Rudolf Hoess, appeared as a defence witness during the Nuremberg trial, although his 'defence' was some of the most incriminating evidence: he gave cold detail of how more than two million people were murdered under his command. (Hoess was hanged in Auschwitz by the Polish authorities in 1946.) At the end of the trial, three of the defendants were acquitted (Papen, Schacht, and Fritzsche), although they were subsequently charged and convicted by German national authorities; two committed suicide in gaol (Goering, who had been sentenced to death, and Ley even before the trial started); one, Bormann, was sentenced *in absentia*; ten were executed; and the others were given prison terms ranging from ten years to life.

The defendants adopted radically different defence strategies. Goering was lucid and eloquent and largely unrepentant about what he had done for Hitler. Larger than life (both in girth and in character, even if the prison regime had caused his clothes to hang more loosely on him than they had before) Goering was a *bon vivant* with a cruel sense of humour. He adopted a cocky, self-assured attitude in court and made no apologies for what he had done for Germany. He sparred successfully with the prosecutors and got the better of the chief United States prosecutor, Robert Jackson.

Hess, Hitler's deputy who had flown alone to Britain in 1941 to try to negotiate a peace deal with the duke of Hamilton, and who had been imprisoned ever since, pleaded incoherently that he could not remember anything. He read out an unintelligible statement at the beginning of the trial, and pleaded that he would say nothing else because he did not want to be embarrassed by being unable to answer the Prosecutor's questions. The remark caused a snigger in the courtroom. He spent most of the rest of the trial looking distracted and reading cheap novels, occasionally leaving the courtroom as a result of stomach cramps. Hess was sentenced to life imprisonment, which he served in Spandau prison in Berlin where he was the only inmate until he eventually hanged himself in 1987, aged ninety-three.

Ribbentrop, the silver-tongued former champagne salesman whom the other defendants evidently regarded with contempt, spun a tangled web of lies in which he soon got caught up. Keitel claimed that he bore responsibility for acts carried out under his command but, as a soldier, said he was himself following orders. (Generally, this defence was not prominent at Nuremberg although it was of course Eichmann's main line of defence in 1962.) Kaltenbrunner, whom commentators described as one of the most sinister, cruel, and hateful of the defendants, denied all knowledge of atrocities. Frank, by then enveloped in religious mysticism, denied personal guilt but seemed to accept the collective guilt of Germany and said that the trial itself was a judgement of God against the German nation. Frick tried to blame his superiors, Himmler and Goering. Saukel said that an abyss separated him from his duties as a minister and a military man from the terrible conditions in the concentration camps. Speer admitted that the defendants bore responsibility for what had happened, even under a dictatorship: he was sentenced to twenty years and died in London in 1981 after meeting a famously bibulous British historian for tea at Brown's hotel, a meeting which led to a night drinking whisky. Speer died of a cerebral haemorrhage the next morning.

There are many popular misconceptions about the Nuremberg trials. One of the most persistent is that it was the trial of the Holocaust, whereas the full extent of the Holocaust in fact became evident only during the course of the trial itself. The Unted States Deputy Chief Prosecutor, Telford Taylor, had himself not even heard of the concentration camps in Poland by the spring of 1945,[1] while Robert Jackson's report to the president of 6 June 1945, which laid out the reasons why Nazi atrocities should be prosecuted, did not even mention persecution of the Jews but instead only crimes committed against Czechs, Poles, and other peoples whose countries were occupied by the Nazis. From this mistaken perception, it is erroneously concluded that Nuremberg was novel because established for the first time the principle that universal 'crimes against humanity' could be punished even if they had been ordered by senior officials in the state or sanctioned by the law of the land.

It is true that Nuremberg applied the concept of crimes against humanity for the first time, but the idea that there is a natural law higher than the dictates of the state is nonetheless one of the oldest ideas in political philosophy. Cicero expounded it perfectly in his *Laws*: 'Even if there was no written law against rape at Rome in the reign of Lucretius Tarquinius, we cannot say on that account that Sextus Tarquinius did not break that eternal law by violating Lucretia.'[2] It is therefore naive to suggest, as so many do, that Nuremberg dealt with this issue for the first time: as even Cicero realized, the problem is that such appeals to natural law can clash with other precepts of natural law, including considerations about the very nature of lawfulness itself. These can be damaged if positive law is amended after an event in order to criminalize it retrospectively. But in any case, the view that the head of state is morally bound to respect the law has enjoyed continuous currency until the beginning of the modern period. It is only with the rise of secularism that the idea has become common that the sovereign – in this case, the people – should be subject to no moral or religious constraints whatever.

Instead, where Nuremberg really broke new ground was that it brought prosecutions against individuals under international law for crimes against peace, that is, for planning and executing a war of aggression. This innovation was really two rolled into one: the notion of a 'crime against peace' was new, as was the application of the criminal law to individual state leaders for violations of international law. Previously, the subjects of international law had been states, not their leaders, and there had been no penal regime to enforce it. The notion of crimes against peace formed the basis for Counts 1 and 2 of the crimes listed in the indictment (conspiracy to commit crimes against peace and aggressive war itself), while war crimes and crimes against humanity were Counts 3 and 4. (The first two counts were effectively treated as the same count in the judgement.)

When Robert Jackson rose to his feet to open the Prosecution, therefore, he did not say that Nuremberg was the first trial for crimes against humanity. He said that it was 'the first trial in history for crimes against the peace of the world'.[3] He said, 'The crime which comprehends all lesser crimes is the crime of making unjustifiable war.'[4] The judges agreed when they came to give their verdict ten months later. In their sentence, delivered on 30 September 1946, they repeated Jackson's words: 'To initiate a war of aggression … is the supreme international crime, differing only from other war crimes in that it contains within itself the accumulated evil of the whole.'[5] The feeling was that the Nazis had committed acts which were not only universally abhorrent but also an attack on the international system. It was but an updated version of the crime for which the Kaiser had been arraigned at Versailles.

Critics argued at the time – and they have continued to argue since – that the London Charter of 1945 which set up the International Military Tribunal (Nuremberg) created a new crime with retroactive effect, and that it was therefore a violation of one of the most fundamental principles of justice. Supporters of the trial, by contrast, argue that the rule against non-retroactivity should give way to the superior interests of justice, in the broadest sense, in extreme cases. But this is a false dichotomy. One can certainly believe that the Nazi leaders broadly got what they *morally* deserved, while at the same time insisting that the Nuremberg trials were *legally* problematic.

The charge of retroactive legislation is a very serious one – so much so that the authors of the London Charter vigorously denied that they were guilty of it. The Universal Declaration of Human Rights, adopted just two years after the Nuremberg trial ended, enunciated not only the rule against retroactivity but also the fundamental rule that everyone has a right to be tried by an impartial tribunal. These rights in any case had an august two-hundred-year-old history in American law, in the 1789 *Déclaration des droits de l'homme,* and in even longer-standing English law and precedent.

Although some jurists, notably Gustav Radbruch,[6] have argued that the law against retroactivity can be waived in extreme cases, the authors of the London Charter energetically denied that they were doing this. They insisted that the law they were using to prosecute the Nazis was well established, basing their claims mainly on the Kellogg–Briand Pact of 1928, which Germany had signed and by which a number of states had renounced war as an instrument of state policy and condemned it. But there were other precedents and statutes. Articles 227 to 230 of the Treaty of Versailles had dealt with Germany's war guilt and called for trials, including of the Kaiser himself. The Hague Convention of 1907 and the Geneva Convention of 1929 both dealt extensively with war crimes, while there was also the Geneva Protocol of 1924, also known as Protocol for the Pacific Settlement of International Disputes but originally entitled 'Outlawry of Aggressive War' by the American jurists who drew it up. This required compulsory arbitration of all international disputes and defined as aggressor any state which refused to accept such arbitration.

However, none of these various treaties in fact established a precedent for criminal prosecutions for crimes against peace. The arraignment of the Kaiser was a Bill of Attainder (a legislative act directed against a specific individual) and, as such, unconstitutional in the United States and in most civilized jurisdictions. A violation of the law cannot itself become a precedent in law: *ex iniuria lex non oritur.* In any case, the United States of America had never ratified the Treaty of Versailles. They could not very well invoke one of its clauses in support of the Nuremberg prosecution.

More to the point, while the Hague and Geneva Conventions regulated the law of war (*ius in bello*) they did not regulate the law of declaring war in the first place (*ius ad bellum*). Instead, they specifically excluded reference to it, in keeping with the long legal tradition established at least with the Treaties of Westphalia that international law does not distinguish between just or unjust wars but instead regards war a legally neutral form of relations between states. Moreover, inasmuch as prosecutions were foreseen for violations of the laws of war, it was the states themselves who were supposed to bring them. Even the 1924 Geneva Protocol (which in any case Britain and America vigorously opposed, and which was eventually ratified by only one state, Czechoslovakia) did not make war a criminal offence, although it 'condemned' it. It remained within the logic of existing inter-state law, and proposed only sanctions against an aggressor state and not criminal prosecution of its leaders.

The question of the legality of war, and the possibility of criminal punishment for it, had therefore been extensively debated in the pre-war period *and it had not been made a crime.* The point is not that the Nazis would have escaped prosecution if the charge of crimes against peace had not been brought. On the contrary, the Nazis' atrocities could easily have been punished under ordinary laws. A defendant would only incriminate himself as a moral idiot if he claimed that there was no law against mass murder, but almost no one at Nuremberg did. (Hermann Goering's defence was not so much that there was no law against what he had done but that the Allies had committed atrocities too, and that the prosecution at Nuremberg was therefore an exercise in hypocrisy.)

Indeed, the prosecution of the Nazis might have been easier if it had been confined to the established laws of war, or even to the German military code in force even under Hitler.[7] However, the Americans, like the Soviets, were determined to bring charges of crimes against peace, and thereby to create a new coercive system of international law – a new world order – which would remove from states their long-held sovereign right to decide whether or not to wage war. This determination flowed from the ultimately similar view which both Americans and Soviets held about foreign policy: Communism was an overtly universalist philosophy which aimed at world revolution and global governance, while Franklin Delano Roosevelt, the American president, who had identified himself with the 'New Deal' in domestic politics, wanted to offer something similar on the international level too, in order to bring the world out of the chaos created by the war.[8]

Those broader political goals were made very clear during the trial itself. As Robert Jackson said on the second day of his opening statement,

> This trial is part of the great effort to make peace more secure. One step in this direction is the United Nations organization, which may take joint political action to prevent war if possible, and joint military action to insure that any nation which starts a war will lose it. This charter and this trial, implementing the Kellogg–Briand Pact, constitute another step in the same direction – juridical action of a kind to ensure that those who start a war will pay for it personally.[9]

The Nuremberg trial was the anvil on which a new international system was to be forged: the Nazis had to die so that the new world order could live.

These were noble goals, even if, as we shall see, the Nuremberg jurisprudence on crimes against peace has in fact remained a dead letter. Unfortunately, however, there were also ulterior motives. At the London Conference which drew up the Nuremberg Charter, Robert Jackson explained rather frankly that a guilty verdict at Nuremberg was necessary in order to justify the legality of the American government's policies before 1941. The United States had been officially neutral until Germany declared war in December 1941, but President Roosevelt had in fact been helping Britain since September 1939 with the policy known as lend-lease, according to which the United States provided war *matériel* in return for land for military bases. For a neutral state to help a belligerent state is a violation of international law and an abuse of its proclaimed neutrality. Jackson knew this and therefore he had to argue that the German war had itself been criminal in the first place, thereby obviating America's need to obey international law. 'There is involved in this the basis on which the United States engaged in its lend-lease operation…,' he said,[10] adding later:

> The justification was made by the Secretary of State, by the Secretary of War, Mr. Stimson, *by myself as Attorney General,* that [Germany's war] was illegal from the outset and hence we were not doing an illegal thing in extending aid to peoples who were unjustly and unlawfully attacked … As President Roosevelt said to the people, as members of the Cabinet said to the people … launching a war of aggression is a crime and that no political or economic situation can justify it. *If that is wrong, then we have been wrong in a good many things in the policy of the United States which helped the countries under attack before we entered the war.*[11]

As Jackson says here, he had himself been a minister in the government which decided to pursue lend-lease, having been attorney general in Roosevelt's cabinet from 1940 to 1941. The fact that Prosecutor Jackson wanted to find *post hoc* justification for the governmental decisions taken by Minister Jackson was bad enough; the fact that Francis Biddle ended up on the Nuremberg bench was even more problematic. The future Nuremberg judge had served as Roosevelt's solicitor general from 1940 to 1941, and as his attorney general from 1941 to 1945 (Jackson's successor).

Even though they were determined to base their prosecution of the Nazis on the concept of aggressive war, the delegates at the London Conference could not agree on what aggressive war actually was. Jackson admitted, 'It is a rather difficult subject to analyse without taking a good deal of time to do it,' while the Soviet judge, General Ioan Timofeevich

Nikitchenko, said sarcastically, 'If we start discussion on that again, I am afraid the war criminals would die of old age.' He was right: how could one criminalize the German attack on Norway (a pre-emptive strike against Britain's planned occupation of that country) or de-criminalize the British attack on the French fleet at Mers-el-Kébir in July 1940, an attack which occurred when Britain and France were formally allies? Indeed, it is clear that the Allies did not want aggressive war to be declared illegal for themselves. Nikitchenko said, 'Is it supposed then to condemn aggression or initiation of war in general or to condemn specifically aggressions started by the Nazis in this war? If the attempt is to have a general definition, that would not be agreeable.'[12]

Nikitchenko brought a cruel Soviet realism to the discussions which Jackson pretended piously to have difficulty stomaching. The Russian knew a thing or two about rough justice: he had been one of the judges at Moscow's notorious show trials, sentencing Zinoviev and Kamenev to death in 1936, for which he had been decorated with the Order of Lenin.[13] Jackson may have had a gift for the soundbite – phrases from his opening speech, such as 'stay the hand of vengeance' and 'one of the most significant tributes that power has ever paid to reason', are quoted even today by supporters of international criminal tribunals – but intellectually he was not impressive. He tried, for instance, to protest when Nikitchenko said that the Germans 'already been convicted ... by the Moscow and Crimea declarations'[14] and that, 'The fact that the Nazi leaders are criminals has already been established.'[15] But he later had to admit that, 'There is a great deal of realism in Mr. Nikitchenko's statement. There could be but one decision in this case, that we are bound to concede.'[16]

And even though Jackson had also initially protested when the Russians demanded that the Charter specify that the crime of aggression had been 'carried out by the European axis' (he complained that it was unacceptable for a law to be framed in such as way that it applied to one group of countries but not to another) the London Charter did end up restricting the jurisdiction of the Nuremberg tribunal to the Germans and their allies alone. Articles 1 and 6 of the Nuremberg Charter specified that the tribunal was responsible for judging 'the major war criminals of the European axis'. Jackson had said, 'We are not prepared to lay down a rule of criminal conduct against others which we would not be willing to have invoked against us,'[17] and 'We think the clause "carried out by the European Axis" so qualifies the statement that it deprives it of all standing and fairness as a juridical principle.'[18] But in the end this is exactly what happened.

Jackson could hardly have pretended for long that the guilty verdict was not a foregone conclusion. Not only did he have a personal stake in ensuring a guilty verdict; he himself devoted considerable effort to ensuring it. First, the preparatory London Conference was attended by judges and prosecutors alike: Jackson became a prosecutor but the Soviet and French delegates (Nikitchenko and Robert Falco) became judges. This was a highly irregular collusion between the Prosecution and the bench. Second, Jackson himself made sure that the Charter, and especially its definition of 'a war of aggression', was structured so that it closed down certain potential lines of defence. He specifically said that the definition should be framed so that states would not be able to plead 'political, economic, or other considerations' in justification of aggressive war. He also did not want the Germans to be able to argue that Britain and France had been the first to declare war on Germany, although in fact they had. He said, 'I don't want to be in a position where the United States is obliged to enter into a discussion at this trial of the acts or policies of our allies ... Too many recriminations would result ... Why should the court stop it [discussion of the origins of the war] if we four men are not willing to stop it?'[19]

These flaws were bad enough. Worse still was the decisive role played by the Soviets in the Nuremberg trials, a role which was an inevitable consequence of the alliance between the Western allies and Stalin. That role started with the invention of the concept of crimes against peace. Throughout the 1920s, the Soviets had been enthusiastic supporters of disarmament treaties and international agreements outlawing war, most notably the Kellogg–Briand Pact of 1928 and the supplement to it, the Litvinov Protocol of 1929 signed between Russia and six other Eastern European and Middle Eastern states. Stalin helped draw up the Convention for the Prevention and Punishment of Terrorism and the Convention for the Creation of an International Criminal Court, which the Council of the League of Nations approved in 1937. Indeed, one of the Soviet representatives at the London Conference, Aron Naumovich Trainin, who was one of the main theoreticians of the concept of crimes against peace, had proposed 'interventionism' to combat international crimes in a book in 1935.[20] (In the event, neither the Convention on Terrorism nor the Convention for the Creation of an International Criminal Court ever came into force.)

The Soviets acted in this way largely because they were ideologically in favour of world government. Under Communism and world revolution, the world was to be politically united, and the difference between international and domestic law would vanish as surely as the difference between town and country; when Trotsky's friends suggested to Lenin in 1917 that he should be put in charge of foreign affairs (as he soon was), Lenin retorted, 'What foreign affairs will we have now?'[21] Criminalizing the acts of states was one way of discrediting the very idea of nationhood, which, as Marx and Engels had hoped in *The Communist Manifesto*, progressive forces would destroy.

Trainin worked closely with Andrei Yanuarevich Vyshinskii, the prosecutor general of the Soviet Union and the notorious architect of the great show trials held in Moscow in the 1930s. But Vyshinskii was interested in the political value of coercive law at the international level as well as the domestic. In addition to writing eulogies to Lenin and Stalin as theoreticians of the state, Vyshinskii (who became the Soviet minister for foreign affairs after the war) devoted many speeches and books to the relationship between international law and world peace, and he was general editor of the series of books in which Trainin's work on 'The Defence of Peace and the Criminal Law' was published in Moscow in 1937. Vyshinskii wrote the preface, in which he argued that international crimes were precisely crimes against peace.[22] He praised Trainin for attacking the fact that international law had not criminalized aggressive war: Trainin said its permissive attitude to war was proof of its 'bourgeois' and 'imperialist' character.[23] 'Anti-imperialism' was one of the central tenets of Soviet ideology and both Trainin and Vyshinskii wrote extensively on the Soviet Union's role in preventing imperialist aggression and therefore maintaining the peace of the world.[24] This conception of international law, according to which war should be criminalized, was at the very heart of Soviet ideology.

These arguments were advanced all the more vehemently once Germany attacked the Soviet Union in 1941, in violation of the 1939 non-aggression pact between the two countries. The Soviets lost no time in calling the German attack criminal: the Soviet foreign minister, Vyacheslav Molotov, did so in November 1941 and January 1942, saying that a special international tribunal should be set up to try the fascist invaders. This position was repeated in July 1942, when Stalin also called for the creation of such a tribunal,[25] and again in the autumn of 1942 when the 'United Nations War Crimes Commission' was inaugurated for the investigation of German atrocities. This position differed from that expressed by Churchill in the House of Commons on 8 September 1942: he foresaw only national trials when he called for German crimes to be punished 'in every land where atrocities have been committed'.[26] Indeed, when on 12 November 1942, the Soviet ambassador to the United Kingdom, Ivan Maisky, sent a note to the British foreign secretary, Sir Anthony Eden, suggesting that the Nazis be tried by 'an international tribunal', Eden rejected the idea as 'premature'.[27]

In late 1942 the Soviets set up their own commission to investigate and prosecute Germans accused of war crimes in the Soviet Union and

Soviet citizens accused of collaborating with them. With thirty-eight branches around the Soviet Union, this commission brought prosecutions against Germans in Kharkov in December 1943, and against a staggering total of 2.5 million Soviet citizens, some 200,000 of whom were executed. The Moscow Declaration of October 1943 and the conclusions of the Yalta Conference in 1945, both produced under Soviet chairmanship, also solemnly affirmed the need for the Nazis to be put on trial, and when the London Conference convened in the headquarters of the Church of England, Church House, on 26 June 1945, to draft the Nuremberg Charter, Robert Jackson acknowledged the debt to the Soviets when he opened the proceedings by saying, 'We start with the recital of the Moscow declaration [30 October 1943], which is really the beginning of the plan to conduct these trials.'[28]

At Moscow, the prosecutions envisaged were only for 'normal war crimes'. It was only after Stalin's speech 'On the Great Patriotic War of the Soviet Union', delivered on 6 November 1943, the twenty-sixth anniversary of the Bolshevik revolution, that the Allies started to threaten prosecuting the Germans for the war itself.[29] In that speech, to the customary thunderous applause, Stalin outlined several objectives for the Allies, and these included re-establishing the nation-states of Europe subjugated by Nazi Germany, punishing the Germans for their crimes, and 'setting up an order in Europe which completely excludes the possibility of a new aggression by Germany'. Trainin's book *Hitlerite Responsibility under Criminal Law*, edited by Vyshinskii and published in Moscow in early 1944 and then in English translation in London in 1945, duly played a huge role in convincing the Allies to prosecute the Germans for crimes against peace, and in making this the central fact about the Nuremberg trials.

However, Soviet influence was not confined to the all-important concepts of crimes against peace and international tribunals. It also facilitated the Americans' insistence, against French objections, that conspiracy be included as a count on its own (Count 1). Conspiracy is a notoriously elastic concept in law and does not even exist as a crime in many criminal codes; at the London Conference, the French argued in vain that only the offences themselves, towards which the alleged conspiracy is directed, should be punishable. The Soviets, by contrast, had no trouble with the concept of conspiracy.[30] General Nikitchenko said specifically, 'We should not, of course, confine ourselves to persons who have actually committed the crimes *but should also especially reach those who organized or conspired them.*'[31]

The concept of conspiracy was extremely important for the jurisdiction of Nuremberg. It was only because the Prosecution presented crimes against humanity as an integral part of the conspiracy to commit crimes against peace that they were able to prosecute them at all: the judges at the International Military Tribunal read the terms of their own charter very strictly so that crimes against humanity which were not specifically war crimes (e.g. racial persecution) were prosecuted only inasmuch as they were deemed to be part of the conspiracy to commit crimes against peace.[32] This meant that no crimes against humanity committed before Germany invaded Poland on 1 September 1939 were adjudicated at Nuremberg (a point often forgotten today).

In addition to the use of criminal conspiracy theory, the Prosecution and the London Conference also adopted the notion of 'criminal organization' (which was in any case closely linked to the concept of criminal conspiracy). The author of the idea that the Nazi organizations should be proclaimed criminal organizations was Lt Col Murray Bernays, a Lithuanian-born naturalized American appointed by the United States chief of staff to investigate German war crimes. Bernays in turn drew on Raphael Lemkin's view that bodies like the SS were criminal conspiracies; Lemkin was later to formulate the legal concept of genocide. In the event, only a few of the institutions Bernays named were in fact criminalized: the political bureau of the Nazi Party, the SS, and the Gestapo. The court found that the Reichs cabinet, the *Sturmabteilung* (SA), the General Staff, and the Wehrmacht High Command were not criminal organizations.

The allegation of conspiracy has great appeal to prosecutors because it allows the net of indictment to be cast very widely if necessary. The Soviets used it for their show trials. After the Nuremberg trials were over, and as Vyshinskii's reputation rose so high that the Law Institute of the Soviet Academy of Sciences was named after him, Soviet jurists argued that the conspiracy theory applied at Nuremberg and Tokyo had originated with him. P. S. Romashkin, a noted author of various standard textbooks on Soviet law, wrote that the liability theory used at Nuremberg had originally been formulated by Vyshinskii in his concluding speech at the Bukharin trial in 1938.[33] At that trial, Bukharin had complained (after making a long self-accusatory confession of his own 'dastardly crimes') that he was being accused of conspiring with people he had never met. Vyshinskii attacked this line of defence as outdated and un-Soviet.

> To establish complicity we must establish that there is a common line uniting the accomplices in a given crime, that there is a common criminal design. To establish complicity, it is necessary to establish the existence of a united will directed toward a single object common to all the participants in the crime. If, say, a gang of robbers will act in such a way that one part of its members will set fire to houses, violate women, murder and so on, in

one place, while another part of the gang will do the same in another place, then even if neither the one nor the other knew of the crimes committed separately by any section of the common gang, they will be answerable in full for the sum total of the crimes, if only it is proved that they had agreed to participate in this gang for the purpose of committing the various crimes.[34]

Writing in 1949, Vyshinskii returned to the question. 'In our view,' he wrote, 'every participant in a criminal group must be held responsible for each specific crime if it flows from the general aim of the group or if it is in the known plan for the criminal activities.'[35] This applied even if the conspirators did not know each other. The same principle was incorporated into American law via the so-called 'Pinkerton rule' in 1946.[36] Sixty-three years later, and thanks to Vyshinskii's influence at Nuremberg, this doctrine has now been adopted by the International Criminal Tribunal for the former Yugoslavia and the International Criminal Tribunal for Rwanda under the label 'joint criminal enterprise': indeed 'third category joint criminal enterprise' is an even more elastic definition of criminal liability than Vyshinskii's, because under it a defendant can be convicted of a crime committed by others even if the act was not specifically part of the alleged common plan but if it is ruled that it was nonetheless a foreseeable consequence of it.

Vyshinskii rendered one last crucial service to Nuremberg. He visited Nuremberg several times during the course of the trial, although officially he had nothing to do with it, and the other prosecutors and judges allegedly regarded him with suspicion. He did little to allay their fears, and instead behaved with a rather ghoulish sense of humour. At a dinner for the judges and the prosecutors – an event which itself illustrates the cosy relationship between the two – Vyshinskii raised a glass to the swift death of the defendants. The assembled company drank to the toast before the translator had finished, and there were red faces all round when they found out the trap into which they had walked.[37]

Vyshinskii had in fact been appointed by Stalin to a secret commission to ensure that everything at the trial went off as planned, and especially to ensure that no discussion of the Nazi–Soviet Pact was allowed in the courtroom. In keeping with the secret protocol of that pact, the Soviet Union had invaded Poland from the east as Germany invaded from the west, and it had also attacked Finland, the Baltic States, and Bessarabia. The Communists were therefore guilty of exactly the same crimes against peace as the Nazis. They were also guilty of numerous atrocities, most famously the mass slaughter of Poles at Katyn and also of huge-scale deportations (which they continued to practise, as did the Western Allies, after the end of the war).

If they had suspicions about Vyshinskii's presence or role at Nuremberg, the Western judges and prosecutors did not act on them. On the contrary, they collaborated with him and the Soviets generally, for the excellent reason that they wanted to cover up their own war crimes too. Of course the Nazis had committed the most unimaginable atrocities, but the Allies had gone very far in the struggle to defeat them, both by deliberately bombing civilians in German cities and then by ethnically cleansing whole swathes of Central Europe of Germans in 1946, an operation decided at Potsdam which killed two million and uprooted fourteen million people.

Consequently, for instance, the British were happy to accede to Vyshinskii's demand that parts of the speech which Sir Hartley Shawcross intended to give on 3 December 1945 be censored, because they needed the Soviets to support them when their own crimes risked coming under scrutiny.[38] Hermann Goering, Nuremberg's star defendant and (among other things) the head of the Luftwaffe, was not indicted for the terror bombing of British cities (the famous Blitz) because the British did not want their own bomb attacks on German cities to be adduced in a *tu quoque* defence. The whole of Germany lay in rubble by the time the Nuremberg trials had started, and hundreds of thousands of civilians had perished in the firestorms with which Allied bombers deliberately destroyed her cities: the Germans' air raids on Britain 'paled by comparison', according to Prosecutor Telford Taylor.[39] Moreover, the *Enola Gay* had dropped a nuclear bomb on Hiroshima the day after the Nuremberg Charter was promulgated, killing 120,000 Japanese civilians in one go.

By the same token, when the American admiral Chester Nimitz sent a note to the judges saying that the British and American navies had waged naval warfare in exactly the same way as the Germans, the relevant charges against the German admiral, Karl Doenitz, were simply dropped. The illegality of the British, American, and Soviet actions was used to cover up the illegality of the German ones. The case of Katyn was especially disgraceful. The Prosecution knew that the charge against the Nazis for having slaughtered many thousands of Poles, mainly army officers, in the forest in September 1940 was risky because the Goebbels had already publicly blamed the Soviets for the massacre in 1943. The NKVD had indeed actually committed the atrocity, as the Soviet government eventually admitted in 1990, but the Soviets insisted that the charge be included in the indictment against the Nazis, and they were duly convicted of it.

So Nuremberg was a clear case of victors' justice. Other states, especially ones which had been victims of Nazi aggression, asked to be able to appoint judges to the Nuremberg bench, but their requests were rejected, and no judges from neutral states were appointed either. To be sure, there were sound jurisdictional reasons for this – the Allies reasoned that they were the holders of sovereignty in Germany, since the Nazis' unconditional surrender meant that there was literally no German government apart from the Allies themselves – but there can be little doubt that this rejection was also intended to prevent any of the Allies' own misdeeds from coming under scrutiny.

This is doubtless the reason why Nuremberg's great proclamation of the criminality of aggressive war has in fact proved to be a dead letter. No one has ever been prosecuted for crimes against peace since World War II. Those international criminal tribunals which claim supranational or near-universal jurisdiction, like the International Criminal Tribunal for the former Yugoslavia (ICTY) or the International Criminal Court (ICC), have all side-stepped 'crimes against peace'. The ICTY charter makes no reference to the crime of aggression, while the ICC has said it will not conduct prosecutions for it until such time as the term has been defined. Its jurisdiction over this crime has therefore been postponed *sine die*.

It is also for this reason that some of those who initially supported Nuremberg soon turned against it. The great German jurist Hans Kelsen had lobbied hard before the war for the principle of universal jurisdiction and had argued that state sovereignty was the fundamental problem in international relations. His thinking on establishing 'peace through law' has been hugely influential on the creation of international criminal tribunals in the late twentieth century. Yet in 1947 he attacked Nuremberg virulently.[40] He did not mind that the tribunal applied law retroactively but he did feel that the presence of the Soviets on the bench, and the consequent failure to prosecute the Soviet leaders for committing the same crimes as the Nazis, meant that the trials were legally useless. 'If the principles applied in the Nuremberg trial were to become a precedent,' he wrote, 'then, after the next war, the governments of the victorious States would try the members of the governments of the vanquished States for having committed crimes determined unilaterally and with retroactive force by the former. Let us hope that there is no such precedent.'[41] Unfortunately, at least as far as the general principle of prosecuting defeated enemies is concerned, his hopes have been disappointed.

8   Creating Legitimacy: the Trial of Marshal Antonescu

The trial of Marshal Ion Antonescu, *Conducător* (leader) of Romania from 1940 to 1944, took place in less than two weeks in May 1946, as the Nuremberg trials were still continuing in Germany. Antonescu was found guilty and shot on 1 June 1946.

Marshal Antonescu had become head of the Romanian government in September 1940 in much the same way as Marshal Pétain had in France – as a result of national disaster. King Carol, who had established a royal dictatorship before the war, had tried to balance between the Nazis and the Western Allies. His policy collapsed when, as a result of the terms of the secret protocol to the Molotov–Ribbentrop pact signed on 23 August 1939, Romania's northeastern province of Bessarabia was invaded by the Soviet Union and annexed in August 1940. At the same time, the Vienna diktat imposed by Hitler caused part of Transylvania to be ceded to Hungary. The southern Dobruja was ceded to Bulgaria.

This triple loss of territory precipitated a crisis: King Carol made Marshal Antonescu prime minister with full powers on 4 September 1940. Antonescu, who had fought in the Balkan wars in 1912 and 1913 and then in World War I, had been military attaché in Paris and London; he promptly deposed the corrupt and unpopular king, on 6 September 1940, and appointed his son, King Michael, in his place. Romania joined the Axis and helped invade the Soviet Union in June 1941, principally to regain Bessarabia. King Michael remained on the throne as a figurehead throughout the war years, indeed until 1947, and so Antonescu was never actually head of state.

Romania's situation during the war was extremely difficult. Like Norway and Finland, the country had tried to remain neutral; like them too, she was the victim of aggression. The illegality of the secret protocol to the Molotov–Ribbentrop pact, and therefore of the Soviet annexation of Bessarabia and the Baltic States, was finally admitted in 1989; the admission led directly to the secession of the Baltic States and to the collapse of the Soviet Union in 1991. When Romania joined the Axis attack against the Soviet Union in 1941, therefore, she did so in order to recover territory illegally seized from her by Moscow.

Within Romania, Antonescu had to govern in uneasy alliance with the fascist Iron Guard, which tried to overthrow him in 1941 and whose rebellion he suppressed partly with the help of German troops. The Iron Guard was virulently anti-Semitic and Antonescu's relationship to them was rather akin to that between the essentially conservative Marshal Pétain and the overtly pro-Nazi collaborators based in occupied Paris. However, there were very significant deportations of Jews from Romania during the war years for which Antonescu undoubtedly shares blame.[1]

Antonescu remained in power until exactly five years after the signature of the Molotov–Ribbentrop pact. Just as he had overthrown King Carol, so King Michael overthrew him in on 23 August 1944 when, following the Soviet invasion of Romania, he summoned him to an audience and had him arrested on the spot. He and other leading ministers were handed over to a group of Communist partisans who were secretly waiting in another room. Even though the Romanian Communist Party (Europe's smallest, with barely a thousand members) played a mere walk-on part in this royal coup, Communist historiography subsequently elevated it to the status of a glorious proletarian victory, and 23 August became Romania's national day, when the so-called Communist revolution was celebrated.

The marshal remained in Bucharest for eight days until Soviet troops entered the Romanian capital on 31 August. The two generals commanding the Russian troops were under orders from Stalin to find Antonescu, and he was taken to Moscow at the beginning of September 1944, where he was initially held captive in relatively comfortable conditions not far outside the Russian capital.

On 6 March 1945 a government under the pro-Communist Petru Groza was formed in Bucharest. This was thanks to the intervention of none other than the man who had now become deputy people's commissar for foreign affairs, our old friend Andrei Vyshinskii. Vyshinskii travelled to Romania at the head of a Soviet delegation to force the resignation of Nicolae Rădescu, the army general who had governed the country following the fall of Antonescu. Vyshinskii had previously been despatched by Stalin to Italy, where he had been charged with giving the Italian Communists as much chance as possible of participating in the country's political life (the Italian Communist leader, Palmiro Togliatti, was duly appointed minister of justice in June); his visit to Romania at the end of February

1945 had a similar purpose, and it was the beginning of the Soviet Union's consolidation of its influence over Romania.

Vyshinskii had an audience with King Michael on 26 February, where he politely demanded that Petru Groza be appointed in Rădescu's place. The general was not the man to bring Romania into Moscow's orbit. The king initially refused to do as Stalin's envoy asked, so Vyshinskii dropped the politeness. He returned the next day and banged the table so hard that the china rattled, shouting at the young king, 'If this is not done, we cannot guarantee the free existence of the Romanian people'.[2] He got his way, and Groza was installed. For the next seven years, Groza was to preside over the full consolidation of Communist power in Romania until he was succeeded by the vicious Stalinist, Gheorghe Gheorghiu-Dej, in 1952. Two years after Groza's appointment, and presumably in order to thank him for his role, a sycophantic mayor of the Transylvanian town of Sibiu wrote to Vyshinskii to ask him to become an honorary citizen of the town; Vyshinskii accepted, even though he had never even heard of the place until then.

In the run-up to Vyshinskii's visit, the Communists, under the leadership of Ana Pauker, had staged demonstrations against Rădescu for failing to deal harshly enough with 'fascist sympathizers', i.e. Antonescu and his ministers. One of the first acts of new Groza government, therefore, was to pass a law, No. 312, on 21 April 1945, which established the legal basis for the Antonescu trial.[3] This decree-law, which set up the People's Tribunal which was to try him, was drafted specifically to convict Romania's wartime leaders. The text was overtly retroactive because it referred at length to specific historical events and proclaimed 'guilty of the country's disaster' those who had 'campaigned for Hitlerism and fascism and who allowed the advance of German troops on the territory of the country'; who 'after 6 September 1940 acted for the preparation and carrying out of the above deeds by words written or any other means'; who had encouraged the declaration and the continuation of war against the Soviet Union and the United Nations; who had not respected the international laws of war; who had subjected prisoners of war to inhuman treatment; who had ordered acts of terror or repression; who had ordered or condoned collective repression within the framework of racial persecution; who had organized forced labour or the transportation of persons with the aim of exterminating them; and who had committed various other offences during the recently terminated war.[4]

Just as Nuremberg had brought a prosecution against Julius Streicher, one of Nazi Germany's most prominent anti-Semitic journalists, so Romanian intellectuals and journalists who had supported Antonescu or the Iron Guard were also proclaimed guilty by the decree-law. Several pro-Iron Guard writers were tried and sentenced to death (some *in absentia*) in June 1945, in a curtain-raiser to the Antonescu trial itself. In May 1945, indeed, some twenty-nine of Antonescu's ministers and under-secretaries of state were arrested and put on trial,[5] while trials of Antonescu's senior supporters and collaborators went on continuously until 1949.[6]

In addition to its explicit retroactivity, the decree-law included such vague phrases as references to people who had 'served Hitlerism or fascism or who contributed to the realization of their policies or the subjection of the economy of the country to the detriment of the interests of the Romanian people'. None of the offences described were formulated with reference to pre-existing laws in the penal code. There were heavy references to the racial persecutions committed by the previous regime, a difference from Nuremberg where there was much more balance between crimes against humanity (i.e. racial persecution), war crimes, and crimes against peace.

On 10 May 1945, a month after the signature of the decree-law, Antonescu was transferred to the Lubyanka, the KGB headquarters in Moscow, where he was severely interrogated. There was cross-fertilization with the Nuremberg trials, which were then being prepared, just as there had been in the Quisling trial: parts of the information gleaned from Antonescu's interrogation were used by the Soviet prosecutor at Nuremberg, General Rudenko, mainly concerning agreements between Hitler and Antonescu to allow German troops into Romanian territory to help in the attack on the Soviet Union.

Antonescu remained in the Lubyanka until April 1946, when he was sent back to Romania to be put on trial by the People's Tribunal which the May 1945 decree had created. From the very beginning, the prime mover behind the trial was the Soviet Union: Article 14 of the armistice agreement imposed on Romania on 12 September 1944 obliged Romania to arrest and try war crimes suspects in collaboration with the Soviets. The Allied Control Commission which oversaw the terms of the armistice with Romania was chaired by a Soviet general and dominated by Red Army officers. But of course the Romanian Communists who were then gaining power in the country were themselves in full agreement with this Soviet plan. The Romanian Communist Party needed to invent legitimacy for itself as the only bastion against fascism, just as Stalin himself had done in the 1930s.[7] Indeed, it needed to present the arrest of Antonescu on 23 September 1944 as its work alone.

According to the terms of the armistice agreement, two People's Tribunals were set up, in Bucharest and Cluj, to try various army officers and members of the Antonescu regime for war crimes. The tribunals initially examined some 2700 war crimes allegations and a total of 668 persons were found guilty, many of them *in absentia*, even though the tribunals were in existence for only a year (June 1945 to June 1946). The prosecutors were appointed by the Communist minister of justice, Lucreţiu Pătrăşcanu, and most of them were Communist Party members. The chief prosecutor was Avram Bunaciu. Some prosecutors did their work in order to save their own skin: Major Iorgu Popescu had killed a Jewish student during the war but became a public prosecutor in charge of the case against the perpetrators of the anti-Jewish pogroms in Iaşi. Following the closure of the People's Tribunal in June 1946, further prosecutions were carried out for 'crimes against peace' in the ordinary courts in Romania on the basis of a law passed in 1945.

The constitution of the Bucharest People's Tribunal which tried Antonescu reflected the theory and practice of Communist 'people's justice'. The president, Alexandru Voitinovici, was an obscure magistrate from Moldavia[8] and distantly related to the minister of justice, Pătrăşcanu. One of the prosecutors, Dumitru Săracu, had no legal training whatever and had once worked as a cook in the famous restaurant, Capşa, on Calea Victoriei in Bucharest. The members of the panel of judges included Vasile Niţa, a worker representative of the Communist Party; Ion Păuna, another worker representing the Social Democrat Party; Joviţa Dumbravă, a representative of Groza's Ploughman's Front who actually was himself a ploughman, i.e. a 'peasant' in Communist terminology; Constantin Ţiulescu, a worker representing the General Confederation of Labour;[9] and 'a housewife'.[10] In other words, they were not judges at all.

The indictment issued against Antonescu and others on 29 April 1946 expressed the political nature of the trial without embarrassment. Written in the rebarbative tone of Stalinist propaganda, the document was over a hundred pages long and contained accounts of Antonescu's life and political career, and many repetitions of the political accusations against him. It attacked Antonescu for his policies across the board, both for his 'Romanianization' policies involving the expropriation of Jews but also for his 'anti-peasant' policy. It contained rhetorical flourishes and rhetorical questions, referring liberally to Antonescu's 'anti-national' and 'anti-people' policies and of course accusing him of 'chauvinism' and 'anti-Semitism'.[11] Like the decree-law of May 1945, the indictment made little reference to existing penal law and instead accused the defendants of 'bringing about the destruction of the country', of responsibility for 'the national disaster', of belonging to 'reactionary circles', of 'the humiliation and suffering of the Romanian people', 'national betrayal' (treason),[12] and so on. For this reason, the trial was known as the Great National Betrayal Trial, as were later political trials in 1948. The indictment, indeed, specifically said that the Romanian people could never be free until justice was done and until those responsible for the national disaster were condemned.[13]

The indictment also contained the same sort of vigorous personal insults for which Vyshinskii had become famous at the Moscow show trials, for instance, referring to Constantin Vasiliu, one of Antonescu's co-indictees, as 'the most odious, the crudest and the most cynical of the collaborators in Antonescu's criminal government'.[14] It concluded with the affirmation that the chief defendant was guilty under all fourteen of the counts enunciated in the decree-law of 29 April 1945 – not surprising, since the law was drawn up precisely with his conviction in mind. None of these overtly political aspects of the indictment prevented the prosecutor, Vasile Stoican, from interrupting the cross-examination of Antonescu during the trial itself and accusing him of making political speeches.[15]

As at Nuremberg, the prosecution against Antonescu and his supporters made no mention of the aggression committed against Romania by the Soviet Union itself. This meant that the trial was conducted as if Romania had been the initiator of aggression against the Soviet Union, whereas in fact it had been a victim of it. No discussion of the international situation was permitted at the trial, as at Nuremberg, and even Nazi Germany's own threats against Romania were passed over. Like other collaborators, Antonescu pleaded that Romania had been under the threat of direct German occupation and that he had opted for the lesser evil by agreeing to be politically allied to Germany instead.

Romanian troops had certainly committed atrocities, including against Jews, in Iaşi, Odessa, and elsewhere. Hundreds of thousands had been deported from Romania itself. Antonescu was deeply implicated, even though many of the worst atrocities were carried out by the Iron Guard which he did not control. But the effect on the Romanian public of the revelation of these crimes in court was limited because, for nearly two years by the time the trial started, the Romanians had themselves suffered at the hands of the Soviet invaders and of a Communist Party which was widely perceived as a fifth column supported only by Moscow.

The Communists wanted not only to grab legitimacy as anti-fascists; they also used the judicial process to eliminate their non-fascist political rivals. Romania had substantial democratic parties between the wars and the Communists had to destroy them in order to wield full power. Consequently, one of the aims of the Antonescu trial was to present the bourgeois parties as his allies. His trial was in fact only the beginning of a judicial campaign which culminated in the show trial of the National

Peasant Party leaders in 1947. Those leaders – Iuliu Maniu, Ion Michalache, and others – were imprisoned in Sighet prison where in the course of time they died. That prison has since been converted into a memorial museum to the victims of Communism, for the trial of Maniu and the others was itself only the most prominent aspect of a widespread reign of terror, directed by the Soviet Union and involving mass arrests of political enemies.[16]

Those trials sought to present Maniu and the others as members of a conspiracy who, with Antonescu, had plotted to subjugate Romania to Hitler in the interests of world capitalism. The chief prosecutor at the Maniu trial, General Alexandru Petrescu, went on to stage other notable show trials of Romanian Stalinism, notably the anti-Tito espionage trial of various Romanian Serbs, and the trial of those accused of sabotaging the murderous construction of the Danube–Black Sea canal, a project which has become a symbol for the Communist terror. Unfortunately, Petrescu's prosecutorial zeal did not save him when fortune's cruel wheel turned in the end: when Ana Pauker was herself purged, Petrescu was arrested and convicted for crimes he had committed – under the Antonescu regime, when he had been in charge of its prisons and concentration camps.

This, the wider political purpose of the Antonescu trial, was understood immediately by observers, including Burton Y. Berry, the American minister to Romania who observed the Communist takeover in his *Romanian Diaries 1944–1947*. On 3 May 1946 he sent two telegrams to the State Department, the first one reporting on Marshal Antonescu's return to Romania, the second explaining the politics behind the trial and the Soviet political involvement in it. He wrote,

> The war criminal trials of Marshal Antonescu and other ministers scheduled to open May 6 … are reliably reported as being organised to aid a future governmental electoral ticket by seeking to discredit National Peasant and National Liberal leaders, Maniu and Bratianu in the course of the testimony.
>
> It is even reported that Molotov at Paris has requested a selected dossier on the two men to be used in the present sessions of Foreign Ministers and that the Marshal and Mihai Antonescu have been promised certain clemencies if they implicate Maniu and Bratianu during the trials. For political purposes the Government seeks to compromise other personalities in addition to the Papal Nuncio including Jewish leaders and political deputies of Bratianu and Maniu.[17]

During the trial itself, the Communists staged events in Bucharest's central square to give the impression that popular will was being done in the courtroom. Princess Ileana of Romania, who witnessed the events, recalls how loudspeakers were installed in University Square in central Bucharest where demands for Antonescu's death were broadcast. Trucks with Russian soldiers as guards brought workers to demonstrate, to give the impression that 'the people' were demanding that their former leader be executed. Images of the crowd were duly broadcast around the world and even into the courtroom itself where Antonescu was being tried.[18]

The trial started on 6 May 1946 and lasted until 17 May. During his cross-examination by the president of the Tribunal, Antonescu denied ever having ordered deportations or massacres. The film of the trial survives and he appears vigorous and healthy; the transcript of the trial seems to indicate that the discussions were relatively polite. Antonescu claimed that there had been evacuations of population from border areas, but only for reasons of pure military necessity.[19] As far as the invasion of Odessa and the presence of Romanian troops at Stalingrad was concerned, Antonescu responded that it was an ancient principle of warfare to pursue the enemy as far as necessary beyond one's own territory in order to defeat him; he quoted Scipio's pursuit of Hannibal into Africa and Spain and Napoleon's march on Moscow to prove his point.[20] When confronted with the accusation that he had ordered or tolerated the massacre at Odessa, Antonescu claimed not to remember the case. He then said that reprisals were provided for in international law when the enemy failed to obey the laws of war (when the Red Army entered Hungary in 1944, posters were put up in Hungarian towns saying that ten Hungarian civilians would be shot for the death of each Soviet soldier, and that any house from which even a single shot was fired would be summarily burned down[21]) and that he had signed but never carried out orders for reprisals against Soviet citizens if Romanian soldiers were attacked. He said that he had ensured that soldiers who committed war crimes in occupied territory were punished.[22]

Two giants of inter-war Romanian politics, Gheorghe Brătianu and Iuliu Maniu, testified at the Antonescu trial, rather as Léon Blum and Edouard Daladier had testified at the trial of Marshal Pétain the previous year. However, their testimony was not intended to incriminate Antonescu, to whose governments they had suggested ministerial appointments. On the contrary, Maniu, the most respected and popular politician in Romania, shook the marshal by the hand as he left the witness box. This gesture of solidarity with a man who, he knew, had been condemned in advance by the authorities, was ruthlessly exploited by the Communist press which was determined to present Maniu as Antonescu's friend.

A film was taken of the last moments of Marshal Antonescu. It has the quality of Eisenstein about it. An angular-faced court official wearing dark glasses read out the judgement in a jarring voice, finding Antonescu guilty of all the charges in the indictment. Antonescu and his fellow convicts (Constantin Vasiliu, his minister of the interior; Gheorghe Alexianu, the governor of Transnistria; and Mihai Antonescu (no relation), his deputy prime minister) were then marched to a wooded area where they were tied to posts. They were asked for their final requests and Marshal Antonescu asked to be shot by soldiers not by prison guards. His request was refused. As the squad raised its guns, Antonescu seemed to salute by raising his hat in his outstretched right hand. As the shots rang out, he fell to the ground. 'Gentlemen, you have not shot me!' he cried as he lay writhing in agony. An officer holding a pistol administered a *coup de grâce* to each of the four convicts, and two to Antonescu, one in the head and one in the chest.

9 Ethnic Cleansing and National Cleansing in Czechoslovakia, 1945–1947

The Antonescu trial and the subsequent trial of the National Peasant leaders showed how the judicial system was an instrument for enforcing Moscow's rule over Eastern Europe, as of course it had been a tool of political repression in the Soviet Union itself before the war. But Stalin's penchant for political trials had supporters in the West. When the *Ligue des Droits de l'Homme* published its Rosenmark report on the Moscow trials in October 1936, it expressed approval for them and opined that the defendants were probably guilty as charged. In any case, Stalin was an ally. At the London Conference which drew up the Nuremberg Charter, there were differences between the Soviet and American delegations but the American secretary of state, James Byrnes, told Prosecutor Jackson to put his scruples about the Soviets aside because it was 'a matter of national policy' to have them on board.[1]

Czechoslovakia had played a central role in the outbreak of war. Hitler had agitated for the cession of the Sudetenland, and the West capitulated to his demands at Munich on 30 September 1938. The Czech lands were occupied in March 1939, where a Protectorate was established with a Czech government under German tutelage, and Slovakia was made an independent state (although in reality also a puppet) under the presidency of a Catholic priest, Monsignor Jozef Tiso. As the war came to an end, talks on the reunification of the country and the creation of the new Czechoslovak government were held in Moscow in March 1945 between the representatives of the London government in exile under President Edvard Beneš and the other political parties, especially the Communists. The returning government determined at Košice in April 1945 that collaborators would be tried by a new National Court, and that indictees would include 'treacherous journalists' and 'traitors' from banking and industry (as also happened at Nuremberg).

The basis for this trial of members of the Protectorate government and other collaborators was the Decree No. 16 of 19 June 1945 entitled 'On the Punishment of Nazi Criminals, Traitors and their Collaborators, as well as On Extraordinary People's Courts'. This decree is often known as the 'Great Retribution Decree' and was one of the earliest so-called Beneš decrees. Named after the president who signed them, these 143 decrees formed a vast legislative programme which became the legal blunt instrument by which, among other things, the entire German population of Czechoslovakia was ethnically cleansed. There was huge public anger at the role which had been played before and during the war by the Germans in the Czech lands, many of whom supported the Nazis, and the air was thick with demands for vengeance. Three million civilians were expelled as a result of these decrees and the Allies' Potsdam agreement of August 1945, and their expulsion and mass murder is inseparable from the overall programme of 'national cleansing' expressed by the decrees.[238] The political imperatives outlined at Košice were explicitly formulated in the intensely political language of the Great Decree, whose preamble burns with invective against the crimes of the Nazis and their collaborators.

The Great Retribution Decree retroactively criminalized collaboration and created 'Extraordinary People's Courts' to try and convict people accused of it. It was complemented by Decree No. 17, issued on the same day, which created a special court, the National Court, for the specific trial of 'the state president of the so-called Protectorate, the members of the so-called Protectorate government', and other collaborators under the terms of the crimes outlined in the Great Decree. 'Journalists who propagandistically served the invader government'[239] and anti-Communist organizations were also specifically named as potential indictees.

Other important decrees were the 'Small Retribution Decree' (No. 138) of 27 October 1945, which empowered local committees to punish those who 'undermined public morale by behaviour insulting to the national sentiments of the Czech or Slovak people'; and Decree No. 115 of 8 May 1946 which exonerated acts of vengeance committed against the occupiers or their collaborators. The decrees were passed in an atmosphere of extreme vengeance and retribution which indirectly caused the deaths of many hundreds of thousands of Germans and the ethnic cleansing of millions.

The structure of the special people's courts created by Decree No. 16 reflected the political imperatives of the day; they were composed of one professional jurist and four lay associates.[240] These latter were based on the model of soviets in the Soviet Union and were *de facto* controlled by the Communists, since there were two Communist parties in the National Front government: the Communist Party of Czechoslovakia and the Communist Party of Slovakia. Very often, these courts were used to exercise political and personal acts of vengeance and to settle scores. Some 30,000 trials took place in the two-year period on the basis of these decrees before these special people's courts. Around half of those sentenced were Germans, 713 death sentences were handed down, of which two-thirds were Germans, and 741 persons were sentenced to life imprisonment.

As with the Nuremberg Charter, the decree which created the special people's courts proclaimed that certain organizations were criminal and that mere membership of them was itself a criminal offence (Decree No. 16, Article 1.3.2). There was no system of appeal. The courts could hand down death sentences which had to be carried out within two hours of being handed down (Article 31.2). The courts ceased to exist in 1947, the year before the final Communist takeover of the country, and the majority of those imprisoned by them were released in 1955.

In a speech given in December 1945, President Beneš emphasized that the trials were part and parcel of an overall process of engineering change in Czechoslovak society[241] – what we would today call 'transitional justice'. The whole process was proudly called a 'national purge' or 'national cleansing' (*národní očista*), the word 'purge' obviously having clear Stalinist connotations (as did the equivalent term, *épuration*, in France).[242] The Communist leader, Klement Gottwald, was even more candid about the political nature of this process: 'The struggle against traitors and collaborators is a tool which we have today in the fight for the leadership of the nation … It is a very sharp weapon with which we can cut away so many limbs of the bourgeoisie that only its trunk will remain.' Not to use this weapon, he said, would make it rust.[243]

An integral part of this 'cleansing' was ethnic cleansing: expropriations and expulsions of Germans and Hungarians were specifically conditional on whether they had committed crimes defined in the same decrees used to prosecute Monsignor Tiso and other wartime leaders (for instance, the Decree No. 33 of the Slovak National Council, dated 15 May 1945). There is widespread understanding today that the Beneš decrees and the associated decrees passed by the Slovak National Assembly were grossly unfair violations of due process, even if they flowed from the decision taken by the Allies at Potsdam to cleanse Central Europe of Germans.

The trial of former members of the Protectorate government before the specially constituted National Court opened on 29 April 1946. It was to last until 31 July. The defendants included two Protectorate prime ministers, Jaroslav Krejčí and Richard Bienert; the former minister of railways, Jindřich Kamenický; the former minister of finance, Josef Kalfus; and the former agriculture minister, Adolf Hrubý. The Protectorate state president himself, Emil Hácha, a tragic figure whose guilt remains a matter of debate (although 'Hachaism' became a byword for collaboration), had been arrested on 13 May 1945 on the orders of the Communist minister of the interior, Václav Nosek, and in a preliminary interrogation by the National Court, he had pleaded mental instability. He died in a prison hospital on 27 June 1945, before his trial could begin.

Hácha's first prime minister, Alois Eliáš, also never came to trial, for the good reason that he was murdered by the Nazis in 1942. He was never considered a collaborator in the first place, and was finally given a state funeral in 2006. Eliáš worked with the resistance during his terms in office and tried to perform active works of resistance himself; most notably he tried to poison a group of pro-German Czech journalists by inviting them to his office and serving them sandwiches laced with botulism, typhus, and TB bacteria. Others, true collaborators, escaped trial by their own hand. Emanuel Moravec, the hated education minister in the Protectorate government, who was an enthusiastic collaborator with the Nazis and who made energetic propaganda about the future of the Czech lands in a Nazi Europe, committed suicide on 5 May 1945.

By the time the trial of the Protectorate government started, revenge against actual perpetrators was well under way, and the press had started to complain that the 'big fish' were getting away in Czechoslovakia while Quisling, Pétain, Laval, and others had already faced trial.[244] The defendants were accused of supporting the Nazi movement in the media and of executing the occupier's illegal acts. But returning President Beneš wanted and needed the trial for exactly the same reason as the Gaullists in France: to demonstrate that the governments in Prague and Bratislava had been null and void in law, and that only his government in exile was legitimate.[245]

As in France, the press agitated hard for conviction of 'the traitors' and demanded the harshest punishment. The Communists, who headed the government from May 1946, with Gottwald as prime minister, were happy when the Soviet ambassador to Czechoslovakia told the justice minister, Prokop Drtina, that the Soviet Union expected the death sentence to be passed on at least three of the defendants. The other political parties in the government tried to influence the outcome as well; the trial was discussed in cabinet meetings and the government itself recommended the death sentence in at least two cases.

Much of the testimony offered during the trial was favourable to the Defence. Many argued that the destruction of Czechoslovakia had not been caused by national traitors but instead by the Western powers who had thrown the country to the Hitlerian wolf at Munich. Many understood the political imperatives behind the prosecution: the justice minister had to defend himself against the charge that the trial was 'victors' justice'. The defendants succeeded in scoring some points against the exiled ministers who were now their accusers: Bienert declared, 'If I had been clever, I would have left the country too.'[246]

When the court came to deliver its ruling on 31 July 1946, it resisted the government's calls for the death penalty and imposed only prison sentences. No doubt this reflected that there were also sharp divisions within the government, and the fact that public opinion did not support the harsh punishments demanded by the Communists. Richard Bienert got three years and Jaroslav Krejčí twenty-five, the former's light sentence due to the fact that he maintained links with the anti-Nazi underground and indeed had even been arrested by the Gestapo in 1939. Even the agriculture minister, Adolf Hrubý, who was expected to be sentenced to death – the Communists considered him a double traitor since he had fought in the Red Army in World War I – was sent to prison, where he died in 1951. Josef Kalfus, who was finance minister throughout the whole of the Protectorate's existence, was found guilty but not punished since the court recognized that he had also been working with the Czech underground.

The Communist Party organized a vast letter-writing campaign to the justice minister, in an attempt to get the sentences revised and made harsher. Indignant workers protested outside the justice ministry, and the Communist press reported on a 'wave of anger' across factories, resistance groups, and Communist organizations. But the campaign ran up against the buffers of public opinion and its own inconsistencies: it was precisely a feature of the people's courts that they admitted of no appeal. The Communists lost this battle, and there was no review of the sentences.

Rudolf Beran, who had been prime minister of Czechoslovakia from 1 December 1938 until the Nazi occupation of 14 March 1939, was put on trial the following year. Like State President Hácha, he had remained in his post, albeit in only a heavily truncated territory, serving as Protectorate prime minister until Adolf Eliáš took over on 27 April 1939. Beran's trial was an even greater exercise in hypocrisy than that of the members of the Protectorate government. Czechoslovakia had lost the Sudetenland by the time he came to power and, with it, its pre-Munich military fortifications. The subsequent occupation of the Czech lands and the dismemberment of Czechoslovakia were almost a foregone conclusion. But the Communists were determined to eliminate Beran because, as a leading agrarian, he was a conservative and a long-standing opponent both of Edvard Beneš, whose election to the presidency he had tried to thwart in 1935, and of the Communists, whose party he had helped to ban. Most of the charges against Beran were thrown out, especially the claim that he was pro-totalitarian and anti-Communist. But he was still given a twenty-year prison sentence (no doubt as a direct result of political pressure from the ruling Communists), which meant life. Born in 1887, he died in prison in 1954.

Beran's trial played a direct role in the simultaneous trial of Slovakia's wartime leader, Monsignor Tiso. Fearing that the sentence would be light, the judges in the Tiso trial brought forward the announcement of their verdict by a week in order that the Beran sentence could not be cited as a precedent. Beran was sentenced on 21 April 1947, three days after Monsignor Tiso had been hanged.

Jozef Tiso was one of the more extraordinary figures in an age of extremes: a Catholic priest who aligned himself with Hitler and who had run a clerico-fascist state under German tutelage. He continues to be the subject of controversy today, some despising him as an anti-Semite and a collaborator, others insisting he was a patriot and a Christian who did what he could for his country at its most difficult hour.

Tiso had been involved in Czechoslovak politics from the earliest days as a member of the Slovak People's Party of Andrej Hlinka. Like many Slovak nationalists, he became increasingly disenchanted with the failure of the Czechs to grant the Slovaks the autonomy within the common state which they had promised. Once the Nazis started to agitate against Czechoslovakia, the Slovak nationalists became effectively allies of the Germans. Czechoslovakia was dismembered at Munich in September 1938, with both Germany and Poland moving in to take Czech territory, and that agreement contained provisions for Slovak autonomy. But the interim situation lasted only a few months until Hitler summoned Monsignor Tiso to Berlin and told him to proclaim independence. This duly occurred, on 16 March 1939, and the Nazis used this as the pretext for their occupation of the whole of Bohemia and Moravia: 'The Czechoslovak artificial state has collapsed,' was how a pamphlet at the time spun the invasion, 'the Führer is ensuring peace and order.'

Following the defeat of the Axis powers and the invasion of Slovakia by the Red Army, how to resurrect Czechoslovakia became the main political question facing the country's politicians. What to do with Tiso became a major issue within that context. Tiso's fate divided the political parties because the Catholic, anti-Communist and pro-Tiso vote was strong in Slovakia, whereas the Communists had at least 40 per cent of the vote in the Czech lands, twice as much as its nearest competitor, as against only 30 per cent in Slovakia, half that enjoyed by the rival national-ist (and partly pro-Tiso) Democratic Party.[247] The Communists wanted to humiliate and destroy Slovak opponents of Czechoslovak unity by execut-ing Tiso; more liberal politicians wanted to appease them and bring them on board by granting him clemency. One Communist Party leader said, 'With this trial we are going to liquidate the whole reactionary Slovak past and the betrayal of the Slovak bourgeoisie and Slovak reaction.'[248] The Communists also wanted to engineer a split between the two wings of the Democratic Party, one half of which was Catholic, conservative, national-ist, and pro-Tiso, the other half of which was more pro-Czechoslovak and close to Beneš in Prague.[249]

Tiso had fled with the retreating German army to Austria, from where he made a vigorous broadcast pleading for Slovak independence and against the Bolshevik threat. He was turned over to the Czechoslovak authorities in October 1945 and thence to the Communist-dominated Na-tional Committee in Bratislava. He was put on public display in handcuffs, which caused huge protests. Numerous people, from the British ambas-sador to Prague to a group of Slovak bishops, appealed for clemency, on the grounds that a harsh sentence would cause relations between Czechs and Slovaks to worsen. [250]

The principal legal instrument which made provision for Tiso's trial was the explicitly retrospective Decree No. 33 'On the Punishment of Fascist Criminals, Occupiers, Traitors, and Collaborators and on the Creation of People's Justice', passed by the Slovak National Council on 15 May 1945. This decree preceded by a month Beneš's Great Retribution De-cree. As its name suggested, it created people's tribunals as well as a special National Court in Bratislava to try 'the president of the Slovak Republic', 'the members of the Slovak government from 14 March 1939 onwards', and members of Tiso's party; it was a piece of tailor-made legislation. It crimi-nalized (with provision for the death penalty) 'anyone who worked for the destruction of the Czechoslovak Republic … in the period 6 October 1938 to 14 March 1939 …' and anyone who was 'a significant founder, organ-izer, or propagandist of the Slovak People's Party of Hlinka, the Hlinka Guard, or of other fascist organizations … who was a propagandist for fascist ideas, for collaboration with Nazi Germany or for war against the Union of Soviet Socialist Republics; who … took part in anti-democratic, anti-Communist, racist or similar actions and campaigns of hatred …'[251]

The trial began on 2 December 1946. Tiso was charged along with his two deputies, Alexander Mach (his interior minister) and Ferdinand Ďurčanský (his foreign minister who escaped to America and was tried *in absentia*). The leading politicians of the land – President Edvard Beneš in Prague and Dr Jozef Lettrich in Bratislava – had already said they thought Tiso should be executed.[252] Tiso's prime minister, the overtly pro-Nazi Vojtech Tuka, had been executed following a short trial in August, while other potential witnesses – for instance the German Foreign Minister, Joachim von Ribbentrop – had been executed at Nuremberg.[253] The presiding judge, Igor Daxner, was a Communist and a Protestant who had fought in the Slovak National Uprising which Tiso had suppressed, and was thus triply an enemy of the Catholic conservative defendant.

The indictment was 213 pages long and was issued just three weeks before the trial started, which clearly left no time to prepare an adequate defence.[254] It took a day to read it out on the first day of the trial. Tiso was not given the right to choose his own defence counsel but instead had a court-imposed lawyer, Ernest Žabkay, who, like the judge and Prosecutor Anton Rašla, was a member of the Communist Party of Slovakia.[255] Tiso was never granted a proper confidential audience with him. The indictment accused Tiso of 113 crimes under four main charges: treason and conspiracy against the Czechoslovak state; being a fascist and supporting the Nazis; crushing the Slovak National Uprising in 1944; and crimes against humanity. Two hundred witnesses were called, and the total documentation submitted weighed 700 kilograms.[256]

The conspiracy against the unity of Czechoslovakia was alleged to have pre-dated the war and the Germans' ultimatums. This accusation recalled the similar allegations of conspiracy levelled at Pétain and Quisling, and it anticipates the accusation that Slobodan Milošević conspired to carve a Greater Serbia out of the ruins of old Yugoslavia. More than half of the indictment, indeed, was taken up by this alleged pre-war plot, yet there seems little doubt that it was completely invented. Part of the evidence involved alleged links with the Sudeten German leader, Konrad Henlein, but this was hardly a crime since Henlein led a legal party within democratic Czechoslovakia, and in 1937 the then Czechoslovak prime minister had even tried to persuade Henlein to enter the national government. The crimes against humanity with which Tiso was charged, especially the deportation of 60,000 Jews, was included only after much longer charges about the treasonable and anti-democratic character of Tiso's regime, and more emphasis was laid on crimes against Czechs than against Jews or Slovaks. Tiso was also charged with 'preparation for aggression against the first socialist state in the world, against the USSR',[257] a form of words very close to that which the Soviets had asked for at Nuremberg and which had also been included in the indictment against Marshal Antonescu in Romania. In fact, the Prosecution tried all lines of attack. It alleged, for instance, that Tiso was both a Slovak nationalist and a Hungarian agent; that he was both a clerico-fascist and that he had disobeyed the pope over his Jewish policy.

Presiding judge Igor Daxner acted like a prosecutor, bullying witnesses and humiliating the defendant. He even travelled to Prague to ask President Beneš what sentence he thought Tiso deserved, and reported back to the other members of the National Court that the president of the Republic favoured death. Four out of the seven judges were Communists (two Moscow-trained members of the Central Committee of the Communist Party of Slovakia) and one was a former Communist. Indeed, all the judges were members of the resistance against Tiso, just as the juries in the Pétain and Laval trials had also been selected exclusively from among *résistant* or other anti-Pétainist circles. There was fear that Tiso would become a martyr to the cause of Slovak independence from the Czechs, as indeed he has become in some expatriate circles and since the collapse of Communism, and so broadcasts were stopped after the first day, when the charges were read out, and any journalist thought to be too indulgent towards the defendant was barred from the press room.[258]

The Prosecution made its final submissions on 13 and 14 March 1947, the press having already demanded 'an act of revenge and retribution'.[259] Tiso rose to make his final speech for the Defence on 17 March 1947 and, rather like Quisling, was to be on his feet for eleven hours over a period of two days (17–18 March 1947). In contrast to his earlier behaviour, the president of the tribunal made few interruptions and seemed happy to let the defendant speak for as long as he liked. On the first day, Tiso spoke until 9 p.m. The speech was well phrased and fluent but also repetitive in parts. On occasions, he made the court laugh when he ridiculed the Prosecution and the president had to call order. Photographs of the trial show him in apparently robust health and on combative form; in some of the pictures, he appears positively relaxed, chatting to people.

Tiso denounced the lies of the Prosecution case against him and the trial itself as political with a preordained outcome.[260] He claimed that he had been told two days before the trial began that he would convicted in order to be removed from political life. He said that he was convinced that he would be sentenced to death but historians in future would research more deeply into the period. He said that he had attained and remained in office out of a sense of duty towards his country in its hour of need. Even Jews, he said, had asked him to remain in place. He had intervened to restrain the Germans in their attempts to Germanize Slovakia.

Tiso said that his entire political life had been spent working for the Slovak people and for national independence. 'Slovakia for the Slovaks!'

had always been his highest principle.[261] Collaboration with Germany became a necessity, he said, after March 1939 when Slovakia became Germany's neighbour: 'The Germans could have swallowed us as a lion swallows a frog.' Their main fear was occupation by the Germans: they had adopted a pro-German tone in public in order to keep the Germans sweet. He said that he had given the Germans in Slovakia special rights, suppressed the Communist Party, and 'solved the Jewish question in our own way' in order to remove all of the three pretexts which the Germans habitually invoked to justify their various acts of aggression against other countries.[262]

Tiso protested vehemently at the retroactive nature of the decrees under which he was being tried. On the issue of his alleged conspiracy against the Czechoslovak state, Tiso asked why he was not arrested or his party dissolved when both the Sudenten German and the Hungarian parties were banned and their leaders arrested in 1938. He complained that he was unable to call certain witnesses – Ribbentrop for instance, or the German commanders of units in Slovakia – because they were either dead or missing. He complained that the Prosecution had made use of doctored film footage, which it had shown in court, to implicate him falsely in collaboration with the Germans. Indeed, he repeatedly said that the whole indictment was vitiated by the 'false light' which it shed on historical events, making them seem otherwise than they were.

Tiso, who was prolix, became eloquent when he spoke personally about the relationship between his vocation as a priest and his political activity. 'The life of someone who is conscious of a goal,' he said, 'is like a work of art which possesses a particular point of view from which alone it can be understood. Otherwise we stand outside a magic castle without the key.' His commitment to the Christian faith, he said, was what explained everything else. He described how he had worked for the creation of the Czechoslovak state but how he and his colleagues became progressively disappointed when Slovakia's promised autonomy did not materialize. His commitment had always been to the individual, the family, and the people. All his political principles and beliefs, he said, flowed from natural law and the Christian faith. The single slogan of the Slovak People's Party had been 'For God and the nation'. But Tiso also alleged that he had not pursued a confessional policy but that his goal had been for all religions to live together in harmony.

He said that he would never have proclaimed Slovak independence if there had not been the pressure from Hitler, who had ordered him to do it, threatening to occupy the country if he did not, and to let the irredentist Hungarians do so too. He denied emphatically that he was an authoritarian or a fascist, although he admitted that he believed in the principle of and need for authority and in the need for national unity. He said that his whole political action had been devoted to awakening a sense of nationhood among the Slovak people. He claimed that he had fought against the racialism of the Nazis. He claimed to have publicly distanced himself from Nazi theory, for instance at a reception for the diplomatic corps on 7 January 1942.

Tiso admitted that he had wanted to reduce the role of the Jews in the Slovak economy. He supported Jewish emigration to Palestine. But he said restrictions imposed on Jews in the legal and medical professions had been carried out humanely and as a social measure with due compensation paid by the state. Any brutalities committed against Jews were, he said, the fault of Tuka's Nazi-imposed government over whom he tried to use his influence, as indeed even the Vatican had told him to do. He said that it had simply been impossible to halt this 'flow' (by which he meant the rise of anti-Semitism), but that it was possible only to influence and reduce it.

Tiso claimed with some justification that he had mitigated the harsher and more violent aims of the radicals in Slovakia, including those of his own prime minister. (Tuka, with whom Tiso had been in nearly constant conflict, was appointed in 1940 under pressure from Hitler because Tiso was considered too moderate.) Although Tiso denied any murderous intent towards the Jews, he compromised his own credibility when he claimed not to remember having signed deportation orders. He argued energetically that he had granted thousands of presidential exemptions to the government decrees on deportations, saving hundreds or thousands of Jews. Although there is dispute about how many exemptions Tiso actually signed, James Mace Ward has concluded: 'In terms of the radical attempt to Nazify Slovak society, there can be little doubt that Tiso was the main foil to its success.'[263]

The trial finished on 19 March 1947 after seventy-one days, when the court found Tiso guilty on 95 of the 113 charges.[264] In total, 8,000 pages of documents were submitted and the verdict was over two hundred pages long.[265] The judges followed the original structure of the indictment fairly closely in their judgement but exonerated Tiso of large parts of it, especially of the claim that he had conspired for years against Czechoslovakia. The death sentence stood out in marked contrast to the prison sentences given to the collaborators in Prague, and to Tiso's own deputy, Alexander Mach, who was given a sentence of thirty years in prison even though his culpability for treason and crimes against humanity was almost definitely greater than Tiso's.

The verdict and the trial itself caused huge ructions within Slovakia, with the Church and much of the population campaigning for clemency. Tiso's lawyers appealed on a number of grounds, both on the substantive issues about Tiso's guilt (they claimed that he was being punished for events which he did not, in fact, control) and on the basis that the trial was rigged: Tiso had not been able to see his lawyers in private, and the bench was politically biased.

The Presidium of the Slovak National Council had only a very short while to consider the 214-page judgement, and it took only ten minutes to do so. Thanks to one abstention, it unexpectedly referred the matter to the federal president in Prague. President Beneš then in turn unexpectedly decided to refer the matter to the national government, whereas in fact the decision on clemency was his alone as head of state. The national government met later the same day, 17 April 1946, to discuss the matter.[266] It was deluged by petitions and telegrams from both sides of the argument. The governing parties were bitterly divided but also linked to one another by a series of previous promises. The argument went down to the wire, and there were frantic arguments and phone calls between the Democratic Party leader and President Beneš (who clearly wanted Tiso to be executed but who did not seem to want to take responsibility for it). These last-minute attempts failed and Tiso was executed on 18 April 1947.[267]

The decision was not based on arguments about the guilt or innocence of the defendant but instead about how to preserve the unity of Czechoslovakia. The minister of defence, Ludvík Svoboda (later president of Communist Czechoslovakia) made it clear that Tiso should be executed because of what he symbolized: populism, fascism, treason, and collaboration.[268] The Democrats, by contrast, wanted to strengthen Slovak loyalty to Czechoslovakia by granting Tiso clemency.[269] In the end, Tiso's fate was sealed by the fact that he did not have enough friends: the president disliked him and he had too many enemies in both the Slovak and Czechoslovak governments. Having failed to get the Protectorate ministers executed in 1946, the Communists – stronger by now, as their grip on power had tightened – were determined not to let their prey escape this time.

Tiso's trial was the curtain-raiser for widespread abuse of the judicial process by Czechoslovakia's Communists, who used it to seize power and eliminate their enemies, a seamless process which started in 1945 and continued into the 1950s. In this respect, it resembles the trial of Antonescu. The first major conspiracy prosecution against Democratic Party leaders was brought in September 1947, and by the following year the Communists controlled Czechoslovakia completely. But in this as in so many other countries, the revolution devoured its own children: the Communist general secretary, Rudolf Slánský, who was exultant at Tiso's death sentence and declared his hanging a 'victory' for the Party ('We pushed through the government the refusal of Tiso's request for clemency and Tiso was hanged'[270]), lasted only five more years in office until he was prosecuted as a pro-Yugoslav deviationist in the (largely anti-Semitic) so-called Slánský trial of 1952 and hanged too. His colleague in 1947, Vladimír Clementis, the deputy foreign minister, also a Communist, and who had also argued energetically against clemency for Tiso, was tried alongside Slánský and met the same fate.

Meanwhile, the prosecutor of Tiso, Anton Rašla, was prosecuted as a nationalist in the 1950s: as chairman of the Slovak–Yugoslav Friendship Society, he fell victim to the anti-Yugoslav campaign which swept through Stalinist Czechoslovakia after Belgrade's break with Moscow in 1948. He was sentenced to life and found himself in prison with Alexander Mach, Tiso's co-defendant, whom he had also prosecuted. Rašla was released in 1958 and rehabilitated in 1960, while Mach was released in 1968 after Rašla had turned to him to help suppress a prison riot.[271] Rašla himself has on many occasions confirmed the fundamentally political nature of the Tiso trial, and he and the defence lawyer, Žabkay, co-authored a book about it in 1990. A largely unrepentant Rašla said that the National Court was a revolutionary tribunal whose main purpose was to purge the country politically, a statement he repeated on 13 April 2007, shortly after which he died, aged ninety-five.[272]

10   People's Justice in Liberated Hungary

Hungary after World War I was a kingdom without a king ruled by an admiral without a fleet: Miklos Horthy had reigned as regent over the now landlocked country since it lost its Habsburg monarch and its coastline at the end of the war. Hungary entered World War II against the Allies although its only real quarrel was with its neighbours, Romania and Slovakia, which were its allies. Horthy had presided over a national-conservative alliance between the aristocracy, the land and industry. In opposition to this, there grew up a radical anti-establishment fascist movement, the Arrow Cross, based on the lower middle classes, minor officials, and others whose fortunes had waned in the 1930s, creating thereby a 'new right' in opposition to the 'old right' in power, rather as in Romania. Meanwhile, the Communists were strong too, in opposition to both.

All sides of the political spectrum, including many on the Left, burned with resentment at the huge territorial losses suffered by Hungary at Versailles. Hungarians therefore shared with Hitler and the Germans a desire to see the injustices of the postwar settlement overturned. But although this caused Hungary to side with Nazi Germany from the beginning of the war, and although Admiral Horthy's governments were undoubtedly anti-Semitic, the 'old right' under Horthy resisted most of the Germans' demands, for instance on deportations of Jews, especially in the two years from 1942 to 1944 when the government was led by that epitome of the country gentry, Miklós Kállay.

This all changed when the tension between the old and new rights erupted into civil war in 1944. Not trusting Horthy and Kállay, Hitler ordered the occupation of Hungary in March 1944 and forced the appointment of a pro-Nazi Arrow Cross government under General Döme Sztójay. Sztójay was overthrown in August 1944 by a counter-coup led by Horthy in August 1944, after Hungary's bitterest enemy, Romania, changed sides and joined the Allies. Horthy saw the way the wind was blowing and tried to negotiate a separate armistice with the Allies (separate, that is, from

Germany). On 15 October 1944, the leader of the Arrow Cross, Ferenc Szálasi, seized power in a counter-counter-putsch to stop Horthy from doing this, and appointed himself 'Leader of the Hungarian Nation'. The country then broke apart under the twin pressures of civil war and invasion. Soviet and Romanian troops reached the outskirts of Budapest on Christmas Eve 1944. The pro-Nazi government fled to the west of the country and it took a further two months for the country as a whole to be retaken.

The incoming Communists sought to purge the political system of opponents. Hungary, like Czechoslovakia, had been bitterly divided during the war, and Hungarians had fought one another on their own territory. Having been the object of terrible persecution by the pro-Nazi leaders, men who were both Communist and Jewish, like Mátyás Rákosi, especially wanted revenge. Hungary had had the highest rate of deportation of Jews anywhere in occupied Europe. Adolf Eichmann's whole office moved to Hungary in March 1944 and over 400,000 Jews were deported in two months. Like Romania in 1944, defeated Hungary was put under the control of the Allied Control Commission under Soviet chairmanship, after a provisional government under Horthy did sign its ceasefire on 20 January 1945. Partly for this reason, the allies never wanted to see him prosecuted. As in Romania, legal purges of collaborators and other conservatives were required by the terms of that armistice, as were the repeal of anti-Jewish legislation and the banning of all pro-Nazi political parties.[1] But all members of the Hungarian National Independence Front wanted these measures anyway.

As the Red Army entered Hungary, therefore, and as the new authorities seized control of parts of the country, 'people's courts' were set up. The legal basis for these courts was the decree issued by the Provisional National Government in Debrecen on 25 January 1945. Although the provisional government was a coalition of various forces, the Communists dominated it. The December 1944 manifesto of the Independence Front was based heavily on the Communist Party's own manifesto of 30 November, and both made the pursuit of war criminals and traitors one of the central points of their programme of 'democratic reconstruction': the plan was to conduct a full purge of all pro-Nazi elements in Hungarian society, whether in politics, the administration, or the media.[2]

Revolutionary justice was meted out immediately. While the Germans were still in control of parts of Budapest, two non-commissioned officers were hanged in a public square following a sentence by a people's court in February 1945: as Nuremberg was to do, the 'court' rejected the defendants' plea that they had been obeying orders.[3] As soon as Budapest itself was completely liberated, later that month, the Red Army helped the Communists to gain all-important control of the interior ministry and the police.

Heavy emphasis was laid on the concept of 'enemies of the people' and on the need to purge them. The 'people's courts' were *ad hoc* committees who usurped the powers of the country's proper courts of law, and which were set up in areas held by the Communists and retrospectively legalized in the decree of 25 January 1945 (itself subsequently revised and published as Law No. 7 enacted by the Hungarian parliament on 11 September 1945).

The terms of the January 1945 Decree made it clear that the law the people's courts would administer was political, personal, and retroactive, as it was to be in Slovakia (where the relevant decree was voted later, in May). The Hungarian decree defined as a war criminal any senior politician who had led Hungary into war or failed to prevent it or the later armistice; anyone who had aided or belonged to the Arrow Cross government; anyone who had committed war crimes; and any person who 'either in print or in speeches … engaged in activities conducive to the country's entry into the war … or aiming to influence public opinion in a direction harmful to the country'.[4] Acts were also punished if they were deemed 'fascist-friendly' or 'anti-democratic'.[5] Law No. 7 (16 September 1945) made it clear that war criminals would be prosecuted even if the acts alleged had not been crimes when they committed them. The principle of collective responsibility was applied, as at Nuremberg and as at Quisling's trial, for instance when membership of the fascist Arrow Cross was retrospectively criminalized. Prior to the entry into force of this law, trials had been carried out on the basis of government decrees alone, i.e. in contravention of the principle that trials should be carried out by tribunals established by law.

These courts were overtly political, composed of lay people. Although they were chaired by an appointee of the ministry of justice, he had no voting rights; in addition, there were five representatives of each of the political parties which composed the Independence Front (and, from May 1945, six members including a trades union appointee). They could try civilians, soldiers, and foreigners and they could issue sentences ranging from pecuniary fines to death. They acted under the overall aegis of a 'National Council of People's Tribunals' which was similarly composed of five, then six, lay political appointees.

A decree of 16 August 1945 extended the jurisdiction of these tribunals from the war period to the present, prosecuting acts which were deemed to be hindering the government's work or preventing democracy. The concept of 'enemy of the people' became a guiding principle. By 13

September 1945, when the decree on people's tribunals was turned into a law, the state secretary introducing the bill, Kálmán Kovács, said that the trials were also to be an instrument of political change for the future:

> The reactionary and fascist enemy hides not only among the men of the past era, it may raise its head even today when it blocks the development and strengthening of the people's democracy, for instance, when civil service clerks, in bad faith, do not fulfil their prescribed tasks and thus heavily endanger the execution of democratic orders … The people's tribunals are the only suitable weapon to eliminate such enemies of democracy.[6]

The scale of the purges the people's courts were to carry out was enormous. Between February 1945 and April 1950, 90,000 people were investigated; 60,000 were tried; 27,000 were found guilty of war crimes, crimes against humanity, and crimes against the state. The total number of people executed was, however, relatively low: 146, out of 322 death sentences passed. Forty thousand people were interned in concentration camps until 1949, while over 200,000 ethnic German civilians were expelled from Hungary and 62,000 civil servants were dismissed. The total number of Hungarian citizens who suffered in these purges therefore lies between 300,000 and 400,000.[7]

The Communists made no bones about the fact that they wanted political retribution. The first chairman of the Budapest People's Court, Ákos Major, who was unrepentant about the activities of his tribunal even in the late 1980s, sentenced people to death without having any qualifications as a judge; on the contrary, he said specifically, forty years after the events themselves, that the very nature of his tribunal as 'a people's court' meant that it was grounded in politics (having been created by the Communist Party). He said he had allowed 'the whirl of passions, the bereavement, despair and hate to mix freely in front of the people's court – that is why we were the people's court.'[8] A similar sentiment had been expressed by the American prosecutor at Nuremberg, Robert Jackson, in his report to the president of 6 June 1945, a document which was adopted as expressing the official position of the United States government at the opening of the London Conference. Jackson said repeatedly that the Nazis had 'fundamentally outraged the conscience of the American people' and 'affronted the sense of justice of our people' (although he did not mention either the Holocaust or the persecution of the Jews), and he argued that these sentiments should guide the proceedings: 'I believe that those instincts of our people were right and *that they should guide us as the fundamental tests of criminality*.'[9] Identical arguments had been used to justify changing the law to enable the execution of Quisling.

Ákos Major's mentor, Gábor Péter – Soviet agent, head of the secret police, and instigator of the show trials, whose name became a byword for the Communist terror in Hungary – said that the people's judges enforced 'revolutionary legality' and should not get bogged down in 'the marshland of traditional legal practices'.[10] (Péter was himself purged in 1953 and sentenced to life imprisonment.) This same dismissive attitude towards procedure was expressed by Nuremberg which declared that it would not be 'bound by technical rules of evidence' (Article 6 of the IMT charter) or, in our own day, by the International Criminal Tribunal for the former Yugoslavia (ICTY), which has boasted that its theory of criminal liability 'disregards legal formalities'[11] and that it 'does not need to shackle itself to restrictive rules which have developed out of the ancient trial-by-jury system'.[12]

Similarly, the minister of justice, István Ries (who himself was to die in a Communist prison in 1950, the victim of a counter-purge) said in 1945 that the purpose of the people's courts was to force politicians to assume real responsibility for their acts 'before the outraged people'.[13] Ries went on:

> We will not wait for the judgement of history, we will make them [politicians] responsible to the people's tribunal. This judgement must be just, even though we feel that the perpetrators of these crimes should not expect justice but only retribution.
>
> The adjudication of these cases, however, is not so much a legal as in the first place a political question. This means that the regular courts are not suitable for these trials and that the current laws are not appropriate.

He explained that the cause of Hungary's catastrophe lay in the 'counter-revolution that followed the revolution of 1919' (i.e. when Horthy overthrew the Communist Béla Kun) and that the cases would therefore have to be tried by people 'who can represent the new people's democratic Hungary'. In other words, the courts had to be stuffed with pro-Communists. Ries also said that the purpose of the trials was didactic: they were necessary to help 'the misled and stupefied public opinion of the country learn the history of twenty-five years of Hungarian fascism'.[14] Such sentiments form the backbone of much of the theory of 'transitional justice' today, which is similarly supposed to give a definitive account of historical events and to bolster democratization through education. Using the kind of overt political language for which, for instance, the Riom trial was also notable, and which was also to characterize the trial of Antonescu (accused of causing 'national disaster') the death sentence passed on the collaborationist minister of justice, László Budinsky, in December 1945, was justified in the name of 'twenty-five years of an oppressive ruling system that had brought the country to the brink of destruction'.[15]

The trials of the wartime leaders opened in late October 1945 and ended in March 1946. The defendants included four collaborationist or pro-Nazi prime ministers: Béla Imrédy (prime minister from May 1938 to February 1939), László Bárdossy (prime minister from 3 April 1941 to 7 March 1942), Döme Sztójay (prime minister from 23 March 1944 to August 1944), and Ferenc Szálasi ('Leader of the Hungarian Nation' from 15 October 1944 to February 1945). Thirteen ministers in the Szálasi Arrow Cross government were also prosecuted, as were two dozen journalists accused of writing pro-war and anti-Semitic articles. Even General Sztójay's spokesman, the journalist Mihály Kolosváry-Borcsa, was put on trial (and sentenced to death). This policy of including journalists as war criminals has been copied, in our own day, by the International Criminal Tribunal for Rwanda.

The first trial was that of Bárdossy, which lasted just five days (29 October to 3 November 1945) and was held in the Great Hall of the Academy of Music in Budapest. It was timed to coincide with the municipal and national elections in October and November 1945;[16] by demonstrating the corruption of the previous regime, the Communists hoped to consolidate their grip on power. Bárdossy was charged with crimes against peace (the only one of the four prime ministerial defendants to face this charge) and with crimes against humanity. Like the charges brought at Nuremberg, the charges against Bárdossy concerned political decisions such as the decision to wage war: he was accused of violating the Treaty of Eternal Friendship with Yugoslavia by helping the Germans to invade it in April 1941; of leading the country into war without the consent of parliament (in fact, the order to send troops into Trans-Carpathian Ruthenia (Soviet territory) on 28 June 1941 was given by the regent, Admiral Horthy, while Bárdossy had only informed parliament of the regent's decision); and of thwarting attempts to sign an armistice. Bárdossy was also accused of crimes against humanity for his responsibility for massacres of Jews, both because of his role in passing anti-Jewish legislation and also for ordering deportations.[17] The indictment was accompanied by a long 'justification'[18] which gave a detailed (if accusatory) account of Bárdossy's acts and political decisions in the run-up to war and during it.

Bárdossy rose to address the court on 2 November 1945 at the conclusion of the trial.[19] He argued that he had the right to be tried under the terms of Law No. III of 1848 which provided for ministers to be tried by members of parliament, and he protested that he was being tried by *ex post facto* legislation. It was an intelligent and emotional speech, the last words of a man who knew what fate awaited him and who felt considerable remorse. He said that he was responsible for his acts but not a criminal and that, although he understood that peace might require a sacrifice (i.e. his own death) he protested his innocence. His speech, like the original decree which caused his indictment, contained a long account of recent history starting with the overthrow of the Soviet government of Béla Kun in 1919. It contained a review of the whole of Admiral Horthy's foreign policy since the end of World War I. Bárdossy said that Central Europe had come under the domination of Germany thanks to the negligence and even complicity of the Western powers, who had allowed Czechoslovakia to be dismembered at Munich in 1938. Hungary's neighbours, he said – the Czechs, the Romanians, the Yugoslavs – had all naturally become the allies of the 'rising sun of Berlin', partly because that country was developing and strong, partly too because they felt abandoned by the West. Given her geographical situation, Hungary had had no choice but to move into the German sphere. Hungary had tried to recover some of the territories taken from her at Versailles. Bárdossy went painstakingly through the history of war, especially the background to the decision to collaborate with the Germans in the invasion of Yugoslavia in April 1941; he said that Hungary had had no choice but to acquiesce in the German demand to allow her troops to cross Hungarian territory to attack Yugoslavia, and the decision to allow this had been taken to prevent a full German occupation of Hungary. His acts, therefore, had been aimed at the lesser evil. In any case, there were Hungarians in northern Yugoslavia 'waiting for liberation, waiting to be united again with Hungary'. He said that if the Soviet Union had been justified in entering Poland in 1939, on the basis that that country had ceased to exist, then Hungary too had the same right to enter the territory of the defunct Yugoslavia.

The same went for Hungary's participation in the war on the Soviet Union in June: the country effectively had no choice. 'Regardless of how much somebody believes in resurrection, it is still improper to recommend that he commit suicide,' he said, and the same applied to countries. He argued that Hungary had merely tried to keep its participation in the war to a minimum, less than the Germans demanded. He complained that other countries which had collaborated more enthusiastically than Hungary were being given preferential treatment, and that this showed that Hungary could never have relied on the West. 'The fate of the losers is determined by the interests of the victors,' he said in conclusion, 'and only the unity of the nation may provide some protection.' Quoting the Bible, he said that the country should have remained united but that it had not done so. 'In a fragmented country, the forces consume each other and the opposing forces, unwillingly, become the tools of foreign interests.' He implied that his government had failed to unite the nation and that this was why it had failed. 'There is no more repellent sight than passengers on a sinking ship killing each other,' he said. He concluded,

> Allow a man saying goodbye to tell you that even among the ruins you must not look for opposition. Look for what binds together not for what divides. With a hand in a fist, you cannot build, with a heart full of hate you cannot heal. I admit that rightful passions and bitterness must find an outlet. A way must be found to ease the soul so that it may emerge from its pain and find its way back to national unity. No sacrifice is too great if it leads to this. Even if bringing the sacrifice has no relationship to rendering justice. After six months of suffering in body and soul and exposed to continuous attempts to humiliate me, I stand here with a clear and calm conscience. It is only the immense pain and bitterness that this unfortunate nation has suffered that bows my head and fills my heart. I still believe and avow that God will help this nation. Now I am asking you to do your duty.[20]

The tribunal did do its duty, as least as it understood it: Bárdossy was executed on 10 January 1946.

The trial of Béla Imrédy followed, lasting from 14 to 23 November 1945, also in the Academy of Music. He had been Bárdossy's predecessor as prime minister before the war and minister of economic cooperation in the Sztójay government: he was charged with passing the first anti-Jewish laws, with aligning Hungary with Nazi Germany prior to the outbreak of hostilities, with supplying intelligence to the Nazis, and with responsibility for the deportation or killing of Jews. Imrédy was executed on 28 February 1946. A joint trial in which the leader of the fascist Arrow Cross and ephemeral 'Leader of the Hungarian Nation', Ferenc Szálasi, was in the dock alongside five of his ministers and senior military, was held from 5 February to 1 March 1946: the main charges there involved the Arrow Cross's deliberate sabotage of Admiral Horthy's attempt to negotiate an armistice with the invading Soviets and Romanians, and the Arrow Cross's numerous crimes against humanity. The commanders of the German occupying forces in Hungary, Veesenmayer and Winkelmann, testified and tried to put the blame on the Hungarians. Like all the other defendants, Szálasi was condemned to death; he was executed on 12 March 1946.

Finally, General Döme Sztójay faced trial from 14 to 22 March 1946 alongside his ministers, two of whom had later also served under Szálasi. They were charged with treason and crimes against humanity, and with being an accessory to Bárdossy's anti-Soviet policy as ambassador to Berlin from 1936 to 1944. Veesenmayer testified during his trial too and said that the occupation force was only a few hundred men strong while

Eichmann's office had only twenty men: 'We could not have made a move without the help of the Hungarians.' Sztójay was executed by firing squad on 22 August 1946.

Throughout these trials, the public which attended them often broke out in protests, while the press indulged in highly politicized and seemingly hysterical attacks on the defendants. Journalists vied with one another to produce violent and often obscene invective with which to denounce the former leaders now in the dock. Political interference in the trials was also overt and active. During Bárdossy's trial, the Stalinist first secretary of the Hungarian Communist Party, Mátyás Rákosi, sent for the judge, Ákos Major, and told him to stop discussing the Treaty of Trianon during the trial. This was because an appeal in court to Hungarian irredentism counted as a powerful defence, since the desire to regain territories lost at Versailles was very widespread in the country at large and on all sides of the political spectrum. The Defence counsel in Ferenc Szálasi's trial was forbidden from delivering the final speech for the Defence on the express orders of the ministry of justice.[21]

For some of the main actors in these trials, they were part of a seamless whole in the overall process of establishing the Communist grip on power. For others, it was a dangerous game of musical chairs which ended in death whenever the tune changed. Judge Peter Jankó, for instance, sent Szálasi to his death in 1946 and went on to sentence the former Communist minister, László Rajk, to death in 1949 in one of the most notorious show trials of Rakósi's Stalinist regime: Rajk was accused of Titoist, Trotskyite, fascist, and capitalist conspiracy, and his trial lasted from 16 to 24 September 1949.[22] This was part of the anti-Yugoslav campaign initiated across Eastern Europe after Tito's defection from the Soviet camp in 1948. (Before the break with Stalin, Tito himself had also used the judicial system to destroy his opponents, most notoriously in 1946, when Yugoslavia put the royalist leader, General Draža Mihailović, on trial, together with several of the ministers of the government in exile, including the prime minister, Slobodan Jovanović, who was tried *in absentia*.[23] Mihailović was executed. Indeed, the wartime collaborationist leader of Serbia, Milan Nedić, was also due to be put on trial by Tito's Communists but he fell out of his prison window in February 1946 before the proceedings had begun.)

As minister, Rajk himself had 'discovered' a 'conspiracy against the state' by the Smallholders' Party after it had won 57 per cent of the vote in the 1945 elections, and he exploited this 'plot' to liquidate the rival party by prosecuting its leaders in the courts.[24] But the wheel of political fortune turned, and Rajk was hanged on 15 October 1949, the anniversary of the putsch by which Ferenc Szálasi had seized power in 1944. Earlier that year, Judge Jankó had also upheld the life sentence on Cardinal Mindszenty in 1949. Mindszenty, the head of the Catholic Church in Hungary and one of the country's greatest opponents of Communism (he had been arrested by the Arrow Cross in 1944 for his opposition to them too), was sentenced to life imprisonment for counter-revolution and treason by the new Communist power. His case became one of the most important *causes célèbres* of the Cold War. As Mindszenty rightly wrote in his memoirs of the laws and procedures which condemned him, 'The judge is no longer obliged to ascertain objective truths: his business is solely to serve the Communist Party's interests … The sole purpose of my trial was to clear the way for Communist despotism.'[25] But Jankó thought that the cardinal had got off lightly. 'There is not the slightest doubt that Mindszenty should have been sentenced to death,' he said.[26] However, as for Rajk, enthusiastic collaboration with Communism proved to be a poisoned chalice for Jankó. He eventually committed suicide in 1955, when a campaign began to have Rajk posthumously rehabilitated; this succeeded in 1956.

11 From Mass Execution to Amnesty and Pardon: Postwar Trials in Bulgaria, Finland, and Greece

Bulgaria

The judicial bloodletting in postwar Europe was severest in Bulgaria. Some 3,000 people were executed as war criminals, and virtually the entire wartime political class was wiped out. The incoming Communists, helped to power by the Allied Control Commission under the chairmanship of a Soviet general (as in Hungary, Romania, and Finland), regarded all their political enemies as 'fascists'. Even Tito had the honour of this epithet from 1948 onwards. A judicial process was set up to purge the entire country of such 'fascists' which naturally included the wartime regime, and as in Romania, Hungary, and elsewhere, these trials were merely part of a wider civil war pitting Communists, backed by the Red Army, against the wartime elites and their supporters.

The victims of the purges included three heads of state (the three members of the country's Regency Council: Prince Kyril of Preslav, Bogdan Filov, and Nikola Mikhov, who reigned in the boy king Simeon's place on the death of Tsar Boris III on 28 August 1943) and three additional wartime prime ministers (Bogdan Filov having also been prime minister from 1940 to 1943): Petur Gabrovski (who had been prime minister for a week in September 1943), Dobri Bozhilov (prime minister from 14 September 1943 until 1 June 1944), and Ivan Bagrianov (1 June to 2 September 1944). They were accused of their role in bringing Bulgaria into alliance with Germany from 1941 to 1944 and of facilitating the plundering of the Bulgarian economy by the Nazis.

These men had been overthrown in September 1944 by the advancing Red Army and were initially taken to the Soviet Union before being returned to Bulgaria for trial later that year. All five men were shot together in the night of 1 February 1945 and buried in a mass grave that had been a bomb crater. Together with them, the people's tribunals tried and executed ten royal counsellors to Tsar Boris III and thirty-five other former ministers from the wartime governments. They also tried and convicted members of the country's wartime National Assembly from 1941 to 9 September 1944 – a total of 126 people in one trial.

As soon as the Red Army entered Bulgaria, on 8 September 1944, and the Patriotic Front seized power, political police controlled by the Communists were put in place and the Communists quickly started setting up their system of legalized state terror.[1] The terms of the armistice were negotiated in Moscow on 12 October between the British and Soviet foreign ministers, only a few days after Churchill's famous 'percentages' deal with Stalin in Moscow on 9 October (when the British premier divided up Europe into spheres of influence on the back of a piece of paper). The terms of the armistice were eventually promulgated on 28 October 1944, and it effectively gave the Soviet commander unrestricted authority. One of its terms was that 'Bulgaria will cooperate in the apprehension and trial of persons accused of war crimes', but in fact the Communist government had already passed a 'Statutory Ordinance on the Trial of the Culprits for the Involvement of Bulgaria in the War against the Allied Powers and for the Related Crimes' on 6 October. The people's courts it created were to try whole swathes of the population, including (as in Czechoslovakia, France, and elsewhere) journalists, writers, painters, caricaturists, and others in the media who had allegedly helped spread 'fascist' ideas.[2]

As in Hungary, the work of the tribunals was as overtly political as their composition. The prosecutors were elected by the Fatherland Front committees which had been established all over the country and which were the principal vehicle for the Communists' seizure of power. Georgi Petkov, the Chief Prosecutor, proclaimed that, 'The historic activity of the people's court will be conducted under the slogan "death to fascism".'[3] The Bulgarian Communist leader, Georgi Dimitrov (who himself had famously been the star defendant in the Nazis' Reichstag fire trial in Leipzig in 1933), said that he wanted the trials against the regents and prime ministers to uproot all 'German agents' from Bulgaria. When it was all over, in January 1946, Stalin raised a toast to Dimitrov, congratulating him for his judicial purge and comparing it to his own purges in 1937–8 which, he said, had had the same purpose.[4]

The courts started worked in 1944 and carried on until 1946: their most high-profile defendants were the men who had led the country during the war. Their trial opened in Sofia on 21 December. These prosecutions were of course carried out in spite of the fact that the monarchy (and therefore the regents) and the parliamentarians enjoyed legal immunity under the terms of the constitution then in force. The terms of reference of the indictment and conviction were cast very widely: the charges were for 'putting national security and the national interest in jeopardy', 'concluding treaties with the belligerent powers' (the Axis), 'the decision to go to war', 'violating the proclaimed neutrality towards the USSR', 'damaging the international position of Bulgaria', as well as for more conventional war crimes (murder, arson, pillage, and racial persecution of Jews). The defendants (especially the parliamentarians) were accused of failing in their constitutional duty to 'act conscientiously', i.e. not under extraneous influence.[5]

As in Hungary, the defendants put up a spirited defence and, as at Riom, the authorities were unhappy with the fact that they had unwittingly given their mortal enemies one last platform from which to speak. They argued that they had chosen the lesser evil and avoided the worse fate of a full-on attack, such as had happened to Yugoslavia and Greece. The prosecutor called for fifty-two death penalties, and the trial concluded on 1 February. In the event, over twice as many were carried out. The goal was evidently to terrorize the population. Cyril Black, an American diplomat in Sofia at the time, described the scene in the courtroom:

> The defendants prepared to hear the sentences standing in a square in the courtroom surrounded by armed militiamen. The prince looked haughty and defiant, Filov was restless and uneasy, while the others talked and joked nervously with each other while waiting for the judges to appear. The clerk read out the sentence in a loud and clear voice: death for twenty-five regents and ministers, eight counsellors, and sixty-seven members of the National Assembly ... They were shot that evening in batches of twenty.[6]

By March 1945, the people's courts had already handed down over 10,000 verdicts in 131 trials and condemned over 2,000 people to death.[7] Property and money were confiscated and the rulings were subject to no appeal. Industrialists, judges, and journalists were also shot as part of this new Red terror. To these judicial killings one must also add the estimated 30,000 or 40,000 murders carried out as part of the same purge, but which were enacted without any pretence at legal process. This was in spite of the fact that Bulgaria had not attacked the Soviet Union and its leaders had refused the Germans' demand to hand over Jews.

As in Romania and Hungary, other politicians soon fell victim to the legal purges as well: before the October 1946 elections, twenty-four members of the Agrarian Party were assassinated and its leader, Nikolai Petkov, was prosecuted as a traitor and hanged on 23 September 1947.[8] Indeed, the political nature of the purges was perhaps clearest in the prosecution and conviction of Dimitar Peshev, the vice-president of the Bulgarian National Assembly, who in March 1943 had sent a letter to Prime Minister Filov signed by forty-three out of the country's one hundred and sixty members of parliament saying that it was quite unacceptable to accede to the Germans' demands to deport Jews.[9] His protest was astonishingly successful, and Peshev has been posthumously credited with almost single-handedly saving the lives of Bulgaria's 48,000 Jews. But he was no Communist, and so he was soon prosecuted by the people's courts and was sentenced to fifteen years in prison (although he was released after a year and a half for good behaviour). Twenty of the deputies who signed his letter in 1943 were sentenced to death by the same tribunals.

On 26 August 1996, it was announced that the previous April the Bulgarian Supreme Court had revoked the sentences handed down to the regents, the prime ministers, the ministers, the counsellors, and the members of the National Assembly in the ruling of 1 February 1945. All but two were recognized as having been wrongly convicted. In a tightly argued ruling, and drawing on the new international human rights documents (such as the European Convention) which democratic Bulgaria had now recognized, the court found that the people's court had been a special court which had retroactively introduced new legal norms in contravention of the principle *nullum crimen sine lege*. It had erred in law by not allowing certain lines of defence, such as self-defence and extreme constraint, and it had also rigged the rules of procedure to stymie the Defence. The decree creating the court had described the defendants as guilty and thus infringed the presumption of innocence.

The Supreme Court found that the indictments had been one-sided and political; that the people's court itself was 'anti-constitutional', and that the matters adjudicated (matters of state policy) were simply incommensurable with the criminal law. The people's court, the Supreme Court ruled, was little more than a mechanism for settling scores with political opponents, and it found that there were grounds for saying that the regents, ministers, and parliamentarians had indeed acted in what they thought were the best interests of the Bulgarian people. The evidence, the court concluded, was insufficient and legally incorrect.[10]

One of the judges dissented – but only to say that the Supreme Court should not revoke sentences which had been passed by an illegal tribunal in the first place. The 1879 Turnovo constitution of Bulgaria, legally in force during the war years, made no provision for a people's tribunal, said Judge Plamen Tomov, and therefore any sentences issued by it could not be reviewed by the Supreme Court.[11] The political implications of all this were clear. As the speaker of the Bulgarian parliament said on 28 February 2001, in a ceremony to honour Peshev, 'The destiny of Dimitar Peshev and of his fellow deputies to the Twenty-fifth National Assembly is a moral condemnation of the inhuman so-called "people's court".'

Finland

As in Hungary and Bulgaria, it was as a result of Soviet pressure that the wartime head of state of Finland and his two prime ministers were prosecuted for war crimes. Article 13 of the armistice treaty imposed on Finland by the Soviet Union and signed in Moscow on 19 September 1944 required Finland to prosecute war criminals. But the judicial process was also used to eliminate other political enemies too. The head of the Allied Control Commission for Finland was the arch-Stalinist Andrei Alexandrovich Zhdanov, who as Party boss in Leningrad had played a key role in the great Soviet purges.

In October 1944 Zhdanov handed the government in Helsinki a list of people whom Moscow wanted to see in the dock. But the strongman of Finland, Marshal Mannerheim, by then state president, used his good offices in Moscow to see that many of the senior officers' names were removed from the list. The Soviets continued to press their case and, on 5 March 1945, an article appeared in *Pravda* calling the Finnish wartime leaders war criminals and saying they were guilty of aggression against the Soviet Union. Zhdanov ratcheted up the pressure, insisting that a special law be passed to enable the trials to take place: otherwise, he said, an international tribunal would be used to try them instead.

Eventually, in August 1945, the new government reluctantly gave in and agreed to the trials although Mannerheim made it clear that he did not believe the accusation of aggression was justified. The special law entered into force on 12 September 1945, President Mannerheim having authorized Prime Minister Paasikivi to sign it so that his signature would not appear on what was regarded as a shameful concession.

Eight leading politicians were indicted: the wartime president from 1940 to 1944, Risto Ryti; Johan Wilhelm Rangell and Edwin Linkomies, his two prime ministers; and five other ministers including Väinö Tanner, the Social Democratic leader (who had been prime minister in 1926–7 but who was minister of trade, then finance, during the war) and Toivo Kivimäki, another former prime minister who had been Finnish ambassador to Moscow, and whose head the Soviets expressly demanded.[12] The Finnish Communists especially wanted to eliminate Tanner in order better to consolidate their domination of the Left.

As was to be the case in Bulgaria and Hungary, the accusations against the wartime leaders were political and loosely phrased to include the whole gamut of Finland's war policy: that it had allowed German troops to enter and transit through Finland (which Sweden had too, although no Swede was ever prosecuted); that it had declared war on the Soviet Union; that it had rejected Soviet peace offers since 1941; that it had broken off diplomatic relations with the United Kingdom; and that it had actively cooperated with the Nazis by signing a pact with Ribbentrop in the summer of 1944. The terms of the indictment specifically mentioned war against the Soviet Union and other Allies, betraying thereby the special (i.e. not universal) quality of the so-called law under which the defendants were being prosecuted; it also contained the same allegations of behaviour contrary to the interests of the country that had characterized the indictment against Antonescu ('Whoever, in a decisive manner, has helped cause Finland to go to war in 1941 against the Union of the Soviet Socialist Republics, or the United Kingdom of Great Britain and Northern Ireland, or who has, during the war, prevented the achievement of peace, shall be punished for misuse of his office to the detriment of the country...').

Many Finns regarded these trials as an abomination, since of all countries, Finland could not be accused of attacking the Soviet Union: the Soviet Union had attacked Finland on 30 November 1939, a clearly illegal act for which it was expelled from the League of Nations. The Finns referred to the war of 1941–4 as 'the continuation war', a mere continuation of the Winter War of 1939–40. Like Romania, Finland had also changed sides in 1944, and there was bitter fighting against the German troops in Lapland. Finns also resented the retroactive nature of the legislation, especially of course the introduction of the notion of 'crimes against peace'. There was widespread feeling that the prosecutions were contrary to the laws and constitution of Finland, as they undoubtedly were.

The trial lasted from 15 November 1945 to 21 February 1946. Ryti was defended by Hjalmar Procopé, the former Finnish foreign minister who had been ambassador to Washington during the war. In his defence, Ryti denied that Finland had participated in the World War, since its troops had not invaded any other state; they had merely tried to recapture territory seized by the Soviet Union in 1940. During the war, indeed, the Finnish leaders had constantly maintained that they were not in alliance with Nazi Germany but that they were fighting their own war against the same enemy. Like all other wartime collaborationist leaders, Ryti insisted that he had done his best to protect his country's interests and that he had striven to protect it from a greater evil. He also of course argued that Finland had not attacked the Soviet Union, but the Soviets exercised strong pressure on the government and the press to prevent this line of defence from being published. They helped the Prosecution by bringing forth ever more incriminating documents from the Nuremberg trials which were going on at the same time.

The verdicts and sentences were handed down on 16 February 1945. Those convicted were given symbolic prison sentences but Zhdanov's Control Commission protested strongly and Moscow threatened Helsinki with renewed hostilities. The government gave in once again and pressured the court to review the sentencing. On 21 February it did so, and convicted all the defendants. Ryti was found guilty and sentenced to ten years in prison; Linkomies and Rangell were given five years each. This was a profound shock for Finnish public opinion, which even to this day continues to argue that the sentences were unjust.[13] As recently as 2005, a Finnish Social Democrat MEP, Lasse Lehtinen, co-authored a book, *Scapegoats of the Nation*, arguing that the trial was unfair.[14]

However, the relative leniency of these sentences, at least in comparison to those meted out elsewhere in Europe, reflects the weakness of Soviet control over Finland. Economically and socially, Finland was clearly part of the West, even though it pursued a prudent foreign policy and stayed out of overtly anti-Soviet organizations like NATO. This leniency was further emphasized by the fact that the convicted ministers were pardoned in 1949 by the new Finnish president. Ryti was given various honours, including an honorary doctorate from the University of Helsinki, and his official portrait was hung in the Council of State alongside that of Finland's other presidents. But he was an ill and broken man by then, who never re-entered politics; he died in 1956. Johan Rangell was more lucky. He had been national triple jump champion before World War I and president of the organizing committee for the 12th Summer Olympics which had been due to take place in Helsinki in 1940 but which were cancelled because of the outbreak of war; after his release from prison, he became chairman of Finland's National Olympic Committee from 1961 to 1963. Linkomies, meanwhile, a former professor of Latin, became rector and then chancellor of the University of Helsinki until he died in 1963.

Greece

Like Finland, Greece had not been awarded to the Soviet Union's zone of influence by Churchill but instead put into the Western orbit. The political configuration was very different. Although like its Balkan and Central European neighbours, the returning government in exile of Greece created 'people's courts' to try its collaborationist leaders, the political imperatives facing the returning government were precisely the opposite of those in countries dominated by the Red Army: the government there was engaged in a civil war against the (indigenous) Communists; it was not controlled by them. The Communists opposed the Papandreou government as much as they had opposed the Nazis, and 70,000 British troops had to be sent into Greece to help Papandreou retain control. A general strike was called, and a demonstration gathered in Syntagma Square in Athens on the morning of 4 December 1944, just six weeks after the German forces had been driven out. The square was surrounded by British troops and armed police. The order was given: 'Shoot the bastards!', and twenty-five people were shot dead.[15]

So when the trials of the wartime collaborationist leaders finally began on 21 February 1945, the defendants were essentially on the same side of the political divide as the existing government. The wartime collaborators had fought Communist insurgents, just as the new democratic government was doing. The trial lasted until 31 May, with Giorgios Tsolakoglou (prime minister from 1941 to 1942), Konstantinos Logothetopoulos (prime minister from 1942 until 1943), and Ioannis Rallis (1943 to 1944) as defendants. The government's initial enthusiasm for the trials had waned very rapidly, given the difficult internal political situation and the ambiguities of the trial, but the sentences were harsh nonetheless. Tsolakoglou was sentenced to death, though his sentence was commuted to life imprisonment and he died in prison in 1948; Logothetopoulos was also sentenced to life imprisonment, but was released in 1951; Rallis was also given life, but he died in 1946. Ioannis Rallis' son George, who also became Prime Minister, published his father's testimony in 1947, justifying his acts and entitled *Ioannis Rallis Speaks from the Grave*'

The trials were relatively fair. The prime minister and leader of the government in exile, George Papandreou, was forced to testify in the trial, since the defendants claimed that he and other leading Greek politicians had encouraged the collaborators to take up their posts. The argument advanced by the defendants – that they had been defending their country against Communism in their *de facto* alliance with the Nazis, which in any case they had not chosen but which had been forced on them by invasion and defeat – was exactly the same as that adopted by Quisling and Antonescu. Yet it carried considerable weight in a country which was then actually mired in a civil war against Communists. Ioannis Rallis even revealed that he had armed Napoleon Zervas, the anti-Communist Greek general and heroic resistance leader whose troops were even then continuing to fight the Communists on the new government's behalf. The courts in fact treated Communist fighters more harshly than the collaborationist defendants. The Communist press dismissed the proceedings as a farce.[16] As elsewhere in Europe, the Communists wanted blood, but in Greece, at least, they did not get it.

The trial record was destroyed after six months, no doubt a reflection of the government's discomfort at these trials. This was in stark contrast to the huge publicity given to the 'show trials' staged against collaborators in neighbouring or nearby countries controlled by the Communists, and to the associated ideology of 'anti-fascism' which bolstered them in power for the next forty years.[17] Even today, there is not a single transcript, document, article, or book about the trial of these three prime ministers to be found anywhere in any of the court libraries or the libraries of the Law Faculty or the Philosophy Faculty at the University of Athens.[18] All records of that trial have simply been dropped down the memory hole.

12   Politics as Conspiracy: the Tokyo Trials

Tokyo is the forgotten Nuremberg. Whereas today everyone remembers Nuremberg, the sister trial in Tokyo has largely vanished from historical memory and is seldom cited as a judicial precedent. This is in spite of the fact that the president of the International Military Tribunal (IMT) for the Far East proclaimed during the trial itself that there had been no more important trial in history.[1] (Many other trials have been called 'the trial of the century' before being similarly forgotten.) The judgement of the tribunal was not published in full until 1977,[2] and the complete proceedings of the trial not until 1998.[3] This amnesia no doubt reflects the fact that, whereas American fury in 1945 was perhaps even greater at Japanese war crimes than at German ones, a few decades later the principal historical memory of World War II was that of the Holocaust perpetrated in Europe.

By the time the IMT convened in Tokyo on 3 May 1946, the Nuremberg trials had been under way for six months; they were to finish in September 1946. While war crimes trials of European leaders had been going on across the continent, the Tokyo trials did not finish until 1948. They therefore brought to a conclusion the series of postwar trials of heads of state and government.

Inspired by the practice in other states, the choice of the defendants at Tokyo was based on the desire to prosecute a representative cross-section of the wartime regime of Japan as a whole. Four prime ministers were in the dock: Koki Hirota (prime minister from 9 March 1936 to 2 March 1937, minister of foreign affairs from 1933 to 1936 and again from 1937 to 1938, a civilian, hanged in December 1948); Hiranuma Kiichiro (prime minister from 5 January 1939 to 30 August 1939, a civilian, sentenced to life but paroled in 1952); Hideki Tojo (a general in the Imperial Army, prime minister for most of the war, from 1941 to 1944, including at the time of the attack on Pearl Harbor, hanged in 1948); and Kuniaki Koiso (prime minister from 22 July 1944 to 2 April 1945, a general in the Imperial Army, sentenced to life imprisonment and died in 1950).

As at Nuremberg, the process by which indictees were chosen was political. Mamoru Shigemitsu, a former foreign minister and ambassador to London, was included in the list of indictees at the very last moment, and on Soviet insistence. His arrest and trial provoked numerous protests, as many in the West believed him to be a good and innocent man.[4] (Shigemitsu was sentenced to seven years in prison, although he was quickly paroled and then re-entered political life to become foreign minister once again in 1954.) The other indictees were all senior ministers and top military commanders. Meanwhile, hundreds of actual perpetrators were also prosecuted by the Americans, in trials conducted away from the glare of publicity, for having committed crimes under the ordinary laws of war.

However, the head of state himself, Emperor Hirohito, was not in the dock. General MacArthur had decided that if the emperor were indicted, then direct military rule would have to be introduced in Japan, and that this would require 'one million reinforcements'.[5] He was an admirer of the Japanese people and he understood the political repercussions of putting their emperor on trial. But it would have been very easy to convict the emperor on the same basis of command responsibility as that used to convict the prime ministers and other senior figures, especially since he was no mere figurehead. The judges connived in his exoneration, including by actively intervening during the trial to prevent any witnesses or defendants from implicating him or calling into question the policy decision taken by the American occupation authorities.[6] Like Admiral Horthy, the head of state in Hungary, Emperor Hirohito was spared from prosecution by a purely political decision.

There were twenty-eight defendants at Tokyo (two of whom died during the trial, while one was declared unfit to stand trail), compared with twenty-four at Nuremberg (of whom twenty-one actually stood trial). The Tokyo Charter followed the Nuremberg Charter very closely indeed, often verbatim; it was drafted essentially by Joseph B. Keenan, who went on to be the trial's chief prosecutor. Like the Nuremberg Charter, the Tokyo one declared, 'The Tribunal shall not be bound by technical rules of evidence,' and it admitted anything it deemed to be 'of probative value', without saying what, if any, conditions were needed to fulfil this criterion. The charges were divided into the same three categories as at Nuremberg: crimes against peace, war crimes, and crimes against humanity. As at Nuremberg, great prominence was given in the indictment to the concept of criminal conspiracy to initiate aggressive war. All but two of the defendants were convicted of conspiracy to commit crimes against peace, compared with only eight out of twenty-two at Nuremberg. Of those two, one was convicted of war crimes and the other of aggressive war and war crimes. There were no acquittals at Tokyo. Seven men were condemned to death: two prime ministers (Tojo and Hirota) and five generals. This compares with twelve death sentences at Nuremberg (and three acquittals). Although Japan had only the Americans as occupiers, judges were summoned from the United States, the Soviet Union, Britain, China, the Netherlands, France, Australia, New Zealand, Canada, India, and the Philippines – precisely those countries which were said to be victims of Japanese aggression. In other words, the members of the bench were deliberately chosen for their presumed bias.

As is the practice at the International Criminal Tribunal for the former Yugoslavia, some of the judges at Tokyo were not in fact judges at all: the Chinese judge, for instance, was a politician. The Indian judge, Radhabinod Pal, was the only man on the bench with any experience in international law. The Russian judge, a military officer, spoke neither of the tribunal's two official languages, English and Japanese. Judges were frequently absent, and numerous important rulings were carried out by majority vote. Justice Pal himself missed eighty out of the trial's 417 days. The presiding judge, Sir William Webb, returned to his native Australia for a month in November–December 1947, missing twenty-two days of the trial. Other judges came and went according to their availability, and the trial continued with empty seats on the bench.[7]

Like Nuremberg, Tokyo was a city in ruins as a result of Allied bombs. The United States air force had napalmed Tokyo on 9–10 March, killing 80,000 people in the firestorms thus provoked. Indeed, it was partly for this reason that the atomic bombs were dropped on Hiroshima and Nagasaki, killing well over 100,000 people outright, the vast majority civilians, and another 100,000 who died soon afterwards from radiation: there was nothing left in the capital to bomb.[8] It was doubtless precisely because of the terrible violence which the Allies had inflicted on Japan that they concentrated their prosecution on aggression rather than war crimes, of which they had committed plenty themselves. The Americans held the upper hand and they wanted to force the Japanese to admit that they had started the conflict.

However, the accusation of aggression was more difficult to sustain at Tokyo than it had been at Nuremberg. There was little doubt that Japan had attacked its neighbours, and of course the United States, but one of the Allies, the Soviet Union, had also had attacked it, thanks to pressure from the Western Allies at Yalta and at Potsdam. The Soviet Union had agreed to declare war on Japan on 8 August 1945, two days after Hiroshima, and the official justification the Soviets gave for their declaration was that the war in the Pacific would thereby be brought more swiftly to an end. However, the Soviet Union had a non-aggression pact with Japan at the time, and the declaration was therefore a violation of that treaty; it had committed the very same 'international crime' for which the Treaty of Versailles had said that the Kaiser should be arraigned, and of course the same crime as that for which the Japanese leaders were in the dock.

Similar objections also applied to the charge of crimes against humanity. There can be little doubt that the American decision to drop atomic bombs on Hiroshima and Nagasaki were themselves examples of crimes against humanity. But that is not how the Allies saw things then or see them now. Even today, the memory of the bombing of Hiroshima and Nagasaki is cherished. In 2003 the *Enola Gay*, the aircraft which dropped the Hiroshima bomb, and which was affectionately named after the pilot's mother, was restored and exhibited in the Smithsonian National Air and Space Museum at Dulles airport in Washington, DC. The new exhibition replaced an earlier one which had attracted controversy because it spoke about the victims of the attack.

The Americans also decided not to bring any prosecutions against those responsible for the notorious Unit 731, a covert biological warfare research unit run by the Japanese army, in which prisoners were used as human guinea pigs for experiments which seem like something out of the darkest sadistic fantasy. Prisoners were cut open while alive; they were tied to posts and bombarded with chemical and biological weapons; they were horribly tortured to death ostensibly for reasons of medical research. The total number of victims is estimated at between 3,000 and 10,000, but discussion of the camp's horrible practices was suppressed at the trial because General MacArthur granted an amnesty to the camp commander, General Shiro Ishii, in return for his agreement to hand over his findings to the American authorities. Ishii was never prosecuted and died a free man in 1959.

Perhaps because of these difficulties, the issue of aggressive war was debated more intelligently at Tokyo than at Nuremberg, and this was greatly to the detriment of the Prosecution case. One of the defence counsels, Kenzo Takayanagi, relished telling the court that when the Japanese government had sent a note to the American government in 1929, announcing that it agreed to sign the Kellogg–Briand Pact – the very treaty on the basis of which the wartime leaders were now being prosecuted – Tokyo had said that it agreed with Washington's understanding of aggressive war and self-defence, and that according to this understanding Japan would be able legitimately to defend her interests in China.[9]

A further reason why the Japanese defence was more robust than that of the Germans at Nuremberg was that the Cold War was getting under way during the trial. This gave the defendants a perfect opportunity to claim that they had been acting against the Communist threat from the Soviet Union and China.[10] Since the Americans were themselves by then advocating a policy of containment vis-à-vis Communism, and since this included support for war in some parts of the world – as of course it was to do throughout the postwar period – the Japanese defendants argued that they had been doing the same thing themselves, only a little earlier than the Americans. The bench however, chaired by the aggressive and partisan Webb – who had agreed to be a judge even though he had previously carried out three investigations into Japanese war atrocities for the Australian government, and was therefore *parti pris* – refused to admit these remarks or the documents supporting them.[11]

A further issue on which there was strong debate was command responsibility. If the Japanese war crimes trials are remembered at all in modern international humanitarian law, it is because they provided the widest possible interpretation of command responsibility. The Americans (not the IMT at Tokyo) hanged General Tomoyuki Yamashita in 1945 for atrocities committed in the Philippines: the finding was not that he had ordered atrocities, nor even that he had been aware of them, but instead that he had condoned a climate of lawlessness and failed to prevent violations. The case went to the United States Supreme Court and Yamashita's death sentence was upheld by seven votes to two with strong dissenting opinions. The reason why the conviction is controversial is that the language in which the laws of war are formulated is replete with qualifiers which emphasize deliberate intent: phrases such as 'wilful killing', 'wilfully causing great suffering', 'wanton destruction of cities', and so on. Yamashita may have been morally guilty of criminal negligence but the existing laws of war had not been formulated to criminalize this.

This concept of negative criminality – subsequently upheld by the IMT at Tokyo – had been fiercely contested by the American members of the Commission of Responsibilities at Versailles, who had argued in 1919 that it was intolerable to punish people for acts which they had not ordered and of which they may even have been unaware.[12] In modern international humanitarian law, and thanks largely to Tokyo, however, this view has gone unheeded. It is common now for defendants to be convicted on the basis that they 'must have known' or 'should have known' about crimes and that they failed to prevent them, but such claims come dangerously close to a presumption of guilt which any defendant would have difficulty disproving. The tendentiousness of this doctrine of negative liability (failure to prevent breaches of the laws of war) was only emphasized when two of the defendants at Tokyo (Iwane Matsui and Koki Hirota) were hanged for it, having been acquitted of ordering, authorizing, or permitting atrocities.

At Tokyo, the Prosecution alleged that the grand conspiracy of imperialism and aggression which united the defendants dated from as far back as 1927. A document known as the 'Tanaka memorial' named after the then prime minister, Giichi Tanaka, which provided the basis for Frank Capra's propaganda film *Why We Fight*, and which the Prosecution took seriously, was supposed to show how the defendants shared a common plan from 1927 to 1945; it has subsequently turned out to be a fake on a par with the so-called 'Operation Horseshoe' document advanced by NATO and the Prosecution at the ICTY in support of its claims about an alleged conspiracy hatched by Slobodan Milošević and others to drive out the ethnic Albanian population of Kosovo. But the fact that the Prosecution argued (and the judges concurred in their verdict) that the 'common plan' had been hatched in 1927 meant that nearly two decades of Japanese domestic and foreign policy were equated, from the legal point of view, with a private criminal conspiracy to rob a bank or commit a murder. Yet such a version of political events can be advanced only by leaving the acts of other states out of the picture, and by taking the defendants' political decisions out of their true world political context.

One of the reasons why the Prosecution relied on this wide-ranging conspiracy theory was that the indictment was drawn up before it was decided who was going to be indicted.[13] A concept as elastic as conspiracy can be expanded or contracted to fit almost anyone. One of the Defence counsels quoted at length the authoritative article of Francis B. Sayre on 'Criminal Conspiracy':

> Conspiracy is as anomalous and provincial as it is unhappy in its results. It is utterly unknown to the Roman law; it is not found in modern Continental codes; few Continental lawyers have ever heard of it … Under such a principle everyone who acts in cooperation with another may some day find his liberty dependent upon the innate prejudices of an unknown judge. It is the very antithesis of justice according to law.[14]

The use of a body of law gleaned from financial fraud and other forms of organized crime for the purpose of adjudicating political decisions was additionally strange in the case of the Japanese: whereas one could make a case for saying that the Nazi leaders who seized power in Germany in 1933 were in some respects akin to a criminal gang, this thesis hardly applied to the members of the Japanese elite prosecuted at Tokyo. They had risen to positions of power legally and by virtue of their abilities, and without perpetrating any assaults on the constitutional order comparable to the 1933 'enabling law' (*Ermächtigungsgesetz*) in Germany.

At Tokyo, the Defence argued that Japan felt encircled, that she was subject to various forms of blockade or economic discrimination, and that she felt entitled to protect her national and regional interests just as the Americans had done when they waged war against the British naval blockade in 1812. Japan was being squeezed out of trade by barriers put up by the burgeoning regional European imperial economic arrangements in East Asia. The tribunal's refusal to consider the political context not only gave a totally biased account of Japan's pre-war policies, but also led to some amusing inconsistencies in the judgement. For instance, the tribunal found both that the attack on Pearl Harbor in December 1941 had been an act of aggression, and also that China had received help from the United States while she had *de facto* been at war with Japan since 1937. Yet these two findings cannot both be true: if the United States was not neutral but an ally of a belligerent power, then the attack on Pearl Harbor was not entirely unprovoked.[15] Whether one considers it a justified response is another matter.

It was precisely such conundrums which led to Tokyo's most interesting outcome, the lack of unanimity on the bench. The trial lasted two and a half years and the transcript ran to 45,000 pages. There were 818 public sessions, 416 witnesses, and unsubstantiated affidavits from 779 others. The judgement was 1781 pages long and it took no fewer than nine days (4–12 November 1948) for the president of the court to read it out. It was notable for the fact that five judges on the bench offered either separate or dissenting opinions, although these opinions were not read out in court, and the very fact of their existence is buried deep inside the judgement itself.

The dissenters were Henri Bernard of France, Bert Röling of the Netherlands, and Radhabinod Pal of India. (The president of the tribunal, William Webb, had concurred with the guilty verdict but opined that death was not an appropriate sentence; Judge Jaranilla of the Philippines also filed a separate opinion.) As we shall see, Pal's was the most dramatic since he argued that all defendants were innocent on all counts. But Henri Bernard's dissent was perhaps even more forceful than Pal's because it was not politically motivated and because its tone was so measured. Bernard wrote, 'Essential principles, violation of which would result in most civilised nations in the nullity of the entire procedure, and the right of the Tribunal to dismiss the case against the Accused, were not respected … A verdict reached by a tribunal after a defective procedure cannot be a valid one.'[16] Röling agreed (although not in his Opinion); he later explained the failure to publish the transcripts of the proceedings at the time by saying, 'I suppose that they [the United States] were perhaps a bit ashamed of what happened there ...'[17] Röling also agreed with Pal that Tokyo was victors' justice[18]

Bernard published his dissenting opinion because he was angry with his fellow judges for announcing their verdict in the name of the whole tribunal instead of in the name of their majority alone. Bernard also said that he was not convinced of the defendants' guilt of crimes against peace (although he did think the Japanese generally and some of the defendants were guilty of atrocities). He argued that both the law against crimes against peace and the law of conspiracy which underpinned it were too poorly defined to be usable. He bitterly attacked the way in which the findings of fact had been drawn up by the majority seven and then presented to the other judges for approval. This meant that all eleven judges never met to discuss the findings of fact, even though these made up 1050 pages of the judgement.[19]

Bernard even alleged that the findings of fact had been effectively doctored by the majority seven to put things into the mouths of the accused which, he said, they had not said:

> In several parts of the judgement quoting discourses, policies adopted etc., by the Defendants, the word 'war' is accompanied by the epithet 'aggressive' in such a way that the latter seems to emanate directly from the mouth or the pen of the Accused. Never, however, did any of them ... speak of this war as an aggressive war. It is only by substituting the conclusions drawn from the examination of these discourses, policies etc., that the majority was able to write the findings of fact permitting to arrive at the confession on the part of the Defendants of their guilt and implicitly of the cognisance of the law.[20]

Bernard argued that the Prosecution had also failed to demonstrate proof of conspiracy. 'No direct proof was furnished concerning the formation among individuals known, at a known date, at a specific point, of a plot the object of which was to assure to Japan the domination unaccepted by its inhabitants of some part of the world.'[21] This failure, he said, was especially egregious in view of the fact that Emperor Hirohito was not on trial. If Hirohito's case was measured by a different standard, Bernard said, then one was right to wonder whether international justice would merit to be exercised at all.[22]

Radhabinod Pal's long and forceful dissent was not included in the trial record either and he had to publish it himself privately in Calcutta in 1953.[23] It has since become well known among opponents of such international tribunals. He said he thought all the defendants should be acquitted because the IMT was not competent to try them. Pal was adamant that no treaty, statute or part of customary international law made aggressive war a crime. 'The so-called trial held according to the definition of crime *now* given by the victors obliterates the centuries of civilisation which stretch between us and the summary slaying of the defeated in a war. A trial with law thus prescribed will only be a sham employment of legal process for the satisfaction of a thirst for revenge. It does not correspond to any idea of justice.'[24] He insisted, sarcastically but correctly, that 'only a lost war is a crime.'[25]

Pal's view on the wrongness of criminalizing aggression went to the very heart of the matter. His rejection of this charge was not based merely on the 'sterile legalisms'[26] which Justice Jackson had so proudly said would be tossed aside to secure the conviction of the Nazis. Pal argued not only that it was wrong to bring a prosecution for aggressive war without having managed to define the term (as neither Tokyo nor Nuremberg had managed to do) but also that the very desire to introduce a new world order of peace was itself fundamentally flawed. 'I am not sure if it is possible to create "peace" once for all, and if there can be a *status quo* which is to be eternal,' Pal wrote. 'At any rate in the present state of international relations such a static idea of peace is absolutely untenable. Certainly dominated nations of the present day *status quo* cannot be made to submit to eternal domination only in the name of peace … War and other methods of self-help by force can be effectively excluded only when this problem is solved.'[27]

This view had many supporters in Asia, where many countries were hoping to throw off the yoke of colonialism. They resented the introduction of a new principle in international criminal law which seemed designed to preserve the current colonial arrangements indefinitely by outlawing any attack against them. There can be no doubt that the law applied at Tokyo would do this: Japan was accused of attacking Britain and the Netherlands, even though she had, of course, attacked only the Asian colonial possessions of these states, not the states themselves. Indeed, it has also been plausibly argued that the whole purpose of the Tokyo trial was to re-legitimize the postwar American occupation of Japan.[28]

The law against aggression also seemed in danger of legitimizing reprisals against anti-colonial insurgencies: the Dutch, who of course had a judge on the Tokyo bench, were themselves fighting a bitter anti-insurgency operation to retain control of Indonesia as the Tokyo trial was going on, while the French, who also had one, were similarly fighting to retain Indochina. Indeed, when American investigators arrived in Saigon to arrest members of the Japanese colonial police for prosecution for war crimes, they found that the French, British, and Indians who were occupying the country had rearmed them in order to help them fight the Viet Minh.[29] In this context, Allied accusations against the Japanese at Tokyo for having established systems of colonial rule in the countries they invaded must have elicited wry smiles from the defendants and, one hopes, a guilty conscience among the people making them.

Pal made great rhetorical use of the terrible killing caused by the American atomic bombs: he illustrated his *Dissentient Opinion* with graphic photographs of civilians killed and burned at Hiroshima and Nagasaki. More pointedly still, he reminded his readers that, after World War I, a letter had been produced from Kaiser Wilhelm II to the Austrian emperor, Franz Joseph, which was quoted as evidence of the German emperor's criminal intent. Wilhelm had written,

> My soul is torn, but everything must be put to fire and sword; men, women and children, and old men must be slaughtered and not a tree or house left standing. With these methods of terrorism, which are alone capable of affecting a people as degenerate as the French, the war will be over in months, whereas if I admit considerations of humanity, it will be prolonged for years.[30]

This letter was used by those who wanted to hang the Kaiser, yet the reasoning it expressed was the same as that used at the time – and still used today – to defend the American decision to drop the A-bomb on Japanese cities.

The fact that the bench was divided vitiates the validity of the death sentences: it is common in many jurisdictions for unanimity to be required for a death sentence. In the case of Hirota, the vote on the death sentence was six votes to five; it is inconceivable in most jurisdictions to execute a man on the basis of a one-vote majority. Richard Minear compares the laxity of the Tokyo voting rules with that of American military courts, which require a three-fourths majority for the death sentence; he calculates that if these rules had been in force at Tokyo, then there would have been no death sentences *at all*.[31]

Like the trial of Monsignor Tiso in Czechoslovakia, the judgement of the International Military Tribunal for the Far East was subject to appeal to the highest political authority in the land, which was General MacArthur. Within a week of the sentences having been handed down, the defence counsels appealed to him. Given that eleven judges had written six separate opinions, there seemed every reason for an appeal for clemency to be heeded. General MacArthur summoned a meeting of the Allied Council for Japan, composed of the ambassadors of the Allied Powers in Japan: the United States, Australia, France, India, the Netherlands, China, New Zealand, the Soviet Union, and the United Kingdom. The various diplomatic representatives basically copied what their co-nationals on the bench had said: India called for clemency, just as Justice Pal had said all defendants were innocent; the Netherlands recommended that Hirota's death sentence be commuted to life imprisonment, just as Justice Röling had said that Hirota was innocent; the seven nations whose judges composed the majority suggested no change to the majority verdict.

Having heard their opinions, the majority of which upheld the majority view of the bench, MacArthur decided that he could not overrule the tribunal's decisions and the men were sent to their deaths. He issued an emotional statement, concluding his rather agonized reasoning by saying,

> I pray that an Omnipotent Providence will use this tragic expiation as a symbol to summon all persons of good will to the realization of the utter futility of war – the most malignant scourge and greatest sin of mankind – and eventually to its renunciation by all nations. To this end, on the day of execution, I request the members of all the congregations throughout Japan of whatever creed or faith in the privacy of their homes or at their altars of public worship to seek divine help and guidance that the world will keep the peace, lest the human race perish.

The following year, the chief prosecutor, Joseph Keenan, published an account of the trial in which he made the extraordinary claim that what was at issue was not the guilt or innocence of the defendants, but instead the wider issue of forging a new world order based on the criminalization of war. Having disgraced himself during the trial by his heavy drinking – he was often inebriated in court, and was habitually unable to eat dinner since he had already had too much to drink by the early evening – Keenan disgraced himself further by saying that it did not matter if some of the defendants had been unjustly executed because their fate was a means to the 'grander and wider aim of the trial, [i.e.] to advance the cause of peace and right notions of international law'.[32] The punishment of the defendants, he said, was 'relatively unimportant' by comparison. Keenan was angry that the Defence lawyers did not see things this way and instead concentrated on trying to get their clients acquitted. 'In order to facilitate the interests of their clients, it seems that the Defense were willing to sacrifice the common international good,' he wrote. 'Had there been an actual miscarriage of justice with regard to some of the defendants, *there would have been no wrong*. The situation of the defendants was comparable to that of American soldiers about to take a beachhead; that is, *the lives of morally and legally innocent men may be sacrificed in the achievement of the common purpose*.'[33]

13   The Greek Colonels, Emperor Bokassa, and the Argentine Generals: Transitional Justice, 1975–2007

As we have seen, there was a glut of trials of former heads of state and government in the aftermath of World War II. Perhaps this was inevitable after such a worldwide conflagration which had ended in such apocalyptic events as the Holocaust and the detonation of bombs which reduced entire cities to ruins in an instant. The overriding desire was for a new international system which would ensure world peace once and for all, a desire expressed by the slogan 'Never again war!'

The Greek colonels

Unfortunately, war is part of the human condition and the respite from it and the lull in trials of heads of state lasted but three decades – until the trial of the Greek colonels in 1975. The colonels had seized power on 21 April 1967 and governed the country until their regime collapsed after the Turkish invasion of Cyprus in 1974. Although the Greek colonels argued that they were wielding power legally (having been invested in office by the king) they also initially proclaimed themselves to be a revolutionary regime, and the coup leaders operated nominally under the command of a 'Revolutionary Council'. Like Lenin, Stylianos Pattakos, one of the three coup leaders (with Giorgios Papadopoulos and Nikolaos Makarezos), proclaimed that the task of the revolution was 'to fashion a new man', who was supposed to 'have the strength to do Absolute Good'.[1] It was not until 1975, after the regime had been overthrown and the Greek parliament voted a resolution that the revolution had in fact been a coup – and not a legitimate government – that the new government was able to proclaim its predecessor's laws illegal and to initiate a prosecution against it. A political vote abrogating previous laws was needed for the trials to start.

The colonels had seized power ostensibly to prevent the victory of the Centre Left at elections. This, they feared, would have formed a coalition with the United Democratic Left, the front organization for the banned Communist Party of Greece. Greece had emerged from civil war against its Communists only eighteen years previously. Papadopoulos himself was eventually overthrown on 25 November 1973 in a counter-coup internal to the regime, led by Brigadier Dimitrios Ioannides. This followed the notoriously bloody suppression of a rebellion led by a Marxist group based at Athens Polytechnic on 17 November 1973. ('17 November' remains to this day the name of an extreme left-wing terrorist organization which has carried out successful political assassinations, for instance of the British military attaché in Athens in September 2000.) Ioannides then organized the coup against Archbishop Makarios in Cyprus in July 1974, which led to the Turkish invasion, defeat for Greece, and the downfall of the military junta.

The regime was characterized by the commission of numerous atrocities, including widespread arrests and torture, and it waged its own internal war against the Communist threat. Twenty members of the junta were put in the dock before a special court in August 1975 for high treason, insurrection, conspiracy, illegal actions while in office, and for the murders at the Polytechnic. They included two heads of state: Papadopoulos (prime minister from 1967 to 1973, regent from 1972 to 1973, and finally president in 1973) and George Zoitakis (regent until 1972). The trial was itself described as 'Greece's Nuremberg' at the time. Papadopoulos and his co-defendants, who included the man who had overthrown him, refused to defend themselves in protest against the fact that the incoming government had retrospectively declared their 1967 coup to have been illegal. The colonels, indeed, had originally been sworn in as the legal government of Greece by King Constantine, who said at the time that he thought they had acted in the best interests of the country, and they had appointed the attorney general as prime minister. (The king tried to overthrow them in a counter-coup in December 1967, but his failure led to his exile.)

Moreover, one of the colonels, Phaidon Gizikis (who was no put on trial), who succeeded Papadopoulos as president on 25 November 1973, had himself inaugurated the new democratic prime minister, the conservative Constantine Karamanlis, in 1974, whose government was now bringing the prosecution. So there was considerable legal continuity between the democratic regimes which preceded and succeded the junta. Moreover, the colonels' commanding officers had approved their actions in 1967 so they could not really be tried under military law either. The colonels' lawyers walked out of the court, denouncing what they called the climate of terror and violence in which the trial was being conducted. 'I shall answer only to history and the Greek people,' Papadopoulos said, echoing what Pierre Laval, Marshal Pétain, and Vidkun Quisling had said in 1945. The president of the court, Ioannis Deyannis, shot back, 'Do you think history is absent from this courtroom?'

The charge of treason was easier to sustain than the charge of seizing power illegally because the socialists claimed that the colonels had acted with the support of the CIA and the Americans against the perceived Communist threat. When Andreas Papandreou, the future prime minister (and the son of the postwar prime minister), testified, he declared that the Greek intelligence service had been financed and helped by the CIA. 'I can assure you,' he said, 'that these men [the defendants] worked in direct cooperation and correspondence with the Americans.' Papandreou Junior was the Americans' *bête noire*; although he had studied in the United States and served with the American navy, he turned against them in the 1950s and started to attack the American role in Greece in inflammatory speeches. It was his and his father's Centre Union which had been tipped to win the elections halted by the 1967 coup. It has been persuasively argued that the coup was enacted according to plans prepared by NATO's secret cell in Greece and that Papadopoulos was the chief liaison officer between Greek intelligence and the CIA. The coup, in short, was 'a Gladio coup', Gladio being shorthand for the secret armies organized across Europe by NATO to prepare insurgencies against a hypothetical Communist invasion.[351] However, the court president forbade almost all discussion of the question of CIA or American involvement during the trial and therefore the question of treason, in that sense, was largely neglected. Papadopoulos, Pattakos, and Makarezos were sentenced to death, commuted to life imprisonment; Zoitakis was given life.

Emperor Bokassa

In 1979 Jean-Bédel Bokassa of Central Africa, who had crowned himself emperor in 1976 in a ceremony costing $200 million, who had nineteen wives, and who believed himself to have been given the title 'Apostle of Peace' by Pope Paul VI, was overthrown by French paratroopers and fled into exile in Ivory Coast. In December 1980 his trial *in absentia* opened in the same stadium in the capital, Bangui, where he had sat on an eagle throne, wearing a crown and holding a sceptre, only four years previously. There were no cross-examinations and no witnesses for the Defence; even though Bokassa had indicated to the government which had overthrown him that he wanted to return to defend himself, the new republican authorities did not want this. Witnesses appeared before the court and were allowed to say more or less whatever they liked, often on the basis of things they had read in the papers about their former king. The most sensational charge, and one which many believed at the time even though it was invented, was that Bokassa had given instructions to a chef on how to cook human flesh: the chef alleged that he spiced a dead body with onions and Pernod but that it sat up and pointed at him reproachfully once inside the oven. 'It struggled so much that it messed up the whole kitchen,' the cook told the court. 'I begged its forgiveness and pushed it back in the oven.'[352] The trial lasted four days and, after deliberating for two hours, the judge announced the death sentence on 23 December.

Bokassa himself strongly resented the charge of cannibalism and eventually returned from exile in 1986 in an attempt to clear his name. He was imprisoned on arrival, on the pretext that he had returned in order to seize power. By this stage a new one-party state was being set up under General André Kolingba, who had overthrown Bokassa's successor in a bloodless coup in 1981. The decision to try Bokassa in person was a way of bolstering the new regime's legitimacy, stifling what remained of support for Papa Bok by demonstrating his regime's brutality. To this end, the central stadium was again initially chosen as a venue so that thousands could attend, although at the last minute, and for security reasons, it was changed to the Palais de Justice. Bokassa was arraigned on the same list of charges as those for which had been convicted in December 1980. There were fourteen charges: six of murder and associated crimes (including cannibalism); two of arbitrary arrest and imprisonment; and other counts of violent assault, embezzlement (four counts), and treason. He was given Defence lawyers, including an ambitious young barrister from Paris keen to make his name with a difficult case.

This, Bokassa's second trial, began on 26 November 1986. But the presiding judge of the court was the same man, Edouard Franck, who had chaired the farcical first trial in 1980 – and who became General Kolingba's Prime Minister in 1991. Defence objections against him were overruled. Bokassa arrived in the courtroom smiling and he made extravagant upbeat statements to the waiting press. When he was asked to confirm his identity as 'a second-class soldier', the former self-appointed marshal bridled and protested that even Marshal Pétain had kept his rank after his conviction in 1945. He then rose to address the court. 'I am innocent of the charges,' he said. 'I have only ever been motivated by the sincere desire to serve my country.' In a dignified speech, Bokassa argued that France – and especially its president, Valéry Giscard d'Estaing – had violated his country's national sovereignty by overthrowing him and that, to do so, it had orchestrated a propaganda campaign against him. He insisted that he did not now want to regain power but wished his successor (whom he called 'General Kolingba') every success in promoting national unity. There were cries of '*Vive l'Empereur!*' from the crowd outside the Palais de Justice, which listened to the trial broadcast live on loudspeakers – something the government had arranged for educative and propaganda purposes.

The Prosecution asked for an adjournment until 15 December. Bokassa's return had taken everyone by surprise, and it needed more time to prepare its case. When the trial reopened, his grandstanding took a knock as accusations were made that he had ordered or condoned specific murders, in one case like King David in order to sleep with his victim's mistress. Bokassa's claims not to remember the details of these cases were feeble and seemed self-incriminating. Alternatively, he said that while he accepted general responsibility as head of state, he tended to blame his subordinates for their excesses. On occasions he recognized abuses of due process but invoked national security in justification. While Bokassa tended to get up and speak every day – he had a reputation for long-windedness – his Defence team scored impressive points, in particular by successfully undermining the credibility of Prosecution witnesses during cross-examination.

The trial soon took its toll on the former emperor, who grew weak from fatigue and lame from gout. Meanwhile, the Central African capital, Bangui, ground to a halt as people spent whole days listening to the trial on the radio. The evidence presented ranged from the gruesome to the bizarre. The court spent some time debating how many breasts a certain woman had had whom Bokassa had allegedly had murdered (some said three, others four), because more than two breasts was a sign of sorcery and Central African law recognized the right to defend oneself against witches. The cook was brought back and again testified how he had flambéed human flesh in gin and whisky and served it to the former emperor for dinner; the Defence had little difficulty rubbishing this testimony. Witnesses were also heard on the charges of embezzlement, and it became clear that corruption was extremely rife. But clear evidence of specific orders explicitly issued to carry out crimes refused to materialize, no doubt in part because Bokassa's executors who appeared as witnesses themselves tried to cover their own tracks. The presiding judge was overtly biased in favour of the Prosecution, having in any case found Bokassa guilty on the same charges six years previously.

On 1 June 1987 the Prosecution delivered its summing up. The Defence summarized its case by saying that Bokassa bore general political responsibility for the wrongdoings during his regime but that he should be acquitted on all charges since the evidence presented was insufficient to justify conviction. Bokassa's subordinates were to blame. The verdict was given after a week's deliberation on 12 June. Bokassa was found guilty of at least twenty murders, of complicity in an attack on a school when children had been tortured to death, and of embezzling tens of millions of dollars. But he was acquitted of stealing the crown jewels and of cannibalism. Bokassa stood to attention as the judge announced the sentence: death by firing squad. The Defence appealed on the grounds of sovereign immunity and on the basis that the new constitution provided that heads of state could only be prosecuted for treason, and then only by the national congress. On 14 November 1987 the Supreme Court rejected the appeal, saying that the constitution applied only to presidents not emperors, but on 20 February 1988, Bokassa's sentence was commuted by President Kolingba to life imprisonment. Bokassa was freed on 1 September 1993 as part of a general amnesty. He lived in poverty in a rundown villa in Bangui whose roof was falling in, and appeared once or twice in the street dressed up in his marshal's uniform. He died in 1996.

Transitional justice in South America

In February 1986, a congressional indictment was issued against the former military dictator of Bolivia, General Luis García Meza Tejada, who had been president of Bolivia for just over a year (1980–1), and fifty-two of his collaborators (ministers and paramilitaries), on thirty-six charges including sedition, armed insurrection, murder, genocide, and (in García Meza's own case) the illegal sale of the diaries of Che Guevara. For various reasons, the trial itself did not get under way until January 1989 and when it did nearly all the defendants were absent. They had not in fact been arrested. Meza attended some of the early sessions but went into hiding when Congress accused him of stealing and selling the diaries; at some point he fled to Brazil.

The trial dragged on for so long that, in December 1992, the seven-year term of the judges expired before the trial had ended; in February 1993 they were replaced by a new team. These new judges allegedly took just two months to digest the 4,000 pages of evidence which had been accumulated by then, and they gave their verdict in April. The sentence was notable for the fact that the conviction for genocide, which related to a massacre of eight leftist guerrillas in 1981 (the so-called Harrington Street massacre), was punished with a lighter sentence (twenty years) than the other charges of plotting a coup, sedition, armed insurrection, and murder.[353] Garcia Meza was eventually extradited from Brazil in 1995 and is now in prison in Bolivia.

Argentina, meanwhile, was going through a similar process, where the military junta was overthrown in 1983. It had seized power in 1976 for much the same reason as the colonels had in Greece: to fight a left-wing insurgency in what it called 'the war on subversion and terrorism'. Defeated in the Falklands War in 1982, the regime published two legislative acts as it prepared to leave office: the so-called 'Final Document' of 23 April 1983, which argued that the junta's legitimacy had been based on emergency decrees passed by the previous president authorizing the military to crack down on terrorists; and a general amnesty, including for the leftist insurgents, published on 23 September 1983, just five weeks before the elections which brought Raúl Alfonsín to power. On the same day as the 'Final Document', the junta also ratified an instrument reaffirming the legality of acts carried out according to its own decrees in the war on terror, while, in a secret decree, it ordered the incineration of all compromising documents.

When the junta fell, there was a huge outpouring of pent-up public anger against the abuses committed by old regime and a widespread demand that the generals face justice. One of Alfonsín's first acts as president was to pass Decree No. 158 (13 December 1983) entitled 'Presidential Order to try the members of the junta'. The decree resembled Marshal Pétain's proclamation of the guilt of the Third Republic leaders prior to the Riom trial, both in that it dwelt at length in its preamble on the guilt of the previous regime and on its various illegal acts, even naming the defendants who had 'usurped the government' in 1976, and also in that it was backed by a genuine grassroots desire for retribution. The named guilty men included Lt-General Jorge Videla (president of Argentina from 29 March 1976 to 29 March 1981), Lt-General Roberto Viola (president from 29 March to 11 December 1981), and Lt-General Leopoldo Galtieri (president from 22 December 1981 to 18 June 1982, who had invaded the Falkland Islands, to huge popular acclaim, in 1982).

Shortly thereafter, Alfonsín set about purging the judiciary and appointing to all the key courts judges who were, in the words of one of the architects of the trials of the military leaders, 'close friends of the administration'.[354] In order to enable the trials to occur, the amnesty law of September 1983 had to be nullified by Congress, which duly occurred in 1984, in spite of the fact that numerous articles of the Argentine constitution seemed to be violated by this change to the law: Article 2 provided that a defendant had the right to be tried by the most lenient law in force at the time, while Article 18 forbade retroactive legislation. This latter article was also violated by Congress's decision to remove jurisdiction for acts committed during military rule from the country's military courts. (The military courts retained the right to try people, including for human rights abuses, but they were brought under the overall control of the civilian Federal Court of Appeal in Buenos Aires.) Finally, military law in force at the time provided for the defence of superior orders, and yet this was also retroactively changed.

The plan was initially that the junta leaders would be tried by the Supreme Council of the Armed Forces, the highest military court, both for human rights abuses and also – in another aspect reminiscent of the Riom trial – for the planning and execution of the disastrous Malvinas (Falklands) campaign. The government instructed the Supreme Council to proceed with the former trials first, and the hearings started in early 1984. Videla and the others defended their acts as political and as part of Argentina's war on terror. By the end of September the Supreme Council reported to the Federal Court of Appeals that it could find nothing objectionable in the decrees and orders issued by the junta in its military activity against subversives. The Federal Court immediately decided to take over jurisdiction itself, instructing the Supreme Council to hand over its 15,000 pages of files to the prosecutor (whose then deputy is now the chief prosecutor of the ICC in The Hague, Luis Moreno Ocampo). On 4 October 1984 the Federal Court asserted its control over the trial.

The trial eventually started on 22 April 1985. The defendants were charged with 709 specific cases of human rights abuses. The first witness was the last president of Argentina before the junta seized power, Italo Luder, who testified about the decrees he had signed authorizing the army to suppress subversion. Human rights activists from bodies like the United Nations Human Rights Commission and Physicians for Human Rights testified, as did journalists, much in the manner of the so-called 'expert' witnesses at contemporary international criminal tribunals. One defendant testified that when he had been imprisoned by the regime, he had been treated well, but of course testimony was also received about kidnapping and murder. The trials was attended by grandee British and North American philosophers like Ronald Dworkin, Bernard Williams, and Thomas Nagel, who gave lectures on the need for retroactive justice. The Prosecution relied on the contentious Yamashita judgement at Tokyo in 1945 to accuse the junta leaders of criminal liability for the acts of their subordinates, because the defendants argued that they had not ordered any of the atrocities and the Prosecution (like the Supreme Council) could not prove that they had.

The Defence started to present its case on 30 September 1985. It began by attacking presidential Decree 158 of 1983 which, it said, had proclaimed the defendants' guilt in advance. It also attacked the retroactive legislation under which the defendants were being tried, and said that the amnesty law should be respected. It attacked the evidence provided by the National Council on Disappeared Persons as fabricated. General Viola said he was being accused of something of which he was proud, having defeated terrorism. The air force leaders on trial tried to distinguish their force from the army and the navy. Others argued that a state of war had existed in the country, as evidenced by the presidential decrees on subversion signed before the junta took power. The Defence completed its summing-up on 21 October 1985, and four hours later President Alfonsín proclaimed a state of siege as a series of bombs went off around the country, presumably in protest at the trial. Alfonsín then arranged a secret dinner with the judges to discuss their views about the defence of superior orders. Judgement was served on 9 December 1985. Videla was sentenced to life in prison and Viola to seventeen years, while Galtieri was acquitted. One other junta leader (Emilio Eduardo Masasera) was also given life, while the third leader, Orlando Agosti, got four years. The following year, the Supreme Court, to which the defendants appealed, reduced Viola's sentence to sixteen years and but upheld Videla's life sentence. In May 1986 Galtieri was found guilty by the Supreme Council for mishandling the Falklands War and imprisoned.

This was not the end of the story, however. Following another secret meeting between President Alfonsín and the judges of the Federal Court of Appeal in 1986, the president decided that it was time to move on and put an end to prosecutions against members of the former regime. Congress passed the president's so-called 'Full Stop Law' on 23 December 1986, an attempt to ensure national reconciliation and draw a line under prosecutions for acts committed during military rule. The law had the paradoxical effect of speeding up prosecutions, as courts scrambled to meet the deadline, and this in turn provoked a brief rebellion by junior officers within the military shortly before Easter 1987. Alfonsín brilliantly defused this rebellion by going to see the rebels in person, after telling an enormous crowd outside the presidential palace that this was what he was going to do. On his return from his successful mission to the still waiting crowd, he was deliriously acclaimed as a hero; he told everyone to go home and have a happy Easter. In June, and as a result, Alfonsín got Congress to pass a law on due obedience which proclaimed that superior orders were indeed an irrefutable defence for anyone below the rank of colonel; this was a further attempt to pacify the military and its supporters and ensure civil peace. This pacification worked, in spite of the fact that, in January 1989, a left-wing terrorist movement attacked a military garrison and killed eleven soldiers; the discovery that some of the attackers were connected with human rights groups seemed to confirm the military's claims that the original charges against them were politically motivated.

Alfonsín left office later that year to be succeeded by a Peronist, Carlos Menem. Thus began the long political process by which successive presidents ruled first one way and then the other on the fate of the junta leaders. Menem pardoned Videla, Viola, and Galtieri in 1990, but this only threw the country into a new fever of argument about who should be prosecuted for what. The Full Stop Law and the law on Due Obedience were repealed in March 1988 but not with retroactive effect, i.e. they continued to prevent the prosecution of people for acts committed during military rule. This was a red rag to human rights groups like Amnesty International, the United Nations Human Rights Committee, and the Inter-American Commission on Human Rights, as well as to the more activist members of the Argentine judiciary, all of whom protested vehemently against these amnesty laws even though they had been democratically passed in a spirit of peace and welcomed at the time by the people. They agitated for further prosecutions, and their long campaign was successful. Menem lost power in 1999; the laws were eventually proclaimed unconstitutional by various courts, repealed again by the Congress in 2003, and proclaimed null and void by the Supreme Court in 2005.

As the political wind blew first one way and then the next, the former military leaders were either free men or defendants facing serious criminal charges: it was on the basis of a judge's ruling that the two duly voted laws were unconstitutional that General Galtieri was again arrested in 2002 and prosecuted on human rights charges (although he died under house arrest in 2003 before his trial could start) and that warrants were also issued for the arrest of Alfonsín's immediate predecessor, General Reynaldo Bignone, in March 2007. Meanwhile Videla's presidential pardon was struck down in the courts in 2006 and his convictions upheld in 2007. There are few starker illustrations of how the law follows the imperatives of politics than the fate of the military leaders in Argentina.

14 Revolution Returns: the Trial of Nicolae Ceauşescu

The trial and execution of the Romanian dictator, Nicolae Ceauşescu, and his wife, Elena, on 25 December 1989 compressed into a short space of time many of the events which have typified trials of heads of state throughout history: violent revolution; a cathartic trial to judge and anathematize the deposed head of state; and a swift and brutal death. The fact that it was all broadcast live on television – when the entire Western world was sitting at home enjoying Christmas – ensured that the events received maximum publicity. They provided a real-time insight into the sorts of passions which have driven political trials in the more distant past.

Yet the Ceauşescu trial also fired the starting gun for a regrettable trend. The principal charge brought against him by the kangaroo court hastily convened to execute him was for genocide. This same charge of genocide was to be decisive in the trials of the former Bolivian president García Meza Tejada (who, accused of it in January 1989, was convicted in 1993 of genocide for the massacre of eight people); General Pinochet of Chile (originally arrested in 1998 for genocide of under a hundred people); Colonel Mengistu of Ethiopia (who was convicted *in absentia* for genocide in 2006, just as political opponents of the new Ethiopian regime, including human rights activists, also found themselves prosecuted for genocide); Jean Kambanda of Rwanda (convicted of genocide without trial in 1998); and Slobodan Milošević (accused in 2001 of complicity in genocide in Bosnia in 1995). Unfortunately, in an age in which the Nazi Holocaust became the supreme (negative) moral reference point for Western societies, the 'universal' crime of genocide seems in danger of being debased as a legal concept, the very magnitude of the crime itself encouraging prosecutors to believe that it is a 'magic bullet' and that almost any killing can come under this category.

Ceauşescu's overthrow was the dramatic and bloody culmination of a series of stunning coups against Communist leaders all over Eastern Europe in the autumn of 1989. One by one, men who had governed their Warsaw Pact countries for decades were swept aside in what commentators welcomed as 'people's revolutions'. The process started when the Communist government of Hungary opened its border with Austria, thereby allowing hundreds of thousands of East German tourists on holiday near Lake Bálaton to drive to the West. A trickle turned into a flood: the first tourists arrived in West Berlin in early September, while thousands sought refuge in the West Germany embassy in Prague. The East German leader Erich Honecker (himself to face trial in 1992) was overthrown by his comrades in October, and they (or their masters in Moscow) ordered the Berlin Wall itself to be opened on the night of 9 November 1989 – the anniversary of both the revolution against the German emperor in 1918 and the *Reichskristallnacht* in 1938.

One by one, the bulwarks of the post-war Communist regime in Eastern Europe followed. The hardline leader of Bulgaria, Todor Zhivkov, was deposed the day after the Berlin Wall fell, on 10 November 1989. (In February 1991, Zhivkov was put on trial for embezzlement, but not for acts of state. The trial continued until October. He was convicted and sentenced to seven years in prison. The fact that Zhivkov was not prosecuted for 'human rights abuses' elicited protest from Human Rights Watch at the time.) In Czechoslovakia huge crowds jangled their keys in Prague's Wenceslas Square, and the Communist regime of Gustav Husak duly fell. It seemed like modern-day magic – the equivalent of the destruction of the walls of Jericho by trumpets – but the truth behind the regime change was more banal. The decisive moment in Prague came when the Czechoslovak defence minister, General Milan Vaclavnik, was summoned to the Soviet embassy on the morning of 24 November 1989; having declared the previous day that the army was prepared to 'defend socialism', he emerged from his long meeting with the Soviet diplomats to say that the military would not intervene in politics after all. Having lost its main defender, the regime started to crumble the next day.

It is highly likely that the secret services of the respective states, as well as important elements within the Communist hierarchy, played a role in engineering these changes. In other words, there were turncoats. In Prague, the demonstrators swelled to hundreds of thousands on the rumour that a student called Martin Smid had been beaten to death by the police. Photographs emerged of a body being carried away on a stretcher, and the government's denials that this had happened only inflamed passions further. In the event, it turned out that the government was right: Martin Smid was alive and well; no one had been killed; and the role of 'dead body' had been played by an agent of the Czechoslovak secret police.[1]

Not all the Eastern European leaders went quietly. One East German Politburo member denounced the bogusness of Mikhail Gorbachev's new slogans of *glasnost* and *perestroika* when he commented acidly, 'Just because your neighbour puts up new wallpaper, it does not mean you have to do the same thing.'[2] For the most part, though, the new political wind blowing from Moscow provide irresistible. Ceauşescu, however, tried to swim against the tide. His career had been characterized by an apparent political independence from Moscow ever since he had condemned the Warsaw Pact invasion of Czechoslovakia in 1968. His regime was, however, far more tyrannical and eccentric than the others in Eastern Europe.

The Romanian leader's fortunes began to turn when the Yugoslav news agency, Tanjug, started to issue inflammatory reports about events in the western Romanian town of Timişoara, near the Yugoslav border. These reports concerned the fate of a Lutheran pastor, László Tökes, an ethnic Hungarian, whose allegedly anti-government sermons were becoming too popular. His story came against the background of reports in the Western press that Romania was oppressing its Hungarian minority; in reality, the Communist regime oppressed all its citizens, but it is evidently more damaging in the West to be called a nationalist than a Communist.

A crowd gathered outside Tökes's house as the police pre-announced they were going to arrest him. On 17 December, the stand-off turned violent and people were beaten and shot. Although there were no Western journalists in Romania at the time, and although news reports could not be verified by Western agencies, the world's media started to broadcast that there had been massive bloodshed in Timişoara. There were reports of 'cubic metres of corpses'[3] and of 'at least a thousand corpses in the morgue at Timişoara.'[4] Even these huge figures quickly climbed through 4,000 dead and 4,000 wounded, 13,000 arrested and 7,000 condemned to death, 12,000 dead, 63,000 dead, and finally reaching hecatombs of '70,000'. This turned out to be pure invention, comparable to the famous tall tales about German officers tossing Belgian babies on their bayonets or Iraqi soldiers emptying Kuwaiti incubators of premature children and leaving them to die on the floor.[5] It was only when regime change was eventually accomplished in Romania that the real figure for the number of dead in two weeks of clashes across the whole of Romania, including in the capital Bucharest, was established at less than 200. There were perhaps thirty people killed in Timişoara. In France, the media manipulation at that time is now so notorious that the word 'Timişoara' has passed into common usage in French as a byword for propaganda.

These inflated figures nourished the view that 'the people' had risen up against 'the power'. Soon the claim was made that 'genocide' had been committed. The Western media took all their information from news sources which, until only a few weeks previously, they would have dismissed out of hand as mouthpieces for Communist propaganda: the Yugoslav press agency, Tanjug; the Soviet news agency, Tass; the East German news agency; and Hungarian sources. All these countries, including most importantly the Soviet Union, were by now controlled by 'reformers', i.e. senior members of the Communist hierarchy who, by adopting democratic rhetoric, had managed to grab power. This did not stop Western reporters feeding out of these agencies' hands.

In fact, Ceauşescu had given specific orders that there should be no bloodshed.[6] Reports of scores of Soviet 'observers' or 'experts' at the scene in Timişoara[7] suggest for some commentators the hidden hand of Moscow behind the events. The new reformist political agenda being set in Moscow required that the old guard in Eastern Europe be dismissed. The speculation is that someone had an interest in escalating the situation, against Ceauşescu's orders; perhaps it was deemed necessary to have real deaths in order to fulfil the same purpose as that fulfilled by the fictitious death of Martin Smid in Prague the previous month.

Soon the propaganda started about mass graves, and it was here that one of the most macabre acts of the whole disinformation campaign was performed. A number of bodies were removed from the local morgue and lined up to be displayed and photographed, as if they had been taken fresh from the streets. It was actually clear that these people had been dead for some time, and indeed that autopsies had been performed on them, but no one noticed this important detail when it mattered.[8]

Ceauşescu had left the country at the height of these troubles for a state visit to Iran and he returned on 20 December. In an attempt to recover the situation, he went on television to denounce the insurgents as agents of foreign powers. 'It is quite clear,' he said, 'that this campaign against Romania is part of a general plan against the independence and sovereignty of peoples.' He referred to 1968, when he and Romania had stood up against the invasion of Czechoslovakia 'and for the defence of the independence of Romania', a clear indication that he thought that Moscow was behind the events in Timişoara.[9]

In fact, Ceauşescu had understood in advance what was going on in the other countries of the Warsaw Pact. At a meeting of the Politburo, held on 14 December – that is, three days before the trouble even started in Timişoara – Ceauşescu had said,

Everything that is happening now in Germany, in Czechoslovakia and in Bulgaria now and, a while ago, in Poland and Hungary, is organised by the Soviet Union with the help of the Americans and the West ... What is happening in these last three countries, the GDR, Czechoslovakia and Bulgaria, are coups d'état organised with the help of the dregs of society who are themselves being helped from abroad. This is how things should be understood.[10]

In an attempt to retrieve the situation, Ceauşescu ordered that a rally be held in University Square in Bucharest on 21 December. This square had been the scene, fifty years previously, of the 'spontaneous demonstrations' organized by the Communists calling for the death of Marshal Antonescu and witnessed by Princess Ileana in 1946. Ceauşescu gave a now famous speech allegedly interrupted by heckling. According to the version of events given at the time, and widely retained by history, the crowd started to shout 'Timişoara', the dictator stopped in mid-sentence, and the television transmission was cut. His expression of shock has entered history as the dramatic moment when the tyrant stared at a rebellious crowd and realized that the game was up.

The reality is quite different. In fact, the interruption did not consist of heckling but instead of screaming. This is perfectly audible on the video and audio tapes of the event. Evidently something had happened in the square which frightened people badly, and there was mass hysteria. Some have claimed that the loudspeakers broadcast sounds of gunfire, others that there really was gunfire. It seems that people in the crowd thought 'Timişoara' was about to happen to them and they fled the square in panic. Ceauşescu's reaction, moreover, to this was not one of shock or fear but instead one of confusion and concern. He tried to calm the people by raising his hand. Most importantly, what happened at the moment when his face appeared confused was that both the TV transmission and his microphone were cut (or failed). Ceauşescu spent several minutes shouting 'Allo! Allo!' (i.e. 'Can you hear me?' or 'You there!') and 'Wait, comrades, wait!', as if people were indeed leaving the square. After a few minutes, the sound was restored and Ceauşescu resumed his speech, much as if nothing had happened, announcing a rise in the basic salary and other paltry financial incentives for continued social obedience. It is therefore quite wrong to say that the dictator realized that his time had come: on the contrary, he behaved as if nothing was wrong. But the image of the apparently frightened tyrant had been broadcast, and in the country as a whole his reputation was fatally damaged. If the interruption in transmission was deliberate, therefore, it cannot have been Ceauşescu's people who were responsible. Either it was a simple accident or the revolutionaries created the fatal image, and probably the original disturbance in the square itself. The revolution was an inside job.

In any case, the Ceaușescus then remained in the Central Committee building for another day. On 22 December, Ceaușescu emerged again on the balcony overlooking University Square with a megaphone. After this second appearance on the balcony, he allegedly fled in a helicopter which took off from the roof of the Central Committee building, and later in a car, before being caught, arrested, and put on trial. But even this is not certain. If Ceaușescu had tried to flee, why did he put up such a robust defence at his trial, which occurred three days later, when he insisted that he was still president of Romania? Ceaușescu's notorious 'flight to Varennes' may itself have been disinformation. After all, on the morning of 6 October 2000, after the post-election disturbances which overthrew President Slobodan Milošević, a similar claim was made by his now victorious enemies that he had fled to the airport and taken off for Moscow; in fact, the deposed Yugoslav president was sitting quietly at his home in Dedinje. Certainly, during the Ceaușescu trial, the former president and his wife emphatically denied that they had fled, insisting instead that they had been betrayed.

At any rate, in the three days between Ceaușescu's last speech and the broadcast of his trial on 25 December, there was further fighting all over the country, although it was not clear who was shooting at whom. During these days, a maximum sense of hysteria was encouraged by the repeated claim made by the new authorities that 'terrorists' were at large, fighting for Ceaușescu, and that they were being helped by 'Arab mercenaries' – an interesting anticipation of the same rhetoric used by the proponents of the war on terror after 2001. In fact, the real identity of these 'terrorists' has never been conclusively established, while the claim that there were foreign mercenaries is almost certainly a myth. The minister of defence, meanwhile, was found dead, apparently after having committed suicide although many suspect that he was murdered.

The point of all this is to underline what soon became clear during the trial itself, namely that Ceaușescu had been overthrown by a palace coup involving senior pro-Moscow Communists within the Party hierarchy. In November 1989 six former senior Communists had issued a statement attacking Ceaușescu and calling themselves the National Salvation Front. One of their number, the veteran Stalinist, Silviu Brucan, had just returned from visits to Moscow and Washington. National Salvation Front was to be the name taken by the new power headed by the former Stalinist-era general secretary of the Communist Youth, Ion Iliescu, who soon succeeded Ceaușescu as president of Romania.

In order to effect their coup, these insider Communists had to focus attention on the person of Ceauşescu. Just as the six had done in November, they pretended that he, and he alone, was the cause of all of Romania's woes, in order to distract attention from the ills of Communism as a system and from their own heavily compromised past. By ratcheting up the tension, and by pushing the already deeply traumatized Romanians further into hysteria, they baptized their seizure of power in blood. Consequently, for the first time in Romanian history, the people genuinely did acclaim a Communist – Iliescu – when he took power. Although Iliescu romped back home in elections held to confirm him in office the following spring, his democratic credentials became clear in January and then again in June 1990, when he summoned miners from the Jiu valley to Bucharest to crush demonstrations against him. When the miners came in June to quell what they said was a counter-revolution, they killed at least seven people. The purpose of the 'revolution' in Romania was precisely the same as the purpose of the Bolshevik 'revolution' in 1917: to bring to power a gang of ruthless men and to legitimize their seizure of power with the appearance of mass support.

Ceauşescu's trial was an integral part of this process. When he appeared before his accusers in the military barracks in Tîrgovişte on Christmas Day, the revolutionaries' heavy Stalinist mindset was all too apparent. The presiding judge, Gica Popa, opened the proceedings by proclaiming proudly, 'We are a people's tribunal.' No doubt, for him, the historical resonance of this was positive. As the camera swung from the indicted couple to their accusers and judges, one could recognize Gelu Voican Voiculescu, one of the prime movers behind the trial and the revolution, who became a minister in the first government of Petre Roman as director of the newly reconstituted secret police. Present too was General Victor Stănculescu, perhaps the key figure in the conspiracy, who was later charged with giving the order to shoot demonstrators in the streets of Bucharest in June 1990.

The principal accusation against Ceauşescu was that he had committed genocide by killing 63,000 people. The other charges were buried in the Prosecution's rambling invective. The prosecutors' claims ranged from the ridiculous – 'You are faced with charges that you held really sumptuous celebrations on all holidays at your house' – to the sublimely vague – 'Crimes against the people. They carried out acts that are incompatible with human dignity and social thinking; they acted in a despotic and criminal way; they destroyed the people whose leaders they claimed to be.' The Prosecution was also deeply confused, since it both alleged genocide and also said that there had so far been '34 casualties'. Elena Ceauşescu remarked sarcastically, 'Look, and that they are calling genocide.' There was further inconsistency when the judge at first said that the couple would be judged 'according to laws adopted by the Council of the National Salvation Front', whereas of course the new power had had no time to pass any laws at all by then, and the Prosecution in fact quoted only articles from the pre-existing penal code.

Ceauşescu's tactic was to refuse to recognize the authority of the court. He said repeatedly that he would answer questions only at a session of the Grand National Assembly, which alone had the right to call him to account. The Prosecutors and judges replied that the Assembly had been dissolved and that the National Salvation Front was the new power. Ceauşescu addressed his accusers as 'you putschists'. When the National Salvation Front was mentioned, Ceauşescu replied scornfully, 'This gang will be destroyed. They organized the putsch.' He said the new power was 'working for foreigners'. As the exchanges went on, they became more and more surreal.

> PROSECUTOR: Did you know about the genocide in Timişoara?
> ELENA CEAUŞESCU: What genocide? By the way, I will not answer any more questions.

Ceauşescu insisted that he was still president of Romania (as Saddam Hussein was to insist he was president of Iraq at his trial in 2006), and he denied that he had starved his own people. As with the Quisling trial, Ceauşescu and his wife were accused of having lived in luxury – 'They were even worse than the king, the former king of Romania' – and of having bank accounts in Switzerland. This charge, never proved, was also to be made against Slobodan Milošević, also never proved.

> PROSECUTOR: Let us now talk about the accounts in Switzerland, Mr. Ceauşescu. What about the accounts?
> ELENA CEAUŞESCU: Accounts in Switzerland? Furnish proof!
> NICOLAE CEAUŞESCU: We had no account in Switzerland. Nobody has opened an account. This shows again how false the charges are. What defamation, what provocations! This was a coup d'état.

However, in the chaos, the Ceauşescus did clearly say that those who had shot into the crowd in Timişoara were the Securitate, whom they called 'terrorists'.

> NICOLAE CEAUŞESCU: You as officers should know that the government cannot give the order to shoot. But those who shot at the young people were the security men, the terrorists.
> ELENA CEAUŞESCU: The terrorists are from Securitate.
> PROSECUTOR: The terrorists are from Securitate?
> ELENA CEAUŞESCU: Yes.

Ceaușescu insisted, 'Not a single person was shot in Palace Square [i.e. University Square, where he had made his famous speech] ... no one was shot.' In an anticipation of the trial of Slobodan Milošević, the 'people's tribunal' trying Ceaușescu tried to impose a Defence team on the couple, which the former president energetically refused to accept. The 'Defence' then spoke in the manner adopted by the Defence during the great Moscow show trials. Just as, in 1937, Ilya Braude, counsel for the Defence for Knyazev, had dwelt graphically and at length on his client's 'despicable actions', and just as Sergei Kaznacheyev, another Defence counsel, told the judges that, 'the picture of treachery and betrayal which has unfolded before you in the course of these few days is monstrous,' so the three 'Defence' lawyers in the Ceaușescu trial spent half of their speeches expressing disgust at the former president's crimes and the other half extolling the legality of the grotesque charade in which they were participating.[11] Addressing his own client, one of these counsels said,

> You led the country to the verge of ruin and you will be convicted on the basis of the points contained in the bill of indictment. You are guilty of these offenses even if you do not want to admit it. Despite this, I ask the court to make a decision which we will be able to justify later as well. We must not allow the slightest impression of illegality to emerge. Elena and Nicolae Ceaușescu should be punished in a really legal trial ... They will be indicted, and a sentence will be passed on the basis of the new legal system. They are not only accused of offences committed during the past few days, but of offences committed during the past 25 years. We have sufficient data on this period. I ask the court, as the plaintiff, to take note that proof has been furnished for all these points, that the two have committed the offences mentioned. Finally, I would like to refer once more to the genocide, the numerous killings carried out during the past few days. Elena and Nicolae Ceaușescu must be held fully responsible for this. I now ask the court to pass a verdict on the basis of the law, because everybody must receive due punishment for the offences he has committed.

The judges soon concluded that the couple were guilty on all counts and that they merited the death sentence. The initial intention was to separate the couple, but Elena Ceaușescu insisted that they wanted to die together. Their hands were tied in the courtroom and Elena Ceaușescu protested that she was being hurt. 'Why are you doing this when I have been a mother to you all?' In an almost exact repetition of the fate meted out to Marshal Antonescu forty-three years previously, the pair was taken out into the courtyard and shot. Once again, the myth of revolution had triumphed.

15 A State on Trial: Erich Honecker in Moabit

Erich Honecker was born in the Saarland in 1912, the son of a miner. He became a member of a Communist youth group at the age of ten: his only career other than politics was when he became a roofer's apprentice for two years. By 1930 he was attending a Party school in Moscow. He was arrested by the Gestapo in 1935 and spent ten years in Moabit prison in Berlin for treason, before being released by the Soviets in 1945. He founded the Free German Youth in 1946 and was one of the leaders of the Socialist Unity Party (the Communist Party of East Germany based on the forced fusion between the Communist Party of Germany and the Social Democratic Party). He became a member of its Central Committee and of the People's Chamber, the national parliament. When Walter Ulbricht, the East German Communist leader, eventually fell from power in 1971, Honecker became Party boss, president of the National Defence Council, and president of the State Council, i.e. head of state. Honecker was Willy Brandt's opposite number, and the two Germanies signed a Basic Treaty in 1972. Following the arrival to power of Mikhail Gorbachev in Moscow, the upheavals of 1989, and a putsch against him in the Central Committee, he fell from power on 18 October 1989 after seventeen years in office.

An arrest warrant was issued for Honecker and other East German leaders within a month of the reunification of Germany. In March 1991 Honecker fled to Moscow. Following the failed putsch in Moscow in August 1991, and as he realized that Mikhail Gorbachev's star was waning and that of Boris Yeltsin rising, Honecker took refuge in the Chilean embassy in Moscow – thereby recalling the fact that thousands of Chileans had taken refuge in East Germany following the overthrow of Salvador Allende by General Pinochet in 1973. He remained there for seven months until, following the collapse of the Soviet Union, and thanks to massive pressure from the government of Chancellor Helmut Kohl, he was extradited to Germany on 29 July 1992, where he was imprisoned in the same Moabit prison in Berlin where the Nazis had kept him nearly sixty years previously. A 783-page indictment was drawn up in haste: the former East German leader was fatally ill and time was short.

Since the Berlin Wall had been put up in 1961, at least 200 people had been shot dead trying to escape to the West. The barrier extended through the whole of Germany, cutting the city of Berlin in half but also traversing fields and dividing villages in the country. Named an 'anti-fascist protection barrier' by the Warsaw Pact countries, it was widely perceived in the West as the ultimate symbol of Communist tyranny. The border was patrolled by armed guards, it had automatic shooting devices, and the land along it was mined. Many people felt that this tyranny was itself criminal and that it should therefore be condemned as such in a court of law.

Honecker was prosecuted together with five of his colleagues: Erich Mielke, the head of the Stasi; Willi Stoph, the former prime minister; Heinz Kessler, the former defence minister; Fritz Streletz, the head of the army; and Hans Albrecht, a senior local official whose fiefdom was on the border with West Germany. Of the two hundred killings, the indictment listed sixty-eight known deaths. In order to keep the trial short, twelve of these were selected: four deaths on the wall in Berlin itself and eight along the border in the countryside between East and West Germany.

The indictment was therefore tightly framed in the terms of the ordinary criminal law and not based on vague political accusations. However, even with these self-imposed limitations, the indictment faced considerable judicial obstacles. Honecker was a former head of state (and the other indictees senior ministers of that state), and such people cannot generally be tried by the legal system of another state. This, the customary position in law, which is based on the undeniable fact that the world is divided up into different jurisdictions, has been widely treated with contempt by modern human rights activists. However, it was reaffirmed as a core principle of international law in 2001 by the International Court of Justice in a ruling against Belgium: Belgium had issued an arrest warrant for Abdulaye Yerodia Ndombasi, who had been foreign minister of the Democratic Republic of Congo (Belgium's former colony) at the time when Congolese troops allegedly committed war crimes, but the ICJ instructed Belgium to withdraw the warrant, on the basis that one state does not have the right to try ministers or former ministers of another state. The court ruled that immunity and impunity are not the same thing (although opponents of this view try to confuse these two near homonyms) and that 'immunity' simply expresses the undeniable fact that one state does not have jurisdiction over another.[1]

This principle is itself expressed in Paragraph 20 of the Law on Court Procedure of the Federal Republic of Germany: 'German jurisdiction does not extend to representatives of other states ...' Honecker was indubitably a recognized foreign head of state and not, for instance, a criminal usurper, as the Gaullists had said the Vichy government was, or the mere head of the illegal 'Soviet Occupation Zone' of their country as some anti-Communist West Germans maintained. West and East Germany had recognized each another diplomatically and signed a Basic Treaty in 1972; Honecker had been received in West Germany with full honours on his state visit there in 1987.

The second major jurisdictional problem was posed by the maxim *nulla poena sine lege*. The reunification treaty, signed in 1990, which dissolved the German Democratic Republic and annexed its *Länder* to the Federal Republic, had provided that any prosecutions carried out for acts committed on the territory of the former state while it was in existence had to be brought under the law then in force, that of the GDR.[2] This was to prevent the abuses widely associated with retroactive legislation. It was all very well for some West German jurists to argue after the collapse of East Germany that it had been *im Kern ein Unrechtsstaat* ('at the very core a state without law'[3]), or for the judge in the first trial of the border guards who, in 1989, had shot the last victim of the Berlin Wall, Chris Gueffroy, to say in 1991 that the East German leaders had no legitimacy and that therefore the law of the GDR should not have been obeyed. The fact remained that the Federal Republic itself had formally and solemnly recognized the legal validity of East German laws in Article 9 of the treaty on unification, and had then incorporated them into its own legal system when the two states were united. Moreover, retroactive legislation in general is explicitly forbidden by Article 103, Paragraph 2 of the German Basic Law (the constitution of the Federal Republic of Germany).

The problem, of course, was that the positive law of the GDR had effectively permitted shootings on the border, at least since 1982. The Border Law of that year did allow for people to be shot at if they were trying illegally to cross the border of the GDR, although it did not provide for the mines and automatic shooting devices which had, in fact, killed the majority of those who died trying to cross into West Germany. Paragraph 27 of that law provided for the use of firearms in extreme situations, especially (subsection 2) when a crime was about to be committed. The law also provided that human life should be protected as far as possible and that anyone wounded in a shooting had to be given first aid. The use of firearms on the border was thus governed by law, although the law did not provide for a 'shoot to kill' policy. Even if the border guards had shot people dead, therefore, it seemed that their acts were legal.

Before Honecker came to trial, trials were held of the border guards themselves. The first of these was held in September 1991. It was an emotional event: the proceedings were attended by the mother of the young man for whose killing the guards were being prosecuted.[4] The judges in these initial cases reasoned that the positive law of the GDR at the time of the shootings could not be invoked to excuse what was, by any standards, an immoral act. They argued that states should not shoot their own citizens (a bizarre remark in view of the fact that, in every country in the world, policemen carry guns) and they invoked the writings of Gustav Radbruch, the jurist who had argued that an immoral law was no law at all, repeating in German legalese the old maxim adopted by SS Augustine and Thomas Aquinas, the primary philosophers of natural law.[5] Radbruch's theory had been used to justify the widespread use of retroactive legislation in the war crimes trials and purges conducted at the end of World War II. But, as Uwe Wesel cleverly points out in his excellent account of the Honecker trial, Radbruch himself had held the opposite view in 1932, when he was already a senior law professor aged fifty-three. Then he had written that the judge was duty-bound to stick rigorously to the positive law, even if he had personal moral scruples about it. 'However unjust the law may be in its content, it always fulfils the function of legal certainty in virtue of its existence alone ... We despise the priest who preaches against his conscience but we admire the judge who through his feeling for the law does not let himself be led astray from loyalty to the law.'[6] One can see what he meant: it would be the opposite of the rule of law for judges to refuse to apply laws with which they personally disagree. But given that it had required the planetary cataclysm of World War II and the horrors of Nazism to make an eminent jurist change his mind, by what right did judges punish young border guards for failing to come to Radbruch's postwar conclusions on their own?[7]

Finally, it was not clear what theory of liability to use. The members of the National Defence Council had not killed anyone themselves (although Erich Mielke was also prosecuted by the German authorities for killing a policemen in 1931) and East German law required a far higher level of *mens rea* than West German law to convict a person of murder. Yet the Prosecution decided to charge the members of the National Defence Council as co-perpetrators, the highest possible degree of criminal culpability. They were accused of having played a decisive role in erecting the Berlin Wall and in setting up the border regime of guns and mines: Honecker himself, for instance, had been the principal person in charge of the building of the Berlin Wall in 1961, in his then capacity as secretary for state security of the Central Committee of the Socialist Unity Party. This meant that what had begun as a trial for complicity in murder did become, after all, the trial of one of the greatest and most symbolic political events of the Cold War.

Because Honecker was ill and Willi Stoph had had a heart attack, it was decided to reduce the number of homicide cases further to ten in order to ensure that the trial did not drag on indefinitely. The trial eventually opened at the Criminal Court in Moabit on 12 November 1992, nine days after the Federal Court of Justice had upheld the sentence in the second border guards trial. The judge in that trial had convicted the border guards but only on the basis of existing GDR law (she said that the law allowed them to shoot but not to kill) and she gave them suspended sentences. The leniency of this ruling was a natural curtain-raiser to the trial of the East German leaders, since people had been complaining that only the 'small fish' were being prosecuted for executing the criminal orders of their superiors, the Communist leaders themselves.

The bench was composed of three professional judges and two lay ones. The Prosecution was bolstered by lawyers for the relatives of victims, according to a procedure in German criminal law which allows victims or their relatives to play the role similar to that of appellants in a civil suit. There were 13,000 pages of Prosecution documents, which were handed over to the Defence only shortly before the trial began, leaving them no time to prepare an adequate response. The presiding judge, Hansgeorg Bräutigam, was an avowed anti-Communist who used to write a right-wing column in the *Berliner Morgenpost* under a pseudonym. It is indeed normal for judges in Germany to have a declared and official party political affiliation: indeed, the judge in one of the 1991 trials of border guards had also been a political activist, belonging to an organization which smuggled refugees out of East Germany.[8] When, in Britain, one of the Law Lords hearing General Pinochet's extradition case in 1998 turned out to be on the board of Amnesty International, one of the bodies pressing for the former Chilean president's extradition to Spain, the judge in question had to resign and the case was heard again. But the same rules do not apply in Germany.

The first matter for discussion was Willi Stoph's health. The court instructed that a court doctor examine him and, when it met again the following day, it ruled that he was unfit to stand trial. Immediately thereafter the court also ruled that Erich Mielke should not stand trial since he was facing a parallel trial for shooting a policeman in 1931, and he was too old to face two trials simultaneously. So the number of defendants fell from six to four within two days. The next few days were taken up with formalities until, on the sixth day of proceedings, 3 December 1992, Erich Honecker rose to address the court.[9] The courtroom was full and the public was not to be disappointed: the man who was notorious for his dreary Communist logorrhoea, and who was weak from the liver cancer that was growing every day inside him, sprung unexpectedly into eloquence to make the last and perhaps finest speech of his life. He began by saying,

> I am not going to lend this accusation and this court procedure the appearance of legality by defending myself against the evidently unfounded accusation of manslaughter. A defence is also superfluous because I will not live to hear your verdict. The punishment which you evidently have in mind will never reach me. Everybody knows that today. So for this reason alone any trial against me is a farce. It is political theatre.

Honecker therefore adopted the same strategy as Marshal Pétain and others by refusing the accept the validity of the procedure and by denouncing the trial as politically motivated. But also like so many other former heads of state in his position, including Pétain, he wanted to make a final statement for history. Given that Honecker's lifelong political career had started as it was now ending, in the Moabit prison in Berlin, he spoke with the vigour and vehemence of a man writing his own epitaph. For as Samuel Johnson told Boswell, 'Depend upon it, sir, when a man knows that he is to be hanged in a fortnight, it concentrates his mind wonderfully.'

Honecker began by insisting on the basic legitimacy of the state he had led: the German Democratic Republic, he said, had been recognized by more than a hundred states, it was a member of the UN Security Council, and it had even chaired that body and the UN General Assembly. How could it now be dismissed as 'an illegal state' (*ein Unrechtsstaat*)? He then compared his fate to that of other German Communists and socialists who had also been prosecuted and convicted by successive German states including the Third Reich: Karl Marx, August Bebel (one of the founders of the Social Democratic Party), and Karl Liebknecht. Germany had always put leftists on trial, he said, and the Federal Republic of Germany was no different from Imperial Germany or the Third Reich in this respect. He delivered a good one-liner: 'The Federal Republic is not a state of law (*kein Staat des Rechts*) but instead a state of right-wingers (*ein Staat der Rechten*).'

'This trial is as political as a trial against the political and military leadership of the GDR only can be. Whoever denies this does not err; he lies.' Honecker said that everyone had always known that he, as head of the East German state, was politically responsible for the border regime at the wall. Yet West German politicians had received him with full pomp as a legitimate head of state in 1987. 'There are therefore only two possibilities,' said Honecker. 'Either the politicians of the Federal Republic consciously, freely and even eagerly sought out the company of a murderer, or they now consciously take pleasure in the fact that innocent people are accused of murder.'

Honecker said that the political purpose of his trial was comprehensively to discredit the policy of the state he led and 'to suffocate once again the idea of social justice'. 'We are to be branded as murderers for this purpose,' he said. Honecker complained that a major propaganda campaign had been orchestrated against him: 'The journalist who informs and denounces is highly praised,' he said, 'but no one asks what happens to his victims.'

> I am the last person to be against moral and legal standards by which politicians should be judged or condemned. But three conditions must be fulfilled: the standards must be exactly formulated in advance; they must be equally valid for all politicians; and there must be a court which is above party politics, that is to say a court which is occupied neither by friend nor enemies of the defendant must decide.

This trial, he said, satisfied none of these conditions. He then moved to the allegations themselves. He said that he bore full responsibility for the border regime between East and West. 'This is a heavy responsibility and I will explain shortly why I took it upon myself.' He and his colleagues had always regretted any deaths on the border, both from a human point of view and also because these deaths were extremely damaging politically. Honecker insisted that the decision to erect the Berlin Wall had been taken not by the German Democratic Republic but by the Warsaw Pact countries together, at a meeting in Moscow on 5 August 1961. The decision taken in Germany on 12 August 1961 – the one mentioned in the indictment against him and his colleagues – was only the ratification of this previous earlier resolution. For this reason, Honecker argued, the decision had to be seen in a political context. 'I do not say that to exculpate myself or to shift the responsibility onto others. I say it because that is how it was.'

Honecker maintained that the decision to build the wall had avoided the deaths of thousands or even millions by preventing the outbreak of a war between the Warsaw Pact and NATO. It could not be dissociated from the history of the Europe and the Cold War. He traced the decision's origins to 1933, the year of Hitler's ascent to power, and he made a quick review of German history since that fateful year – rather as Lázsló Bárdossy, the Hungarian collaborationist premier, at his trial in 1945, had started his account with 1919. Honecker recalled that the Communist Party had been banned that year, by all political parties, in virtue of their support for the enabling law (*Ermächtigungsgesetz*) voted after the Reichstag fire and by means of which Hitler seized dictatorial power. He gave a quick account of the subsequent war and Germany's defeat and division and said that the division of Germany was the fault of the Western allies, who had created a currency zone and then the Federal Republic on the territory of their zones. 'The creation of the GDR was a logical consequence of the prior creation of the Federal Republic of Germany.' The GDR, he said, had immediately been subjected to an embargo by the West and to 'non-belligerent aggression' by it, the purpose of which was to isolate the Communist German state, and that this was the policy which led to the building of the wall. Germany lay at the centre of the world's division into two blocks, the West was seeking to extend its influence into the territory of East Germany, tension rose, there was a threat of nuclear war, and the wall was built as the only means of preventing the Western aggression from threatening the GDR's very existence.

Honecker then quoted various West German politicians who agreed that the wall had stabilized and then reduced the tension between the two German states and the two world blocs, and that it had ultimately laid the basis for peaceful coexistence between them. He quoted the conservative Bavarian prime minister, Franz-Josef Strauss, who wrote this in his memoirs and also admitted that NATO had plans to drop an atomic bomb on East Germany. 'In my view,' Honecker said, 'there would have been no Basic Treaty between the two Germanies, no Helsinki process and no unification of Germany if the wall had not been built then, or if it had been torn down before the end of the Cold War.' For this reason, he said, neither he nor his colleagues bore any juridical, moral, or political guilt for having built it.

Honecker also advanced the same argument as that which pro-Nazi collaborators had advanced in their trials after 1944, namely that he had acted to forestall a worse outcome, in this case intervention by the Soviet Union. 'You only have to know what happened in Hungary in 1956 and in Czechoslovakia in 1968. Soviet troops, which were in any case present in the GDR, would have intervened in exactly the same way in 1961. Even in Poland, General Jaruzelski declared martial law in order to prevent such an intervention.' (In April 2007 General Jaruzelski, indeed, was himself indicted by a Polish court for this very decision.)

Honecker also advanced a sort of *tu quoque* defence when he said that many political decisions cost human lives. He mentioned the Vietnam War, the Falklands War, the American invasions of Grenada in 1983 and of Panama in 1989. None of the leaders who took these decisions had ever been put on trial, Honecker said. He then implied that it was extremely difficult to make judgements about political decisions at all: 'I believe that political acts can be judged only by the spirit of their time. If you close your eyes to what happened in the world outside Germany in the years between 1961 and 1989, you cannot reach any just judgement.'

He concluded his speech with a long defence of socialism and an attack on what he said was the illusory democracy of the Federal Republic. He said that this trial was supposed to be the Nuremberg trial of Communism but that the GDR had had no concentration camps, no gas chambers, no Gestapo, and no political death sentences. It had waged war against no one. Yet, he said, the Socialist Unity Party was being treated as if it were one of the 'criminal organizations' defined by Nuremberg, all in an attempt to show that the GDR had been a lawless state. Honecker concluded with a vigorous denunciation of the political motives behind the trial.

> If we are to resume the political character of this trial, it represents the continuation of the Cold War and the rejection of the new thinking ... The world has changed but the German legal system stages political trials as if Wilhelm II were still on the throne. It has overcome its liberal political 'weakness' of 1968 and is now back on good old anti-Communist form. We are said to be blockheads and incapable of reform. But in this trial, it is being demonstrated where the blockheads are in charge and who is incapable of reform. On the outside, people appear extremely malleable, Gorbachev is given the honorary citizenship of Berlin and he is forgiven for the fact that he once praised the border guards by writing in their book of honour [when he visited Berlin in 1986]. But, on the inside, people remain 'as hard as Krupp steel' [an allusion to the old Nazi slogan].

Helmut Kohl had once compared Gorbachev to Goebbels, Honecker said, but that had now all been forgotten: although Gorbachev belonged to the Communist world movement just as much as Honecker did, Gorbachev and Kohl were now on first-name terms. The attack on him was therefore pure hypocrisy. Honecker finished speaking after about one hour and sat down. He said nothing more during the rest of the trial.

The other defendants spoke in their turn in the days that followed. General Fritz Streletz argued firmly that there had been no shoot-to-kill policy and that the number of would-be escapees who were caught was 3600, while fewer than 200 were killed, of whom thirty or forty had been killed by gunshots fired by border guards. He said that mines were a recognized military device and that their presence in the ground at the border was heavily advertised by signs, as the relevant international military conventions require. Heinz Kessler also argued vigorously that there had been no order to shoot would-be escapees.

Otherwise, attention was devoted largely to the chief defendant's failing health. On 21 December, a second arrest warrant was issued against Honecker for alleged corruption: perhaps the Prosecutor feared that his prey would escape him on medical grounds and was trying to gain time. On 23 December, in an extraordinary development, the Defence lodged an appeal against the presiding judge on the grounds of partiality, alleging that he had lied in court. Two days previously, indeed, Judge Bräutigam had come briefly into the courtroom and handed a guidebook to East Berlin to Honecker's Defence lawyers. One of the lay judges on the bench wanted an autograph from the former East German leader. The Defence team acquiesced, and the guidebook was handed to Honecker, who obligingly signed it. After the break, one of the Prosecution counsels asked what the judge had said to the Defence, and Bräutigam replied nervously, 'I gave the Defence something that came in the post. It was totally routine.' The Defence counsels remained silent, but, when later that day, the decision went against them not to suspend the trial, they took their revenge by revealing what in fact the judge had done. Bräutigam, the presiding judge, was forced to resign in this historic trial because he had told a fib.[10]

The rest of the trial proceedings were devoted to arguing whether Honecker could live long enough to see the trial through. On 29 December, the Defence appealed to the constitutional court of the *Land* of Berlin against the decision of the court not to suspend the trial. This constitutional court had only been in existence for a few months (since March 1992) because it had taken that long to create the *Land* of Berlin, pass the relevant law, and elect the judges. Uwe Wesel speculates that the Defence tried their luck with the Berlin court because they reckoned that its judges might be tempted to take a dramatic decision in order to make a name for their new body. If so, they were to be proved spectacularly right.

The appeal was made on the basis that the decision to press on with the trial was a violation of the human dignity of the defendant. As it happens, the constitution of the *Land* of Berlin made no specific reference to human dignity, although that phrase is found in Article 1 of the federal constitution of Germany and in that of many of the other *Länder*. The court announced its decision on 12 January 1993, and of course it was a bombshell: the constitutional court ruled that it was indeed a violation of the human dignity of the defendant to continue a trial whose end he would not live to see. It argued that, even though human dignity was not mentioned in the Berlin constitution, the constitutional court of Berlin nonetheless had the right and duty to protect it, even if that meant overruling other courts in the same jurisdiction who were presumably also trying to respect the same *Land* constitution. The court ruled that the protection of human dignity was 'an unwritten principle' of the Berlin constitution: judges of a court in a state with a written constitution invoked 'unwritten parts' of that constitution because the written parts were deemed insufficient.

In spite of various last-minute counter-appeals by the Prosecution, Erich Honecker was released from prision on 13 January 1993 and he went straight to the airport where he boarded a plane for Santiago in Chile, where his wife and children met him on 14 January. He lived in a suburb of the Chilean capital, his health improved, and he wrote his memoirs.

Meanwhile, the trial of the remaining three defendants, Kessler, Streletz, and Albrecht, lasted a further eight months. One Soviet witness testified that it was the Soviet Union which had decided to build the wall following Khrushchev's failed meeting with Kennedy and the collapse of attempts in 1959 to solve the German question. Walter Ulbricht and Erich Honecker had only been obeying orders from Moscow, just as the border guards had ultimately been obeying orders (or laws) issued by them. Gorbachev was asked to testify about the entry he had written in the border guards' visitors book when he had visited the Berlin Wall in 1986, in which he had praised them for their work; although he was attending the Bayreuth festival in 1993, and was therefore in Germany and therefore presumably available to testify, he declined to come. Evidence was heard about mines and the unanimous view was that a state has the right to protect its border with mines. On 16 September 1993 the verdict was handed down: Kessler got seven and a half years, Streletz five and a half, and Albrecht four and a half. The judge ruled that there had been no direct order to shoot, in the sense that the Prosecution had argued, but that of course the practice was at least tolerated. He ruled that the GDR was by no means independent from Moscow, but that it did have some room for manoeuvre, especially on this issue. The grandest trial of a Communist regime to date ended with the release of the most important defendant and symbolic sentences for his most senior colleagues. Honecker did live to see the end of the trial from which he escaped; he died in Chile in 1994.

16   Jean Kambanda, Convicted without Trial

On 6 April 1994 an aircraft carrying the presidents of Rwanda and Burundi, the chief of staff of the Rwandan army, and other senior Rwandan and Burundi officials, was shot down as it came into land at Kigali airport. All the passengers and three French crew were killed. By common consent, it was this event which triggered what has become known as the Rwandan genocide, a three-month massacre in which hundreds of thousands of people, mainly ethnic Tutsis, were murdered, often with machetes. The fighting ended with the victory of the Tutsi-dominated Rwanda Patriotic Front (RPF), which managed to overthrow the Hutu government in July and has remained in power ever since.

The Rwandan genocide has become the defining event in the canon of modern military and judicial interventionism. It inspired – and continues to inspire – huge revulsion, as hundreds of thousands of men, women, and children were hacked to death. A number of Hollywood feature films have been made about it (in contrast to the roughly contemporaneous events in Bosnia, which have generated no equivalent entertainment). The few months between the shooting down of the plane in April and the RPF victory in mid-July 1994 have been elevated to the supreme reference point for the two main claims of the interventionists: first, that the West stood idly by while the killing took place (there were UN soldiers in Rwanda at the time and yet they did not stop the killing) and that, therefore, it should instead intervene in other places in the future; and second, that the immunity customarily given to heads of state should, like state sovereignty itself, be cast aside in favour of the superior commands of universal morality so that the people responsible for organizing such atrocities can be put on trial as war criminals.

Rwanda is a small state in East Africa which, like many other countries on that continent, has been beset by ethnic problems which are partly inherited from the age of colonialism. Until 1961 Rwanda was governed by first Germany and then Belgium via a Tutsi monarchy and aristocracy ruling over a huge Hutu majority. When the monarchy was overthrown, in a classic democratic postcolonial revolution, many Tutsis fled, fearing repression by the new majority in power. Throughout the 1960s and 1970s Tutsi guerrillas attempted to wreak revenge by terrorizing the population, attacking at night and killing civilians. Hutus accused Tutsis of wanting to re-establish the monarchy and their servitude under it.

In addition to its own basic internal instability, Rwanda is prey to larger geopolitical forces outside its territory, especially since its indigenous ethnic groups also live in the neighbouring states of Burundi, Uganda, and Congo (the former Zaire). In the 1990s those larger geopolitical forces included the push by the United States to increase its influence in the Great Lakes region, including at the expense of France; this was one of the factors behind the wars in Congo, which cost three million lives. Finally, there was also an ideological aspect to the conflict in Rwanda: the RPF, led by General Paul Kagame (now president of Rwanda), was essentially an outgrowth of the Maoist guerrillas in neighbouring Uganda who had fought to bring President Museveni to power there in 1986. By contrast, many of the Hutu leaders from whom Kagame seized power in July 1994 were devout Catholics. For instance, Jean Kambanda – the focus of this chapter, since he was prime minister of Rwanda during the genocide, and who made international humanitarian law history in 1998 when he became the first head of government to be convicted of genocide by an international tribunal – is a daily communicant, while the late President Juvénal Habyarimana (the one killed in the plane crash), had been introduced to charismatic Catholicism by the extremely devout late Belgian royal couple, King Baudouin and Queen Fabiola, and they used to pray together whenever they met.[1]

In 1990 the RPF, most of whose leaders were officers in the Ugandan army, invaded Rwanda with Uganda's backing. Kagame himself was chief of Ugandan military intelligence at that time, having been trained in the United States at Fort Leavenworth in Kansas. Some have speculated that the United States encouraged the invasion, President Habyarimana having refused to toe a pro-American line in foreign policy. The invasion was also partly directed at Congo (Zaire) to the west of Rwanda, and at seizing control of its vast natural resources, especially diamonds and coltan (a metallic ore used in mobile phones and DVD players). Following the events of 1994, indeed, the new American-backed Tutsi Rwandan army did take part in the invasion of Congo, together with Ugandan forces, an invasion which represented the beginning of the First Congo War of 1996–7 and which led directly to the overthrow President Mobutu of Zaire and to the installation of Laurent Kabila in his place.

After the 1990 RPF-Ugandan invasion of Rwanda (to which the world paid little attention, since it was more interested in the contemporaneous Iraqi invasion of Kuwait), there followed four years of violence and insurrection. The RPF forces used classic Maoist guerrilla tactics, roaming in and out of Uganda and driving huge numbers of Hutus out of the territory they seized. The resulting conflict eventually caused President Habyarimana to seek peace by signing the internationally backed Arusha Accords in August 1993. These accords provided for the RPF rebels to be included in the government, together with other political parties. Shortly after they were signed, however, the (also Hutu) president of neighbouring Burundi, Melchior Ndadaye, was assassinated in October 1993 by Tutsis in the army of Burundi, after only three months in office, and this caused hundreds of thousands of Hutus from Burundi to flee into Rwanda.

In spite of the signature of the Arusha Accords, RPF attacks continued in the first four months of 1994. UN troops had been despatched in late 1993; as in Bosnia, the worst killings in Rwanda occurred on the UN's watch. But it was on return from a meeting in Tanzania to discuss the implementation of the accords that two presidents (the recently appointed President Cyprien Ntaryamira of Burundi was, like Habyarimana, a Hutu) and the Rwandan chief of staff were killed when their plane was shot down. The RPF blamed Rwandan Hutu extremists for murdering their own president in order to sideline him and to have a pretext for committing genocide against the Tutsis (the Tutsis had been alleging Hutu 'genocide' against them since 1961), while the Hutus blamed the RPF and the Tutsis.

Whatever the truth, the killing sparked off was on a huge scale. It is not known how many people died and it is not known what percentage of Hutus and Tutsis were killed. One figure which has gained currency is 800,000 killed but even the human rights activists who advance this figure say that they do not know the real tally. Certainly such a figure is enormous; for comparison the highest rate of deportation to Auschwitz which the Nazis achieved was 400,000 from Hungary in two months in 1944. Others claim that 200,000 or so were killed between 6 April 1994 and mid-July 1994 when the RPF seized the Rwandan capital, Kigali. Whatever the truth, these are huge figures, especially considering that the method of killing was primitive rather than industrial. But the resulting claim of genocide, however plausible, has been politically exploited by the RPF Tutsi government to justify its return to the situation which prevailed before the referendum against the monarchy in 1961: Rwanda is now once again governed exclusively by the Tutsi minority, although this time with heavy backing from the United States rather than Belgium.

As a result of the outrage at the killing, the UN Security Council created the International Criminal Tribunal for Rwanda (ICTR), by means of Security Council Resolution No. 955 on 8 November 1994. Like its sister tribunal, the International Criminal Tribunal for the former Yugoslavia (ICTY), the ICTR was therefore not established by law, a violation of a key legal principle outlined in nearly all authoritative international documents on human rights (e.g. Article 14 of the 1966 United Nations Covenant on Civil and Political Rights, Article 6 of the European Convention on Human Rights). The purpose of this prohibition is to prevent the creation of *ad hoc* tribunals to prosecute specific people. In its 2003 report on the trial of the 'Grenada 17' – the sixteen men and one woman including the former prime minister of Grenada, Bernard Coard, who were sentenced to death (commuted to life imprisonment) in 1986 for murdering Coard's predecessor, Maurice Bishop, in 1983 – Amnesty International denounced that trial as an act of political vengeance conducted under pressure by the Americans who had invaded Grenada in 1983 to overthrow a Marxist government there. Amnesty stressed the inherent illegality of ad hoc tribunals.[2] Today, by contrast, one does not hear the same criticism of the more recently created international tribunals which are just as ad hoc as the ones which convicted Coard. On the contrary: when the trial of Charles Taylor, the former president of Liberia, opened on 4 June 2007 in a specially constituted branch at The Hague of the UN-backed 'Special Court for Sierra Leone' – today's supporters of such trials do not blush to call their courts 'special' – Amnesty 'welcomed' the fact that he was on trial, and exhorted the Special Court to broadcast the trial for maximum educative effect back home.[3]

The normal and constitutionally correct method for establishing an international criminal tribunal would have been for a treaty to be submitted to ratification. This was done when the International Criminal Court (ICC) was created in 1998. Even though the United Nations lawyers fully understood the constitutional implications of what they were doing when they created the ICTY and the ICTR,[4] they decided to create these tribunals by executive fiat for reasons of pure political expediency. They knew that the ratification process would be slow and that it would probably fail thanks to resistance by the states concerned (especially in the case of Yugoslavia). Given that both these tribunals are international, and that the judges on their benches come from all over the world – embodying the principle that 'the peoples of the world' are sitting in judgement over those who flout the basic principles of humanity – these tribunals also bear a constitutional and ideological resemblance to those *ad hoc* 'people's tribunals' which Communists used to purge postwar Europe, also in the name of that nebulous concept, 'the people'.

The Charter of the ICTR gives the court temporally limited jurisdiction, namely the period 1 January to 31 December 1994. This means that few acts committed by the RPF and Tutsis, for instance massacres of Hutu refugees in Congo when Rwanda invaded Zaire in 1996, can be adjudicated. Indeed, no one from the RPF and no Tutsi has ever been prosecuted by the tribunal: all the defendants are from the defeated regime, even though the RPF undoubtedly also committed atrocities when it seized power. Rather as at Nuremberg, which limited aggressive war to that committed by the Axis, the genocide referred to in the indictment is only the genocide of Tutsis by Hutus, not genocide in general: the Commission of Experts which reported to the UN general secretary in 1994, and whose report was used as the basis for the creation of the ICTR, said that there was overwhelming evidence that genocide had been committed against the Tutsis, but none for genocide against Hutus.[5] So one side was proclaimed guilty as charged even before the tribunal was created, and that proclamation of guilt became one of the founding documents of the tribunal.

Because the ICTR prosecutes only Hutus, it is a clear example of victors' justice. Just as the Yugoslavia war crimes tribunal refused to open an investigation into whether NATO had committed war crimes in Yugoslavia in 1999 for fear that information from NATO sources to the prosecutor's office would dry up immediately, so Kigali made it absolutely clear to the ICTR prosecutors that the supply of witnesses and information from Rwanda would dry up immediately if there was so much as a hint of any impending prosecutions against members of the RPF. It is for this reason that one of the most prominent expert witnesses who used to work with the Office of the Prosecutor, Professor Filip Reyntjens of the University of Antwerp, wrote in 2005 that he was refusing to do so any more: there was, he said,

> compelling evidence on a number of massacres committed by the RPF in 1994. These crimes fall squarely within the mandate of the ICTR, they are well documented, testimonial and material proof is available, and the identity of RPF suspects is known. If they are left unprosecuted, the ICTR will have failed to eliminate one of the root causes of genocide and other crimes – impunity. Indeed, it is precisely because the regime in Kigali has been given a sense of impunity that, during the years following 1994, it has committed massive internationally recognised crimes in both Rwanda and the DRC. Article 6(2) of the Statute explicitly rules out immunity, including for Heads of state or government or for responsible government officials.

This principle is contravened when, as is currently the case, a message is sent out that those in power need not fear prosecution. In addition, by meting out victors' justice, the ICTR fails to meet another stated objective, namely to 'contribute to the process of national reconciliation and the restoration and maintenance of peace'.[6]

This structural presumption of guilt was reinforced in June 2006 when the Appeals Chamber of the ICTR instructed the Trial Chamber to 'take judicial notice' of the 'fact of genocide'.[7] To take judicial notice of something is a device in legal procedure by which the need for proof is waived when the facts in question are uncontested and uncontroversial, and usually when they do not bear on the matter in hand. Examples of the kinds of things of which judicial notice can be taken include the location of a place or the day of the week on which a certain date falls. When judicial notice is taken of a fact, it means that that fact can no longer be disputed in court.

To instruct the Trial Chamber to take judicial notice of the fact of genocide, however, is to remove from defendants the right to plead that genocide did not occur. The Prosecution case is that the Hutu Rwandan government planned, instigated and carried it out. If it turns out that what occurred was not genocide but mob violence, then obviously there can be no convictions for genocide. Genocide is widely regarded as a crime committed only by states.[8] Three of the five acts defined as genocide in the ICTR's own statute can only be committed by organizations wielding state power or claiming to. Moreover, the ICTR's statute, like the other relevant international humanitarian law documents including above all the Genocide Convention of 1948, stipulates that genocide means acts committed 'with intent to destroy, in whole or in part, a national, ethnical, racial or religious group': the *mens rea* or guilty intent is crucial. In order to prove command responsibility on the part of people who were not actual perpetrators, therefore, it would be necessary, first to show that genocide was committed and then to show that the non-perpetrator defendants were guilty of complicity in it or of conspiracy to commit and organize it. Genocide allows the prosecutorial net to be cast very widely, for instance to prosecute people for allegedly instigating it through the media or, in one case, through pop songs, but such prosecutions become futile if there was no genocide. By contrast, if it is assumed that genocide did occur, then it follows (as a matter of law) that someone must have planned it, or that other non-perpetrators bear criminal liability for it according to the various forms of liability for genocide listed in Article 2(3) of the ICTR statute.

The political nature of this ruling was admitted when the ICTR itself said that it would 'put the occurrence of the genocide beyond legal dispute' because it meant that genocide should be taken 'as established beyond any dispute and not requiring any proof'. The ruling, it said, would 'silence the "rejectionist" camp which has been disputing the occurrence of genocide' and relieve the Office of the Prosecutor 'of a substantial burden of proof'. Henceforth, the role of each trial would only be to establish 'the personal involvement of the accused person in genocide'.[9] The similarity with the Riom trial was striking, of which Marshal Pétain said the function was only to establish the appropriate sentence for the pre-established guilt.

The decision smacked of desperation. Perhaps it was an indication that the Prosecution case was precisely having difficulty proving its original claims. The Prosecution initially alleged that President Habyarimana's regime had had genocidal plans as early as 1990, and that it was merely waiting for the pretext to implement them. Somewhat inconsistently, it also argued, at least in the early trials, that Habyarimana's murderers killed him in order to get him out of the way so as to enable the genocide to happen. However, both these (contradictory) theories have been progressively abandoned in Prosecution arguments, as it becomes more difficult to pin the blame for the shooting down of the plane on Hutus.

In 1997, indeed, the ICTR's investigations into the event were abruptly terminated. The UN investigator, the Australian Michael Hourigan, has alleged that this happened when it became clear that the finger pointed not at the Hutus but at Paul Kagame, the former Tutsi rebel leader and now president of Rwanda.[10] This claim has also been made by a French investigating magistrate, Jean-Louis Brugière, acting for the families of the deceased French citizens. In November 2006 Brugière issued an international arrest warrant for nine senior Rwandan officials: the sixty-four-page warrant is a highly detailed and damning indictment of Kagame's role in precipitating the crisis in Rwanda.[11] It is only because French law prohibits arrest warrants against serving heads of state that Kagame's name itself is not on the list of indictees. But Brugière has accused Kagame of obstructing all investigations into the shooting, and also alleges that the CIA is the author of the original 'disinformation' that the plane was shot down by Hutus, which he describes as 'political' and 'intended to discredit France'. Brugière's arrest warrant was signed on 17 November 2006 and Rwanda broke off diplomatic relations with France within a week.[12]

The reason why the responsibility for the shooting down of the plane is so important is that, if it is demonstrated that the order was in fact given by the Tutsis, then the theory of a pre-planned genocide, central to the original charge against the Hutus, collapses. More generally, the question of responsibility for the shooting down of the plane occupies the same position in the legal reasoning (of both the Prosecution and the Defence) as did the charges for starting the war made against the Kaiser in 1918 and the Nazis and the Japanese after 1945, who were indicted for the crime of aggression or of violating the sanctity of international treaties, i.e. for starting those conflicts.

By the same token, only if the attacks were 'widespread and systematic' can they constitute 'crimes against humanity'; if they were spontaneous and inchoate, then convictions cannot be obtained for crimes against humanity. Worse, the ICTR itself has an institutional self-interest in proving these graver 'international' crimes because if the killings were simply 'ordinary' war crimes, committed by ordinary people, then there would be little or no legal justification for the existence of an international tribunal at all. The centrality of 'genocide' to the ICTR's *raison d'être* is emphasized by the fact that it is the first crime listed in the tribunal's charter, before all the others, whereas in the ICTY it is the third (after grave breaches of the Geneva Conventions and War Crimes).

To these fundamental problems of ideological prejudice must be added the procedural weaknesses which are the hallmark of the ICTR, even more so than of the sister tribunal for Yugoslavia in The Hague.[13] The rules of procedure at both the ICTY and the ICTR are heavily stacked against the Defence. The Prosecution is structurally part of both tribunals (together with the judges and the registrar) while the Defence is outside it. Indeed, the full title of the ICTR is 'International Criminal Tribunal for *the Prosecution of Persons Responsible* for Genocide and Other Serious Violations of International Humanitarian Law Committed in the Territory of Rwanda', not 'for the *trial* of persons *accused* of … etc.', The ICTR is prosecutorial in its very essence.

Perhaps the most obvious erosion of defendants' rights is the length of the trials. The trial of the man alleged to be the main ringleader of the genocide, Théoneste Bagosora, started when he was arrested in 1996, yet the Prosecution did not deliver its closing submissions until over ten years later, on 1 June 2007. The trial is not expected to end until 2008, twelve years after his arrest. Other defendants have been in detention for similar periods of time. Such periods of detention are simply incompatible with the presumption of innocence, or with the right to a swift trial.

Secondly, there is very heavy reliance on 'expert witnesses'. 'Expert witnesses' are people who have not, in fact, witnessed anything but who present themselves as experts about the events in question. This is an abuse of the process of cross-examination, the purpose of which is to test forensically whether or not a defendant's testimony is reliable. Expert witnesses are typically Europeans or Americans who regard themselves as activists fighting for a cause, but who were many thousands of miles away when the events occurred. Their opinions should have no probative value whatever in establishing whether or not a crime was committed.

In addition to expert witnesses, the ICTR (again like the ICTY) relies heavily on anonymous witnesses. This infringes one of the most basic rights of a defendant in a criminal trial, the right to cross-examine witnesses for the Prosecution. If the defendant does not know who the witness is, then it is very difficult to establish his credibility. Worse, in the ICTR, the same people have testified anonymously on repeated occasions in different trials, with different code names on each occasion, sometimes giving different or even conflicting evidence about the same events. The Defence has no way of knowing that this is taking place, precisely because the identity of these witnesses is hidden. The difficulty of knowing what has been said in trials is also aggravated by the widespread use of *in camera* sessions, in which what has been said in court is simply secret. Defence lawyers suspect that such anonymous witnesses are simply paid agents of the Rwandan government who travel to Arusha in Tanzania (where the ICTR is located) to spin whatever yarns they are required to spin for the purposes of a particular trial. The justification for this widespread use of anonymity is that Prosecution witnesses are said to be in danger of their lives, but in fact it is Defence witnesses who are more at risk: six of them have been killed shortly after giving testimony.

Much of the ICTR's procedural laxity was laid down in the first judgement, that against Jean-Paul Akayesu, a schools inspector and mayor found guilty on nine counts including genocide and crimes against humanity. The ICTR ruled then that no corroboration was needed for allegations of rape; that hearsay evidence is admissible; that it does not matter if witnesses' written statements differ from their testimony in court; and that inconsistencies in witness testimony can be explained by trauma (but that it can still be used to convict people).[14] The reasoning, therefore, is fatally circular: if a Prosecution witness's testimony is contradictory, this is adduced as evidence that he or she was a victim. Inconsistency becomes proof of credibility rather than a sign of unreliability. The very fact that the ICTR has a 'Witness *and Victim* Protection Unit' shows that the institutional assumption is that witnesses are by definition victims, an assumption which is incompatible with the presumption of innocence of the defendant.

Last but not least, there are surreal problems of translation which reflect huge cultural differences between the Western-backed law of the ICTR and the state of Rwandan society. Many concepts at the heart of the Prosecution case simply do not exist in the Rwandan language, Kinyarwanda. The Kinyawanda term for the RPF army is a vague and imprecise historical term; there is no distinction in the language between rape and consensual sex; and there is no distinction between an accomplice and a supporter. A large part of the Prosecution case turned on the fact that the Hutus referred to the Tutsis as 'cockroaches', although it was not always clear that the Kinyarwanda word, 'inyenzi', actually meant this or whether it had the same repulsive connotations as in European languages. (The term was sometimes used by the rebels themselves, because they came out at night, while 'inyenzi' was also a merely derogatory form of 'Inkotanyi', a word referring to a nineteenth-century tribe.) Finally, as the Akayesu judgement itself noted but was happy to ignore, the African tradition makes little or no distinction between events which a person has actually witnessed himself and events of which he has only heard speak.

Although the Prosecution alleges that the main ringleader of the genocide was Colonel Théoneste Bagosora, who helped form the provisional government after the assassination of President Habyarimana, the man who in fact became prime minister following the assassination was Jean Kambanda, who in 1998 pleaded guilty to genocide and was sentenced to life. Kambanda thus made history – and delighted international humanitarian law activists – by becoming the first person ever to be convicted of genocide, the supreme international crime, by an international tribunal, since the ratification of the UN Convention on Genocide in 1948. Since he was a head of government, his conviction is said to herald a milestone in the fight against sovereign immunity and therefore a major victory in the ICTR's own struggle for self-justification.

On closer inspection, the story is more complicated. Kambanda was originally arrested on 18 July 1996 in Kenya (in a spectacular round-up of suspects who included one case of mistaken identity[15]). Nearly two years later, and after having been held in Dodoma, away from the other defendants, Kambanda appeared before the Trial Chamber on 1 May 1998 and pleaded guilty to all six counts against him: genocide, conspiracy to commit genocide, direct and public incitement to commit genocide, complicity in genocide, and crimes against humanity for murder and extermination. Because of the guilty plea, there was no trial and no legal examination of the charges themselves. A hearing was held on 3 September 1998 and the following day Kambanda was sentenced to life imprisonment.

The text of a 'Plea Agreement between Jean Kambanda and the OTP [Office of the Prosecutor]' was published in the sentencing and judgement decision of 4 September 1998.[16] The agreement contained admissions of guilt by omission and of guilt by association but at no point did Kambanda admit that he ordered genocide or that he was party to a deliberate conspiracy to commit it. Three days after his sentence, Kambanda announced that he was appealing. On 11 September, he wrote a five-page letter revoking his guilty plea, and denouncing the tribunal and the way it operated. He complained that his family had not received protection, as he said he had been promised by his lawyer, Oliver Michael Inglis, and that he had in any case not instructed this court-imposed lawyer. 'I do not recognize Maître Inglis as having been my lawyer or as able to be it in the future. At best, he has been working for the Prosecution.'[17] It was indeed the case that Inglis had known the prosecutor, his compatriot from Cameroon, for thirty years and that they had previously worked for the same law practice.

In other words, Kambanda denied that he had meant it when he pleaded guilty. Maybe he had acted under duress, hoping to obtain protection for his wife and children in return for cooperation with the prosecutor, or fearful that they would come to harm if he did not cooperate. He may not have cared what he signed; Kambanda had a drink problem and he was plied with booze by the investigators while in Dodoma. Alternatively, Kambanda or the lawyer may have gambled with the plea bargain for rational reasons. Only a few weeks before the agreement was signed on 28 April 1998, Dražen Erdemović had pleaded guilty at the ICTY on 5 March 1998 to killing over a hundred people personally. He too had agreed to cooperate with the prosecutor. Erdemović was sentenced to five years in prison, an astonishingly light sentence given that he had himself committed mass murder. He has since appeared as a Prosecution witness in numerous ICTY cases, including the trial of Slobodan Milošević.[18] If Kambanda knew about this sentence, he may have thought he could expect the same leniency. As the first defendant at the ICTR to be sentenced, he could not have known that the sentences handed down at Arusha were to be far harsher than those at The Hague.

It later transpired that, during the period of his detention in Dodoma, Kambanda had repeatedly asked to see his family and his own lawyer, the Belgian Johan Scheers (who had also been Habyarimana's lawyer). He was given assurances on both counts. In fact, his contacts with Scheers were restricted to a phone conversation in the company of the Quebec police inspector who was de-briefing him. When he was finally brought to Arusha, a lawyer was assigned to him with whom he had never previously spoken, Inglis. He repeatedly asked about his family and Scheers and asked to be able to put his side of the story. According to his later version of events, Kambanda signed what Inglis asked him to sign on the basis that there would be later hearings in the presence of Scheers.

Following his life sentence, Kambanda formally requested that Johan Scheers represent him for his appeal. On 5 October this request was denied. The justification was that there had been a dispute between Scheers and the registrar (he had been Defence counsel for Akayesu and there had been an argument over fees). On 9 October Kambanda again demanded that Scheers represent him; this was again rejected and Kambanda was forced to pick a Dutch lawyer instead. The matter dragged on for another year until the new counsel, Tjarda Eduard van der Spoel, submitted further grounds for appeal on 24 November 1999. He alleged that the Trial Chamber had erred in law by not examining whether the guilty plea had been obtained under duress. Kambanda said he wanted the verdict overturned and a proper trial. The counsel added that Kambanda had been illegally detained at Dodoma, rather than at Arusha, and that he had not been represented by the lawyer of his choice.

It took another six months for the Appeals Chamber to come to Arusha from The Hague to hear Kambanda's case. The hearing was held on 27 June 2000. Kambanda told the court that he had agreed to enter a guilty plea under duress. He deplored the fact that the authors of massacres against Hutus were going unpunished and that the tribunal refused to recognize the international nature of the Rwanda conflict, treating it entirely as an internal civil war. He said that he had signed the guilty plea only on the basis that it would lead to a trial with the lawyer he wanted, Scheers. 'Maybe if I had had a lawyer worthy of the name, he would have advised me not to sign the documents. I never felt myself bound by those documents, they were documents produced by the prosecutor for the prosecutor.' He repeated that he was ready to cooperate with the tribunal and the prosecutor 'in order that the whole truth of the Rwandan affair be known'. He said, 'Since the very beginning, I have said that I feel politically responsible and that I wanted to explain why there were so many deaths in Rwanda. I was prime minister during the genocide, whence my political responsibility, and it is that I am talking about.' He said that there had been 'millions of deaths on both sides in the Rwanda conflict' but that he was not at the origin of what happened.

His pleas were in vain. Following counter-arguments by the prosecutor, Carla del Ponte, who said that she was satisfied by what Kambanda had said on appeal that the verdict and sentence should be upheld, the Appeals Chamber ruled on 19 October 2000 that the appeal should indeed be rejected. The Appeals Chamber made a very cursory review of whether the 'confession' had been made voluntarily and it found that it had been, without testing the evidence or even taking the defendant's protests on board at all. So the landmark conviction of a former head of government for genocide by an international tribunal – a conviction which was itself used to obtain guilty verdicts in subsequent trials – was in fact made on a rather confused man who immediately rescinded his guilty plea, on the basis that it had been made under duress, out of concern for his family's safety, and following bad advice from a lawyer who was an old friend of the prosecutor and whom he had not instructed.

As one commentator writes, the judges knew that Kambanda's appeal came at a politically difficult time. The RPF government of Kigali was refusing to cooperate with the ICTR on another case (Barayagwiza), and there was felt to be popular resentment in Rwanda against the UN, of which the ICTR is a part, and whose soldiers had been in Rwanda during the genocide. Because Kambanda had been the head of the government during those events, his name and face had become a symbol of them. It was politically impossible for the sentence to be overturned. 'In order to preserve and strengthen the ties between the ICTR and the government of Rwanda ... the Court needed a sacrifice. Like Isaac, blood needed to be spilled in order to preserve what justice was left.'[19]

Three years later, Kambanda, by then a lifer doing time in Mali, sent a formal affidavit to the Defence team in the 'Military II' trial (where the defendants are the former army chief of staff, the gendarmerie chief of staff and two other junior officers) in which he recalled that the massacres started as soon as the plane was shot down and the president killed on 6 April 1994. By the time he was appointed prime minister (as a result of intervention by the UN representative and the American ambassador) the massacres had been going on for three days. 'In virtue of the fact that the massacres had been going on for three days,' he wrote,

> it is impossible that the government I led could have planned them. Its members had nothing in common ideologically ... all planning between the parties was impossible. At no point, during my time in office as prime minister, did I have any knowledge of the conception of any plan for these massacres, neither before nor after the assassination of President Habyarimana. I would have known about this since I had the Central Intelligence Service under my supervision. Without the assassination of President Habyarimana, interethnic massacres on this scale would definitely not have taken place. It is therefore essential to find those responsible for that attack and he or they must be held responsible for the consequences of their crime.[20]

Three years later, Kambanda was called as a witness in the mammoth trial of Théoneste Bagosora and he eventually got a chance to tell his story in court. But by then it was too late. He said this:

> The events that took place in my country were so serious and so difficult to understand that as a former prime minister, I had the duty to explain

them and politically assume that responsibility. That is what I recognize. I did not perpetrate any crimes. I did not send anybody to kill anybody. But I was an authority. I had a duty to protect all my people, all the segments of the population: Tutsis, Hutus, and Twas. I did not succeed in doing this, in spite of my efforts which are unfortunately not recognized, and that is why I have taken on this responsibility to explain what I saw that other people did not see or do not want to see.

I am not one of those who deny the genocide of the Tutsis. Obviously, I am not a legal expert to give you a definition of what is meant by genocide. But during the period between April and July 1994, I saw that people … were hunted down and killed for what they were, specifically, because they were Tutsis. There were men, women, children, young people, and old people who were killed. I am not a legal expert, but I believe that that is genocide.

Unfortunately, Mr President, during the same period and under the same circumstances, I saw that people from the Hutu ethnic group were massacred because they were Hutus. Men, women, elderly people, young people and children were killed. They were hunted down and killed. If the first was a genocide, then the second was too. So I believe there was a double genocide in Rwanda: genocide of the Hutus, and genocide of the Tutsis. Now, the question that arises is who perpetrated these genocides, and I have answers for that.

Regarding the genocide of the Hutus, this is easy to demonstrate. It's much easier because one does not need a lot of information to know that the genocide of the Hutus was committed by the current president of Rwanda, his regime, his army, his militia. I have evidence which has been forwarded to you, Mr President. [21]

17 Kosovo and the New World Order: the Trial of Slobodan Milošević

Like Jean Kambanda's conviction for genocide in 1998, the accusation published the following year (on 27 May 1999) against the president of the Federal Republic of Yugoslavia, Slobodan Milošević, by the International Criminal Tribunal for the former Yugoslavia (ICTY), made legal history. As supporters of international humanitarian law and judicial and military interventionism enthusiastically pointed out, this was the first time that an indictment had been issued against a sitting head of state by an international tribunal. In fact, of course, Marshal Pétain and Vidkun Quisling had also been indicted while in office, albeit by national authorities.

Slobodan Milošević was indicted at the height of the seventy-four-day bombing campaign (25 March 1999 to 4 June 1999) by NATO, the world's most powerful military alliance. He had become a hate figure in the West by that time, blamed for all the Balkans' woes and accused of being a nationalist, a racist, and a determined war criminal. Like the indictment, the 1999 NATO bombing campaign was itself legally novel. The postwar international system, created out of the ruins of World War II, was based on the 'Nuremberg principles' that starting a war is the supreme international crime, and on the concomitant principles of the sovereign equality of states and the rule against intervention in the internal affairs of other countries. NATO's attack on Yugoslavia was precisely intended to overthrow these rules and replace them with new principles which would permit what had previously been solemnly forbidden. Whereas the Nuremberg judges had ruled that, 'War is an essentially evil thing',[1] now the NATO powers were determined to show that it could instead be the instrument of the highest morality, and rightfully deployed against states committing human rights abuses. So completely was NATO convinced of the morality of its war, indeed, that its supreme commander, General Wesley Clark of the United States, attributed to it divine qualities, when he said that for Slobodan Milošević, the vast air power being deployed against him 'must be like fighting God'.[2]

Various Western leaders spoke eloquently about the innovatory quality of the NATO war against Yugoslavia. The Czech president, Václav Havel, said, 'This war places human rights above the rights of the state.'[3] The British prime minister, Tony Blair, said that 'twenty years ago' there would have been no intervention over Kosovo but that the world had changed and the international system needed to change with it. 'Globalisation has transformed our economies and our working practices,' he said. 'But globalisation is not just economic. It is also a political and security phenomenon ... On the eve of a new Millennium we are now in a new world. We need new rules for international co-operation and new ways of organising our international institutions.' He went on, 'The most pressing foreign policy problem we face is to identify the circumstances in which we should get actively involved in other people's conflicts ... The principle of non-interference must be qualified in important respects.'[4] This was in fact none other than the doctrine of interventionism which others had formulated long before Blair[5] and it became the hallmark of his term in office.[6] Two days later, NATO incorporated the new doctrine into its 'New Strategic Concept' promulgated in Washington on 24 April 1999; according to this, the alliance's old policy of only defending the sovereignty and security of its member states from external attack was jettisoned in favour of a new self-given right to intervene all over the world.

The war was waged ostensibly in support of the ethnic Albanian population of the southern Serb province of Kosovo, which was said to be suffering persecution at the hands of the Yugoslav authorities. Following an alleged massacre of Albanians in the village of Račak in January 1999, the Americans brought the Yugoslavs and Kosovars together at Rambouillet, south of Paris, in February 1999. At that meeting, NATO issued an ultimatum to Yugoslavia, demanding a radical constitutional change (autonomy for Kosovo) and the right for NATO troops to occupy the entire territory of Yugoslavia.[7] It was an ultimatum designed to be rejected as unacceptable, and it was. The Yugoslav parliament voted against the country's proposed occupation by NATO on 23 March 1999, and the bombing started the following night.

Three days after the bombing started, people started to arrive in large numbers at the borders between Yugoslavia and Macedonia and Albania. The propaganda value of their arrival was enormous: it allowed NATO to claim that Yugoslavia was trying to expel all its ethnic Albanian citizens in a vast programme of racial persecution. Indeed, the official line soon became that the NATO attack had started *in response* to the arrival of the refugees, whereas in fact it was the other way round.[8] Soon, camps in Macedonia and Albania were full of hundreds of thousands of refugees, and the world was horrified by the stories they told. No story seemed too ghoulish to be believed, and atrocity reporting spread like wildfire in the world's media. A sense of hysteria gathered momentum as public opinion was whipped up against the Serbs in general and Milošević in particular, and a lynch-mob mentality was created by NATO's war propaganda, which was intense. Comparisons with the Nazis abounded. The British prime minister, Tony Blair, wrote, 'It is no exaggeration to say what is happening in Kosovo is racial genocide.'[9] In April 1999 the United States ambassador for war crimes, David Scheffer, said he thought 100,000 Albanians had been killed,[10] and the American defense secretary, William Cohen, repeated this figure the following month.[11] It was widely claimed that Serbia was committing mass murder on a scale not seen in Europe since World War II.

It soon turned out, however, that these claims were exaggerated. When the ICTY's own forensic investigators travelled to Kosovo in the summer of 1999, they discovered that the body count fell massively short of the hecatombs they had been promised. In most cases of alleged 'mass grave' sites, there were no bodies at all while, in the cases where people had been killed, the numbers were a fraction of what had been claimed. Some of the most lurid stories, such as that the Serbs had been burning the bodies of dead Albanians in the furnaces at the mining complex at Trepča, which deceived self-appointed Balkan experts at the time,[12] turned out to be complete fabrications.[13] The total death toll turned out to be about 500, not including the several hundred Serb and Albanian civilians whom NATO had killed with its bombs. This author was the first journalist to reveal the exaggerations.[14] Although the ICTY prosecutor, Louise Arbour, had said shortly after the NATO bombing had ended that she expected to indict Milošević for genocide in Kosovo, this charge never materialized.

As things settled down, it became clear what had actually happened. Kosovo had long been home to an extremely powerful Mafia.[15] To do battle with Milošević and the Serbs, NATO formed an alliance with a paramilitary rebel group which was itself heavily involved in drug- and people-smuggling and had roots in the Maoist regime of Enver Hoxha in neighbouring Albania, the Kosovo Liberation Army. The KLA was heavily armed and ruthless. It had over ten thousand men under arms. It received money, weapons, and training from the Americans, especially via the CIA's favourite 'deniable' mercenary company, MPRI (as even the Prosecution counsel, Geoffrey Nice, was himself later to admit during the Milošević trial).[16] The KLA was courted by Western leaders rather as the

Contras had been in Nicaragua in the 1980s, and glamorized even more so. Madeleine Albright famously kissed the tall, handsome KLA leader, Hashim Thaci, who later became prime minister of Kosovo in 2007 and whom Tony Blair was also happy to receive at Downing Street in 1999.

The mass exodus of people from Kosovo was not, in fact, the result of a programme of racial persecution but instead of three factors. First, there were some localized military operations, especially near Yugoslavia's borders, in which people had been told to leave their homes.[17] This was because Yugoslavia feared a land invasion and was afraid that its forces would be unable to fight a NATO invasion if the local population was in favour of it. Some of these people will have chosen to leave Yugoslavia completely. Others will have fled NATO's bombs, and the fighting between the KLA and Yugoslav forces, as did many ethnic Kosovo Serbs. Once these people started to arrive on the borders, and once the KLA and NATO realized what a sensation and a propaganda coup their arrival created, it was imperative to keep up the flow of 'refugees', and there is compelling evidence that the KLA itself told the Albanians to leave, or encouraged them to do so by spreading fear of what would happen to them if they did not.[18] In the words of one authoritative reporter, quoting a KLA source, 'It was KLA advice, rather than Serbian deportations, which led some of the hundreds of thousands of Albanians to leave Kosovo.'[19] It was for this reason, indeed, that none of the refugees had any of the injuries one would expect if people had fled a marauding genocidal army. One report quoted a Red Cross worker thus: '"These men don't look as though they have walked 20 miles," she said, staring pointedly at Kucu's spotless white running shoes. "They look as though they arrived by Mercedes."'[20]

The problem was that the same propaganda which was being generated by the KLA and NATO to support the war was also being fed to the Office of the Prosecutor at The Hague to encourage an indictment to be issued against Milošević. The same governments who were arming and funding the KLA were also driving forward the policy of indicting the Yugoslav president: United States ambassador David Scheffer (one of the early authors of the doctrine of military and judicial interventionism) admitted in 2006 that the indictment was part and parcel of the United States' overall policy towards Milošević: 'As a subtext to our diplomatic engagement with Milošević was the possible indictment of him.'[21] During the bombing, moreover, the NATO spokesman, Jamie Shea, was also happy to say that NATO countries were funding the ICTY and supporting its activities.[22] Just as the chief prosecutor, Louise Arbour, on 21 April 1999, said that she welcomed the decision of Western states 'to provide *intelligence-based information* to my Office',[23] so Shea said, 'NATO countries are those who have provided the finance to set up the Tribunal [the ICTY], we are amongst the majority financiers'[24] and, 'Without NATO countries, there would be no ... International Criminal Tribunal for the former Yugoslavia.'[25] During the Milošević trial, even the lead Prosecution counsel, Geoffrey Nice, referred to the Western powers as 'the forces and powers that established this tribunal',[26] while the president of the ICTY, Judge Gabrielle Kirk McDonald, hailed Madeleine Albright, the American secretary of state (who many believe was the prime mover behind the attack on Yugoslavia in 1999) as 'the mother of the tribunal'.[27] It was hardly surprising, therefore, that the Office of the Prosecutor refused in June 2000 even to open an investigation into whether NATO had committed war crimes during the Kosovo war.

The alliance between NATO, the KLA, and the ICTY was therefore not just tactical or even strategic, it was ideological at the deepest level. NATO leaders based their arguments for war on their claim that, in the face of terrible atrocities, the rules of national sovereignty had to give way to the right of intervention and the superior claims of human rights. Only this enabled them to claim that their attack was justified, since it was patently illegal under international law, having not been authorized by the UN Security Council.[28] The argument anticipated the similar argument in favour of the 2003 attack on Iraq, which also relied crucially on a false claim, namely that there were weapons of mass destruction in Iraq. NATO's anti-sovereignist philosophy was identical to that of the ICTY, and to emphasize the total harmony of interests, the ICTY carried two links at the centre of its home page during the bombing, one to the UN of which it is an organ, and the other to NATO.

This harmony of interests between so-called international justice and the foreign policies of the most powerful Western states, especially the United States of America, had in fact led to the creation of the ICTY in the first place. Its origins lay in a speech made by the incoming United States secretary of state, Lawrence Eagleburger, on 16 December 1992. Eagleburger said that an international war crimes tribunal should be created to try Serb and Yugoslav leaders including Slobodan Milošević.[29] The UN Security Council duly created the ICTY on 25 May 1993, when it passed UN Security Council Resolution 827.

Curiously, the theological issues which were at the heart of the trials of Charles I and Louis XVI were also not far below the surface in this decision. Eagleburger said in his 1992 speech that he had been prompted to press for the creation of an international war crimes tribunal after speaking to Elie Wiesel, the Holocaust survivor and author.[30] It so happens that Wiesel had long been fascinated with the idea that God should be condemned for permitting the Holocaust. Drawing on Hasidic lore – in Judaism, there is a strong tradition of haggling with God, of addressing Him in the manner of a plaintiff addressing a judge in court, and even of rabbis issuing judgements against Him in rabbinical trials[31] – and expressing precisely the attitude of metaphysical revolt described by Albert Camus, Wiesel's play, *The Trial of God (as it was held on February 25, 1649 in Shamgorod)* (1979) deals with how minstrels in a seventeenth-century East European shtetl decided to put God on trial for allowing the Jews to be killed in a pogrom. Wiesel allegedly got this idea after he had actually witnessed three rabbis in Auschwitz pronouncing God guilty for His silence in the face of the Nazis' crimes against humanity. Wiesel continued his interest in the ICTY long after influencing Eagleburger: he appeared as a witness – disembodied, via video link – at the sentencing hearing of the former Bosnian Serb president, Biljana Plavšić, in December 2002, during which he issued various pronouncements on the need for crimes against humanity not to go unpunished.

Eagleburger's speech, and the subsequent creation of the tribunal, had the immediate political effect of scuppering the peace proposals which were then being drawn up by David Owen and Cyrus Vance, the EU and American negotiators, proposals to which Slobodan Milošević had appended his signature. Supporters of international humanitarian law, indeed, have always energetically insisted that their 'just' wars are preferable to an 'unjust' peace. In the face of what they say is aggression, they denounce peace agreements as 'appeasement'.[32] The destruction of the Vance–Owen peace plan, like the destruction (also thanks to American pressure[33]) of the similar Cutileiro plan of March 1992, ensured that the fighting in Bosnia continued.

The reason for the determination not to cut a deal with the Bosnian Serbs lay in political ideology. Bosnia had been elevated by New Left Communists in Yugoslavia and their Western allies to an icon of multinationalism, at the very moment when the Western European powers were forging a new multinational political order in the European Community by turning it into a federal quasi-state, the European Union. Agreement on the Maastricht treaty was reached at the same European summit as the decision to recognize the secessionist states of Yugoslavia, a decision which dismembered that state in the hope of fashioning a new order out of the resulting chaos. These Yugo-nostalgics had tossed Yugoslavia itself aside as soon as the Serbs had started to grumble about the old 1974 Titoite constitution which divided and weakened them. For the EU leaders, and for the Americans under Clinton, Bosnia stood for precisely that postnational and postmodern future which they wanted for their own states, and which many of them had seen in Communist Yugoslavia. Opposed to the project of creating an independent Bosnia, and not wanting to belong to it, the Serbs represented an apparently reactionary and atavistic national force, an existential threat to the new European ideology.

The incoherent Western policy of insisting that Bosnia remain united as a state – incoherent because multinational Yugoslavia had been allowed to collapse, precisely in the name of the very right to self-determination that was then denied to the Bosnian Serbs – ensured that the fighting in Bosnia lasted for three years (1992–5). It ensured, in particular, that the 'ethnic cleansing' which is the inevitable consequence of all wars of partition continued on an large scale. If Bosnia had been allowed to collapse as Yugoslavia had done, the fighting might have been over in three months. Bosnia had never in history existed as a state, and its claim to existence was therefore much weaker than Yugoslavia's. Its Serb population (42 per cent) never wanted to secede from Yugoslavia in the first place, and the manner in which the various votes on independence were taken was brazenly illegal and corrupt, effectively a *coup d'état*. (The vote on the independence referendum was taken in the parliament at 3 o'clock in the morning, after the Bosnian Serb delegates had been told to go home, while the Islamist president, Alija Izetbegović, remained in power even though his term in office had expired.[34]) Just as millions had died for Bolshevism, therefore, many tens of thousands of lives were sacrificed to the West's determination to see the postmodern and postnational constructivist project of Bosnian state-building succeed.[35] To this day, indeed, the West doggedly persists in its pretence that Bosnia-Herzegovina does and can exist as a state, even though in reality it exists on paper only because the presence of an international governor, and the division of the state into totally autonomous entities, mean that its three constituent peoples are not, in fact, governed by its government.

The same effect of scuppering peace was achieved by the indictment of Milošević in 1999. By denouncing the Yugoslav president as a war criminal, NATO upped the ante and boxed itself into an extremist corner from which it had difficulty extricating itself. As a result, the bombing continued for seventy-four days, inflicting terrible damage and costing NATO billions, whereas the initial intention had been for the Yugoslavs to capitulate within a week. In the event, it took over a year for the West to achieve its original aim in attacking Yugoslavia and supporting the KLA, namely to overthrow Milošević. Over a hundred million dollars were poured into the coffers of opposition politicians, mafiosi, and professional technicians of 'regime change' to help organize the violent putsch which occurred against Milošević on 5 October 2000, against the background of the disputed outcome to the presidential election.[36]

Milošević was duly imprisoned in Belgrade on corruption charges (the substance of these never materialized, and proof for them was never provided) and the American government lobbied hard for him to be transferred to the ICTY at The Hague. Although Yugoslav law, like the law of many states, did not permit the extradition of its nationals to other jurisdictions, although the Yugoslav parliament had rejected a bill to change the law to allow it, and although the Yugoslav constitutional court had issued an injunction against a decree passed by the government of the Republic of Serbia to enable Milošević to be so transferred, the Serb prime minister, Zoran Djindjić, ordered his police simply to take the former president out of prison and bundle him into the helicopter bound for Bosnia and The Hague. Djindjić did this on 28 June 2001 – St Vitus' Day, the anniversary of the Battle of Kosovo Field in 1389 and Serbia's national day.

Milošević made his first appearance in court on 3 July 2001. The hearing was short and he used it to denounce the ICTY and the case against him. The judge switched off his microphone on several occasions, as he was to do throughout the trial. In November 2001, over two years after the initial indictment for Kosovo had been issued, the Prosecution brought out two new indictments, on Bosnia and Croatia, no doubt because it realized that the case on Kosovo was so weak. Milošević had been investigated by the Office of the Prosecutor in 1995 for his alleged involvement in the Bosnian civil war, but the decision had been taken then that there was no evidence to press for a prosecution. Milošević had been president of Serbia at the time when the Yugoslav federation was breaking up; during the fighting between secessionist Croats and the Yugoslav National Army, in the latter half of 1991 and the early months of 1992, Milošević had no command at all over the Yugoslav army. By the time the Bosnian civil war started, in April 1992, he had a post on the national defence council but Yugoslavia very quickly (in May 1992) recognized Bosnia-Herzegovina as an independent state and announced that it had no territorial claims on it. To be sure, Yugoslavia gave help to the Bosnian Serb army, and therefore incurred some indirect responsibility for what that army did in Bosnia. But the link between it and Milošević in Belgrade was tenuous.

Apart from the fact that the addition of indictments for Bosnia and Croatia meant that the trial would now cover over ten years of Balkan history, the original Kosovo indictment was also amended in a very important way on 29 October 2001. Whereas in the first two versions of the Kosovo indictment, Milošević was charged with individual criminal responsibility (i.e. command responsibility) for the acts alleged, now, instead, it was alleged that he had participated in 'a joint criminal enterprise' and that his culpability was based on this, for all three indictments. Two months previously, the Prosecution had secured the conviction of a Bosnian Serb commander, Radislav Krstić, for genocide, on the basis of this new theory of liability for his indirect role in the Srebrenica massacre in Bosnia in 1995. This concept of 'joint criminal enterprise' had been invented by the ICTY in July 1999 when it ruled on its first case, that of a low-level perpetrator called Duško Tadić, who had been convicted (on appeal) for a number of murders, even though the tribunal admitted that there was no evidence that he had actually committed them. It ruled instead that he had been part of a small group of soldiers which had entered a village and killed some Muslim men, and that he had shared the common criminal intent of the group. He was therefore equally responsible for all acts committed by its members. This is the theory of criminal liability formulated by Vyshinskii at the Bukharin trial in 1938.

The ICTY statute itself said nothing about the concept of joint criminal enterprise. On the contrary, it stipulated that its theory of liability was 'individual criminal responsibility', i.e. precisely not collective responsibility. It listed five such types of liability in its Article 7(1), both principal and accessorial: planning, instigating, ordering, committing, or aiding and abetting.[37] In contrast to these forms of liability, and in contrast to the theory of command responsibility – according to which a defendant is deemed guilty if he ordered a crime or in some way bears responsibility for the acts of his subordinates – joint criminal enterprise does not trace vertical lines of responsibility from commanders to perpetrators, but instead horizontal ones, linking all members of a group to each other and making them equally responsible, as co-perpetrators, for all the crimes committed by the group. It is a form of guilt by association.

In support of this new theory of criminal liability (of which even the Nuremberg judges had taken a dim view) the ICTY judges invoked two international treaties which had not even existed at the time when the events themselves occurred, the International Convention for the Suppression of Terrorist Bombing (1997) and the Statute of the International Criminal Court (1998).[38] For that matter, joint criminal enterprise had not even been alleged in the original allegations against either Tadić or Krstić, which made it somewhat difficult for them to defend themselves against the charge.

Further rulings of the ICTY have emphasized that a defendant may be convicted by means of 'joint criminal enterprise' for crimes which he did not commit, order, know about, or intend. In 2004 the Appeals Chamber explicitly removed the requirement of *mens rea*, which is normally considered to be the *sine qua non* for a criminal conviction, when it ruled, 'The third category of joint criminal enterprise ... [does] not require proof of intent to commit a crime.'[39] In 2005 it ruled, 'A participant in a joint criminal enterprise need not physically participate in any element of any crime.'[40] In Milošević's own case, the Trial Chamber ruled on 16 June 2004, 'It is not necessary for the Prosecution to prove that the Accused possessed the required intent for genocide before a conviction can be entered on this basis of liability [i.e. third category joint criminal enterprise].'[41]

By applying this doctrine to Slobodan Milošević, the Prosecution took a vague and fragile doctrine of criminal liability, originally conceived to adjudicate acts of group violence committed by a small number of people on a specific occasion, and applied it to a vast series of events spanning more than a decade, covering a huge territory, and involving a large and unspecified number of 'persons known and unknown'. During the cross-examination of his co-defendant and former minister, Vojislav Šešelj, Milošević – like Bukharin in 1938 – established that he and Šešelj had not even met each other until April 1992, by which time they were supposed, according to the Prosecution, to have been members of the same joint criminal enterprise for eight months.

Moreover, it was on the basis of this theory of liability, and the conspiracy theory which underpinned it, that the Prosecution applied to have the three separate indictments against Milošević joined into one monster trial, presumably in the hope that if it threw enough mud, some of it would stick. The Prosecution claimed that the 'joint criminal enterprise' in question was a plan to create a Greater Serbia from the ruins of Yugoslavia by expelling non-Serbs from the territories of Croatia and Bosnia.[42] In fact, not one of the three indictments had even mentioned 'Greater Serbia' with reference to Milošević. The prosecutor, Geoffrey Nice, admitted during the relevant hearing that the purpose of joining the three trials into one was to distract attention from the weakness of the Kosovo indictment, and to prevent Milošević from saying that NATO had attacked his country and committed war crimes there. The 'counter' to this, said Nice, was to look at the defendant's conduct 'from the end of the 1980s right the way through to 1999 as a whole'.[43] This amounted to an admission that the purpose of the trial was to provide justification for the NATO attack: by arguing that Milošević had pursued his joint criminal enterprise 'since the end of the 1980s', the Prosecution could show that NATO's illegal war was in fact a response to Milošević's acts, not a war of aggression.

Although it was clear to some that the prosecutor's case was weak, not even sceptics could have anticipated how quickly the Prosecution case was to unravel. Milošević, who defended himself, turned out to be an excellent advocate and very well-informed. Mahmut Bakalli, a former

Communist Party boss in Kosovo, appeared as the first witness for the Prosecution on 12 February 2002. By asking simple questions, the former president exploded a number of the myths told about Kosovo by Bakalli and repeated endlessly in the West: there had been no system of 'apartheid' between Serbs and Albanians in Kosovo, nor any other form of racial persecution; that public officials in Kosovo had not been required to sign 'loyalty oaths' to him to keep their jobs; and that there had been full provision for education in Albanian and other extensive cultural rights. Bakalli's most difficult moments came when he had to admit that, as Communist Party boss of Kosovo, he had himself called in the tanks from Belgrade in 1981 to suppress a demonstration in favour of Kosovo independence. Milošević also got him to admit that he had worked as an adviser to the then spokesman of the KLA, Adam Demaçi, although he had declared himself an independent politician in his opening statement to the court.

Other witnesses quickly followed, and although much of the testimony was gripping, the world's media ignored it after the initial thrill of seeing Milošević in the dock had worn off. The Prosecution called 298 witnesses, divided essentially into four categories: perpetrators, victims, senior politicians and military figures, and insiders. The purpose was to demonstrate the 'Greater Serbia' conspiracy theory. Milošević countered that Serbia had never sought war; that the war was one of secession; that Serb civilians in Croatia and Bosnia had been attacked first and that the Yugoslav National Army (over which he had no control until May 1992) had acted as a neutral force, where it tried to keep the two sides apart and protect people from attack by secessionist paramilitaries; and that in Bosnia he had always supported peace while trying to help his brother Serbs across the border. He added a conspiracy theory of his own: that the Western powers had plotted to break up his country, Yugoslavia, whose survival he had always supported.

Throughout the trial, the Prosecution would often announce to the media that a 'star witness' or 'key insider' was about to appear. Most of these backfired. Ratomir Tanić claimed to be a close adviser to Milošević but in cross-examination it turned out that they had actually never met; Tanić was rumbled in the Serbian media, and was even attacked by the new interior minister, Dušan Mihajlović, as a swindler, a fantasist, and a liar.[44] Yet there was never any investigation or prosecution of him for perjury. The judges, instead, systematically sided with the Prosecution, frequently interrupting Milošević to prevent him from undermining the credibility of Prosecution witnesses.

Other 'insiders' were no better. Radomir Marković, the former head of the Yugoslav secret services, testified at length, as a Prosecution witness, that the Prosecution case against Milošević was completely untrue: there had been no plan to expel the Albanians from Kosovo, and everything had been done to protect civilians and to respect the laws of war in the fight against the KLA. General Alexander Vasiljević, another Prosecution witness, gave the same evidence. The testimony of Zoran Lilić, Milošević's predecessor as president of the Federal Republic of Yugoslavia, was also massively exculpatory of Milošević and a severe blow to the Prosecution case even though he too was a Prosecution witness. The same went for Borisav Jović, the Serb member of the Yugoslav federal presidency from 1989 to 1991, who was particularly interesting on Milošević's role in the wars in Slovenia and Croatia, when he blamed the secessionist states for the violence and said that Milošević's influence over events at that time (1991) had been minimal. Although a Prosecution witness, his testimony therefore also contradicted the Prosecution's case in every essential respect. Bizarrely, Geoffrey Nice never mentioned the alleged 'joint criminal enterprise' during the testimony of Jović, even though Jović is specifically named as a member of the alleged conspiracy in both the (amended) Bosnia and Croatia indictments, and he has never been indicted for it either.

Other witnesses were embarrassing for the Prosecution in other ways. There was the Kosovan Albanian who showed a shirt riddled with bullets which he said he had been wearing when the Serbs tried to massacre him: he had played dead and then crawled away from under the bodies when the coast was clear. How, the former president asked, could his shirt have been riddled with bullets if he escaped? God had preserved him, came the reply, so that he could come and tell his tale. Anonymous witness K41, himself a supposed perpetrator of war crimes, insisted that he had come to the tribunal motivated only by a desire to tell the truth because his conscience could no longer bear the memory of what he had done. Although he had explicitly denied during the examination-in-chief that he had a criminal record, Milošević established quickly that he did. The relevant questions put by Milošević during cross-examination have been censored from the trial transcript, and therefore it is impossible for the public now to know what this witness was convicted of.[45] The Serbian press, however, managed to identify him and revealed that he was a thug on the run who had beaten up and robbed an old lady at the very time he said he was suffering from pangs of conscience. In spite of the fact that the witness had apparently given false evidence about his own criminal record – therefore of course calling into question the reliability of his evidence about atrocities – the judges again made no attempt to investigate or prosecute him for perjury. Milošević put it to him that he agreed to testify in return for a guarantee of immunity from prosecution by the ICTY, something which, as transpired during his cross-examination of Captain Dragan Vasiljković, the Office of the Prosecutor is in the habit of offering.

As with K41, it soon became very clear that the Prosecution had fished in very murky waters to obtain its witnesses. The court froze in silence when anonymous witness K2 admitted that he had murdered Arkan, the notorious paramilitary and war profiteer who had been shot dead in a Mafia killing in the Intercontinental hotel in Belgrade in January 2000. Officially, Arkan's murder remains an unresolved mystery to this day. However, it is only because of reports by one observant journalist that we know that this is what K2 said.[46] You cannot tell that he made this astonishing admission in open court from reading the transcript, because the relevant passages have been censored, thus:

> MILOŠEVIĆ: Tell me, please, is the reason why you believe your life is in danger your statement to the investigators or the fact [redacted] [redacted] Why is your life in danger?
> WITNESS K2: Now for both reasons.
> [...]
> MILOŠEVIĆ: I didn't hear your answer.
> WITNESS K2: The answer is yes.
> MILOŠEVIĆ: So because you're involved in the [redacted].
> WITNESS K2: Yes.
> MILOŠEVIĆ: So that is the main reason why you're no longer living in Serbia and why you're concealing your identity; is that right?
> WITNESS K2: Yes.[47]

In other evidence, it became painfully clear what a ruthless organization the Kosovo Liberation Army had been. Several sessions were devoted to the alleged massacre at Račak in January 1999: this event was the direct cause of the Rambouillet meeting which in turn led to the bombing of Yugoslavia. The Albanians alleged that Račak was a massacre of civilians; the Yugoslavs countered that there had been a firefight with KLA guerrillas and that the people killed were KLA soldiers. Witness Shukri Buja, the KLA commander at Račak, confirmed that he had over 1,000 men in the region at the time and that they were heavily armed: 'Our soldiers were equipped with automatic rifles, mortars, machine-gun of 7.9 calibre, machine-gun 12.7, 60-millimetre grenade launcher, and rifles M-48, AK-47, the mortar of 500 millimetres as well,' he said.[48] Much to the astonishment of Judge May, Buja later confirmed that the KLA had attacked the police with hand-held rocket launchers.[49] As Milošević pointed out, an earlier witness had claimed that the KLA had only hunting rifles.

Some of the most intriguing testimony came from Dražen Erdemović, a mercenary who had fought on all three sides in the Bosnian civil war and who pleaded guilty in 1996 to taking part in the murder of over 1,000 Bosnian Muslims, of which he said he had personally murdered over 100. Erdemović has testified in four other trials and hearings (his own, a hearing against Radovan Karadžić and Ratko Mladić, the trial of General Krstić, and the Milošević trial), and his testimony has been crucial to the case against these men. Yet his account is simply incredible. He claims that 1200 men were shot dead in less than five hours: they arrived in buses, they were taken out of the buses in groups of ten, lined up in a field, and then shot. But a simple calculation is enough to see that it is impossible to kill so many people in such a short time, at least in the manner described. If it took ten minutes to take each group of ten men out of a bus to the place of execution, some 100 metres away, and then kill them, then the killing would have had to have gone on for twenty hours, not five. The judges never asked about this simple inconsistency in this key evidence on any of the occasions when Erdemović testified (and the issue was not raised by Milošević either). Worse, none of the men whom Erdemović repeatedly named as his accomplices in this massacre have ever been contacted by the Prosecution, still less indicted, even though one of them was arrested in the United States in August 2004. Erdemović happened to mention on one occasion that he feared for his life because a man he had had a fight with was trying to kill him; had he agreed to become a Prosecution witness in order to benefit from the generous witness protection programme? He now lives in a Western European country under an assumed name, after having been given the disgracefully light sentence of five years for the atrocity he says he committed.[50]

One of the most damaging sessions for the Prosecution was when Vojislav Šešelj testified in August 2005. Geoffrey Nice was forced to admit that Milošević himself had never once used the term 'Greater Serbia', even though, as shown above, it was on the basis that he had embarked on a joint criminal enterprise of creating a Greater Serbia that the three indictments against Milošević had been joined into one. Even the normally indulgent judges could not believe their ears when Nice made this admission: how could he suddenly say that Milošević had never embraced the Greater Serbia concept, when that charge lay at the heart of the case against him? Nice got into terrible confusion at this point, saying both that 'Greater Serbia' was a historical concept different from Milošević's policy and also that the two were essentially the same. He also said that Milošević was both allied with Šešelj over Greater Serbia and at odds with him on it.[51]

The Prosecution realized from the outset that Milošević knew the case better than any lawyer and that he was an excellent advocate. It therefore tried to get the judges to impose a lawyer on him, even though the ICTY statute, and every authoritative human rights document in the world, recognizes the right of a defendant to defend himself as a 'minimum guarantee'. These requests were rejected by the judges, on the basis of long and detailed judicial rulings, in 2002. In 2004, however, the bench changed its mind and decided to force Milošević to accept a lawyer after all. It tossed all its previous legal reasoning aside and said that expediency – Milošević's poor health – required the imposition of a lawyer. In fact, the real reason why the trial had taken so long was that the Prosecution had ignored the judges' instructions to finish its case within a year. As the judges themselves admitted when they imposed the lawyer, there is no precedent anywhere in any jurisdiction in the world for imposing a lawyer against a defendant's will because he is sick. Moreover, the decision was taken specifically to allow trial *in absentia*, which is normally frowned upon or illegal. The court, by taking a decision which, as it itself admitted, had no basis in law or precedent, was therefore behaving quite lawlessly.

As it turned out, the decision was a disaster. Milošević had lined up over ninety Defence witnesses and most refused to come, saying that they would testify only if Milošević himself cross-examined them. The trial effectively ground to a halt, although not before the judges prosecuted and sentenced a seventy-year-old academic for contempt of court for politely telling them that he would answer questions only from Milošević himself. Within three months of having taken the decision to impose counsel, the Appeal Chamber convened to overturn the arrangements and effectively restore the *status quo ante*, while confirming the Trial Chamber in the original rightness of its decision. The imposed counsel was officially retained but in practice Milošević regained the right to conduct his own defence. The Appeals Chamber ruled, in other words, that the Trial Chamber did have the right to violate the tribunal's own statute. But if a court is created which can ignore the terms of its own statute, as well as the law and precedent which is supposed to guide it, then the rule of law has come to an end and the court is simply a law unto itself.[52]

Milošević died in custody in the night of 10–11 March 2006. He was the seventh Hague defendant to die in custody or shortly after leaving it. He had been complaining of poor health since the beginning of the proceedings and his supporters claimed in 2002 that the judges were turning a blind eye to his appeals in order to kill him. There were also reports in 2002 that the doctors at The Hague had given him the wrong medicine, worsening his condition.[53] His health deteriorated until, in March 2006, he discovered to his astonishment that the results of a blood test carried out in January had been withheld from him, even though – or, as he suspected, because – they revealed the presence in his blood of dangerous substances which were impairing the effect of his other medication. He hand-wrote a letter to the Russian foreign minister, Sergei Lavrov, on 8 March 2006, saying that someone in The Hague was taking 'active, wilful steps to destroy my health'.

In December 2005 Milošević had applied to go to Russia to be treated at a heart clinic there. Doctors from that clinic had examined him and recommended treatment. The ICTY requested a written undertaking from the Russian government that Milošević would be returned to the Netherlands for the rest of his trial following any such treatment, and they received this written guarantee on 18 January 2006. Yet on 23 February 2006, the judges refused to let Milošević go. One of the reasons why Milošević therefore wrote to Lavrov was that he felt that whatever mistreatment he was being administered in The Hague would be discovered in Russia. His brother, Borislav Milošević, who lived in Moscow, speculated on 24 February 2006 that he was being poisoned, as did Momir Bulatović, federal prime minister when Milošević had been president of Yugoslavia, who said later that Milošević's death had prevented him from giving clinching evidence which would have demonstrated Milošević's innocence. For his part, the Russian cardiologist squarely blamed the judges: 'If Milošević had been taken to any specialized Russian hospital, the more so to such a stationary medical institution as ours … he would have lived for many long years to come. Unfortunately it is an absolutely banal fact that he died due to lack of medical treatment.'[54]

18   Regime Change and the Trial of Saddam Hussein

Unlike the NATO attack on Yugoslavia in 1999, the Anglo-American attack on Iraq in 2003 was one of the most hotly contested political decisions of modern times. Inspired by the Manichaean, millenarian,[1] and neo-Jacobin ideology of the neo-conservatives,[2] some of whom demanded that the US pursue 'an end to evil' on the basis that 'there is no middle way for Americans – it is victory or Holocaust,'[3] and by the neo-Trotskyite dogma of 'global democratic revolution' which President George W. Bush often said was the centrepiece of his foreign policy[4] (for instance, 'The establishment of a free Iraq at the heart of the Middle East will be a crushing defeat to the forces of tyranny and terror, and a watershed event in the global democratic revolution'[5]), the invasion of Iraq was attacked by opponents as illegal because, like the Kosovo war, it was never authorized by the United Nations Security Council. Supporters of the war, London and Washington in first place, replied that the attack was covered by existing UN Security Council resolutions. The question of the legality of the war cannot be dissociated from the question of the legality of the subsequent trial and execution of the Iraqi president, Saddam Hussein.

The international system ratified after World War II in the charter of the United Nations bans the use of force in international relations (war) except when a state is acting in self-defence or when authorized by the Security Council voting under its Chapter 7 powers on operations designed to maintain peace and security. These rules of positive international law reflect the long-standing principle that states do not have a right to attack one another, a principle which can be traced back at least to the signature of the Treaties of Westphalia in 1648.

It was in order to bypass this rule that the British and American governments alleged that Iraq was building 'weapons of mass destruction' (WMD). It has subsequently been revealed that this was not the case, and it is now certain that both Washington and London knew as much. But George Bush devoted much of his State of the Union address in 2003 to exaggerating and inventing the threat from Iraq's WMD. The reason for this tactic was that there were Security Council Resolutions dating from the First Gulf War in 1991 which forbade the country to produce such weapons. Britain and America claimed that these old resolutions remained active and that Iraq's continued breach of them made their 2003 attack legal.

According to both the British and American governments, Iraq was in breach of UN resolutions 678 and 687. (We shall leave aside, for the sake of argument, the fact that in reality Iraq was not in breach because it was in fact not manufacturing WMD.) They argued that Resolution 1441, voted on 8 November 2002, referred back to those two resolutions from 1990 and 1991 and thereby legalized the attack which eventually occurred in March 2003. Britain and America had advanced exactly the same arguments about Resolution 678 in early January 1998, in justification of their attack on Iraq in December of that year – an attack known as Operation Desert Fox, which for some reason was named after the nickname given to the Nazi field marshal, Erwin Rommel, for his success in North Africa in 1941.[6]

In fact, Resolution 678 (voted on 29 November 1990) said that 'all necessary means' (i.e. war) could be used to enforce Resolution 660 (2 August 1990) and the other resolutions voted since then. Resolution 660 called on Iraq to withdraw from Kuwait. Resolution 678, the one which authorized the use of military force, did so only with the single aim of liberating Kuwait, which duly happened in 1991.

None of the resolutions voted on Iraq between 660 and 678 said a word about 'weapons of mass destruction'.[7] These were not mentioned until Resolution 687 was passed, on 3 April 1991, after Kuwait had been liberated. Resolution 687 did impose heavy sanctions on Iraq to force it to abandon its weapons programme but there was never any suggestion that this condition should be imposed by war. Instead, it insisted that Iraq notify the UN that it had accepted the terms laid down, at which point a ceasefire would come into force. Iraq did this in a letter to the UN Secretary General on 6 April 1991, at which point the ceasefire came legally into effect. The Security Council decided 'to remain seized of the matter' and this in turn led to the weapons inspection team and the burdensome regime of UN sanctions which lasted, on and off, until 2003. But Resolution 687 did not authorize war; on the contrary, it contained the mechanism for the end of war.

Resolution 1441, voted on 8 November 2002, did rule that Iraq was in breach of Resolution 687. However, it did not conclude that the ceasefire was therefore no longer in force, as the British and American governments said it did, but on the contrary sent a reinforced weapons inspections mission to Iraq and determined 'to remain seized of the matter'. By no stretch of the imagination, therefore, can Resolution 1441 be said to authorize war: on the contrary, it gave Iraq another chance to comply with 687, and the weapons inspectors were sent back into Iraq shortly thereafter.

Far from being legal in terms of UN resolutions, therefore, the Anglo-American attack on Iraq interrupted and destroyed the very weapons inspection mission which Resolution 1441 had reintroduced. The inspectors were told to get out by the Americans, just as they had been in 1998 when the team was about to conclude that Iraq had complied with the disarmament requirements, and shortly before the four-day bombing operation known as Desert Fox. The illegality is emphasized by the fact that phrases in the draft resolution presented by the Americans, which would have authorized the use of force, were removed from what became Resolution 1441 after protest by other Security Council members.

It was precisely because 1441 did not authorize war that Britain and America tried to introduce a further Seucrity Council Resolution in February 2003. Their attempts were thwarted by announcements from Moscow and Paris that any resolution authorizing war before the weapons inspection team had reported would be vetoed. It was therefore absolutely clear that the attack, which commenced on 20 March 2003, was illegal under the terms of the United Nations Charter and that, as such, it was a criminal war of aggression.

In any case, all the arguments about weapons were blown out of the water by President Bush himself when he issued an ultimatum to Iraq on the eve of the attack. He said that Saddam and his sons had to leave the country within forty-eight hours or the bombing would start.[8] The ultimatum is a recognized device in the customary international laws of war: by issuing it, George Bush made formally clear, as a matter of law, that the purpose of the war was to remove Saddam Hussein and to effect 'regime change', not to disarm the country. The day the attack was launched, the British prime minister, Tony Blair, broadcast to the nation that, 'Tonight, British servicemen and women are engaged from air, land and sea. Their mission: to remove Saddam Hussein from power …'[9] (although he had earlier misled the House of Commons by saying that Saddam could remain in power if he disarmed[10]). Since no UN Resolution had ever authorized war to remove Saddam from power or even to invade Iraq (George Bush Senior had refused to 'go to Baghdad' in 1991 for this very reason), the war was clearly illegal according to Bush's and Blair's own terms. Subsequent to the invasion, indeed, and to the failure to find any of the supposed weapons, supporters of the war fell back on the 'regime change' argument to justify their acts.

Regime change obviously was the whole point of the exercise. But it is not only unlawful as a *casus belli*, it is also unlawful after war has been waged and a country occupied. The Hague and Geneva conventions of 1907 and 1949 regulate what countries are allowed to do when they occupy other states. Article 43 of the 1907 Hague Convention says that an occupying power should respect 'unless absolutely prevented, the laws in force in the country'. Article 54 of the Fourth Geneva Convention of 1949 says, 'The Occupying Power may not alter the status of public officials or judges in the occupied territories, or in any way apply sanctions to or take any measures of coercion or discrimination against them, should they abstain from fulfilling their functions for reasons of conscience', and Article 64 provides that the penal laws of the occupied country should remain in force unless they represent a threat to the security of the occupier, and that 'the tribunals of the occupied territory shall continue to function.' The authoritative Commentary to the (IV) Geneva Convention edited by Pictet emphasizes that these security-based derogations from the general inviolability of the occupied country's legal system may not be extended to other areas: 'The occupation authorities cannot abrogate or suspend the penal laws for any other reason – *and not, in particular, merely to make it accord with their own legal conceptions.*' [11] Article 65 provides that any new penal laws brought in by the occupier should not be retroactive, a principle repeated in Article 67.

In direct violation of these provisions, the Americans in Iraq conducted a wholesale purge of the judicial system, including for the purpose of trying Saddam. The process started when the Occupation Authority led by Paul Bremer abrogated the 1971 constitution of Iraq, but radical political change in Iraq had in fact been the goal of the invasion in the first place. It is now known that the decision to invade Iraq was taken long before 2003, and even before the attacks in New York and Washington on 11 September 2001, and that the idea of promoting regime change in Iraq by means (*inter alia*) of a criminal trial of Saddam and his colleagues dated as far back as 1998, when the Iraq Liberation Act was passed. Its Section 3 stated, 'It should be the policy of the United States to support efforts to remove the regime headed by Saddam Hussein from power in Iraq and to promote the emergence of a democratic government to replace that regime.' Section 6 stated, 'The Congress urges the President to call upon the United Nations to establish an international criminal tribunal for the purpose of indicting, prosecuting, and imprisoning Saddam Hussein and other Iraqi officials.' In 2002 the United States ambassador-at-large for war crimes, Pierre-Richard Prosper, announced that his office had a whole room devoted to collecting material for a future indictment of the then incumbent Iraqi president.[12]

The goal – apart from controlling Iraq's vast oil wealth – was to engineer the political transformation of Iraq and the whole Middle East. Many neo-conservative commentators admitted that a 'democratized' Iraq was to be the centrepiece of this new geopolitical arrangement.[13] Former treasury secretary Paul O'Neill has written in his memoirs how an invasion of Iraq was part of the strategy of the Bush team immediately it took office, and that it was discussed at the very first meeting of the new National Security Council on 30 January 2001.[14] At the second NSC meeting, on 1 February 2001, Donald Rumsfeld, the then secretary of defense, explained that getting rid of Saddam should be a key part of US foreign policy: 'Imagine what the region would look like without Saddam and with a regime that's allied with US interests,' Rumsfeld said. 'It would change everything in the region and beyond it. *It would demonstrate what US policy is all about.*'[15]

The trial of the Ba'athist leaders, especially Saddam Hussein, was a key part of this programme. Detailed planning for this began in the State Department in October 2001, shortly after 9/11, where seventeen working groups were set up to make plans for changing everything in Iraq, from health policy, local government, defence policy, education, media, water, agriculture, the economy and infrastructure.[16] The so-called Transitional Justice Group, created within the State Department, produced a 248-page report in March 2003,[17] which proposed a wholesale destruction of Iraq's existing legal system and its replacement by a new one. The very first issue discussed in this long report was the need to prosecute the Ba'athist leaders, Saddam in first place.

It was because there had been so much advance preparation for a judicial purge of Iraq that the occupying powers, known as the Coalition Provisional Authority (CPA), shortly after 9/11, were able to set about arranging the trial of Saddam immediately after the invasion. On 23 June 2003, Paul Bremer issued Order No. 15, entitled 'Establishment of the Judicial Review Committee'. (The decree was promulgated in English, an Arabic translation not being produced until over 100 days later.) It announced the immediate and general suspension of the existing Iraqi laws on the judiciary, and the creation of a judicial committee composed of three Iraqis and three 'international' members to review all judicial appointments in Iraq. It would be difficult to imagine a more flagrant violation of the Article 54 of the Fourth Geneva Convention forbidding the sacking of judges.

This new judicial committee was created to operate 'at the discretion of the Administrator', i.e. it was under direct political control. These measures went hand in hand with the de-Ba'athification orders, including the very first order, Order No. 1, issued on 16 May 2003, which removed all senior Ba'ath Party members from public office. The effect of these measures was to purge the judiciary of anyone but enemies of Saddam's regime, and to ensure total American control over the Iraqi judiciary. The CPA, incidentally, vested itself with 'all executive, legislative and judicial authority'[18] in an act of constitutional pre-modernism in striking conflict with the widely held principle that the separation of powers is a key condition of the rule of law.

On 10 December 2003, Bremer signed Order No. 48 creating the Iraqi Special Tribunal to try Iraqis accused of war crimes, crimes against humanity, and genocide. The order also promulgated the Statute of the Tribunal, which stipulated that it had jurisdiction over the period 17 July 1968 to 1 May 2003, the exact dates during which the Ba'ath Arab Socialist Party held power in Iraq. Order No. 48 therefore violated several fundamental legal principles at one go. It created a tribunal by decree instead of by law. It created a 'special tribunal', in violation of Dicey's principle that people should be tried only by ordinary courts, and also in violation of the rules later set down by the CPA's own 'constitution', the 'Law of Administration for the State of Iraq for the Transitional Period', promulgated on 8 March 2004, Article 15(1) of which stipulated (as had the State Department's March 2003 report by the Transitional Justice Group[19]) that, 'Special or exceptional courts may not be established.' (In the event, the new Iraqi government issued a law on 9 October 2005, renaming the Special Tribunal 'Supreme Iraqi Criminal Tribunal'.) It restricted the jurisdiction of the tribunal in time in order to frame specific individuals, the leaders of the Ba'ath regime, a goal in any case affirmed in numerous official statements by American officials, which means that Order No. 48 was effectively a Bill of Attainder, a legislative act directed at the punishment of specific people, something prohibited by every accepted canon of due process including by Article 1, Section 9 of the United States Constitution of 1787. Finally, it ensured that the tribunal would be stuffed with Saddam's enemies, since Article 33 of the tribunal's statute specified that no one who had ever been a member of the Ba'ath Party could serve as an official of the tribunal.

The retroactive jurisdiction of the Special Tribunal was also problematic. Unfortunately, the practice of creating tribunals to adjudicate acts which occurred before they existed has become common in modern international humanitarian law: the International Criminal Tribunals for the former Yugoslavia and Rwanda both adjudicate events which occurred before they were created. Indeed the Rwanda tribunal adjudicates exclusively such events. But this is generally regarded as incompatible with the rule of law. The International Criminal Court, for instance, cannot adjudicate any events which occurred before its statute entered into force and this is why its president said that his court could never try Saddam.[20]

By the time Saddam's trial started, on 15 October 2005, the CPA had been dissolved and power handed over to a new 'sovereign' Iraqi government headed by Iyad Allawi. The formal handover of power occurred on 28 June 2004. However, the reality of continued American control over the judicial process (and indeed over the government of Iraq) was obvious. In July 2004 the United States government announced that it was spending $75 million on the trial.[21] When Saddam appeared for the first time in court, on 1 July 2004 for a pre-trial hearing, the TV images which CNN broadcast (without sound) helpfully carried the words 'Cleared by US Military' at the top of the screen. The footage had indeed passed first through the hands of the American military censor. The reality and perception of American control of the trial lasted until Saddam's execution in January 2007: the former Iraqi leader remained in American, not Iraqi custody, throughout and when the Egyptian president, Hosni Mubarak, realized that the execution was imminent, he sent a message to the American president, George W. Bush, to try to obtain a stay of execution.[22] If Iraq had been a truly sovereign state, then Mubarak would presumably have petitioned the Iraqi president, Jalal Talabani, instead.

Although the new 'sovereign' Iraqi government passed a law re-establishing the tribunal (re-naming it 'Iraqi High Tribunal' instead of 'Special Tribunal', having called it 'Supreme Iraqi Criminal Tribunal' for a few months in August–October 2005), its statute was essentially the same as that drawn up by the Americans in 2003. It was re-promulgated only on 18 October 2005, one day before Saddam's trial started. The American authors of the original statute had cherry-picked from pre-Ba'athist Iraqi law a 1958 law (No. 7) which criminalized acts of war or threats of war against another Arab state, and they inserted this as a specific crime as Article 14 of the tribunal statute (2003 version). This allowed the tribunal to prosecute Saddam for invading Kuwait in 1990 but not for invading Iran in 1980. The Iran–Iraq war, which lasted eight years, claimed nearly a million lives, and plunged the Gulf into crisis for nearly a decade, was the judicial equivalent of an elephant in the room which no one was permitted to mention. As is well known, the Americans provided help to the

Iraqis during that period, and Ronald Reagan's personal envoy to the Middle East, Donald Rumsfeld – the man who, as George W. Bush's defense secretary, masterminded the 2003 attack – visited Iraq on two occasions to meet Saddam Hussein, in December 1983 and in April 1984. According to a Senate report published in 1994, the United States supplied chemical and biological weapons to the Iraqis from 1983 right up to the invasion of Kuwait in 1990.[23] Naturally the Americans did not want such uncomfortable facts to come out in court, and so all discussion of the Iran–Iraq war (which had been one of the proximate causes of the invasion of Kuwait) was ruled out. Moreover, as if to emphasize the fact that this was victors' justice, the CPA Order No. 17 (27 June 2004) specifically awarded the occupying forces immunity from prosecution by the Iraqi courts.

The Prosecution in the Saddam trial decided to adopt the opposite tactic of that adopted by the Prosecution of Slobodan Milošević. Whereas the Prosecution in the Milošević trial insisted that three separate indictments be bundled together, for Saddam, the decision was taken instead to separate them out into individual trials. Some of the people, especially Americans, who had been advisers on the Milošević trial also advised the Iraqi Special Tribunal on the Saddam trial, and it seems that the lessons of the failure of the Milošević trial, which had by then been in difficulty for years, were learned. Instead of focusing on the whole of Saddam's political career, the Prosecution started with one event in the early 1980s which formed the basis of one trial, reserving other alleged crimes for future trials if the verdict of the first one (by some miracle) turned out to be an acquittal.

The tribunal was a hybrid between a national and an international court, a pattern which has since been copied by the Special Court in Sierra Leone and which was prefigured by the constitution of the War Crimes Chamber of the Court of Bosnia and Herzegovina. Like those two courts, the Iraqi Special Tribunal (renamed Iraqi High Tribunal) has national (i.e. Iraqi) judges but they are 'assisted by international advisers'. This is a euphemism for American political control. The judges were sent on a training course in London before the trial started and the tribunal is 'special' (in spite of its new name) to the extent that it is structurally separate from the rest of the Iraqi court system.[24] The first general director of the Iraqi Special Tribunal was Salem Chalabi, an Iraqi exile and nephew of the neo-conservatives' favourite exile, Ahmed Chalabi, the leader of the opposition party, the Iraqi National Congress. (Chalabi Junior resigned his post after a warrant was issued for his arrest for murder, in September 2004, but not until he had participated in the appointment of judges to the bench.)

The trial opened on 19 October 2005, and was devoted to events in the town of Dujail in 1982. There had been widespread reprisals against inhabitants of that town after an assassination attempt against Saddam. Saddam was only one of eight defendants: the others included actual perpetrators of or direct accessories to the alleged events in Dujail, for instance local informers and the head of the local revolutionary court which had sentenced 148 people to death. The phrasing of the indictment underlined the reality that the tribunal was an essentially prosecutorial body: the opening phrase says that the presiding judge, by then Abdul Rahman, accuses Saddam Hussein of various crimes: 'Judge Rauf Rashid Abdul Rahman accuses you (Saddam Hussein Al-Majid) of the following: ...'

The occupying authorities and their cheerleaders in the international humanitarian law industry welcomed the trial of a head of state widely reviled in the West as a monster. But the spectacle of such a high-profile trial was less novel for Iraqis themselves. All political change in Iraq in the twentieth century had been violent (with the single exception of the 1968 Ba'athist coup), and it had invariably been accompanied by the elimination of enemies, often by means of trials. When the monarchy was overthrown in the coup of 14 July 1958, the king and a score of members of the royal family were murdered; the corpse of the regent, Abdul Ilah, was dragged through the streets of Baghdad and his remains were dismembered and hung outside the ministry of defence. Other political figures such as the prime minister were also torn apart limb from limb. But the Committee of Free Officers who seized power then established a People's Court to put 'enemies of the people' on trial; Colonel Ahmad Hassan al-Bakr, the future president of Iraq and Saddam's mentor, himself served on it. The court sent people to the gallows for years: in 1960 Judge Fadhil al-Mahdawi said his special tribunal was unique in history and 'a light to the world'.[25]

When Brigadier Kassem, the coup leader, was himself overthrown in the first Ba'athist coup of 1963, the Ba'athists organized a massive purge of political opponents, mainly Communists, the lists of people to be executed having been supplied to them by the CIA.[26] After the second (and decisive) Ba'athist coup in 1968, Saddam Hussein (by then Bakr's deputy, but an all-powerful one) 'discovered' a CIA-Zionist plot against the new regime and staged a show trial of conspirators in December: Saddam was in charge of the propaganda and the media was saturated with coverage of the trial. Fourteen of the alleged conspirators, nine of them Jews, were sentenced to death in January 1969, and their bodies were left to hang in Liberation Square for a day. Radio Baghdad urged people to come and see 'what happens to enemies of the revolution', and hundreds of thousands did.[27] Indeed, when Saddam himself was eventually hanged, he was executed alongside the chief justice of his own Revolutionary Court which had itself meted out death sentences liberally, and for political purposes. Show trials and abuse of the judicial process as a means of enforcing political power were the norm in Iraq, not some new development. Indeed, the slightly amended version of the statute of the Iraqi High Tribunal, which the Iraqi government promulgated one day before Saddam's trial started, included offences from the deliciously named law on the 'Punishment of Conspirators against Public Safety and Corrupters of the System of Governance' of 1958 – the very laws administered by the notorious Mahdawi court in its show trials after the overthrow of the monarchy by Brigadier Kassem.

The indictment against Saddam made liberal use of the latest developments in international humanitarian law, especially the doctrines of crimes against humanity and 'joint criminal enterprise', invented at the Rwanda and Yugoslav tribunals. 'Joint criminal enterprise' allows convictions for persons of the worst crimes on the basis of inferred intent (inferred, for instance, from his position of authority), a far lower threshold of proof than that required by other theories of liability.

From the very beginning, the trial was more an *opera buffa* than a solemn procedure. Saddam, like Charles I, refused brazenly to recognize the authority of the court to try him and he was rude and truculent towards the judge.[28] His arrogant tone, and the chaotic nature of the proceedings, were soon overtaken, however, by the assassination of two Defence lawyers, Sadoon al-Janabi and Adil Mohammad Abbas Zubaidi, acting for Saddam's co-defendants, who were killed on 21 October 2005 (two days after the trial started) and 9 November 2005 respectively. A third Defence lawyer, Thamer Hamoud al-Khuzaie, was injured in the second attack; it is to be assumed that he had also been a target for assassination.

One of Saddam's own lawyers, Khamis al-Obeidi, was then assassinated on 21 June 2006. Reports at the time said that he was abducted by people wearing police uniforms, and the rumour in Baghdad was that the government had been involved in the killing. Saddam's chief Defence counsel, indeed, alleged that the interior ministry troops had been infiltrated by Shiite death squads.[29] During the trial, the Defence argued that witnesses had also been killed. Throughout the trial, Saddam Hussein was unable to obtain a single confidential audience with his own Defence lawyers, while a full account of the charges against him was not presented until 15 May 2006, six months into the proceedings.[30]

On 14 January 2006 the presiding judge, Rizgar Amin, suddenly announced his resignation, denouncing government interference in the trial and saying he was in fear of his life; by then one of his other colleagues on the bench had also resigned. Judge Amin was replaced by Rauf Rashid Abdul Rahman, a Kurd from Halabja who lost relatives in the famous 1988 attack for which Saddam would also have faced trial: he was hardly a disinterested party. (It had been expected that Amin would be replaced by his deputy, Saeed al-Hammash, but he too was quickly sidelined following a political campaign against him.)

While Saddam's trial for the events in Dujail was still under way, in August 2006, proceedings started in the second trial, which concerned the notorious Anfal campaign in 1988. This was the occasion of the famous chemical weapon attack on Halabja. This time Saddam was in the dock along with his cousin, Ali Hassan al-Majid ('Chemical Ali'), the man credited with masterminding Saddam's weapons programme. This trial, which was interrupted by the conviction and execution of Saddam for his role in the Dujail events, was remarkable mainly for the fact that the presiding judge, Abdullah al-Amiri, made a throwaway remark during Saddam's cross-examination of a witness. The witness, who said that his family had been a victim of the Anfal campaign, said that he had visited Saddam to ask about their fate. The former president asked the witness, 'I wonder why you wanted to meet me, if I was a dictator?' Judge al-Amiri interjected, addressing Saddam, 'You were not a dictator. People around you made you look like a dictator.' Saddam bowed his head in thanks, and the judge was promptly sacked from the case.

When the tribunal came to rule on the Dujail case, on 5 November 2006 (it did not produce its written judgement until seventeen days later, on 22 November 2006, and the judgement ran to 300 pages), it convicted Saddam and sentenced him to death. But it did so without even having bothered to demonstrate that Saddam did, in fact, have knowledge of or culpability for the events in Dujail. It inferred his culpability (and that of his co-defendants) from their various official positions. The court concluded that the defendants 'must have known' about the various acts, without actually providing any proof that they did.[31] Similarly, it offered no proof for the existence of a joint criminal enterprise but just said that there must have been one. The Trial Chamber ruled that Saddam must be guilty for Dujail because he was generally guilty of ordering arrests, even though it admitted that no actual evidence had been presented that he ordered the torture or the killings. At one point, the chamber absurdly found that a report submitted to Saddam in 1987 saying that forty-two people had died during interrogation after Dujail in 1982 proved that he had known about these crimes at the time and failed to prevent them.

In the case of Barzan al-Tikriti, whose actual participation in some of the acts of torture and murder in Dujail are not reasonably in dispute, the tribunal concluded that he was responsible for all the acts committed in Dujail, even those committed after he had left the national government in Iraq to become the Iraqi government representative on the UN Commission on Human Rights in Geneva. Other grounds adduced for his criminal liability were that he was Saddam's half-brother – not exactly judicially watertight reasoning. It was on the basis of such unacceptably low standards of proof that al-Tikriti, like Saddam himself, was executed.[32] No doubt people will feel that men like Saddam and Barzan al-Tikriti deserved their fate, but the same cavalier attitude to evidence was also applied to the very low-level perpetrators who stood alongside them in the Dujail dock: a farmer, a postman, and a mechanic. These local men may have contributed to arrests, but the tribunal found that they were in fact co-perpetrators of the joint criminal enterprise and therefore guilty of crimes against humanity as well. It reached this conclusion on the basis that 'everyone knew' what would happen to people who had been arrested. They were given long prison terms.

These low standards of proof were aggravated by the fact that the identity of the Prosecution witnesses was unknown to the Defence until the moment they appeared in court. Most of them were physically invisible to the court. This practice of using anonymous witnesses has become widespread in international tribunals, and it is extremely dangerous because it seriously hampers cross-examination by the Defence. In addition, exculpatory evidence was withheld from the court: Another defendant, Anwad al-Bandar, the former president of the Revolutionary Court, insisted that his own court's procedures had been fair. He asked repeatedly, from April 2006 onwards, for the relevant file to be submitted to the court, but it was withheld until after the close of the Defence case.

When the verdict was read out, Saddam refused to stand to hear it. The judge ordered a court official to make him stand, and they forced him to his feet. 'Stop twisting my arm, you oaf!' Saddam complained, and stood up. When the death sentence was read out, Saddam shouted, 'Long live the great Iraqi people! Long live the nation! Down with the traitors! Down with the occupiers! Allahu Akbar! You are the servants of the colonizers! Long live the people and death to its enemies!' One of his Defence lawyers, the former United States attorney general, Ramsey Clark, handed the judge a written motion denouncing the trial and its irregularities. The judge glanced at the document and said to Clark, 'Get out!'[33]

The case went to appeal. The Appeals Chamber itself was constituted only on 12 December, and it delivered its ruling on 22 December. It issued a seventeen-page ruling on the Trial Chamber's 300-page judgement, dealing with the procedural aspects of the trial in one nine-line paragraph. This recalled the cavalier manner in which the Defence counsel at the trial of Nicolae Ceauşescu had repeatedly stated that those proceedings were legal. As at Vidkun Quisling's appeal, the Appeals Chamber embellished the 'findings' of the Trial Chamber (although without any evidential justification) saying that Saddam had personally supervised and ordered the torture and the killings at Dujail, whereas in fact the Trial Chamber had simply said that he must have known about them.[34]

Saddam Hussein was executed in the early hours of 30 December 2006, Iraqi time. Hooded men tied the noose and cries of 'Moqtadr' went up as he prepared to die: Moqtadr al-Sadr was the radical Shiite cleric whose followers had represented a threat to Saddam even when he had been in power.[35] Saddam looked down disdainfully at the men baying for his blood and said, 'Is this the way Iraqi men behave?'[36] The trap door opened and he was filmed as his neck cracked and his head swung from the noose; video images of the execution circulated immediately on YouTube. The international outcry was nearly unanimous, at least in Europe, where leaders shed crocodile tears at the carrying out of a death penalty long since banished from the old continent. The American president, however, welcomed the hanging. 'Today, Saddam Hussein was executed after receiving a fair trial,' George W. Bush said in a prepared statement, 'Bringing Saddam Hussein to justice … is an important milestone on Iraq's course to becoming a democracy that can govern, sustain, and defend itself, and be an ally in the War on Terror.'[37]

Saddam, meanwhile, spoke from the grave when a letter he had written on the eve of his execution was published. He wrote,

> Here, I offer my soul to God as a sacrifice and if He wants, He will send it to heaven with the martyrs, or, He will postpone that … so let us be patient and depend on Him against the unjust nations … Remember that God has enabled you to become an example of love, forgiveness and brotherly co-existence … I call on you not to hate because hate does not leave a space for a person to be fair and it makes you blind and closes all doors of thinking and keeps away one from balanced thinking and making the right choice.[38]

Conclusion

When we cast our thoughts back over three hundred years of trials of former heads of state, there is perhaps one conclusion which imposes itself above all others: there has never been a single acquittal. The only former heads of state who have escaped conviction have been Erich Honecker and Slobodan Milošević, the first by being about to die, the second by actually dying during his trial. General Galtieri of Argentina was acquitted by the military court which tried him first, but then immediately convicted by the civilian Supreme Court instead, which in any case had acquired the right of oversight over the whole procedure. The three men acquitted at Nuremberg were not heads of state or government, and they were in any case immediately rearrested and convicted by the German de-Nazification authorities instead (although then amnestied again shortly thereafter). Danton's grim prediction in 1792 that one cannot save a king who is on trial (printed as an epigraph to this book) has proved absolutely correct.

This zero per cent acquittal rate can be explained by the fact that, in most cases, the conviction of the former sovereign is an indispensable source of legitimacy for the new regime, which seeks by organizing the trial not only to destroy its enemy but also, much more importantly, to affirm its status as the new sovereign. This is as true of modern international tribunals as it was of the High Court of Justice in 1649. The right to prosecute criminals and the right to make new law are two core attributes of sovereignty, and in these trials those rights are very often wielded in a particularly dramatic and public way in order ceremonially to found the new regime. The new regime's laws are said to apply not only now but also retroactively, projecting themselves back in time to condemn the old regime's laws as illegitimate. By declaring the old order suspended and the new order in force, the new sovereign affirms his rule and his status as lawgiver.

Regime trials are designed to found new regimes. This revolutionary agenda is as visible today as it was in the revolutionary tribunals of eighteenth-century France or seventeenth-century England. Just as earlier revolutionaries said they wanted to ensure that nothing would henceforth be as before in the political order, so those individuals and organizations who campaign now for the work of international tribunals insist that they want 'to put an end to impunity'. They say that, in the past, tyrannical heads of state could kill and steal and then look forward to a quiet retirement, whereas in the future, they will be held to account for their actions. They argue that international tribunals will herald a new reign of accountability in which sovereigns will no longer be able to think of themselves as above the law.

No doubt it is part of human nature to think that political change can lead to improvement, and of course sometimes it does. But the revolutionary nature of these trials makes one thing certain: they never conform to the definition of the rule of law offered by Dicey, 'that no man is punishable or can be made to suffer in body or goods except for a distinct breach of law established in the ordinary legal manner before the ordinary courts of the land.'[1] On the contrary, nearly all such trials have occurred either before specially created tribunals, or on the basis of new laws promulgated by the new regime and imposed retroactively, or both. Regime trials are 'trials of rupture', designed precisely to emphasize a break in the regime and the law, not a continuity in it. The paradigm is therefore completely different from that of an ordinary criminal trial. Whereas when a common felon commits a crime, the institutions of state remain untouched before and afterwards, in these trials it is the institutions of state themselves which change or have changed.

In an ordinary trial, the prosecuting authorities, and especially the judge, have no particular connection to the defendant: the judge's job is to establish whether a crime was committed and, if so, to hand down the sentence stipulated by the law. In a regime trial, by contrast, the prosecuting authority and the judiciary cannot acquit the defendant because the sources of their own power would thereby be compromised. The new sovereign never allows the process by which the defeated opponent ended up in the dock to be adjudicated, i.e. the means he used to obtain his power. The acts of 'the international community' never come under scrutiny by the international tribunals which it has set up. Whereas in an ordinary trial, the judicial system (like the sovereign) is neutral and above the fray, in a regime trial it is an integral part of it. Political trials are the continuation of war by other means.

It is not possible to escape or neutralize this political element of regime trials because of the very nature of the crimes alleged. The acts adjudicated in trials of heads of state or government are political acts, not private ones. Heads of state are not direct perpetrators: instead, they are accused of acts physically committed by their subordinates. Heads of state are prosecuted either for decisions which they have taken in their official, public capacity or on the basis of the modern doctrines of command responsibility and joint criminal enterprise. These doctrines can work only because the acts for which the ex-leaders are said to bear criminal responsibility are imputed to them because they took place within the framework of a recognized public structure (usually an army).

Acts of state – including acts of war – are precisely public acts: as Stephen Neff rightly notes, 'Perhaps the single most obvious and widely agreed feature of war, throughout its long history, has been its character as a public and collective enterprise.'[2] This public character of acts of state is actually emphasized in war, because war is a conflict between two (or more) adversaries: acts of war are determined by the acts of the adversary and they cannot be understood or even honestly discussed without reference to them. To give an account of the acts of one side in a conflict without mentioning the *political* rationale behind them (however morally inexcusable we may consider that rationale to be, or the decisions and acts which flowed from it) is to present the facts in a frankly dishonest light.

The essentially public nature of war, and the impossibility of dissociating conflict from its context – specifically, from the acts of the adversary – mean that it is extremely problematic to compare state policy to a criminal conspiracy. From the *armoire de fer* discovered in Louis XVI's study to the modern formulation of the concept of conspiracy as 'joint criminal enterprise' or 'common plan' (now the cornerstone of the jurisprudence of the Yugoslav and Rwanda tribunals, and of the International Criminal Court), accusations of conspiracy have formed a key part of regime trials throughout history. At Nuremberg and Tokyo, the defendants were convicted of a conspiracy to start wars; Quisling and Pétain were accused (the former convicted) of conspiracy to seize power; the Milošević trial was based on the allegation of a conspiracy to create Greater Serbia.

These charges relied on a partial interpretation of the facts, the partiality consisting precisely in the fact that the other side's motives were downplayed or ignored, in order to bolster the claim of a pre-existing plan. But when an individual plots to commit an act of financial fraud (it is from fraud that the law on conspiracy largely derives) there is never any sense that his acts should be understood with respect to those of his victims. On the contrary, the fraudster who claimed that he stole because he was disadvantaged by society would only be emphasizing his status as a moral idiot.

In cases of human conflict, this is not so. Just as in private conflicts, a murder can in some circumstances be understood (if not necessarily excused) by the prior behaviour of the victim (in the case of the murder of a violent spouse, for instance), all the more so can the other side's behaviour be taken into account in most if not all public acts of conflict (war). Only when this has been done can a judgement be made about the proportionality or reasonableness of the acts alleged. Yet when reading accounts of war crimes in the indictments drawn up by international tribunals such as the ones under discussion in this book, one often has the same disturbing impression that one would have of a description of one man beating another man unconscious which omitted to mention that the acts occurred during a boxing match.

It is precisely this difference between private criminal acts and public acts of war which is at stake when insurgents demand the right to be treated as soldiers, and when the state against which they are fighting refuses and treats them merely as private criminals instead. The argument about whether the acts are ones of war, or simply crimes, is quite simply an argument about political legitimacy. Such arguments, as we have seen, are the Archimedean point of all regime trials: the trial's function is to establish the legitimacy of the new regime and the illegitimacy of the old.

It is this difficulty of subsuming statecraft into the terms laid down by the criminal law which vitiates all the political trials under consideration in this book. It is one thing to allege that an unscrupulous tyrant has exploited his rule for personal private gain, and quite another to allege that acts carried out in the name of the state, and for no personal gain, are 'criminal' in the sense of an ordinary domestic crime. To be sure, a body of law can be elaborated to deal specifically with war crimes, and indeed such *ius in bello* is very ancient and has existed on the statute books of most states since ancient times. But trials of state leaders tend to become absurd, and the law breaks down, when the attempt is made to bring together two spheres, the public sphere of state acts and the private sphere of private delicts. The law on conspiracy is simply incommensurable with acts of state.

It is because of this, the public nature of political acts, that contemporary attempts to individualize guilt in international tribunals, and thereby to defuse all sense of collective national guilt, invariably fail. Whereas a Serb would not normally identify with an ordinary Serb murderer or bank robber, he is more likely to identify with a man who was fighting in a Serb army because he will typically believe that his people were collectively the victims of unjust aggression by Croats or Bosnians. The specific quality of human conflict is that it simply cannot be understood without reference to the enemy, and to the perceived injustices he has committed.

This designation of the victim is therefore the key to all violent conflict. Once one side is believed to have attacked an innocent victim, then that attack demands a response. The innocence of the original victim then blinds the responding party to the exactions he commits in reply: NATO cannot see that its bombs on Yugoslavia were themselves an act of violence, because it believes that they were being dropped only to prevent violence. The other side is then in turn outraged by this escalation of the conflict. Blinded by their equal but opposite perceptions of innocence and victimhood, the parties to violent conflict then start to resemble each other. Each side's collective focus is on the perceived source of the original poison of violence, which must be sought out and destroyed so that the poison can be removed: this is the scapegoat, onto whom all evil is projected. It is this anthropological mechanism which is in operation in regime trials: prosecutors sustain their belief in their own immaculateness precisely by seeking to pin the blame for all the violence committed in the conflict (including their own) onto the one who started it. It is because violence is equated with poison that such trials are often equated with a 'purge'; and it is because there is indeed a sense in which the one who started it truly is guilty of the totality of the conflict that the ritual destruction of the defeated enemy (the scapegoat) is so compelling. Unfortunately, however, such ceremonies rarely if ever lead to reconciliation.

Because all regime trials occur after a period of war, civil war, revolution, or all three, immense collective passions are invariably unleashed by them. Very often the public bays for the defendants' blood outside the courtroom (and occasionally inside it too). Accusation itself is very instrumentalized precisely in order to create social cohesion after a period of internal division.[3] The act of accusation becomes more powerful and intoxicating the more public and collective it is. The intensity of the passions generated, combined precisely with the desire to use them to create a new political order on the ruins of the old one, has often meant that the charges brought are exaggerated or wrong. To be sure, many of the men in the dock whose trials are discussed here had acted venally, vainly, dishonestly, cruelly, evilly, and often illegally. Nonetheless, they were often prosecuted for other things or on the basis of newly invented laws and convicted for things which they had not done.

This special quality of trials of heads of state and government means that we must be very careful about what claims are being made when new political and judicial structures are set up which are aimed specifically or largely at prosecuting them. In particular, it is quite false to say that modern international war crimes tribunals bring about an end to immunity. Regime trials merely displace the locus of immunity from the old regime to the new: international tribunals merely displace it from the national level to the international. This is the inescapable logic of sovereignty. The judges on today's international tribunals are just as immune from prosecution for the things they do while on the bench as King Louis XVI or

Charles I were according to their respective constitutions. Article 30 of the Statute of the International Criminal Tribunal for the former Yugoslavia and Article 48 of the Rome Statute of the International Criminal Court accords this immunity to the prosecutor as well: 'The judges, the Prosecutor and the Registrar shall enjoy the privileges and immunities, exemptions and facilities accorded to diplomatic envoys, in accordance with international law.' Moreover, there is no right of appeal or any legal recourse against the decisions of the United Nations Security Council which created the Yugoslav and Rwanda tribunals: they were imposed on those respective countries by unimpeachable executive fiat.

Politics has in that sense not moved on since the arguments over legitimacy between Charles I and Bradshaw – for the simple reason that it can never move on. It is a basic constitutional truth, overlooked by modern activists of international humanitarian law, that all political orders, including the one they support, are based, in the final analysis, on unimpeachable power. Indeed, if there has been any development between 1649 and now, it has surely been negative: the prosecutions of the English and French kings, like the prosecutions at Nuremberg, were brought by the new *government* of those states at the time. International tribunals, by contrast, are not part of any government: they are precisely separate from the government of the states over which they claim jurisdiction. International tribunals wield their power without even attempting to fulfil the side of the bargain usually regarded as an inherent part of the social contract: the government's duty to use its power to protect its citizens. International tribunals, indeed, have no 'citizens' at all. They are subject to no system of political accountability which ties their actions back to the people over whom they have jurisdiction; they are not controlled by a national legislature or subject to indirect control by political culture or public opinion. They are the judicial equivalent of military bombardment from 30,000 feet: the peoples under their writ cannot fight back.

The goal of this book has been to show the constitutional questions raised by political trials, in particular that such trials are themselves political, not judicial acts, designed to create a new sovereignty and a new immunity. What, then, is the alternative? The answer comes in two stages. First, it is relatively easy to prosecute ordinary war crimes (*ius in bello*), and it is neither legally nor constitutionally problematic to prosecute actual perpetrators. The laws of war are well established on national statute books; the international treaty law on war is abundant. States have prosecuting authorities and they should, of course, prosecute an unscrupulous leader who gives an illegal command. The same goes for prosecutions for treason. Second, the use of courts martial should be encouraged for such prosecutions: one of the reasons for the current distortions and abuses of international war crimes tribunals, indeed, is that they are run by civilian intellectuals, lawyers who have never been professional soldiers and who do not know what it is like to be in the heat of battle. It is a core principle of law that a defendant be tried by his peers, and it is very important to resurrect this principle in the contemporary application of the laws of war. National tribunals are preferable to international ones because they are more deeply embedded in the national culture of the country concerned, and therefore more open to the checks and balances which come from public opinion, and because the new regime of which they are a part has to govern the country in question and take any political consequences of its prosecutions.

The problems arise when trials leave these limited domains and attempt to forge a new political order instead. When political acts hide behind judicial forms, the judicial forms invariably become politicized. Prosecution is itself an aspect of political power – a core aspect – and, like all political power, it needs to be wielded with great care. A good regime trial would be one in which the new sovereign displayed the political virtues as Aristotle defined them: courage, moderation, magnanimity, and prudence. Today's human rights activists, by contrast, are inspired by a punishment ethic which sits ill with these virtues and which often prefers war over peace in the name of 'justice'. The project to create new international tribunals is a political project – to create a new system of law and a new jurisdiction, with human rights activists in charge – just as the punishment of allegedly tyrannical kings was the blunt instrument by which revolutionary republican regimes were set up at national level in the past.

It is certainly desirable that all societies have systems by which to guard their core values, and that justice and peace be preserved. Punishment is due to the wicked and redress to the wronged. But the values needed to ensure these things lie beyond the realm of the law, in ethics and culture and religion. The goal of this book has therefore not been to provide an answer to the question of what to do with an unscrupulous leader, for the simple reason that to the questions raised no simple answer can ever be given. If, as Carl Schmitt says, the sovereign is the one who decides on the exceptional situation,[4] then the rules by which the new ruler adjudicates his predecessor's acts can by definition not be laid down in advance. What to do is a political matter – a matter of judgement which cannot be subsumed under pre-planned or fixed rules. For it is the very essence of the human condition itself that there is no escape from the oldest conundrum of political philosophy: if we appoint guardians to protect our supreme values, who will guard the guardians themselves?

Notes

Introduction

1. Human Rights Watch's various reports on the respective trials. See www. hrw.org.
2. President George H. W. Bush, 'Toward a New World Order', speech to Congress, 11 September 1990.
3. 'L'ère de « la contrainte des états» s'est ouverte, estime Louise Arbour', *Le Monde*, 6 August 1999, 4.
4. Geoffrey Robertson, *Crimes against Humanity: The Struggle for Global Justice* (London: Penguin, 1999; 2nd edn, 2000), xviii.
5. Robertson, *Crimes against Humanity*, 338.
6. Trials of War Criminals before the Nuremberg Military Tribunal under Control Council Law no. 10, vol. III, 'The Justice Case' (Washington, DC, 1951), 969–70. See ch. 3, 'Inverting Nuremberg', in John Laughland, *Travesty: the Trial of Slobodan Milošević and the Corruption of International Justice* (London: Pluto Press, 2007).
7. On this, see Kjetil Tronvoll et al. (eds), *The Ethiopian Red Terror Trials: Transitional Justice Challenged* (Oxford: James Curry Publishers, forthcoming).

Chapter 1: The Trial of Charles I and the Last Judgement

1. Michael Walzer, *The Revolution of the Saints* (London: Weidenfeld & Nicolson, 1965).
2. Geoffrey Robertson, *The Tyrannicide Brief: The Story of the Man who sent Charles I to the Scaffold* (London: Chatto & Windus, 2005; Vintage Books, 2006), 21.
3. Christopher Hill, *The Bible in Seventeenth Century English Politics*, The Tanner Lectures on Human Values, delivered at the University of Michigan, 4 October 1991, esp. 94 (published online at www.tannerlectures.utah.edu).
4. A. L. Rowse, *The Regicides and the Puritan Revolution* (London: Duckworth, 1994), 18.
5. William L. Sachse, 'England's "Black Tribunal": an Analysis of the Regicide Court', *Journal of British Studies*, 12 (1973). Other critics of the trial include Otto Kirchheimer, *Political Justice: The Use of Legal Procedure for Political*

Ends (Princeton, NJ: , 1951), 304, and Ron Christenson, *Political Trials: Gordian Knots in the Law* (New Brunswick, NJ and Oxford: Transaction Publishers, 1986), 234.

6.   This quotation, and much of the account of the trial which follows, is taken from the transcript and account of the trial in *A Complete Collection of State Trials and Proceedings for High Treason*, with a new preface by Francis Hargrave Esq. (London, 1776).

7.   Leon Trotsky, *Collected Writings and Speeches on Britain*, eds R. Chappell and A. Clinton (New York: New Park Publications, 1974); see ch. 6 'Two traditions: the seventeenth-century revolution and Chartism'.

8.   H. L. A. Hart, *The Concept of Law* (Oxford: Clarendon Press, 1961), 66.

9.   The most brilliant writing on this is that of Ernst Kantorowicz. See especially his great work *The King's Two Bodies: A Study in Medieval Political Theology* (Princeton, NJ: Princeton University Press, 1957) and his essay 'Mysteries of State: An Absolutist Concept and its Late Mediaeval Origins', in *Selected Studies* (Locust Valley, NY: J. J. Augustin Publisher, 1965), 381.

10. See on this, John Laughland, 'The Crooked Timber of Humanity: sovereignty, jurisdiction and the confusions of human rights', *The Monist*, vol. 90, no. 1 (January 2007).

11. *A Complete Collection of State Trials and Proceedings for High Treason*, 1043.

12. Patricia Crawford, 'Charles Stuart, That Man of Blood', *Journal of British Studies*, 16/2 (1977), 41–61.

13. William Allen, *A Faithful Memorial of that Remarkable Meeting of Many Officers of the Army of England, at Windsor Castle, in the Year 1648* (1659); available e.g. in Clarendon Historical Society Reprints, series 2, no. 6 (Edinburgh, 1885).

14. René Girard, *Le bouc émissaire* (Paris: Editions Grasset, 1992), 65.

15. Girard, *Le bouc émissaire*, 62.

16. Henry Scudder, *Gods Warning to England*, 23; quoted in Crawford, 'Charles Stuart, That Man of Blood', 48. See Crawford, 48–9, for many other similar passages.

17. Ernst Lee Tuveson, *Redeemer Nation: The Idea of America's Millennial Role* (Chicago, IL.: University of Chicago Press, 1968); Norman Cohn, *The Pursuit of the Millennium: Revolutionary Millenarians and Mystical Anarchists of the Middle Ages* (London: Paladin, 1970); Mark Bell's Oxford D.Phil. thesis, 'The Theology of Violence' (2002), to which excellent work I am greatly indebted.

18. Stephen Marshall, *A Divine Project to Save a Kingdom ... A Sermon to the Lord Maior and Court of Aldermen of the Citie of London* (1644); quoted by Mark Bell.

19. Thomas Case, *Josephat's Caveat to his Judges Delivered in a Sermon* (1644); quoted by Bell.

20. Thomas Manton, *A Practical Commentary ... on the Epistle of St. James*, 422–4; quoted by Bell.

21. For Marshall's apocalypticism, see also his *The Song of Moses and the Song of the Lambe* (1643).

22. Sermon preached, *inter alia*, in the House of Commons on 23 February 1641.

23. Ian Gentles, *The New Model Army in England, Ireland, and Scotland, 1645–1653* (Oxford: Blackwell, 1992), 93.

24. Quoted in Robert S. Paul, *The Lord Protector* (London: Lutterworth Press, 1955), 217.

25. John Calvin, *Institutes* 4: 20.4; see Bell, 'The Theology of Violence', 67 & 103.

26. Quoted in Bell, 'The Theology of Violence', 274.

Chapter 2: *The Trial of Louis XVI and the Terror*

1. Carl Schmitt, *Politische Theologie, Vier Kapitel zur Lehre von der Souveränität* (Berlin: Duncker & Humblot, 1922; repr. 1990), 49.

2. Albert Camus, *L'homme révolté* (Paris: Gallimard, 1951). See also Edmund Burke, *Reflections on the Revolution in France* (London, 1790); Jean Dumont, *Les prodiges du sacrilège* (Paris: Criterion, 1984).

3. Burke's great tract, *Reflections on the Revolution in France*, is shot through with such overtly religious language. See Dumont, *Les prodiges du sacrilège* (the title is itself a quotation from the *Reflections*), and John Laughland, 'The Prodigies of Sacrilege: Edmund Burke on Money', *The Salisbury Review* (autumn 1999) and *The University Bookman* (spring 2000).

4. Marc Bloch, *Les rois thaumaturges, études sur le caractère surnaturel attribué à la puissance royale, particulièrement en France et en Angleterre* (Strasbourg: Publications de la Faculté de Lettres, 1924; 2nd edn, Paris: Librairie Armand Collin, 1961; Paris: Gallimard, 1983).

5. For this and the succeeding account of the way the trial evolved, see Paul and Pierette Girault de Coursac, *Enquête sur le procès du roi* (Paris: F.-X. de Guibert), 1992. I am greatly indebted to this work. For this reference see page 18, quoting *Moniteur* 1792, no. 186 (xiii–35).

6. Girault de Coursac, *Enquête*, 29; quoting *Moniteur* 1792, no. 267 Sup. (xiv–17).

7. Girault de Coursac, *Enquête*, 43; quoting *Moniteur* 1792, no. 238 bis (xiii–518).

8. Girault de Coursac, *Enquête*, 35; quoting *Moniteur* 1792, no. 230 (xiii–430).

9. Girault de Coursac, *Enquête*, 35; quoting *Moniteur* 1792, no. 230 (xiii–432).

10. Girault de Coursac, *Enquête*, 36.

11. Girault de Coursac, *Enquête*, 42–3.

12. Quoted in Edwin Bannon, *Refractory Men, Fanatical Women: Fidelity to Conscience during the French Revolution* (Leominster: Gracewing, 1992), 47–8.

13. Girault de Coursac, *Enquête*, 64.

14. For the text of Mailhe's speech and of the other key speeches, see Michael Walzer, *Regicide and Revolution: Speeches at the Trial of Louis XVI* (Cambridge: Cambridge University Press, 1974).

15. Quoted in Walzer, *Regicide and Revolution*.

16. On this, see Carl Schmitt, *Der Nomos der Erde im Völkerrecht des Jus Publicum Europaeum* (Berlin: Duncker & Humblot, 1950), 15 and *passim*, as well as in other shorter works, e.g. *Land und Meer* (Leipzig: Philipp Reclam, 1942); transl. S. Draghici, *Land and Sea* (Washington, DC: Plutarch Press, 1997).

17. Quoted in Jacques Vergès, *Les crimes d'État: la comédie judiciare* (Paris: Broché, 2004), ch. 6 'Un procès sacrilège', 140, emphasis added.

18. Girault de Coursac, *Enquête*, 71; quoting *Moniteur 1792*, no. 340 (xiv–646). See also Walzer, *Regicide and Revolution*, for an English translation.

19. Quoted in Vergès, *Les crimes d'État*, 141.

20. Girault de Coursac, *Enquête*, 76; quoting *Moniteur 1792*, no. 343 (xiv–673 to 674).

21. Girault de Coursac, *Enquête*, 99; quoting *Moniteur 1792*, no. 348 (xiv–713).

22. See ch. 3 below.

23. Quoted in Vergès, *Les crimes d'État*, 148.

24. Girault de Coursac, *Enquête*, 101; quoting *Moniteur 1792*, no. 348 (xiv–718 to 720).

25. Jacques Isorni, *Le vrai procès du roi* (Paris: Atelier Marcel Jullian, 1980), 12.

26. The transcript of the interrogation of 11 December has been republished in Paul and Pierette Girault de Coursac (eds), *La défense de Louis XVI par Malesherbes, Tronchet et Desèze, précédée du procès-verbal de l'interrogatoire du roi* (Paris: F.-X. de Guibert, 1993), 39–50.

27. Girault de Coursac, *Enquête*, 112; quoting *Journal de la République française*, 12 December 1792.

28. Girault de Coursac, *Enquête*, 112–13; quoting *Convention*, Procès-verbaux (iv–187) and *Moniteur 1792*, no. 348 (xiv–722).

29. Girault de Coursac , *Enquête*, 113; quoting *Moniteur 1792*, no. 348 (xiv–723); *Le Journal universel* quoted by *Les révolutions de Paris*, no. 179, 550.

30. Girault de Coursac, *Enquête*, 114; quoting *Convention*, Procès-verbaux (iv–205).

31. Girault de Coursac, *Enquête*, 105–9.

32. Girault de Coursac, *Enquête*, 118; quoting *Moniteur 1792*, no. 349 (xiv–728 to 729)

33. Isorni, *Le vrai procès du roi*, 24.

34. Isorni, *Le vrai procès du roi*, 26.

35. Isorni, *Le vrai procès du roi*, 28.

36. De Sèze's whole speech is reprinted, together with the amendments he made on his own notes, in Girault de Coursac (eds), *La défense de Louis XVI*.

37. Quoted in Isorni, *Le vrai procès du roi*, 175.

38. Isorni, *Le vrai procès du roi*, 209.

39. L. Saintmichael, *Vie politique de tous les deputes à la Convention nationale pendant et après la Révolution, par M. R., ouvrage dans lequel on trouve la preuve que dans le procès de Louis XVI la peine de mort avait été rejetée à une majorité de six voix* (Paris, 1814).

40. Marc Roche, *Le Monde*, 11 April 2006.

Chapter 3 : War Guilt after World War I

1. On these two competing approaches to law, see John Laughland, 'The Crooked Timber of Humanity: sovereignty, jurisdiction and the confusions of human rights', *The Monist*, vol. 90, no. 1 (January 2007), drawing on the works of Michel Villey, esp. *Le droit et les droits de l'homme* (Paris: Presses Universitaires de France, 1983). For the transition from land-based law to sea-based universalism, see Carl Schmitt, *Der Nomos der Erde* (Berlin: Duncker & Humblot, 1950) and *Land und Meer* (Stuttgart: Philipp Reclam, 1942).

2. Gary Bass, *Stay the Hand of Vengeance: The Politics of War Crimes Tribunals* (Princeton, NJ: Princeton University Press, 2000), 123. What follows is drawn from his ch. 4, 'Constantinople'.

3. James F. Willis, *Prologue to Nuremberg: The Politics and Diplomacy of Punishing War Criminals of the First World War* (Westport and London: Greenwood Press, 1982), 30. I am greatly indebted to this excellent book for the following account.

4. Willis, *Prologue to Nuremberg*, 31.

5. Willis, *Prologue to Nuremberg*, 28–9.

6. On this, see Hans-Hermann Hoppe, *Democracy, The God that Failed: The Economics and Politics of Monarchy, Democracy and Natural Order* (New Brunswick, NJ, and London: Transaction Publishers, 2001), ix–xiv; Erik von Kuehnelt-Leddihn, *Leftism Revisited: From De Sade to Pol Pot* (Washington, DC: Regnery, 1990), 209–10.

7. Willis, *Prologue to Nuremberg*, 55.

8. Willis, *Prologue to Nuremberg*, 57.

9. Willis, *Prologue to Nuremberg*, 59.

10. Emphasis added.

11. Otto von Stülpnagel, *Die Wahrheit über die deutschen Kriegsverbrechen* (Berlin: Staatspolitischer Verlag, 1920).

12. Woodrow Wilson, *Presidential Messages and Addresses and Public Papers (1917–1924)*, eds. Ray S. Baker and William E. Dodd (New York and London: Harper & Brothers, 1927), vol. 2, 414; quoted in Ernst Lee Tuveson, *Redeemer Nation: The Idea of America's Millennial Role* (Chicago, Il. and London: University of Chicago Press, 1968), 211, emphasis added.

13. Margaret Macmillan, *Paris 1919* (New York: Random House, 2001), 13.

14. Alain Besançon, *Les origines intellectuelles du léninisme* (Paris: Calmann-Lévy, 1977), 17.

15. See for instance, V. I. Lenin, *On Dialectics*, in *Marx. Engel. Marxism* (7th revised edn, Moscow: Progress Publishers, 1965), 271–2.

16. Trotsky's Diary, entry for 9 April 1935, in Houghton Library, Harvard; quoted by Richard Pipes, *The Russian Revolution 1899–1919* (London: Harvill Press, 1997), 763. See also Isaac Deutscher, *The Prophet Armed: Trotsky 1879–1921* (Oxford: Oxford University Press), 418.

17. Elizabeth A. Wood, *Performing Justice: Agitation Trials in Early Soviet Russia* (Ithaca, NY: Cornell University Press, 2005).

18.   V.I. Lenin, 'The Question of the Bolshevik Leaders Appearing in Court', in *Collected Works* (Moscow: Progress Publishers, 1960–70, vol. 25, 174 (first published in *Proletarskaya Revolyutsia*, no 1 (36), 1925) .

19.   Quoted by Michael Llewellyn Smith, *Ionian Vision: Greece in Asia Minor 1919–1922* (London: Allen Lane, 1973; facsimile edn, Hurst, 1998), 321.

20.   This account is taken from the diplomatist Frangulis, quoted in Llewellyn-Smith, *Ionian Vision*, 329.

Chapter 4: Defeat in the Dock: the Riom Trial

1.   Frédéric Pottecher, *Le procès de la défaite, Riom Février–Avril 1942* (Paris: Fayard, 1989), 19.

2.   Maurice Ribet, *Le procès de Riom* (Paris: Flammarion, 1945), 21.

3.   Robert Badinter, *Un antisémitisme ordinaire, Vichy et les avocats juifs (1940–1944)* (Paris: Fayard, 1997).

4.   See ch. 1 of my book *The Tainted Source: the Undemocratic Origins of the European Idea* (London: Little, Brown, 1997; 2nd edn, London: Warner Books, 1998), for a discussion of the pro-European groups in France before and during the war. On Abetz, see Barbara Lambauer, *Otto Abetz et les Français, 1930–1958* (Paris: Fayard, 2001).

5.   Text quoted by Pierre Béteille and Christiane Rimbaud, *Le procès de Riom* (Paris: Plon, 1973,) 33.

6.   Appeal, 8 August 1940; quoted in Ribet, *Le procès de Riom*, 13.

7.   Charles de Gaulle, preface to Pierre Tissier, *Le procès de Riom* (London: Harrap, 1943), 5.

8.   Pottecher, *Le procès de la défaite*, 17.

9.   Ribet, *Le procès de Riom*, 16.

10.   This and the other key constitutional laws of the Vichy government can be consulted at http://mjp.univ-perp.fr/france/co1940.htm.

11.   Henri Michel, *Le procès de Riom* (Paris: Albin Michel, 1979), 42–3. Michel's is probably the best book on the Riom trial.

12.   Michel, *Le procès de Riom*, 71.

13.   Maurice Ribet, who gives a vibrant account of hearing the broadcast which was to affect him so deeply (*Le procès de Riom*, 23), gets the date wrong and says the speech was on 15 October.

14.   Michel, *Le procès de Riom*, 51–2.

15.   Michel, *Le procès de Riom*, 55–63.

16.   Pottecher, *Le procès de la défaite*, 31.

17.   James de Coquet, *Le procès de Riom* (Paris: Arthème Fayard, 1945), 20–1.

18.   Pottecher, *Le procès de la défaite*, 117.

19.   Pottecher quotes from Déat's articles in *L'Oeuvre* of 24 February 1942 and a few days later in *Le procès de la défaite*, 65.

20.   De Coquet, *Le procès de Riom*, 19–20.

21.   De Coquet, *Le procès de Riom*, 30.

22.   See Blum's speech at the opening of the trial in de Coquet, *Le procès de Riom*, 27ff.

23. Ribet, *Le procès de Riom*, 18.
24. Pottecher, *Le procès de la défaite*, 48.
25. Michel, *Le procès de Riom*, 244.
26. Michel, *Le procès de Riom*, 369.
27. The military commander in France, General Carl-Heinrich von Stülpnagel, sent Hitler a secret report on the political situation in France on 31 March 1942, 'Lagebericht Februar / März 1942'.

Chapter 5: Justice as Purge: Marshal Pétain Faces his Accusers

1. Vichy apologists say that the figure was nearer 100,000; the figure of 30,000 to 40,000 is from Robert Aron. Official French government statistics put the figure at 10,000, with which some historians agree. See Robert Aron, *Histoire de Vichy* (Paris: Fayard, 1954); see also Yves Beigbeder, *Judging War Crimes and Torture: French Justice and International Criminal Tribunals (1940–2005)* (Leiden and Boston, MA.: Martinus Nijhoff, 2006), 174–5.
2. For Renthe-Fink's writings on European unity, especially his 1943 'Note on the Establishment of a European Confederation', see John Laughland, *The Tainted Source: the Undemocratic Origins of the European Idea* (London: Little, Brown, 1997, and Warner Books, 1998), 33–4.
3. See Gaston Schmitt, *La vérité sur le procès Pucheu* (Paris: Plon, 1963), 37–8. Schmitt was the judge who had condemned Pierre Pucheu, formerly Vichy minister of the interior, to death.
4. José Augustin Martinéz, *Les procès criminels d'après guerre: documents pour l'histoire contemporaine*, trans. from Spanish by Francis de Miomandre, preface by Jacques Isorni (Paris: Albin Michel, 1958), 29–30.
5. See my essay on the trial of Maurice Papon: 'Bad Judgment at Bordeaux', *The National Interest* (summer 1998). For a Gaullist defence of Papon, see Maurice Papon, *La vérité n'intéressait personne: entretiens avec Michel Bergès sur un procès contre la mémoire* (Paris: F.-X. de Guibert, 1999) and Hubert de Beaufort, *La Contre-Enquête* (Paris: F.-X. de Guibert, 1999).
6. For these figures, see Henri Rousso, *Le Syndrome de Vichy de 1944 à nos jours* (Paris: Éditions du Seuil, 1987, 2nd edn 1990), 16. See also Beigbeder, *Judging War Crimes and Torture*, 176.
7. Henri Amouroux, *La page n'est pas encore tournée* (Paris: Robert Laffont, 1994), 483.
8. Jacques Isorni, preface to Pétrus Faure, *Un procès inique* (Paris: Flammarion, 1973), 20.
9. Jacques Isorni, *Philippe Pétain* (Paris: La Table Ronde, 1973), vol. 2, 459; see also Fred Kupferman, *Le procès de Vichy* (Brussels: Éditions Complexe, 1980), 79.
10. *Procès du Maréchal Pétain: compte rendu officiel* (Paris: Éditions Louis Pariente, 1976), 12–15.
11. *Procès du Maréchal Pétain: compte rendu officiel*, 15–16.
12. Charles de Gaulle, *Mémoires de Guerre: L'Appel 1940–1942* (Paris: Plon, 1954), 57; see also Jean Lacouture, *De Gaulle* (Paris: Éditions du Seuil, 1969), 71.

13.   Joseph Kessel, *Jugements derniers: les procès Pétain et Nuremberg*, préface de
      Francis Lacassin (Paris: Christian de Barthillat, 1995), 27.
14.   Isorni read the letter out in the session of 24 July 1945; see *Procès du Maré-
      chal Pétain: compte rendu officiel*, 43.
15.   *Procès du Maréchal Pétain: compte rendu officiel*, 61.
16.   *Procès du Maréchal Pétain: compte rendu officiel*, 173; for Reynaud's reply, see
      187.
17.   *Procès du Maréchal Pétain: compte rendu official*, 175.
18.   Hearing of Wednesday 1 August 1945, *Procès du Maréchal Pétain: compte
      rendu officiel*, 210.
19.   *Procès du Maréchal Pétain: compte rendu official*, 131–2.
20.   *Procès du Maréchal Pétain: compte rendu official*, 133.
21.   Kessel, *Jugements derniers*, 80ff.
22.   Pétrus Faure, *Un procès inique*, 46.
23.   'The court was totally biased against Pétain: the trial was a political trial, in
      a general atmosphere in France of revenge stirred up by the Communists,'
      Yves Beigbeder, *Judging War Crimes and Torture*, 188.
24.   Faure, *Un procès inique*, 218.

Chapter 6: Treachery on Trial: the Case of Vidkun Quisling

1.   This sequence of events is taken from ch. 7 of Paul M. Hayes, *Quisling: The
      Career and Political Ideas of Vidkun Quisling 1887–1945* (Newton Abbot:
      David & Charles, 1971).
2.   I am greatly indebted to Hans Fredrik Dahl, *Quisling: A Study in Treachery*
      (Cambridge: Cambridge University Press, 1999), for this account.
3.   Dahl, *Quisling*, 377.
4.   Dahl, *Quisling*, 379.
5.   The Gaullist reasoning is well explained in Charles Zorgbibe, *De Gaulle,
      Mitterrand et l'esprit de la constitution* (Paris: Hachette, 1993).
6.   Hayes, *Quisling*, 299 & 303.
7.   Hans Fredrik Dahl, 'Dealing with the Past in Scandinavia: Legal purges and
      popular memories of Nazism and World War II in Denmark and Norway
      after 1945', in Jon Elster (ed.), *Retribution and Restitution in the Transition to
      Democracy* (Cambridge: Cambridge University Press, 2006).
8.   Stein Ugelvik Larsen, 'Die Ausschaltung der Quislinge in Norwegen', in
      Klaus-Dietmar Henke and Hans Woller (eds), *Politische Säuberung in Eu-
      ropa* (Munich: Deutscher Taschenbuch Verlag, 1991), 245 n.3.
9.   Para. 51 in *Provisorisk anordning om tillegg til straffelovgivningen om forræderi*
      (Provisional Decree on Supplements to the Penal Code), 15 December
      1944; quoted in Dahl, 'Dealing with the Past in Scandinavia'.
10.   Antonio Cassese, 'Introduction' to B. V. A. Röling, *The Tokyo Trial and Be-
      yond: Reflections of a Peacemonger*, ed. A. Cassese (Cambridge: Polity Press,
      1993), 9.
11.   Telford Taylor, *The Anatomy of the Nuremberg Trials* (New York: Knopf,
      1992), 193.

12. Taylor, *Anatomy*, 413 & 578.
13. J. L. Brierly, *The Law of Nations: An Introduction to the International Law of Peace* (6th edn, Oxford: Clarendon Press, 1963), 405.
14. Maurice Hankey, *Politics, Trials and Errors* (Oxford: Pen-in-Hand, 1950), ch. 4.
15. Dahl, *Quisling*, 384.
16. Dahl, *Quisling*, 385.
17. Quoted by Franklin Knudsen, *I was Quisling's Secretary* (London: Britons Publishing Company, 1967), 62.
18. The text is in Hans Werner Neulen, *Europa und das 3. Reich: Einigungsbestrebungen im deutschen Machtbereich 1939–1945* (Munich: Universitas, 1987), 356.
19. Quoted in Ralph Hewins, *Quisling: Prophet without Honour* (London: W. H. Allen, 1965), 21–2; see also Hayes, *Quisling*, 12.
20. The best account of the trial itself is in Dahl, *Quisling*.
21. Dahl, *Quisling*, 393.
22. Dahl, *Quisling*, 396–7.
23. Dahl, *Quisling*, 403.
24. Hewins, *Prophet without Honour,* 367
25. Hayes, *Quisling*, 302.
26. Dahl, *Quisling*, 404.
27. Dahl, *Quisling*, 406.
28. Quoted in Hayes, *Quisling*, 302; for a longer version of the same quotation, see Hewins, *Prophet without Honour,* 367–8.
29. Quoted in Hewins, *Prophet without Honour,* 367–70.

Chapter 7: Nuremberg: Making War Illegal

1. Telford Taylor, *The Anatomy of the Nuremberg Trials* (New York: Knopf, 1992), xi.
2. Cicero, *De Legibus*, II, iv.
3. Taylor, *Anatomy*, 167.
4. Taylor, *Anatomy*, 54.
5. Quoted in Taylor, *Anatomy*, 575.
6. In his famous essay 'Gesetzliches Unrecht und übergesetzliches Recht', *Süddeutsche Juristen-Zeitung* 1 (1946), 105–8.
7. Istvan Déak makes this point in his excellent article 'Misjudgement at Nuremberg', *New York Review of Books*, 7 October 1993.
8. Elizabeth Borgwardt, *A New Deal for the World: America's Vision of Human Rights* (Cambridge, MA.: Harvard University Press, 2005).
9. Robert H. Jackson, opening address before the International Military Tribunal, 21 November 1945 (second day).
10. International Conference on Military Trials, London, 1945, Minutes of Conference Session [hereafter London Conference], 29 June 1945; see www.yale.edu/lawweb/avalon/avalon.htm.
11. London Conference, 25 July 1945; emphasis added.
12. London Conference, 25 July 1945.

13. Arkady Vaksberg, *The Prosecutor and the Prey: Vyshinsky and the 1930s Moscow Show Trials* (London: Weidenfeld & Nicolson, 1990), 101.

14. London Conference, 29 June 1945.

15. London Conference, 19 July 1945.

16. London Conference, 29 June 1945.

17. London Conference, 23 July 1945.

18. London Conference, 23 July 1945.

19. London Conference, 25 July 1945.

20. Aron Naumovich Trainin, *Ugolovnaia interventsiia* (Moscow, 1935); repr. in *Izbrannye proizvedeniya: Zashchita mira i ugolovnyi zakon*, ed. R. A. Rudenko (Moscow: Izdatel'stvo Nauk, 1969), 17–69.

21. Leon Trotsky, *My Life* (New York: Charles Scribner's Sons, 1930, ch. 29, 'In Power'; also available on www.marxists.org.

22. *Zashchita mira i ugolovnyi zakon* (Moscow: 1937). I am greatly indebted to George Ginsburgs, *Moscow's Road to Nuremberg: The Soviet Background to the Trial*, (The Hague: Martinus Nijhoff, 1996), 20 and *passim*.

23. Ginsburgs, *Moscow's Road to Nuremberg*, 21.

24. See for instance Vyshinskii's speech to the UN General Assembly, 25 September 1948, 'The USSR on Guard over the Peace and Security of Nations'.

25. Taylor, *Anatomy*, 26.

26. Ginsburgs, *Moscow's Road to Nuremberg*, 36.

27. Taylor, *Anatomy*, 28–9.

28. London Conference, 26 June 1945.

29. Antonio Cassese, 'Introduction' to B. V. A. Röling, *The Tokyo Trial and Beyond: Reflections of a Peacemonger*, ed. A. Cassese (Cambridge: Polity Press, 1993), 10.

30. Taylor, *Anatomy*, 80, and Bradley Smith, *Reaching Judgement at Nuremberg* (New York: Basic Books, 1977), 51, are surely wrong on this point.

31. London Conference, 19 July 1945; emphasis added.

32. Taylor, *Anatomy*, 583.

33. P. S. Romashkin, *Voennye prestupleniia imperializma* (Moscow: Nauk, 1953), 273.

34. See *Report of Court Proceedings in the Case of the Anti-Soviet 'Bloc of Rights and Trotskyites'* (Moscow: People's Commissariat of Justice of the USSR, 1938), 695. See also Ginsburgs, *Moscow's Road to Nuremberg*, 65.

35. A. Ya. Vyshinskii, *Voprosy teorii gosudarstva i prava* (2nd edn, Moscow: Gosudarstvennoe izdatel'stvo yuridicheskoy literatury, 1949), 110.

36. See Aaron Fichtelberg, 'Conspiracy and International Criminal Justice', *Criminal Law Forum*, vol. 17, no. 2 (June 2006).

37. Taylor, *Anatomy*, 211.

38. Vaksberg, *The Prosecutor and the Prey*, 259.

39. Taylor, *Anatomy*, 326.

40. Hans Kelsen, 'Will the Judgement in the Nuremberg Trial constitute a Precedent in International Law?', *The International Law Quarterly*, vol. 1, no. 2 (summer 1947).

41. Kelsen, 'The Judgement in the Nuremberg Trial', 171.

Chapter 8: Creating Legitimacy: the Trial of Marshal Antonescu

1. *Report of the International Commission on the Holocaust in Romania*, submitted to President Ion Iliescu in Bucharest on 11 November 2004.

2. Arkady Vaksberg, *The Prosecutor and the Prey, Vyshinsky and the 1930s Moscow Show Trials* (London: Weidenfeld & Nicolson, 1990), 246.

3. The decree-law is published as Document 3 in *Procesul Mareşalului Antonescu, Documente*, ed. Marcel-Dumitru Ciucă, 3 vols (Bucharest: Editura Saeculum, 1996–8), 55ff. (all references to this work are to vol. 1).

4. For a full translation of the charges, see *Report of the International Commission on the Holocaust in Romania*, ch. 12, 'The Trials of the War Criminals', 6.

5. *Procesul Mareşalului Antonescu*, 'Introducere', 32–3.

6. See *Report of the International Commission on the Holocaust in Romania*, ch. 12, 'The Trials of the War Criminals', 7–8.

7. François Furet, *Le passé d'une illusion: essai sur l'idée communiste au XXe siècle* (Paris: Robert Laffont/Calmann-Lévy, 1995), ch. 7.

8. Iosif Constantin Drăgan, 'Cuvânt înainte', in *Procesul Mareşalului Antonescu*, 6.

9. *Procesul Mareşalului Antonescu*, 'Introducere', 23.

10. *Report of the International Commission on the Holocaust in Romania*, ch. 12, 'The Trials of the War Criminals', 13.

11. *Procesul Mareşalului Antonescu*, 'Actul de Accusare', 64.

12. *Procesul Mareşalului Antonescu*, 'Actul de Accusare', 68 & 116.

13. *Procesul Mareşalului Antonescu*, 'Actul de Accusare', 63.

14. *Procesul Mareşalului Antonescu*, 'Actul de Accusare', 133.

15. *Procesul Mareşalului Antonescu*, 'Interogatoriul lui Ion Antonescu', 6 May 1946', 201.

16. See for instance Romulus Rusan, *Geografia si cronologia Gulagului românesc* ('The geography and chronology of the Romanian gulag'), which begins with a quotation from an NKVD directive (i.e. from Moscow), dated 2 June 1947, instructing the Romanian Communists to liquidate the political opposition. www.memorialsighet.ro.

17. *Procesul Mareşalului Antonescu*, document no. 6, 186.

18. Ileana, Princess of Romania and Archduchess of Austria, *I Live Again* (London: Victor Gollancz, 1952), 262–3.

19. *Procesul Mareşalului Antonescu*, 'Interogatoriul lui Ion Antonescu', 203.

20. *Procesul Mareşalului Antonescu*, 'Interogatoriul lui Ion Antonescu', 205.

21. Quoted by István Déak, 'Retribution or Revenge: War Crimes Trials in Post World War II Hungary', in *Hungary and the Holocaust: Confrontation with the Past*, symposium proceedings (Washington, DC: U. S. Holocaust Memorial Museum, Center for Advanced Holocaust Studies, 2001), 39.

22. *Procesul Mareşalului Antonescu*, 'Interogatoriul lui Ion Antonescu', 206–8.

Chapter 9: Ethnic Cleansing and National Cleansing in Czechoslovakia, 1945–1947

1. Telford Taylor, *The Anatomy of the Nuremberg Trials* (New York: Knopf, 1992), 69.
2. 'National cleansing' is appropriately the title of an excellent book on this. See Benjamin Frommer, *National Cleansing: Retribution against Nazi collaborators in post-war Czechoslovakia* (Cambridge: Cambridge University Press, 2005).
3. Decree No. 17, para. 2.
4. Decree No. 16, 19 June 1945, para. 22.1.
5. Edvard Beneš, *Světová krise, kontinuita práva a nové právo revoluční* ('The World Crisis: the continuity of law and new revolutionary law'), speech at the Charles University in Prague, December 1945 (Prague: V. Linhart, 1946); quoted in Frommer, *National Cleansing*, 'Introduction', 1.
6. Frommer, *National Cleansing*, 2.
7. Gottwald in April 1945; quoted in Frommer, *National Cleansing*, 6.
8. Frommer, *National Cleansing*, 271.
9. Frommer, *National Cleansing*, 281.
10. Frommer, *National Cleansing*, 283.
11. Bradley Abrams, 'The Politics of Retribution: the Trial of Jozef Tiso in the Czechoslovak Environment', in István Déak, Jan T. Gross, and Tony Judt (eds), *The Politics of Retribution in Europe* (Princeton, NJ: Princeton University Press, 2000), 262.
12. Viliam Široký, Central Committee Meeting of the Czechoslovak Communist Party, 16 December 1946; quoted in Abrams, 'The Politics of Retribution', 262.
13. Abrams, 'The Politics of Retribution'.
14. Abrams, 'The Politics of Retribution', 263-4.
15. The text of the decree is published in Slovak and German in *Němci a Maďaři v Dekretech Prezidenta Republiky, Studie a Dokumente 1940–1945 / Die Deutschen und Magyaren in den Dekreten des Präsidenten der Republik, Studien und Dokumente 1940–1945*, ed. Karel Jech (Prague and Brno: Ústav pro soudobé dějiny AV ČR, Doplněk, 2003), 462–6. See also the official journal of the Slovak National Council, *Sbierka nariadení Slovenskej národnei rady 1946* (Decrees 57 and 58 of 14 May 1946), 67–78.
16. *Petition of the Slovak Action Committee to the United Nations in the Trial of Dr. Jozef Tiso, President and Other Representatives of the Slovak Republic Before the International Military Tribunal* (New York: Slovak Action Committee, 1947), 10. This document is signed by Ferdinand Ďurčansky, Tiso's foreign minister and co-defendant tried *in absentia*, who had fled to America.
17. I am greatly indebted to James Mace Ward, who kindly sent me his unpublished paper, 'The Trial of Jozef Tiso', which is to be included as the basis for a chapter in his forthcoming work on Tiso.
18. Ward, 'The Trial of Jozef Tiso', section entitled 'The Indictment'.
19. See Anton Rašla and Ernest Žabkay, *Proces s dr. J. Tisom, Spomienky* (Bratislava: Tatra Press, Slovak Union of Journalists, 1990).

20. František Vnuk, *Dr. Jozef Tiso, President of the Slovak Republic, in Commemoration of the Twentieth Anniversary of his Death at the Hands of the Enemies of Slovak Independence* (Sydney: The Association of Australian Slovaks, Orbis Publishing, 1967), 34.
21. Ward, 'The Trial of Jozef Tiso'.
22. Ward, 'The Trial of Jozef Tiso'. On the decision about broadcasts, see Abrams, 'The Politics of Retribution', 267, quoting Joseph Mikus, *Slovakia: A Political History* (Milwaukee, WI: Marquette, 1963), 176.
23. *Pravda*, Bratislava, 4 March 1947; quoted in Vnuk, *Dr Jozef Tiso*, 37 n.2.
24. Tiso's speech is printed in German as *Die Wahrheit über die Slowakei*, ed. Jon Sekera (1948). The paragraphs which follow are a short summary of that long speech.
25. Tiso, *Die Wahrheit über die Slowakei*, 44.
26. Tiso, *Die Wahrheit über die Slowakei*, 48.
27. James Mace Ward, 'People Who Deserve it: Jozef Tiso and the Presidential Exemption', *Nationalities Papers*, vol. 30, no. 4 (December 2002), 571–601.
28. James Ramon Felak, 'The Democratic Party and the Execution of Jozef Tiso', *Slovakia*, vol. 38, nos 70–71(2005).
29. Abrams, 'The Politics of Retribution', 267.
30. On this, see Felak, 'The Democratic Party and the Execution of Jozef Tiso', n. 5.
31. Abrams, 'The Politics of Retribution', 273.
32. Felak, 'The Democratic Party and the Execution of Jozef Tiso'.
33. Abrams, 'The Politics of Retribution', 274.
34. Quoted in Frommer, *National Cleansing*, 323.
35. Ward, 'The Trial of Jozef Tiso'.
36. Radio Slovakia International German Service, Nachrichten, 13 April 2007.

Chapter 10: People's Justice in Liberated Hungary

1.   Karl P. Benziger, 'The Trial of László Bárdossy. The Second World War and Factional Politics in Contemporary Hungary', *Journal of Contemporary History*, vol. 40, no. 3 (2005), 472.
2.   Margit Szöllösi-Janze, 'Pfeilkreuzler, Landesverräter und andere Volksfeinde, Generalabrechnung in Ungarn', in Klaus-Dietmar Henke and Hans Wolle (eds), *Politische Säuberung in Europa* (Munich: Deutscher Taschenbuch Verlag, 1991), 320 n. 17.
3.   István Déak, 'Retribution or Revenge: War Crimes Trials in Post World War II Hungary', in *Hungary and the Holocaust: Confrontation with the Past*, symposium proceedings (Washington, DC: United States Holocaust Memorial Museum, Center for Advanced Holocaust Studies, 2001), 37–8.
4.   The decree is quoted in Eugene (Jenö) Lévai, 'The War Crimes Trials Relating to Hungary', in Randolph L. Braham (ed.), *Hungarian-Jewish Studies* (New York: World Federation of Hungarian Jews, 1969), 260–1.
5.   Szöllösi-Janze, 'Pfeilkreuzler, Landesverräter und andere Volksfeinde', 326.
6.   *Nemzetgyülési Napló* (Diaries of the Temporary National Assembly), Eighth

Session, 13 September 1945; quoted in Anna Wessely, 'Overcoming the Fascist Legacy in Hungary', in Stein Ugelvik Larsen (ed.), *Modern Europe after Fascism* (New York: Columbia University Press, 1998), 992.

7. Déak, 'Retribution or Revenge'.
8. Lázlo Karsai, 'Crime and Punishment: People's Courts, Revolutionary Legality and the Hungarian Holocaust', www.sipa.columbia.edu. Karsai quotes Major's memoirs, *Népbíráskodás, forradalmi törvényesség* ('People's justice, revolutionary legality') (Budapest: Minerva K., 1988), and a TV documentary from 1984, *In the Name of the Hungarian People*.
9. Robert H. Jackson, report to the president, 6 June 1945.
10. László Karsai, 'The People's Courts and Revolutionary Justice in Hungary, 1945–46', in István Déak, Jan T. Gross, and Tody Judt (eds), *The Politics of Retribution in Europe: World War II and its Aftermath* (Princeton, NJ: Princeton University Press, 2000) 237, quoting Major, *Népbíráskodás*, 147.
11. ICTY Appeals Chamber, Prosecutor v. Duško Tadić, Judgement, 15 July 1999, para. 121.
12. ICTY Annual Report, 29 August 1994, para. 72.
13. Quoted in Lévai, 'The War Crimes Trials Relating to Hungary', 256.
14. István Ries, 'A népbíróság védelmében', in *Népbírósági Közlöny*, 8 November 1945; quoted in Karsai, 'People's Courts', 245.
15. Karsai, 'People's Courts', 235, quoting the Documents of the National Council of the People's Courts.
16. Karsai, 'People's Courts'.
17. The indictment and Bárdossy's defence speech are published in Pál Pritz, *The War Crimes Trial of Hungarian Prime Minister László Bárdossy* (Boulder, CO: Center for Hungarian Studies and Publications, 2004), 77–81. See also Benziger, 'The Trial of László Bárdossy', 471.
18. Repr. in Pritz, *War Crimes Trial*, 81–116.
19. Repr. in Pritz, *War Crimes Trial*, 116–59.
20. Pritz, *War Crimes Trial*, 159.
21. Karsai, 'People's Courts', 239.
22. Szöllösi-Janze, 'Pfeilkreuzler, Landesverräter und andere Volksfeinde', 311–12 esp. n.3.
23. See *The Trial of Dragoljub-Draža Mihailović: Stenographic Record and Documents from the Trial of Dragoljub-Draža Mihailović* (Belgrade: Union of the Journalists' Associations of the Federative Republic of Yugoslavia, 1946).
24. Stéphane Courtois, *Le livre noir du communisme* (Paris: Robert Laffont, 1997), 435.
25. Cardinal Mindszenty, *Memoirs* (London: Weidenfeld & Nicolson, 1974), 127.
26. *Time Magazine*, 18 July 1949, www.time.com.

Chapter 11: From Mass Execution to Amnesty and Pardon: Postwar Trials in Bulgaria, Finland, and Greece

1. I take this phrase from Vesselin Dimitrov, *Stalin's Cold War: Soviet Foreign Policy, Democracy and Communism in Bulgaria, 1941–48* (Basingstoke: Palgrave Macmillan, 2007), ch. 3.

2. Nikolai Poppetrov, 'Defascification in Bulgaria from 1944 to 1948: Real Dimensions and the Functions of Propaganda', in Stein Ugelvik Larsen (ed.), *Modern Europe after Fascism* (New York: Columbia University Press, 1998), 797.

3. Quoted in Dimitrov, *Stalin's Cold War*, ch. 3 n. 40.

4. Dimitrov, *Stalin's Cold War*, ch. 3.

5. The terms of the sentence no. 2 of 1945, dated 1 February 1945, is quoted by the 1996 ruling of the Bulgarian Supreme Court overturning it; see *Vrkhoven Sud na RB, Biuletin, Sudebna praktika*, vol. 9 (1996, Year XII), 7–11 (Sofia: Vurkhoven sud, 1991–6), court ruling no. 243, dated 12 April 1996.

6. Cyril E. Black, 'The Start of the Cold War in Bulgaria: a Personal View', *Review of Politics*, vol. 41, no. 2 (April 1979), 174. Black seems to have got the numbers of the defendants slightly wrong.

7. Stéphane Courtois, *Le Livre noir du communisme* (Paris: Robert Laffont, 1997), 430.

8. Courtois, *Le Livre noir du communisme*, 436.

9. The letter is reproduced in French translation in Tzvetan Todorov, *La Fragilité du bien: le sauvetage des juifs bulgares* (Paris: Albin Michel, 1999), 96–9.

10. Supreme Court of the Republic of Bulgaria, court ruling no. 243, dated 12 April 1996 (see n. 5 above).

11. Bulgarian Telegraph Agency, 26 August 1996.

12. See the excellent article by Klaus Reichel, 'An Hitlers Seite', *Die Zeit*, 2 March 2006.

13. Reichel, 'An Hitlers Seite'.

14. Lesse Lehtinen and Hannu Rautkallio, *Kansakunnan sijaiskärsijät* (Helsinki: WSOY), 2005).

15. Daniele Glaser, *Nato's Secret Armies: Operation Gladio and Terrorism in Western Europe* (London and New York: Frank Cass, 2005), 213–14.

16. C. M. Woodhouse, *The Struggle for Greece, 1944–1949* (London: Hart-Davis MacGibbon, 1976), 147.

17. Mark Mazower, *After the War Was Over: Reconstructing the Family, Nation and State in Greece, 1943–1960* (Princeton, NJ: Princeton University Press, 2000), 35.

18. I am grateful to Takis Nitis for looking.

Chapter 12: Politics as conspiracy: the Tokyo trials

1. *Official Transcript of the Proceedings of the International Military Tribunal for the Far East*, 29 April 1946–12 November 1948, 21.

2. B. V. A. Röling and C. F. Rüter (eds), *The Tokyo Judgement* (Amsterdam: APA-Amsterdam University Press), 1977.

3.   R. John Pritchard (ed.), *The Tokyo Major War Crimes Trial* (Lewiston and, New York: Edwin Mellen Press, 1998), 124 vols.

4.   Maurice Hankey devotes an entire chapter to Shigemitsu in *Politics, Trials and Errors* (Oxford: Pen-in-Hand, 1950).

5.   Douglas MacArthur, *Reminiscences* (New York: McGraw-Hill, 1964), 288.

6.   Kirsten Sellars, *The Rise and Rise of Human Rights* (Stroud: Sutton Publishing, 2002), 55.

7.   Richard H. Minear, *Victors' Justice: The Tokyo War Crimes Trial* (Tokyo: Charles E. Tuttle Company, 1971), 88–9.

8.   Barton J. Bernstein, 'The Atomic Bombs Reconsidered', *Foreign Affairs*, January/February 1995; quoted in Sellars, *The Rise and Rise of Human Rights*, 48.

9.   Minear, *Victors' Justice*, 53.

10. Sellars, *The Rise and Rise of Human Rights*, 51.

11. Sellars, *The Rise and Rise of Human Rights*, 52.

12. *Commission on the Responsibility of the Authors of the War and on the Enforcement of Penalties, Report Presented to the Preliminary Peace Conference*, 29 March 1919.

13. Pritchard, *The Tokyo Major War Crimes Trial*, General Preface, xxxv.

14. Francis B. Sayre, 'Criminal Conspiracy', *Harvard Law Review*, 35 (1922), 393–427.

15. Minear, *Victors' Justice*, 156–8.

16. Henri Bernard, 'Dissenting Opinion', in Pritchard (ed.), *The Tokyo Major War Crimes Trial*, vol. 105, 18 & 20.

17. Antonio Cassese, 'Introduction' to B. V. A. Röling, *The Tokyo Trial and Beyond: Reflections of a Peacemonger*, ed. A. Cassese (Cambridge: Polity Press, 1993), 81.

18. Cassese, 'Introduction', 87.

19. Minear, *Victors' Justice*, 89–90 & 141.

20. Bernard, 'Dissenting Opinion', 20–1.

21. Bernard, 'Dissenting Opinion', 21.

22. Bernard, 'Dissenting Opinion', 19.

23. Radhabinod Pal, *International Military Tribunal for the Far East: Dissentient Judgment* (Calcutta: Sanyal & Co., 1953).

24. Pal, *Dissentient Judgment*, 17.

25. Pal, *Dissentient Judgment*, 59.

26. Robert H. Jackson, report to the president, 6 June 1945.

27. Pal, *Dissentient Judgment*, 114–15.

28. Pritchard, *The Tokyo Major War Crimes Trial*, General Preface, li.

29. Sellars, *The Rise and Rise of Human Rights*, 54.

30. Pal, *Dissentient Judgment*, 620.

31. Minear, *Victors' Justice*, 92–3.

32. Joseph Keenan and Brendan Francis Brown, *Crimes Against International Law* (Washington, DC: Public Affairs Press, 1950), 155.

33. Keenan and Brown, *Crimes Against International Law*, 156 & 157, emphasis added.

Chapter 13: *The Greek Colonels, Emperor Bokassa, and the Argentine Generals: Transitional Justice, 1975–2007*

1. C. M. Woodhouse, *The Rise and Fall of the Greek Colonels* (New York: Franklin Watts, 1985), 31; quoting Richard Clogg's essay in Richard Clogg and George Yannopoulos, *Greece Under Military Rule* (London: Secker & Warburg, 1972).

2. On Gladio, see Daniele Glaser, *Nato's Secret Armies: Operation Gladio and Terrorism in Western Europe* (London and New York: Frank Cass, 2005); on Greece, see ch. 16.

3. Quoted in Brian Titley, *Dark Age: The Political Odyssey of Emperor Bokassa* (Montreal: McGill-Queens University Press, 1997), 157, to whom I am indebted for the account of this trial and of Bokassa's trial in person in 1986. Titley's source for this quotation is Bokassa's *Ma vérité*, 95–6, who in turn was quoting an article by Jacques-Marie Bourget published in the French weekly magazine, *VSD* (December 1980), to show how absurd the charges were. Bokassa's book was banned by the French courts in 1985, on the grounds that it violated the privacy of the former president, Valéry Giscard d'Estaing, and most copies were destroyed.

4. See Human Rights Watch report, *Bolivia: The Trial of Responsibilities, The García Meza Tejada Trial*, 10 September 1993.

5. Carlos Santiago Nino, *Radical Evil on Trial* (New Haven, CT: Yale University Press, 1996), 72. I am indebted to Nino for the account which follows.

Chapter 14: *Revolution Returns: the Trial of Nicolae Ceauşescu*

1. See e.g. Krishan Kumar, 'The Revolutions of 1989: Socialism, Capitalism, and Democracy', *Theory and Society*, vol. 21, no. 3 (June 1992), 309–56.

2. Kurt Hager (member of the Central Committee of the Socialist Unity Party), interview, *Stern*, 28 March 1987.

3. Austrian agency, Kathpress; quoted in Radu Portocala, *Autopsie du coup d'état roumain, au pays du mensonge triomphant* (Paris: Calmann-Lévy, 1990), 59.

4. *International Herald Tribune*, 19 December 1989.

5. Philip Knightley, *The First Casualty: The War Correspondent as Hero and Myth-Maker from the Crimea to Kosovo* (1st edn 1975; London: Prion Books, 2000), 86.

6. Transcripts of the Politburo meeting of 17 December 1989; quoted in Portocala, *Autopsie*, 43.

7. Victor Loupan, *La révolution n'a pas eu lieu: Roumanie, l'histoire d'un coup d'État* (Paris: Robert Laffont, 1990), 92.

8. Portocala, *Autopsie*, 67.

9. The text of the speech is given in Portocala, *Autopsie*, 74–6.

10. Quoted in Loupan, *La revolution n'a pas eu lieu*, 25.

11. For the quotations from Braude and Kaznacheyev, see Arkady Vaksberg, *The Prosecutor and the Prey: Vyshinsky and the 1930s Moscow Show Trials* (London: Weidenfeld & Nicolson, 1990), 96–7.

Chapter 15: A State on Trial: Erich Honecker in Moabit

1. Case concerning the Arrest Warrant of 11 April 2000 (Democratic Republic of Congo v. Belgium), Judgement, 14 February 2000; see esp. para. 60.
2. *Vertrag zwischen der Bundesrepublik Deutschland und der Deutschen Demokratischen Republik über die Herstellung der Einheit Deutschlands (Kapitel IX, Anlage I Kapitel III C II Sachgebiet C – Strafrecht und Ordnungswidrigkeitenrecht).*
3. Horst Sendler, 'Über Rechtsstaat, Unrechtsstaat und anderes', *Neue Justiz,* no. 9 (1991), 379–81.
4. Roman Grafe, *Deutsche Gerechtigkeit: Prozess gegen DDR-Grenzschützen und ihre Befehlshaber* (Munich: Siedler Verlag, 2004).
5. St Augustine, *De libero arbitrio,* I, 5; St Thomas Aquinas, *Treatise on Law,* question 96, article 4 (*Summa theologiae, Prima Secundae Partis*).
6. Gustav Radbruch, *Rechtsphilosophie* (3rd edn, Leipzig: Quelle & Meyer, 1932), 32; quoted in Uwe Wesel, *Ein Staat vor Gericht: Der Honecker-Prozess* (Frankfurt: Eichborn, 1994), 39. I am greatly indebted to Wesel for his excellent account of the trial.
7. Wesel, *Ein Staat vor Gericht,* 40.
8. A. James McAdams, 'The Honecker Trial: The East German Past and the German Future', *Review of Politics,* vol. 58, no. 1 (winter 1996). See also McAdams, *Judging the Past in Unified Germany* (Cambridge: Cambridge University Press, 2001), 35–41.
9. Transcript in Wesel, *Ein Staat vor Gericht,* 64–83.
10. This extraordinary episode is recounted in Wesel, *Ein Staat vor Gericht,* 95–7.

Chapter 16: Jean Kambanda, Convicted without Trial

1. Paul Belien, *A Throne in Brussels: Britain, the Saxe-Coburgs and the Belgianisation of Europe* (Exeter: Imprint Academic, 2005), 295.
2. Amnesty International Report, 'The Grenada 17: The Last Cold War Prisoners?', 2003 (AI Index: AMR 32/001/2003).
3. Amnesty International, Public Statement, 1 June 2007 (AI Index: AFR 34/005/2007 (Public)), 'The trial of Charles Taylor must be made relevant to Sierra Leoneans and Liberians'. See also Human Rights Watch, 31 May 2007, www.hrw.org.
4. Report of the Secretary-General Pursuant to Paragraph 2 of Security Council Resolution 808 (1993), presented 3 May 1993 (S/25704), para. 19. See also ch. 4 of my book *Travesty: the Trial of Slobodan Milošević and the Corruption of International Justice* (London: Pluto Press, 2007).
5. *Final Report of the Commission of Experts Established Pursuant to Security Council Resolution 935 (1994),* UNSC, UN Doc. S/1994/1405 (1994), Annex.
6. Letter from Filip Reyntjens to Hassan B. Jallow, Office of the Prosecutor, ICTR, 11 January 2005. The author wishes to thank Professor Reyntjens for giving him a copy of this letter. See also Filip Reyntjens, 'Rwanda, Ten

Years on: from Genocide to Dictatorship', *African Affairs*, vol. 103, no. 411, 177–210.

7. Prosecutor v. Édouard Karemera, Mathieu Ngirumpatse, Joseph Nzirorera, *Case No. ICTR-98-44-AR73(C)*, Decision on Prosecutor's Interlocutory Appeal of Decision on Judicial Notice, Appeals Chamber Decision, 16 June 2006.

8. Alex Obote-Odora, 'Conspiracy to Commit Genocide: Prosecutor v. Jean Kambanda and Prosecutor v. Alfred Musema', *Murdoch University Electronic Journal of Law*, vol. 8, no. 1 (March 2001), para. 39.

9. ICTR press release, 20 June 2006, 'ICTR Appeals Chamber takes Judicial Notice of Genocide in Rwanda'.

10. 'Rwanda "plane crash probe halted"', Mark Doyle, BBC News, 9 February 2007.

11. Délivrance de Mandats d'arret internationaux, Tribunal de Grande Instance de Paris, Cabinet de Jean-Louis Brugière, Premier Vice-President, Paris, 17 November 2006.

12. 'Rwanda breaks diplomatic relations with France', Associated Press, *International Herald Tribune*, 24 November 2006.

13. On these procedural shortcomings, see my book *Travesty*, ch. 5.

14. The Prosecutor v. Jean-Paul Akayesu, *Case No. ICTR-96-4-T* , Judgement, 2 September 1998, paras 130–44.

15. Statement from Dr Agwu U. Okali, Registrar of the ICTR, Concerning the Case of Mr Esdras Twagirimana, 20 September 1997.

16. The Prosecutor v. Jean Kambanda, *Case No. ICTR 97-23-S*, para. 39.

17. The letter is quoted by www.hirondelle.org.

18. ICTY Prosecutor v. Dražen Erdemović, 5 March 1998.

19. Kelly Ranasinghe, 'The Sacrifice of Jean Kambanda', *Chicago-Kent Journal of International and Comparative Law*, vol. 5 (spring 2005), 32.

20. Jean Kambanda, Déclaration, signed at Bamako on 23 September 2003, submitted to the ICTR on 31 May 2006 as Document ID32 (Ndindiliyimana). The author is grateful to Chris Black for sending him this document.

21. Testimony in trial of Bagosora et. al., *Case No. ICTR-98-41-T*, 11 July 2006.

Chapter 17: Kosovo and the New World Order: the Trial of Slobodan Milošević

1. Judgement, 30 September 1945; quoted in Telford Taylor, *The Anatomy of the Nuremberg Trials* (New York: Knopf and Little, Brown, 1992), 575.

2. SHAPE (Supreme Headquarters Allied Powers Europe), News Summary and Analysis, 12 May 1999.

3. Václav Havel, 'Kosovo and the End of the Nation-State', *New York Review of Books*, 10 June 1999.

4. Tony Blair, 'Doctrine of the International Community', speech, Chicago, 22 April 1999.

5. See for instance David Scheffer, later Bill Clinton's ambassador for war crimes, 'Toward a Modern Doctrine of Humanitarian Intervention', *University of Toledo Law Review*, 23 (winter 1992).

6. In 2007 he boasted of 'liberal interventionism' as the thing of which he was most proud (interview in the *Guardian*, 26 April 2007).

7. 'Interim Agreement for Peace and Self-Government in Kosovo', Rambouillet, February 23, 1999, Appendix B: Status of Multi-National Military Implementation Force.

8. This revisionist version of history has proved stubbornly popular. It was peddled, for instance, in the *Independent* on 11 December 2007, which had in a chronology: '1998: Serbs crack down on the separatist Kosovo Liberation Army (KLA), and hundreds of thousands of Albanian Kosovans begin to flee across the border. This prompts Nato to warn Milosevic on the treatment of Albanians.' In fact, there were no refugees until after the bombing started in March 1999.

9. Tony Blair, 'My pledge to the refugees', BBC News Online, 14 May 1999.

10. Fox News, 18 April 1999. See also 'U.S. fears 100,000 Kosovar men slain', Detroit News wire service, 19 April 1999.

11. CBS News, Face the Nation, 16 May 1999.

12. Noel Malcolm, 'Yes, there were mass killings', *Spectator*, 4 December 1999, 25.

13. 'No bodies at rumoured grave site in Kosovo', Reuters, 13 October 1999. Kelly Moore, a spokesperson for the ICTY, said after ICTY investigators had examined Trepča, 'They found absolutely nothing.' See my book *Travesty: the Trial of Slobodan Milošević and the Corruption of International Justice* (London: Pluto Press, 2007), ch. 1.

14. John Laughland, 'The Massacres that Never Were', *Spectator*, 30 October 1999, and 'I was Right about Kosovo', *Spectator*, 20 November 1999. Other journalists who wrote about this include Daniel Pearl, the *Wall Street Journal* reporter who in 2002 was decapitated on video by Islamist extremists in Pakistan. See Daniel Pearl and Robert Block, 'Body Count: War in Kosovo was Cruel, Bitter, Savage: Genocide it Wasn't. Tales of Mass Atrocity Arose and Were Passed Along, Often With Little Proof, No Corpses in Mine Shaft', *Wall Street Journal*, 31 December 1999.

15. See for example Xavier Raufer, 'Albanian Organised Crime', *Geopolitical Affairs*, vol. I, no. 2 (summer 2007), *The Long March to the West*, eds Michel Korinman and John Laughland (London and Portland, Oregon: Vallentine Mitchell Academic, 2007), 395–404.

16. Trial transcript, 24 November 2004, 33, 849.

17. In December 1999 I personally interviewed a Serb witness in Peć, near the Montenegrin border, who had seen such an operation.

18. This hypothesis was discussed in the Milošević trial and in that of his co-indictee, Milan Milutinović. See testimony of Patrick Ball in Milošević trial, 13–14 March 2002 and cross-examination of Ball in the Milutinović trial, 21 February 2007; transcripts available on www.un.org/icty. For other evidence, see Eve-Ann Prentice, *One Woman's War: Life and Death on Deadline* (London: Duckworth, 2000), 113; also the German TV documentary, *Es began mit einer Lüge* ('It began with a lie') broadcast on ARB on 8 February 2001, transcript available at: http://www.wdr.de/online/news/kosovol-

uege/sendung_text.pdf. See also the discovery of Serb police uniforms in a KLA arms cache, reported by Agence France Presse on 3 December 1999, 'Illegal arms cache found in homes of Kosovo Corps members'.

19.   Jonathan Steele, 'KLA Player Longs to Retire from World Stage', *Guardian*, 30 June 1999.

20.   Tony Allen-Mills, 'Truth Chokes on the Fog of War', *Sunday Times*, 28 March 1999.

21.   Scheffer was speaking at the International Conference on the Trial of Slobodan Milošević, National University of Ireland in Galway on 29–30 April 2006.

22.   See Laughland, *Travesty*, 26–7.

23.   ICTY press briefing, 21 April 1999.

24.   Press conference given by NATO spokesman Jamie Shea and SHAPE spokesman Major General Walter Jertz, NATO HQ, Brussels, 16 May 1999, www.nato.int/kosovo.

25.   Press conference given by NATO spokesman Jamie Shea and SHAPE spokesman Major General Walter Jertz, NATO HQ, Brussels, 17 May 1999, www.nato.int/kosovo.

26.   Milošević trial, 24 January 2005, transcript, 35550–1, emphasis added.

27.   Remarks at the US Supreme Court, 5 April 1999; see ICTY Press Release Archive, www.un.org/icty.

28.   On the illegality of the Kosovo war, see Professor Ian Brownlie, QC, Kosovo Crisis Inquiry: Memorandum on the International Law Aspects, 6 October 1999, and UK Parliament Foreign Affairs Select Committee, Report, 23 May 2000; Antonio Cassese, 'Ex iniuria ius oritur: Are we Moving towards International Legitimation of Forcible Humanitarian Countermeasures in the World Community?', *European Journal of International Law*, 10 (1999), 23–30; International Commission on Kosovo, *The Kosovo Report*, 1 October 2000.

29.   Lawrence Eagleburger, 'The Need to Respond to War Crimes in the Former Yugoslavia', speech, 28 December 1992.

30.   Lawrence Eagleburger, opening statement from a news conference, Geneva, en route to Brussels, 17 December 1992.

31.   Anson Laytner, *Arguing with God: a Jewish Tradition* (Northvale, NJ and London: Jason Aronson, 1990); Louis I. Newman, *The Hasidic Anthology: Tales and Teachings of the Hasidim* (New York and London: Charles Scribner's Sons, 1934), 56–9, 'Controversy with God', esp. '1. A Judgement for the Rabbi' and '10. A Trial with God'; Elizabeth A. Wood, *Performing Justice: Agitation Trials in early Soviet Russia* (Ithaca, NY: Cornell University Press, 2005).

32.   See Paul R. Williams and Michael P. Scharf, *Peace with Justice? War Crimes and Accountability in the Former Yugoslavia* (Lanham, MD and Oxford: Rowman & Littlefield, 2002), *passim*.

33.   Lord Carrington, the then EU envoy for Bosnia, has testified in private correspondence that the United States government sent a telegram to Alija Izetbegović in 1992 advising him to rescind his signature on the Cutileiro

agreement. So has Cutileiro himself: see his letter to the *Economist*, 9–15 December 1995.

34. See Robert M. Hayden, *Blueprint for a House Divided: the Constitutional Logic of the Yugoslav Conflicts* (Ann Arbor, MI: University of Michigan Press, 2000), ch. 5.

35. On Bosnia see David Chandler, *Bosnia: Faking Democracy after Dayton* (London: Pluto Press, 1999).

36. On the events of 5 October 2000, see my paper, 'The Technique of the Coup d'État', on www.sandersresearch.com; 'Anatomie einer Revolution, Zoran Djindjić im Gespräch mit Paul Lendvai', *Europäische Rundschau*, 2001/4, pp. 3–20; Dragan Bujošević and Ivan Radovanović, *October 5: a 24-hour coup* (Belgrade: Media Center, 2000); Michael Dobbs, 'U.S. Advice Guided Milošević Opposition; Political Consultants Helped Yugoslav Opposition Topple Authoritarian Leader', *Washington Post*, 11 December 2000; and Tim Marshall, *Shadowplay* (Belgrade: Samizdat B92, 2003).

37. On joint criminal enterprise, see the excellent paper by Allison M. Danner and Jenny S. Martinez, 'Guilty Associations: Joint Criminal Enterprise, Command Responsibility and the Development of International Criminal Law', *California Law Review*, vol. 93 (2005).

38. On joint criminal enterprise generally, see my book *Travesty*, ch. 6.

39. Prosecutor v. Brdjanin, Appeals Chamber Decision on Interlocutory Appeal, 19 March 2004, para. 7.

40. Kvočka, Appeals Chamber Judgement, 28 February 2005, para. 99.

41. Trial Chamber Decision on Motion for Acquittal, 16 June 2004, para. 291.

42. Prosecution's Motion for Joinder, 27 November 2001, para. 13.

43. Trial transcript, 12 February 2002, 30–1; quoted in my *Travesty*, 138–9.

44. Tanić testified on 14 and 15 May 2002, and on 15 May 2002 Dušan Mihajlović denounced him; see Beta Press Agency report, 15 May 2002. A video of Mihajlović's statement was played in court on 21 May 2002. For the text of his intervention, see Milošević Trial transcript, 21 May 2002, 5170.

45. Trial transcript, 6 September 2002, 9806.

46. Germinal Civikov, *Der Milošević-Prozess: Bericht eines Beobachters* (Vienna: Pro Media, 2006), 69–70. This book is an excellent account of the trial.

47. Trial transcript, 9 January 2003, 14605.

48. Trial transcript, 6 June 2002, 6365.

49. Trial transcript, 6 June 2002, 6386–7.

50. On all this, see the excellent account in Civikov, *Der Milošević-Prozess*, 89–99.

51. See ch. 7 of my book *Travesty*.

52. On all this, see ch. 9 of my book *Travesty*.

53. 'Milošević given wrong medicine', by Cees Banning and Petra de Koning, *NRC Handelsblad*, 23 November 2002.

54. Itar-Tass, 15 March 2006.

Chapter 18: Regime change and the trial of Saddam Hussein

1. On American millenarianism and its influence on politics, see Ernest Lee Tuveson, *Redeemer Nation: the Idea of America's Millennial Role* (Chicago, Ill.: University of Chicago Press, 1968).

2. Claes G. Ryn, *America the Virtuous: The Crisis of Democracy and the Quest for Empire* (New Brunswick, NJ: Transaction Publishers, 2003).

3. Richard Perle and David Frum, *An End to Evil: How to Win the War on Terror* (New York: Random House, 2003), 9.

4. See 'President Bush Discusses Freedom in Iraq and Middle East', remarks to the National Endowment of Democracy, 6 November 2003.

5. 'President Discusses War on Terror at Fort Hood', 12 April 2005; also remarks to the National Endowment of Democracy, 6 November 2003; both available on www.whitehouse.gov.

6. Jules Lobel and Michael Ratner, 'Bypassing the Security Council: Ambiguous Authorizations to Use Force, Cease-Fires and the Iraqi Inspection Regime', *American Journal of International Law*, 124 (1999).

7. See the excellent analysis of the legal situation in Michael Mandel, *How America Gets Away with Murder* (London: Pluto Press, 2004), ch. 1.

8. 'President Says Saddam Hussein Must Leave Iraq Within 48 Hours', remarks by the president in address to the nation, The Cross Hall , 8:01 p.m. EST, 17 March 2003, Office of the Press Secretary, The White House, www.whitehouse.gov.

9. Prime minister's address to the nation, 20 March 2003, http://www.number-10.gov.uk.

10. *Hansard*, House of Commons, 25 February 2003.

11. Jean S. Pictet (ed.), *Commentary to the (IV) Geneva Convention Relative to the Protection of Civilian Persons in the Time of War* (1958), 336, emphasis added. This is the official commentary to the Geneva Convention, published alongside the Convention itself on www.icrc.org/ihl.

12. James Bone, 'US Builds Case against Iraq', *The Times*, 29 March 2002.

13. See for instance anon., 'Overthrowing Saddam "just the first step"', *Sydney Morning Herald* (quoting *Boston Globe* and *Washington Post*), 11 September 2002.

14. Ron Suskind, *The Price of Loyalty: George W. Bush, the White House and the Education of Paul O'Neill* (New York: Simon & Schuster, 2004). The agenda of the National Security Council meeting of 1 February 2001 is published on the internet as part of 'The Bush Files' from Paul O'Neill's archive on Ron Suskind's web page, http://thepriceofloyalty.ronsuskind.com/the-bushfiles.

15. Suskind, *The Price of Loyalty*, 85, emphasis added.

16. See the National Security Archive posted on www.gwu.edu.

17. *The Future of Iraq Project*, Transitional Justice Working Group, United States Department of State, March 2003.

18. CPA, Regulation No. 1, Section I (2).

19. Section II B 2 a (Institutional reform, the Judiciary), 21, said, 'The following

steps are proposed after a regime change: 1. Abolishing all special courts …'

20. M. R. Kropka, 'International court's Canadian president says court can't try Saddam', Canadian Press, 7 November 2005.

21. Nicholas Kraley, 'U.S. Denies Interference in Saddam's Trial', *Washington Times*, 2 July 2004.

22. 'Cairo Dismayed as "primitive" Saddam Death', *Guardian*, 5 January 2007.

23. 'United States Dual-Use Exports to Iraq and Their Impact on the Health of the Persian Gulf Veterans', hearing before the Committee on Banking, Housing and Urban Affairs, United States Senate, 103rd Congress, 25 May 1994.

24. 'Ten Lessons from the Saddam Trial', generated from the 7 October 2006 Cleveland Experts Meeting chaired by Michael Scharf, co-rapporteurs: Gregory McNeal, Christopher Rassi, and Brianne Draffin, http://www.law.case.edu/saddamtrial/index.asp.

25. Sadakat Kadri, 'They'd Do Better Sticking Saddam's Head on a Pole', *Guardian*, 4 April 2006.

26. Said K. Aburish, *Saddam Hussein: The Politics of Revenge* London: Bloomsbury, 2000), 58.

27. Aburish, *Saddam Hussein*, 82.

28. See the transcripts of the opening day quoted in *Guardian*, 20 October 2005.

29. 'Saddam on hunger strike after lawyer killed', Associated Press, 21 June 2006.

30. Ramsey Clark and Curtis F. J. Doebbler, 'The Iraqi Special Tribunal, A Corruption of Justice', Partnership for Civil Justice, September 2006, part 2, 32 & 67.

31. Human Rights Watch, *The Poisoned Chalice: A Human Rights Watch Briefing Paper on the Decision of the Iraqi High Tribunal in the Dujail Case*, June 2007, 15.

32. For a fascinating account of how Barzan al-Tikriti was the intermediary who helped broker an agreement between President Mitterrand and Saddam Hussein which would have avoided the first Gulf War of 1991, see Marc Boureau d'Argonne, *Irak: guerre ou assassinat programmé. La France pouvait-elle empêcher la guerre du golfe?* (Paris: F.-X. de Guibert, 2002).

33. *Guardian*, 6 November 2006.

34. Human Rights Watch, *The Poisoned Chalice*.

35. John Laughland, 'We will not Surrender', *Spectator*, 21 September 2002.

36. The author is grateful to Ramsey Clark, former American attorney general and a member of Saddam Hussein's Defence team, for this information.

37. President Bush's statement on execution of Saddam Hussein, 29 December 2006, www.whitehouse.gov.

38. Text published in e.g. *Daily Telegraph*, Sydney, 30 December 2006.

Conclusion

1. A. V. Dicey, *Introduction to the Study of the Law of the Constitution* (first published London: Macmillan, 1885), ch. 4.
2. Stephen Neff, *War and the Law of Nations: A General History* (Cambridge: Cambridge University Press, 2005), 13.
3. François Tricaut, *L'Accusation: recherche sur les figures de l'agression ethique* (Paris: Dalloz, 1977; repr. 2001).
4. Carl Schmitt, *Politische Theologie* (1922; 5th edn, Berlin: Duncker & Humblot, 1990), 11.

Bibliography and Further Reading

General

Émile Benveniste, *Vocabulaire des institutions indo-européennes* (Paris: Les Éditions de Minuit, 1966–74).

Ron Cristenson, *Political Trials: Gordian knots in the law* (New Brunswick, NJ and Oxford: Transaction Publishers, 1986).

A. V. Dicey, *Introduction to the Study of the Law of the Constitution* (London: Macmillan, 1885).

René Girard, all works, especially *Le bouc émissaire* (Paris: Grasset, 1982) and *La violence et le sacré* (Paris: Grasset, 1972).

H. L. A. Hart, *The Concept of Law* (2nd edn, Oxford: Clarendon Press, 1994).

Ernst Kantorowicz, *The King's Two Bodies: A Study in Medieval Political Theology* (Princeton, NJ: Princeton University Press, 1957).

Otto Kirchheimer, *Political Justice: The Use of Legal Procedure for Political Ends* (Princeton, NJ: New Jersey University Press, 1961).

Alisdair Macintyre, *Whose Justice? Which Rationality?* (Notre Dame, IN.: University of Notre Dame Press, 1988).

Armand Mattelart, *Histoire de l'Utopie planétaire: de la cité prophétique à la société globale* (Paris: Éditions de la Découverte, 1999).

Maurice Mégret, *La guerre psychologique* (Paris: Collection Que Sais-Je?, 1963).

Murray Rothbard, *Economic Thought Before Adam Smith* (Aldershot: Edward Elgar, 1995).

Carl Schmitt, *Politische Theologie* (1922; 5th edn, Berlin: Duncker & Humblot, 1990).

——, *Der Begriff des Politischen: Text von 1932 mit einem Vorwort und drei Corollarien* (1932; 3rd reprint of the 1963 edn, Berlin: Duncker & Humblot, 1991).

Michel Villey, *Le droit et les droits de l'homme* (Paris: Presses Universitaires de France, 1983).

——, *La formation de la pensée juridique moderne* (Paris: Presses Universitaires de France, 2003).

Chapter 1: The Trial of Charles I and the Last Judgement

A Complete Collection of State Trials and Proceedings for High Treason, with a new preface by Francis Hargrave, Esq., London 1776.

Mark Robert Bell, 'The Theology of Violence: Just war, Regicide, and the End of Time in the English Revolution', Oxford University D. Phil. thesis, 2002.

Hilaire Belloc, *Oliver Cromwell* (London: Benn, 1927).

Norman Cohn, *The Pursuit of the Millennium: Revolutionary Millenarians and Mystical Anarchists of the Middle Ages* (London: Paladin, 1970).

Patricia Crawford, 'Charles Stuart, That Man of Blood', *Journal of British Studies*, 16/2 (1977), 41–61.

John Figgis, *The Divine Right of Kings* (1914; repr. Bristol, Thoemmes Press, 1994).

Ian Gentles, *The New Model Army in England, Ireland and Scotland, 1645–1653* (Oxford: Blackwell, 1992).

Christopher Hill, *The Bible in Seventeenth Century English Politics*, The Tanner Lectures on Human Values, delivered at University of Michigan, 4 October 1991 (published online at www.tannerlectures.utah.edu).

John Morrill and Philip Baker, 'Oliver Cromwell, the Regicide and the Sons of Zeruiah', in Jason Peacey (ed.), *The Regicides and the Execution of Charles I* (Basingstoke: Palgrave, 2001). Article available online at www.blackwellpublishing.com.

Joseph G. Muddiman, *The Trial of King Charles the First* (London: William Hodge, 1928).

Jason Peacey (ed.), *The Regicides and the Execution of Charles I* (Basingstoke: Palgrave, 2001).

Geoffrey Robertson, *The Tyrannicide Brief: the Story of the Man who sent Charles I to the Scaffold* (London: Chatto & Windus, 2005; Vintage Books, 2006).

A. L. Rowse, *The Regicides and the Puritan Revolution* (London: Duckworth, 1994).

William L. Sachse, 'England's "Black Tribunal": an Analysis of the Regicide Court', *Journal of British Studies*, 12 (1973), 69–85.

Leon Trotsky, *Collected Writings and Speeches on Britain*, eds R. Chappell and Alan Clinton (New York: New Park Publications, 1974).

Michael Walzer, *The Revolution of the Saints: A Study in the Origins of Radical Politics* (London: Weidenfeld & Nicolson, 1965).

——, 'Regicide and Revolution', *Social Research*, vol. 40, no. 4 (winter 1973), 617ff. [not to be confused with Walzer's book of the same title on the trial of Louis XVI]

C. V. Wedgwood, *The Trial of Charles I* (London: Collins, 1964; repr. 1966).

Hugh Ross Williamson, *The Day They Killed the King* (London: Frederick Muller, 1957).

Chapter 2: The Trial of Louis XVI and the Terror

Edwin Bannon, *Refractory Men, Fanatical Women: Fidelity to Conscience during the French Revolution* (Leominster: Gracewing, 1992).

Marc Bloch, *Les rois thaumaturges: études sur le caractère surnaturel attribué à la puissance royale, particulièrement en France et en Angleterre* (Paris and Strasbourg: Publications de la Faculté des Lettres de l'Université de Strasbourg, 1924.

Albert Camus, *L'homme révolté* (Paris: Gallimard, 1952).

Jean Dumont, *Les prodiges du sacrilège* (Paris: Criterion, 1984).

Paul and Pierette Girault de Coursac, *Enquête sur le procès du roi* (Paris: F.-X. de Guibert, 1992.).

―― (eds), *La défense de Louis XVI*, with a preface by Jean-Marc Varaut (Paris: F.-X. de Guibert, 1993).

Jacques Isorn, *Le vrai procès du roi* (Paris: Atelier Marcel Jullian, 1980).

Théodore de Lameth, *Mémoires* (Paris: Eugène Welvert, 1913).

Jacques Vergès, *Les crimes d'État: la comédie judiciare* (Paris: Broché, 2004),

Michael Walzer, *Regicide and Revolution: Speeches at the Trial of Louis XIV* (Cambridge: Cambridge University Press, 1974).

Chapter 3: War Guilt after World War I

Jacques Bainville, *Les conséquences politiques de la paix* (1920; Paris: Éditions de l'Arsenal, 1995).

Gary Bass, *Stay the Hand of Vengeance: The Politics of War Crimes Tribunals* (Princeton, NJ: Princeton University Press, 2000).

Michael Llewellyn Smith, *Ionian Vision: Greece in Asia Minor 1919–1922* (London: Allen Lane, 1973; facsimile edn, Hurst, 1998).

Margaret Macmillan, *Paris 1919* (New York: Random House, 2001).

Carl Schmitt, *Der Nomos der Erde im Völkerrecht des Jus Publicum Europaeum* (Berlin: Duncker & Humblot, 1950).

Otto von Stülpnagel, *Die Wahrheit über die deutschen Kriegsverbrechen* (Berlin: Staatspolitischer Verlag, 1921).

Ernest Lee Tuveson, *Redeemer Nation: The Idea of America's Millennial Role* (Chicago, IL. and London: University of Chicago Press, 1968).

James F. Willis, *Prologue to Nuremberg: The Politics and Diplomacy of Punishing War Criminals of the First World War* (Westport and London: Greenwood Press, 1982).

Elizabeth A. Wood, *Performing Justice: Agitation Trials in Early Soviet Russia* (Ithaca, NY: Cornell University Press, 2005).

Chapter 4: Defeat in the Dock: the Riom Trial

Pierre Béteille and Christiane Rimbaud, *Le procès de Riom* (Paris: Plon, 1973).

James de Coquet, *Le Procès de Riom* (Paris: Librairie Arthème Fayard, 1945).

Hector Ghilini, *A la barre de Riom* (Paris: Jean Renard, 1942).

Henri Michel, *Le procès de Riom* (Paris: Albin Michel, 1979).

Frédéric Pottecher, *Le rocès de la Défaite, Riom Février–Avril 1942* Paris: Fayard, 1989).

Maurice Ribet, *Le procès de Riom* (Paris: Flammarion, 1945).

Pierre Tissier, *Le procès de Riom* (London: Harrap, 1943).

Chapter 5: Justice as Purge: Marshal Pétain Faces his Accusers

Procès du Maréchal Pétain, Compte rendu officiel (Paris: Éditions Louis Pariente, 1976).

Plaidoirie pour le maréchal Pétain, prononcée par le Batonnier Fernand Payen, Maîtres Jacques Isorni et J. Lemaire (Paris: Imprimerie Jacques Haumont, 1946).

Documents pour la révision, préface de Jacques Isorni et Jean Lemaire (Paris: André Martel, 1948).

Yves Beigbeder, *Judging War Crimes and Torture: French Justice and International Criminal Tribunals (1940–2005)* (Leiden and Boston, MA: Martinus Nijhoff, 2006).

René de Chambrun, … *Et ce fut un crime judiciaire: le Procès Laval* (Paris: Éditions France-Empire, 1984).

Pétrus Faure, *Un procès inique*, préface de Jacques Isorni (Paris: Flammarion, 1973).

Général Héring, Commandant Le Roc'h, *Révision* (Paris: Les Iles d'Or, 1949).

Joseph Kessel, *Jugements derniers: les procès Pétain et Nuremberg*, préface de Francis Lacassin (Paris: Christian de Barthillat, 1995).

Fred Kupferman, *Le procès de Vichy: Pucheu, Pétain, Laval* (Brussels: Éditions Complexe, 1980).

José Augustin Martinéz, *Les procès criminals d'après guerre: documents pour l'Histoire contemporaine*, translated from Spanish by Francis de Miomandre, Preface by Jacques Isorni (Paris: Albin Michel, 1958).

Jules Roy, *Le grand naufrage: chronique du procès Pétain* (Paris: Albin Michel, 1966 & 1995).

Léon Werth, *Impressions d'audience: pe procès Pétain* (Paris: Viviane Hamy, 1995).

Jean-Marc Varaut, *Le procès Pétain* (Paris: Perrin, 1995).

Chapter 6: Treachery on Trial: the Case of Vidkun Quisling

Hans Fredrik Dahl, *Quisling: A Study in Treachery* (Cambridge: Cambridge University Press, 1999).

Hans Fredrik Dahl, 'Dealing with the Past in Scandinavia: Legal Purges and Popular Memories of Nazism and World War II in Denmark and Norway after 1945', in Jon Elster (ed.), *Retribution and Restitution in the Transition to Democracy* (Cambridge: Cambridge University Press, 2006).

Yves Durand, *Le nouvel ordre européen nazi 1938–1945: la collaboration dans l'Europe allemande (1938–1945)* (Brussels: Éditions Complexe, 1990).

Paul M. Hayes, *Quisling: The Career and Political Ideas of Vidkun Quisling 1887–1945* (Newton Abbot: David & Charles, 1971).

Ralph Hewins, *Quisling: Prophet without Honour* (London: W. H. Allen, 1965).

Franklin Knudsen, *I was Quisling's Secretary* (London: Britons Publishing Company, 1967).

Stein Ugelvik Larsen, 'Die Ausschaltung der Quislinge in Norwegen', in Klaus-Dietmar Henke and Hans Woller (eds), *Politische Säuberung in Europa* (Munich: Deutscher Taschenbuch Verlag, 1991).

Stein Ugelvik Larsen, 'The Settlement with Quisling and his Followers in Norway: Denazification as a Legal – and Political – Process', in Larsen (ed.), *Modern Europe After Fascism* (New York: Columbia University Press, 1998).

Chapter 7: Nuremberg: Making War Illegal

Istvan Déak, 'Misjudgement at Nuremberg', *New York Review of Books*, 7 October 1993.

Hans Fritzsche, *Das Schwert auf der Waage, Hans Fritzsche über Nürnberg*, ed. Hildegard Springer (Heidelberg: Kurt Vowinckel Verlag, 1953).

George Ginsburgs, 'Laws of War and War Crimes on the Russian Front during World War II: The Soviet View', *Soviet Studies*, vol. 11, no. 3 (January 1960).

——, *Moscow's Road to Nuremberg: The Soviet Background to the Trial* The Hague: Martinus Nijhoff, 1996).

Maurice Hankey (Lord Hankey), *Politics, Trials and Errors* (Oxford: Pen-in-Hand, 1950).

José Augustín Martínez, *Les procès criminels de l'après-guerre* (Paris: Albin Michel, 1958).

Carl Schmitt, *Das internationalrechtliche Verbrechen des Angriffskriegs und der Grundsatz 'Nullum crimen, nulla poena, sine lege'* (Berlin, 1945; new edn, Berlin: Duncker & Humblot, 1994).

Telford Taylor, *The Anatomy of the Nuremberg Trials* (New York: Knopf and Little, Brown, 1992).

Arkady Vaksberg, *The Prosecutor and the Prey: Vyshinsky and the 1930s Moscow Show Trials* (London: Weidenfeld & Nicolson, 1990).

Danilo Zolo, *La giustizia dei vinctiori, Da Norimberga a Baghdad* (Rome and Bari: Editori Laterza, 2006).

Chapter 8: Creating Legitimacy: the Trial of Marshal Antonescu

Ioan Dan, *Procesul Mareşalului Ion Antonescu* (Bucharest: Editura Lucman, 2005).

Marcel-Dumitru Ciucă (ed.), *Procesul Mareşalului Antonescu, Documente*, 3 vols (Bucharest: Editura Saeculum, 1996–8).

Chapter 9: Ethnic Cleansing and National Cleansing in Czechoslovakia

Dr Jozef Tiso, Dr Ferdinand Ďurčansky a Alexander Mach, Pred Súdom Noroda (Bratislava: Vydalo Poverebíctvo informacíi, Tlačila Slovenská Graifca, 1947).

Bradley Abrams, 'The Politics of Retribution: the Trial of Jozef Tiso in the Czechoslovak Environment', in István Déak, Jan T. Gross, and Tony Judt (eds), *The Politics of Retribution in Europe: World War II and its Aftermath* (Princeton, NJ: Princeton University Press, 2000).

Ferdinand Ďurčansky, *Petition of the Slovak Action Committee to the United Nations in the Trial of Dr. Jozef Tiso, President and Other Representative of the Slovak Republic Before the International Military Tribunal* (New York: Slovak Action Committee, 1947).

James Ramon Felak, 'The Democratic Party and the Execution of Jozef Tiso', *Slovakia*, 38, nos 70–1 (2005).

Benjamin Frommer, *National Cleansing: Retribution against Nazi Collaborators in post-war Czechoslovakia* (Cambridge: Cambridge University Press, 2005).

Karel Kaplan, *Dva Retribuční Procesy, Komentované Dokumenty Protektorní vláda, Dr. Jozef Tiso* (Prague: Ústav pro soudobé dejiny Čsav, 1992).

Anton Rašla and Ernest Žabkay, *Proces s dr J. Tisom, Spomienky* (Bratislava: Tatrapress, 1990).

Dr Jozef Tiso, *Die Wahrheit über die Slowakei* (no place/publisher indicated: 1948) [his closing Defence speech at his trial].

František Vnuk, *Dr. Jozef Tiso, President of the Slovak Republic, in Commemoration of the Twentieth Anniversary of his Death at the Hands of the Enemies of Slovak Independence* (Sydney: The Association of Australian Slovaks, Orbis Publishing, 1967).

James Mace Ward, 'People Who Deserve it: Jozef Tiso and the Presidential Exemption', *Nationalities Papers*, vol. 30, no. 4 (December 2002).

———, 'Blank Pages: Slovakia's Struggle to Reevaluate Jozef Tiso, 1989–2001', University of Washington M.A. thesis, 2001. [the basis of Ward's forthcoming biography of Tiso which includes a chapter on the trial]

Chapter 10: People's Justice in Liberated Hungary

Karl P. Benziger, 'The Trial of László Bárdossy: The Second World War and Factional Politics in Contemporary Hungary', *Journal of Contemporary History*, vol. 40, no. 3 (2005), 465–81.

István Déak, Jan T. Gross, and Tony Judt (eds), *The Politics of Retribution in Europe: World War II and its Aftermath* (Princeton, NJ: Princeton University Press, 2000).

István Déak, 'Retribution or Revenge: War Crimes Trials in Post World War II Hungary', in *Hungary and the Holocaust, Confrontation with the Past*, symposium proceedings (Washington, DC: United States Holocaust Memorial Museum, Center for Advanced Holocaust Studies, 2001).

László Karsai, *Crime and Punishment: People's Courts, Revolutionary Legality and the Hungarian Holocaust*, www.sipa.columbia.edu.

——, 'The People's Courts and Revolutionary Justice in Hungary, 1945–46' in Déak etal. (eds), *The Politics of Retribution in Europe*.

Eugene (Jenö) Lévai, 'The War Crimes Trials Relating to Hungary', in Randolph L. Braham (ed.), *Hungarian-Jewish Studies* (New York: World Federation of Hungarian Jews, 1969).

Pál Pritz, *The War Crimes Trial of Hungarian Prime Minister László Bárdossy* (Boulder, CO.: Centre for Hungarian Studies and Publications, 2004).

Margit Szöllösi-Janze, ' "Pfeilkreuzler, Landesverräter und andere Volksfeinde", Generalabrechnung in Ungarn', in Klaus-Dietmar Henke and Hans Wolle (eds), *Politische Säuberung in Europa* (Munich: Deutscher Taschenbuch Verlag, 1991).

Anna Wessely, 'Overcoming the Fascist Legacy in Hungary', in Stein Ugelvik Larsen (ed.), *Modern Europe After Fascism* (New York: Columbia University Press, 1998).

Chapter 11: From Mass Execution to Amnesty and Pardon: Postwar Trials in Bulgaria, Finland, and Greece

Cyril E. Black, 'The Start of the Cold War in Bulgaria: a Personal View', *Review of Politics*, vol. 41, no. 2 (April 1979).

Stéphane Courtois, *Le Livre noir du communisme* (Paris: Robert Laffont, 1997).

Vesselin Dimitrov, *Stalin's Cold War: Soviet Foreign Policy, Democracy and Communism in Bulgaria, 1941–48* (London: Palgrave Macmillan, 2007).

Mark Mazower, *After the War Was Over: Reconstructing the Family, Nation and State in Greece, 1943–1960* (Princeton, NJ: Princeton University Press, 2000).

Nikolai Poppetrov, 'Defascification in Bulgaria from 1944 to 1948: Real Dimensions and the Functions of Propaganda', in Stein Ugelvik Larsen (ed.), *Modern Europe After Fascism* (New York: Columbia University Press, 1998).

Petur Semerdzhiev, *Narodniiat sud v Bulgaria, 1944–1945: komu i zashto e bil neobkhodim* (Sofia: Makedonia Press, 1998).

Tzvetan Todorov, *La fragilité du bien: le sauvetage des juifs bulgares* (Paris: Albin Michel, 1999).

Chapter 12: Politics as Conspiracy: the Tokyo Trials

Joseph Keenan and Brendan Francis Brown, *Crimes Against International Law* (Washington DC: Public Affairs Press, 1950).

Richard H. Minear, *Victors' Justice: The Tokyo War Crimes Trial* (Tokyo: Charles E. Tuttle Company (by special arrangement with Princeton University Press), 1971).

Radhabinod Pal, *International Military Tribunal for the Far East: Dissentient Judgment* (Calcutta: Sanyal & Co., 1953).

R. John Pritchard (eds), *The Tokyo Major War Crimes Trial* (Lewiston and New York: Edwin Mellen Press, 1998), 124 vols.

B. V. A. Röling, *The Tokyo Trial and Beyond: Reflections of a Peacemonger*, ed. and with an Introduction by Antonio Cassese (Cambridge: Polity Press, 1993).

B. V. A. Röling & C. F. Rüter (eds.), *The Tokyo Judgement* (Amsterdam: APA-Amsterdam University Press, 1977).
Kirsten Sellars, *The Rise and Rise of Human Rights* (Stroud: Sutton Publishing, 2002).

Chapter 13: The Greek colonels, Emperor Bokassa, and the Argentine Generals: Transitional Justice

Carlos Santiago Nino, *Radical Evil on Trial* (New Haven, CT: Yale University Press, 1996).
Brian Titley, *Dark Age: The Political Odyssey of Emperor Bokassa* (Montreal: McGill-Queens University Press, 1997).
C. M. Woodhouse, *The Rise and Fall of the Greek Colonels* (New York: Franklin Watts, 1985).

Chapter 14: Revolution Returns: the Trial of Nicolae Ceauşescu

Victor Loupan, *La révolution n'a pas eu lieu: Roumanie, l'histoire d'un coup d'État* (Paris: Robert Laffont, 1990).
Radu Portocala, *Autopsie du coup d'état roumain: au pays du mensonge triomphant* (Paris: Calmann-Lévy, 1990).

Chapter 15: A State on Trial: Erich Honecker in Moabit

Roman Grafe, *Deutsche Gerechtigkeit: Prozess gegen DDR-Grenzschützen und ihre Befehlshaber* (Munich: Siedler Verlag, 2004).
A. James McAdams, 'The Honecker Trial: the East German Past and the German Future', *Review of Politics*, vol. 58, no. 1(winter 1996), 53–80.
A. James McAdams, *Judging the Past in Unified Germany* (Cambridge: Cambridge University Press, 2001).
UWE Wesel, *Ein Staat vor Gericht: Der Honecker-Prozess* (Frankfurt: Eichborn, 1994).

Chapter 16: Jean Kambanda, Convicted without Trial

Thierry Cruvellier, *Le tribunal des vaincus: un Nuremberg pour le Rwanda?* (Paris: Calmann-Lévy, 2006).
Alex Obote-Odora, 'Conspiracy to Commit Genocide: Prosecutor v. Jean Kambanda and Prosecutor v. Alfred Musema', *Murdoch University Electronic Journal of Law*, vol. 8, no. 1 (March 2001).

Chapter 17: Kosovo and the New World Order: the Trial of Slobodan Milošević

David Chandler, *Bosnia: Faking Democracy after Dayton* (London: Pluto Press, London, 1999).

Germinal Civikov, *Der Milošević-Prozess: Bericht eines Beobachters* (Vienna: Pro-Media, 2006).

Allison M. Danner and Jenny S. Martinez, 'Guilty Associations: Joint Criminal Enterprise, Command Responsibility and the Development of International Criminal Law', *California Law Review*, vol. 93 (2005).

Robert M. Hayden, *Blueprint for a House divided: The Constitutional Logic of the Yugoslav Conflicts* (Ann Arbor, MI: University of Michigan Press, 2000).

John Laughland, *Travesty: The Trial of Slobodan Milošević and the Corruption of International Justice* (London: Pluto Press, 2007).

Tim Marshall, *Shadowplay* (Belgrade: Samizdat B92, 2003).

Chapter 18: Regime Change and the Trial of Saddam Hussein

Said K. Aburish, *Saddam Hussein: The Politics of Revenge* (London: Bloomsbury, 2000).

Marc Boureau D'Argonne, *Irak: guerre ou assassinat programmé. La France pouvait-elle empêcher la guerre du golfe?*(Paris: F.-X. de Guibert, 2002).

Ramsey Clark and Curtis F. J. Doebbler, 'The Iraqi Special Tribunal, A Corruption of Justice', Partnership for Civil Justice, September 2006.

Human Rights Watch, *The Poisoned Chalice: A Human Rights Watch Briefing Paper on the Decision of the Iraqi High Tribunal in the Dujail Case*, June 2007.

Michael Mandel, *How America Gets Away with Murder* (London: Pluto Press, 2004).

Index

Abetz, Otto   67, 71, 72, 75
absolute values, concept of   35
absolutism   28
accountability   255
   and international tribunals   256
Action française   82
Agosti, Orlando   183, 184
Agrarian Party, Bulgaria   155
Akayesu, Jean-Paul   215, 216, 218
Albania   222, 223
Albrecht, Hans   196, 205
Albright, Madeleine   224, 225
Alexianu, Gheorghe   127
Alfonsín, President Raúl   181, 183–4
Alibert, Raphael   65, 68, 83
Allawi, Iyad   243
Allen, William   30, 31
Allende, Salvador   195
Allied Control Commission (WWII)
   122, 144, 153
   for Finland   157
Allied Council for Japan   172–3
Allies:
   WWI   52, 54, 55
   post-WWI   57
   WWII   83, 93, 109, 117–18, 119, 143,
     154, 166, 202
   and Nuremberg   75, 103, 104, 109
   Potsdam agreement   130, 131, 165
   and Soviets   111, 112, 114, 158
   and Japan   165, 172
Alsace and Lorraine, German rule of
   WWII   66

American constitution   37
Amin, Rizgar   246–7
Amiri, Abdullah al-   247
Amnesty International   184, 199, 210
Anfal campaign, Iraq   247
anti-Semitism   92, 104, 105, 120, 121,
   123, 124, 139, 141, 143, 148
   anti-Semitic legislation   65, 66–7,
     150, 155
Antonescu, Marshal Ion   119ff, 129,
   136, 147, 158, 189, 193
   appointment   119
   arrest   120
   charges against   123–4
   trial   126–7120, 121, 122
Antonescu, Mihai   127
Arbour, Louise   14, 223, 224
Argentina   181–4
Aristotle   257
Arkan (Željko Ražnatović)   233
Armenian massacres of 1915   52–3
Arrow Cross, Hungary   143, 144, 145,
   148, 150, 152
Arusha Accords   209
Asquith, Herbert   54
Atatürk, Kemal   53
Auschwitz   105, 209, 226
Australia   167, 173
Austria   186
Axis powers, WWII   111, 119, 120, 134,
   155, 211

Ba'ath Arab Socialist Party, Iraq   241,
   243, 245
   trial of party members   241, 242ff
Bagosora, Théoneste   214, 216, 219
Bagrianov, Ivan   153
Bainville, Jacques   56
Bakalli, Mahmut   230–1
Bakr, Colonel Ahmad Hassan
   al-   245
Baltatzis, Georgios   59, 61
Bandar, Anwad al-   248
Bangui, Central African Republic
   177, 178, 179, 180
Baralong incident (1915)   54
Barayagwiza   219
Bárdossy, László   148–50, 151, 202
Barthélemy, Joseph   69–70, 74
Bastille, storming of   36, 37
Batthyány, Count Lajos   18
Battle of Britain   71
Battle of France   85, 87
Battle of Kosovo Field (1389)   228
Baudouin, King of Belgium, and
   Queen Fabiola   208
BBC   72, 79
Bebel, August   200
Beer Hall Putsch   57
Belgium   54, 64, 74, 91, 196, 210
Belsen   104
Beneš, President Edvard   129, 131,
   132, 134, 135, 137, 140, 163
Beran, Rudolf   133, 134
Berg, Paal   92–3, 101
Berlin Wall   186, 196, 197, 201, 202
   trial of guards   198–9, 203, 205
   Soviet Union and   201, 205
Bernard, Henri   169–70
Bernays, Lt Col Murray   115
Berry, Burton Y.   125
Bessarabia   119, 120
Bethmann-Hollweg, Theobald von
   57
Bey, Kemel   52
Bible   32
Biddle, Francis   110
Bienert, Richard   132, 133

Bignone, General Reynaldo   184
Billoux, François   86
Bills of Attainder   23–4, 56, 108, 242
biological warfare   166
Bishop, Maurice   210
Bismarck, Otto von   56
Black, Cyril   155
Blair, Tony   222, 223, 224, 239, 240
Blum, Léon   63, 67, 68, 70, 71, 72, 73,
   75, 126
   and Pétain trial   85, 87
Boegner, Marc   88–9
Bokassa, Jean-Bédel/Emperor
   Bokassa- trial of   177–80
Bolivia   180, 185
Border Law, GDR   197
Boris III, Tsar of Bulgaria   153, 154
Bormann, Martin   104, 105
Bosnia-Herzegovina   207, 209,
   226–7, 228, 230
   independence of   227, 228
Bozhilov, Dobri   153
Bradshaw, John   24, 25, 26, 27, 28,
   47, 256
Brandt, Willy   195
Brasillach, Robert   78
Brătianu, Gheorghe   125, 126
Braude, Ilya   193
Bräuer, Kurt   92
Bräutigam, Judge Hansgeorg   199,
   204
Brazil   180
Bremer, Paul   240, 241, 242
Brinon, Fernand de   78, 82
Brucan, Silviu   190
Brugière, Jean-Louis   213
Brunswick, duke of   36, 38
Budinsky, Lázló   147–8
Buja, Shukri   233
Bukharin, Nikolai   115–16, 229
Bulatović, Momir   236
Bulgaria   78, 153–7, 158, 186, 189
   and Soviet Union   155
   monarchy in   154–5
   people's courts in   156, 157
   post WWII trials in   154–6

purge in   155
revocation of sentences   156
Turnovo constitution (1879)
    156–7
Bunaciu, Avram   123
Burke, Edmund   35
Burundi   207, 208, 209
Bush, President George H. W.   14,
    239
Bush, President George W.   237, 238,
    239, 240, 243, 244, 249
Byrnes, James   129

Cagoule, La (France)   65, 82, 83
Calvin, John   33, 34, 51
Cambodia   17
Camus, Albert   35, 226
Caous, Pierre   72, 87–8
Capra, Frank   168
Carol, King of Romania   119, 120
Case, Thomas   33
Cassese, Antonio   97
Cavell, Edith   52
Ceauşecu, Elena   185, 191–2, 193
Ceauşecu, Nicolae   185–93, 249
    fall of   189–90
    charges against   185, 191, 192, 193
Central African Republic/Central
    African Empire   177, 178, 179
Chalabi, Ahmed   244
Chalabi, Salem   244
Chamberlain, Neville   98
Charles I, King of England   16, 21ff,
    36, 44, 47, 58
    trial of   23–9, 30, 43, 225, 246, 251,
        256
    defence strategy   26
    decision to execute   30–1, 32
    execution of   57
    on relationship of Law and Power
        29
    and the law   26–7, 29
    significance of trial   30
Chautemps, Camille   68
Cheynell, Francis   33
Chile   13, 14, 185, 195, 205

China   166, 167, 169, 173
Chresteil, Georges   79–80
Christianity and sacrifice   31
Churchill, Winston   55, 84, 87, 98,
    113, 154, 159
CIA   177, 213, 223, 245
Cicero   106
Civil Constitution of the Clergy
    (France, 1791)   37
Clarendon, Earl of   24
Clark, General Wesley   221–2
Clark, Ramsey   248
Clemenceau, Georges   55, 81
Clemenceau, Michel   81
Clementis, Vladimir   141
Clinton, President Bill   18, 226
Coalition Provisional Authority
    (CPA), Iraq   13, 241, 242, 243
Coard, Bernard   210
Cohen, William   223
Cold War period   104, 152, 167, 201,
    202
    post Cold War period   13, 14, 198,
        203
collaboration and internal resistance
    97
collective acts of violence   31
collective responsibility   145, 229, 253
colonialism   171–2, 208
command responsibility, theory of
    229, 253
*Commentaries on the Last Four Books
    of Moses* (Calvin)   33
Committee of Twenty Four (France,
    1792)   40
Committee on the Responsibility of
    the Authors of the War (1919)   55
Communism   58, 88, 109, 112, 203
    and foreign policy   109
    and 'people's justice'   123, 211
    communism and Nuremberg trials
        103
Communist Manifesto, The   113
Communist Party
    Bulgaria   153, 154
    Czechoslovak   129, 131, 132, 133ff

East Germany   195, 202
Finnish   157
French   77, 79, 80, 86
Greek   160, 161, 176, 177
Hungarian   143, 144, 146, 148, 151,
  152
Italian   120
Norwegian   92, 101
Romanian   120, 121, 122, 123,
  124–5, 143, 190–1
Slovakian   131, 135, 136
Congo, Democratic Republic of
  (DRC, formerly Zaire)   196, 210,
  211
  First Congo War   208
conséquences politiques de la paix, Les
  (Bainville)   56
conspiracies, claims of, and trials of
  heads of state   40–1, 230, 253
  and Tokyo trials   168–9, 170
  and Nazis   115, 168
  relationship to fraud   253
conspiracy, law and   114–16, 168, 170,
  253
Constantine, King of Greece   59,
  60, 176
Contras, Nicaragua   224
Convention for the Creation of an
  International Court   112
Convention for the Prevention and
  Punishment of Terrorism   112
Cooke, John   22, 28, 29, 34
corruption   17
courts martial   256–7
Couve de Murville, Maurice   97
Crimea Declaration   111
crimes against humanity   14, 16, 42,
  52, 139, 146, 148, 166, 226, 246, 248
  Japan, WWII   166
  monarchy as crime against
    humanity   41–2
  Nuremberg trial and   106–7, 115,
    121
  piracy as crime against humanity
    53

crimes against peace   107, 109, 110,
  112, 113, 114, 118, 122, 123, 148, 158,
  164–5, 170
criminal law   17
Croatia   228, 230, 232
Cromwell, Oliver   23, 25, 30, 32, 33–4
Cutileiro plan (1993, Yugoslavia)
  226
Cyprus, Turkish invasion of   175, 176
Czechoslovakia   109, 129ff, 144, 149,
  154, 186, 189
  German occupation, WWII   129
  Protectorate, WWII   129, 130, 131
    2, 133, 140
  Košice settlement   129, 130
  post WWII anti-German activities
    130–1
  ethnic cleansing in   131
  post-WWII settlement   129–30,
    135
  National Court (1946)   131ff
  Communist takeover (1948)   131,
    140–1
  trial of wartime leaders   131ff
  Sudetanland   133, 138
  Prague Spring   187, 188, 202
  see also Slovakia, Jozef Tiso

Dahl, Hans Fredrik   100
Daladier, Edouard   63, 67, 68, 70, 73,
  75, 126
  and Pétain trial   85, 86, 87
Danton, Georges   251
Darlan, Jean Louis   83
Daxner, Igor   136, 137
de Gaulle, General Charles   67, 77,
  78, 79, 84, 89, 97
  and Marshal Pétain   64, 86, 96
  Gaullists   64, 71, 77, 79, 80–1, 83,
    86, 87, 89, 132, 197
  and Communists   77, 80
de Gaulle, Philippe   64
de Sèze, Raymond   46–7, 48, 49
Déat, Marcel   72, 83
Debré, Michel   97

Declaration of the Rights of Man and the Citizen, France   36, 48, 108
Della Rocca, Ambassador Peretti   69
Demaçi, Adam   231
Democratic Party, Slovakia   135, 140
Denmark   97
Deyannis, Ioannis   177
Dicey, A.V.   242, 252
Dimitrov, Georgi   154
Dissentient Opinion (Pal)   172
divine right of kings   21, 22, 26
Djindjić, Zoran   228
Doenitz, Admiral Karl   103, 104, 117
double jeopardy, concept of (*non bis in idem*)   57
Drtina, Prokop   132
Due Obedience, Law on, Argentina   183, 184
Dufriche-Valazé, Charles Éléonor   40, 41
Dujail, Iraq   245, 247, 248, 249
Dumbravă, Jovița   123
Ďurčanský, Ferdinand   135–6
Dworkin, Ronald   182

Eagleburger, Lawrence   225, 226
Eastern Europe:
   Soviet influence in   129
   Communism in   103, 186, 211
   events of 1989   185ff
   see also specific states
Eden, Sir Anthony   113
Edward II of England   25
Eichmann, Adolf   106, 144, 151
Eilifsen, Gunnar   94, 95, 96
Eliáš, Alois   132, 133
Elverum authorization, the (Norway)   95–6
empires, development of   51
enemy of the people, concept   145
   of humanity   42
Engels, Friedrich   113
English Civil War   21–2; 23, 25, 29, 30, 33
   religious component   21–2, 32, 33, 34

English rebellion   35
Enola Gay   166
épuration (France, post-Liberation)   77, 78
   commissions d' épuration   78
Erdemović, Dražen   217, 233–4
Estates General, French   36, 48
Esteva, Admiral   79–80
Ethiopia   17–18, 185–6
European Community of Peoples   99
European Convention on Human Rights   156, 210
European Union   226
   Quisling's proposals for union of Europe   98–9
expert witnesses, defined   214–5

Falco, Robert   112
Falkenhorst, General von   94
Falklands War (Malvinas)   181, 182, 183, 203
fascism   147, Communist designation   153
Fatherland Front, Bulgaria   154
Faure, Pétrus   89
Fifth Monarchy Men, England   32
Filov, Bogdan   153, 155, 156
Finland   78, 119, 153, 157–9
   and Germany   158
   and Soviet Union   157, 158–9
   and war criminals   157
France   56, 132, 173, 187
   Third Republic   63, 64, 65, 66, 68, 70, 79, 81, 82, 83, 85, 91, 97, 114, 132, 181
   Battle of France   85, 87
   German invasion of 1940 and influence   63, 64, 70–1, 72, 73–5, 78, 83, 85
   Vichy France   63, 65–6, 75, 77, 78, 85, 86, 197, 213
      armistice with Germany   85
      anti-Semitic legislation and activities   65, 66–7, 78, 80, 86

Court of Political Justice   69,
    70
declaration of nullity of   79
and Jews   65, 86, 87, 88–9
Resistance   75, 78, 79, 86, 89,
    96
Supreme Court of Justice
    65–6, 67, 68, 69, 70, 88–9
suspension of habeas corpus
    66
Liberation of   77, 78
female suffrage   78
Fourth Republic   154, 171
Fifth Republic   64, 187
High Court of Justice   79, 80,
    82, 88
l'épuration   77, 78
and Rwanda   213
and Nuremberg trials   104, 114
see also de Gaulle, Pétain, Riom
    Trial
French Committee for National
    Liberation   78, 80
French Revolution   35ff, 43, 47, 51
and priests   37–8, 39–40
anti religious aspects of   37–8, 45
Constitution   47
executions during   39–40
French National Convention   36,
    40, 41, 42, 44, 45–6, 47, 48, 49
influence of   51
National Assembly (French
    Revolution)   35, 36–7, 38–9, 47
Revolutionary Tribunal   39
Surveillance Committee/
    Committee of Police and
    General Security   38–9
the Terror   39
see also Louis XVI
Franck, Edouard   178
Franco, General Francisco   79, 85
Frank, Hans   104, 106
Franz Joseph, Emperor of Austria-
    Hungary   172
Franz-Ferdinand, Archduke   55
Frederick Barbarossa   18

Free German Youth movement   195
Frick, Wilhelm   104, 106
Fritsche, Hans   104, 105
Front populaire (France, 1936)   71, 73
Fryatt, Captain   54
Fujimori, Alberto   13, 14
'Full Stop Law', Argentina   183, 184
fundamentalism, religious   31
Funk, Walther   104

Gabrovski, Petur   153
Galtieri, Lt-General Leopoldo   181,
    183, 184, 251
Gamelin, General Maurice   63, 67,
    70, 72, 81
García Meza Tejada, General Luis
    180, 185
Geneva Convention (1929)   108, 210,
    214, 240
and legal systems   240, 242
Geneva Protocol (1929)   108, 109
Geneva   51
genocide, legal concept of   115, 180,
    185, 187, 191, 193
concept defined   212
Iraq   242
Rwandan genocide and impact
    207–20
George, General   87
George, Lloyd   54, 55
Germany   43, 92, 108, 110, 149, 96
German Empire   52, 200
prosecution of for WWI   53, 55,
    56–7
Ermächtigungsgesetz (enabling
    law, 1933)   169, 202
Nazi Germany   75, 87, 93–4, 103ff,
    124, 158 200
and Hungary   149
and Norway   91, 92
attack on Soviet Union   113
intervention in Romania   120,
    121, 122, 124
invasion of and intervention in
    France   63, 64, 68, 70–1, 72,
    73–5, 83

invasion of Belgium   74
invasion of Poland   74, 115
of Yugoslavia   148–49, 155
Basic Treaty between East and
   West Germany (1972)   195,
   197, 202
creation of Land of Berlin   204–5
German sphere of influence   149
reunification treaty   197
see also Adolf Hitler, Erich
   Honecker, Nuremberg trials,
   Wilhelm II
Germany, East (GDR)   186, 187, 188,
   189, 196, 197, 199, 200, 201, 202, 203
border law in   197–8
trial of border guards   198–9, 203,
   205
see also Berlin Wall, Erich
   Honecker
Germany, West (FDR)   186, 196, 200,
   202, 203
Gestapo   94, 133, 195
Gheorghiu-Dej, Gheorghe   121
Girard, René   31
Giraud, General   78
Girondins, French   38, 43, 45, 48–9
Giscard d'Estaing, Valéry   178
Gizikis, Phaidon   176
global democratic revolution, concept
   of   237
globalisation, impact of   222
Goebbels, Joseph   72, 104, 117, 203
Goering, Hermann   87, 95, 104, 105,
   106, 109, 117
gold standard, 1930s collapse of   71
Gorbachev, Mikhail   187, 195, 203,
   205
Gottwald, Klement   131, 132
Goudas, Admiral Michalis   59
Gounaris, Dimitrios   59, 60, 61
Great National Betrayal Trial,
   Romania   124
Great Retribution Decree,
   Czechoslovakia   130, 134
Greece   78, 155, 159–61, 181
in WWI   53, 54

1922 revolution in   59–60
trial of Greek colonels   175–7, 181
seizure of power   176
17 November Group, Greece   176
war trial in (Trial of the Six)
   59–61
war trials   160
Greek-Turkish war   59
Grenada, American invasion of   203,
   210
Groza, Petru   120, 121, 123
Gueffroy, Chris   197
Guevara, Che   180
guilt, collective national   106, 254

Habyarimana, President Juvénal
   208, 209, 213, 216, 219
Hácha, Emil   132, 133
Hague Conventions   56, 108, 240
and collaboration in occupied
   countries   97
Hague, The   13, 51
Halabja, Iraq, chemical weapon attack
   on   247
Hamilton, Duke of   105
Hammash, Saeed al-   247
Hankey, Maurice   98
Hansson, General Halvor   100
Harrington Street massacre, Bolivia
   180
Hart, H. L. A.   27
Hatzianestis, General   59, 61
Havel, Václav   222
Hayes, Paul   100
heads of state   13, 16
   heads of government   16
   trials of heads of state and
      government   13, 17, 52, 59, 175,
      196, 208, 210, 213, 218–19, 251, 253,
      254, 255
   accountability of   14, 252–3
   and conspiracy theories   40
   and genocide   216, 218
   and justice   41–2
   and law on conspiracy   254
   non-acquittal of   26, 251

prosecution of and concepts of
political philosophy   16–7
and regime trials   251
and war crimes   55
Helsinki process   202
Henlein, Konrad   136
Henri IV of France   22
Henry the Lion, Duke of Saxony and
Bavaria   18
Henry VIII of England   21
Herriot, Edouard   81
Hess, Rudolf   104, 105
Hewins, Ralph   100
Heydrich, Reinhard   93–4
High Court of Justice, England and
Charles I   21, 23, 28, 29, 34, 36, 251
Hill, Christopher   22
Himmler, Heinrich   106
Hindenburg, Field Marshal Paul von
57
Hirohito, Emperor, of Japan   164, 170
Hiroshima and Nagasaki, atomic
bomb and   117, 165–6, 172
Hirota, Koki   163, 165, 168, 172, 173
Hitler, Adolf   105, 106, 125, 202
Beer Hall Putsch   57
and Czechoslovakia   129, 133,
expansionist activities   73, 74
and France   65, 67, 75, 87
and Hungary   119, 143
and Norway   92, 93, 94, 95, 100
and Nuremberg Trials   103, 104,
109, 122
Pétain and   77, 79, 83, 85, 86, 88
Slovakia   134, 138, 139
and Treaty of Versailles   73
Hitler Youth   104
*Hitlerite Responsibility under Criminal
Law* (Trainin and Vyshinskii)   114
Hlinka, Andrej   134, 135
Hoess, Rudolf   105
Holocaust   106, 146, 163, 175, 185,
225–6
Honecker, Erich   186, 195–205, 251
biography   195
and Berlin Wall   196, 198–9

on GDR   200–1, 203
trial of   196–205
Horthy, Admiral Miklos   143–4, 147,
148, 149, 150
Hourigan, Michael   213
Hoxha, Enver   223
Hrubý, Adolf   132, 133
Human Rights Watch   186
human rights   15, 156, 182, 186
activists   16, 19, 184, 196, 209, 257
and governments   14
human rights law   14
universal human rights   14
Hungary   126, 143ff, 155, 158, 186, 189,
202
WWII   143–4
and Germany WWII   143, 149, 150
and Yugoslavia   149
post-WWII period   144–5, 157
purges in   146, 155
people's courts in   145–6, 147
trials in   148ff, 154, 155
Hungarian National Independence
Front   144, 145
Huntziger, Charles   83
Husak, Gustav   186
Hutus   207ff

Ibrahim, Deputy Prime Minister
Anwar   17
Ilah, Abdul   245
Ileana, Princess, of Romania   125–6,
189
Iliescu, Ion   190–1
immunity and impunity, distinction
between   196
impeachment   18
Imperial War Cabinet, UK, WWI   54
Imrédy, Béla   148, 150
India   165, 173
Indonesia   171–2
Inglis, Oliver Michael   217
Inter-American Commission on
Human Rights   184
international affairs and domestic
affairs   15

International Convention for the
  Suppression of Terrorist Bombing
  (1997) 229
International Court of Justice 196
International Criminal Court (ICC,
  est 2002) 13, 118,182, 210, 253, 256
  and Sudan 15
  Statute of the International
    Criminal Court (1998) 229
International Criminal Tribunal for
  Rwanda (ICTR, est 1994) 13, 72,
  116, 148, 210, 211–12, 243, 246, 253,
  256
  and concept of genocide 212–13
  problems with 214–15
  use of anonymous witnesses 215
International Criminal Tribunal for
  the former Yugoslavia (ICTY, est
  1993) 13, 14, 15, 72, 82, 97, 116, 118,
  165, 168, 210, 211, 214, 215, 217, 221,
  223, 224, 243, 246, 253, 256
  creation of 225
  statute 23
  Milošević and 221ff
  theory of criminal liability 147,
  198
  see also 'joint criminal enterprise'
international law:
  development of coercive role of
    14, 109, 113
  humanitarian law 167, 221, 226,
  246, 256
  and individuals 107
  innovations of Nuremberg Trials
    106–7
  in modern period 42
  and neutrality 110
  and peace 107, 113, 173
  and pre-emptive action 98
  prosecution of heads of state and
    political leaders 55, 56, 107,
    208, 254
  relationship with domestic law
    56
  and states 14–15, 56
  subject of 56

and war 113, 51, 55, 107, 108, 113,
  121, 126, 171, 225, 239, 237
  see also Nuremberg trials, war
international tribunals 35, 72, 111
  and heads of state and government
    255
  and international community
    252
  international war crimes tribunals
    225, 257
  lack of political accountability
    256–7
  opposition to 170
  rights and capabilities of 16–17,
    27, 28, 252, 256
  and separation from government
    256
International Military Tribunal
  see Nuremberg Trials, Tokyo Trials
international system, development
  of 21
interventionism, military and judicial
  13, 15
Ioannides, Brigadier Dimitrios 176
Iraq 13, 15, 182, 225, 237
  invasion of Kuwait, 1990 209,
    238, 243, 244
  Anglo-American invasion of, 2003
    15, 237, 238, 239, 240
  legality of invasion 2003 238–40,
    regime change in 239, 240,
    Occupation Authority 240
Iran-Iraq war 243–4
Iraq Liberation Act (US, 1998)
  240–1
Iraq National Congress 244
Iraqi Special Tribunal/Iraqi High
  Tribunal/Supreme Iraqi Criminal
  Tribunal (est 2003) 13, 242, 244,
  246
Iron Guard, Romania 120, 124
Ishii, General Shiro 166
Isorni, Jacques 80, 81, 82, 86, 88
Italy 56, 87
ius ad bellum 108
ius in bello 108, 254, 256

Ivory Coast (Côte d'Ivoire)   177
Izetbegović, Alija   227

Jackson, Robert   105, 106, 107, 109,
    110, 111–12, 114, 129, 171
    views of   146
Jacobinism   237
Jacobins   41, 43, 45, 47, 48
Jacomet, Robert   63, 67, 70
Janabi, Sadoon al-   246
Jankó, Peter   151
Japan   56, 163ff
    war trials   214
    see also Hiroshima and Nagasaki,
        Tokyo trials
Jaranilla, Delfin   169
Jaruzelski, General Wojciech   202
Jeanneney, Jean-Jules   81
Jews, in WWII   146, 153, 226
    in Bulgaria   155, 156
    in Vichy France   65, 78, 80, 86, 87,
        88, 89
    in Nazi Germany   105, 106
    in Hungary   143, 144, 148, 150
    in Romania   120, 123, 124, 125
    in Slovakia   136–7, 138, 139
Jiu valley miners, Romania   191
Joan of Arc   82
Jodl, Alfred   95, 104
Johnson, President Andrew   18
'joint criminal enterprise', concept of
    116, 228, 229–30, 232, 234, 246, 247,
    248, 253
Jovanović, Slobodan   151
Jović, Borisav   232
justice, global   14
    and politics   86
    vengeance and justice   16

Kabila, Laurent   209
Kagame, General Paul   208, 213
Kalfus, Josef   132, 133
Kállay, Miklós   143
Kaltenbrunner, Ernst   104, 106
Kambanda, Jean   13, 185, 207ff, 221
    trial of   216–20

Kamenev, Lev   111
Kamenický, Jindřich   132
Karadžić, Radovan   234
Karamanlis, Constantine   176
Kassem, Brigadier Abdul-Karim
    245, 246
Katyn   116, 117
Kaznacheyev, Sergei   193
Keenan, Joseph B.   164, 173
Keitel, Field Marshal Wilhelm   95,
    104, 105–6
Kellogg-Briand Pact (1928)   108, 109,
    112, 166
Kelsen, Hans   118
Kennedy, John F   205
Kenya   216
Kessel, Joseph   88
Kessler, Heinz   196, 204, 205
KGB   122
Khmer Rouge   17
Khruschev, Nikita   205
Khuzaie, Thamer Hamoud al-   246
Kiichiro, Hiranuma   163
Kivimäki, Toivo   157
Knyazev   193
Kohl, Chancellor Helmut   195, 203
Koiso, Kuniaki   164
Kolingba, General André   178, 179,
    180
Kolosváry- Borcsa, Mihály   148
Kosovo Liberation Army (KLA)
    223–4, 225, 227, 231, 232, 233
    propaganda by   224
    and Račak massacre   222, 233
Kosovo   168, 222, 223, 224, 231, 232,
    237
Kovács, Kálmán   146
Krejčí, Jaroslav   132, 133
Krstić, General Radislav   229, 234
Krupp, Alfried   104
Krupp, Gustav   104
Kun, Béla   147, 149
Kuwait, Iraqi invasion of (1990)   14,
    209, 238, 244
Kyril, Prince, of Preslav   153, 155

La Chambre, Guy   63, 67, 70
Lamballe, Princesse de   39
Lameth, Théodore de   48
Lanjuinais, Jean-Denis   48
Lansing, Robert   55
Laporte, Arnaud de   39
Laud, Archbishop William   22
Laval, Pierre   18, 66, 83, 132, 137, 177
    and Pétain trial   79, 88
Lavrov, Sergei   235, 236
law:
    ex iniuria lex non oritur   108
    and justice   41
    law against aggression   171
    law of declaring war   108, 109, 111
    laws of war   51, 54, 56, 126, 164,
        167, 256
    and political power   256, 257
    nature of lawfulness   106–7
    rule of law   66, 235
    violations of laws   108–9
Laws (Cicero)   106
Le Troquer, André   71–2, 73
League of Nations   51, 55, 57–8, 112,
    158
Lebrun, Albert   81
legislation, retroactive   106–8, 251,
    252
    and international tribunals   17,
        107, 108, 118, 182, 242–3
    Argentina   181, 182–3
    Bulgaria   156
    Czechoslovakia   130, 134, 135
    Finland   158
    France   66, 68, 72, 78
    Geneva Convention on   240
    Germany   56, 57
    and German reunification   197, 98
    Greece   176
    Hungary   145, 148
    Iraq   240, 242
    Norway   94, 96, 98
    Nuremberg   78, 107, 118, 198
    retroactive jurisdiction   17, 78, 79,
        96–7, 145, 252
    retroactive justice   182

Romania   121, 122, 124
legitimacy, political   35
Lehtinen, Lasse   159
Lemaire, Jean-Marie   82
Lemkin, Raphael   115
lend-lease   110
Lenin, Vladimir I   25, 58–9, 101,
    112–13, 175
Lessel, Joseph   88
Lettrich, Dr Jozef   136
Ley, Robert   104, 105
Liberia   13, 210
Liebknecht, Karl   200
Ligue des Droits de l'Homme   129
Lilić, Zoran   232
Linkomies, Edwin   157, 159
Lithuania   18
Litvinov Protocol (1929)   112
Logothetopoulos, Konstantinos   160
London Charter (1945)   107, 108, 111
London Conference   110, 114, 115, 129
Louis XIII of France   22
Louis XVI of France   35ff, 58, 65, 73,
    82, 251, 253, 255
    and the law   38
    attempt to restore   36
    flight to Varennes   37
    trial of   37, 38, 39, 40, 42, 43–6,
        225, 255
    revolutionary press reports on
        trial   45
    execution   36, 49–50
Ludendorff, General Erich   57
Luder, Italo   182

Maastricht Treaty (EU)   226
MacArthur, General Douglas   164,
    166, 172–3
Macedonia   222, 223
Mach, Alexander   135, 139, 141
Maginot line   74
Mahdawi, Judge Fadhil al-   245, 246
Mailhe, Jean   41
Maillard, Stanislas-Marie   40
Maisky, Ivan   113

Majid, Ali Hassa al (Chemical Ali) 247
Major, Ákos 146, 147, 151
Makarezos, Nikolaos 175, 177
Makarios, Archbishop 176
Malaysia 17
Malesherbes, Chrétien-Guillaume Lamoignon de 46, 48
Mali 219
Mandel, Georges 68, 69, 70
Manichaean views and Manichaeism 23, 52, 58, 103, 237
Maniu, Iuliu 125, 126
Mannerheim, Marshal Carl 157
Manton, Thomas 33
Manuel, Pierre 38
Marat, Jean-Paul 43, 45
Marie-Antoinette of France 18
Marin, Louis 81
Marković, Radomir 231–2
Marshall, Stephen 33
Marx, Karl 113, 200
Mary, Queen of Scots 18, 25
Masasera, Emilio Eduardo 183
Mata Hari 79
Matsui, Iwane 168
Maurras, Charles 78, 82
McDonald, Judge Gabrielle Kirk 225
Menem, Carlos 184
Mengistu Hailemariam, Colonel 17–18, 185
mens rea, concept of 198, 212, 229
Meroz Cursed (Marshall) 33
Michael, King of Romania 119, 120, 121, 192
Michalache, Ion 124
Michel, Henri 76
Middle East 112, 237, 241
Mielke, Erich 196, 198, 199
Mihailović, General Draža 151
Mihajlović, Dušan 231
Mikhov, Nikola 153
'Military II' trial 219
millenarianism 237
Milošević, Borislav 236

Milošević, Slobodan 13, 73, 136, 167, 185, 190, 192, 193, 217, 244, 251, 253
    trial of 221ff
    charges against 228, 229
    weaknesses of charges against 230–3, 234
    death of 235
Mindszenty, Cardinal József 152
Minear, Richard 172
Mitterrand, François 81
Mladić, Ratko 234
Mobutu, President 209
Molotov, Vyacheslav 113, 125
Molotov-Ribbentrop Pact (1939) 119–20
monarchy 25
    changing role of 51
    inviolability of 41, 44, 47
    legal aspects of 27, 28
    relationship of monarch to the law 41
Mongibeaux, Judge Paul 81
Moore, John 44
Moravec, Emanuel 132
More, St Thomas 18
Mornet, André 79, 80, 82–3, 85, 88
Moscow Declaration (1943) 111, 114
Moscow show trials 111, 113, 115, 129, 193
Moustiers, Marquis de 75
MPRI (Military Professional Resources Incorporated) 223
Mubarak, Hosni 244
Munich agreement (1938) 129, 133, 134, 149
Museveni, President of Uganda 208

Nagel, Thomas 182
Nansen, Fridtjof 91
Napoleon 82
Nasjonal Samling (National Unity Party, Norway) 91, 92, 93, 94, 96
nation and contract 47
National Council of People's Tribunals, Hungary 145

National Council on Disappeared
    Persons, Argentina   183
National Defence Council, GDR
    198
National Peasant Party, Romania
    124–5, 129
National Salvation Front, Romania
    190, 191, 192
national sovereignty and international
    law   14–15, 255
NATO   15, 159, 177, 201, 202
    and Milošević   227, 230
    'New Strategic Concept'   222
    propaganda by   224
    and Yugoslavia   15, 168, 211, 221,
        222–3, 227, 230, 237, 254–5
Nazis   59, 70, 75, 77, 96, 97, 106, 107,
    108, 109, 114, 119, 136, 146, 153, 154,
    168, 196, 198, 202, 209, 214, 223, 226,
    238
    Beer Hall Putsch   57
    coming to power   73
    in Czechoslovakia   132, 133, 134,
        135, 136, 139
    and Finland   158
    and Greece   160
    and France   85, 120
    and Hungary   143, 144, 148, 150
    Nazi-Soviet Pact   80, 116
    and Norway   91–2, 94, 95
    and Nuremberg Trials   113, 114,
        117, 118, 121, 124, 130, 171
    and Soviet Union   80, 117, 118
    see also Holocaust, Jews,
        Nuremberg Trials
Ndadaye, Melchior   209
Ndombasi, Abdulaye Yerodia   196
Nedić, Milan   151
Neff, Stephen   253
negative criminality, concept of
    167–8
Netherlands   4, 56, 64, 86, 91, 97, 104,
    171, 173
Neurath, Konstantin von   104
neutral states and international law
    110

New Deal, USA   109
New Left Communists   226
New Model Army, England   23, 24
New Zealand   165, 173
Nicaragua   224
Nice, Geoffrey   223, 225, 230, 232, 234
Nicholas II, Tsar of Russia   58
Nikitchenko, Ioan Timofeevich
    110–11, 112, 114
Nimitz, Admiral Chester   117
9/11 attacks, United States   240
Niţa, Vasile   123
NKVD   117
non-interference, principle of,
    qualifying   222
Noriega, General Manuel   17
Norway   91ff, 119
    attitudes towards Germany   94
    Communism in   92
    constitution   96
    German intervention in   91, 92–4,
        95, 97–8, 111
    king   93, 101, 102
    legal position as occupied state
        97
    post-WWII executions in   97
    treason ordinance   96–7
Nosek, Václav   132
Nuremberg trials (1947)   75, 88,
    103ff, 122, 124, 130, 136, 144, 145, 146,
    147, 148, 159, 176, 203, 211, 214, 256
    acquittals at   241, 251
    charges, and evidence used   99,
        106
    and concept of conspiracy   114,
        253
    context   18
    and creation of new world order
        110
    and crimes against humanity   106,
        107, 114–15, 121, 122, 242
    and crimes against peace   105, 107,
        108, 110, 114, 122
    defendants   104–5, 117, 121
    extent defined   15–16, 111, 115

International Military Tribunal
  (Nuremberg)   104, 107, 115
innovations introduced   106–7,
  109, 110, 147
legal and moral aspects   107
nature of Nuremberg trials   106
Nuremberg Charter   110, 111, 114,
  117, 129, 131, 147, 164
Nuremberg jurisprudence   110
Nuremberg principles   221
and other WWII-related trials   18,
  59, 63, 95, 97, 99, 103–4, 119, 122,
  124, 147, 159
participants   104
as regime trial   103
retroactive aspects   78, 96, 118
Soviet role   111, 112, 116–17, 118,
  122, 136
Tokyo Trial compared   163, 164,
  165, 166, 167, 171
as victors' justice   103, 117–18
and war crimes/waging war   66,
  97–8, 118, 122, 221
see also Nazis, theory of criminal
  liability
Nygaardsvold, Johan   92, 93, 95, 99,
  101

O'Neill, Paul   241
Obeidi, Khamis al-   246
Ocampo, Luis Moreno   182
officers of state   17
Operation Desert Fox   238, 239
Operation Gladio   177
'Operation Horseshoe'   168
Operation Wilfred (1940)   98
Owen, David (Lord Owen)   226

Paasikivi, PM Juho Kusti   157
Paine, Thomas (Tom)   49
Paksas, President Rolandas   18
Pal, Radhabinod   165, 169, 170–1,
  172, 173
Panama   17, 203
Papadopoulos, Giorgios   175, 176, 177
Papandreou, Andreas   177

Papandreou, George   160
Papen, Franz von   104, 105
Paris Commune (1791), Surveillance
  Committee of   40
Parliament, British   22, 23
Pasha, Enver   53
Pasha, Said Halim   52–3
Pasha, Talaat   53
Pătrăşcanu, Lucreţiu   123
Patriotic Front, Bulgaria   154
Pattakos, Stylianos   175, 177
Pauker, Ana   121, 125
Paul VI, Pope   177
Păuna, Ion   123
Payen, Fernand   81, 82, 85
Pearl Harbor   164, 169
People's Tribunals, Romania   122–3
Peru   13, 14
Peshev, Dimitar   156, 157
Pétain, Marshal Henri Philippe
  63–5, 67, 68–70, 74, 75, 96, 97, 119,
  177, 178, 181
after Liberation   77
assignation of les pleins pouvoirs
  (1940)   64, 65, 80, 81
and de Gaulle   64, 96
and Franco   85
and Hitler   65, 77, 83, 85, 86, 88
oath of fidelity to   87–8
and Riom Trial   65, 66, 70, 73, 78,
  86, 87, 88, 181, 213
trial of   72, 77ff, 91, 126, 132, 136,
  137, 200, 221, 253
Péter, Gábor   147
Petkov, Georgi   154
Petkov, Nikolai   155
Petrescu, General Alexandru   125
Philippe Égalité, duke of Orléans   49
Philippines   165, 167
Physicians for Human Rights   182
Pictet, Jean S.   240
'Pinkerton Rule'   116
Pinochet, General Augusto   13–14,
  185, 195, 199
piracy   42
as 'universal crime'   42, 53

Plavšić, Biljana   226
Pol Pot   17
Poland   106, 116, 189, 202
police state   38, 66
political acts and judicial forms   257
political acts, public nature of   254
political legitimacy   27
   254, and political trials   251
political purges   23, 131
   Soviet   154, 157
political systems, legitimacy and
   values   35
political trials and acts of state   17
   constitutional questions raised by
      19, 36, 256
   context of   18–19
   Soviet Union and   58–9
Ponte, Carla del   218
Popa, Gica   191
Popescu, Major Iorgu   123
Potsdam agreement (1945)   117, 130,
   131, 165
Pride, Thomas and 'Pride's Purge'   23
Procopé, Hjalmar   158
Prosper, Pierre-Richard   241
Protocol for the Pacific Settlement
   of International Disputes (1924,
   originally 'Outlawry of Aggressive
   War')   108, 109
Protopadakis, Pretros   59, 61
Prussia   38
Pucheu, Pierre   79
Puritan Solemn League and Covenant
   30
Puritans, English   21, 22, 23, 30–1,
   32–3, 57, 58

Quisling, Vidkun   73, 91ff, 132, 136,
   137, 146, 160, 177, 253
   becoming head of government
      92, 93
   accusations of treason   91, 97, 101
   arrest of   94
   charges against   95, 98
   and European union   98–9
   and Germany   92, 94, 95, 96, 97,
      100
   and Hitler   92, 93, 94, 95
   philosophy of   102
   and Soviet Union   91, 92
   trial of   94ff, 122, 145, 192, 221, 249
   charges of treason   91, 95, 96–7,
      98, 101
   see also Nasjonal Samling

Račak, Yugoslavia, massacre at   222,
   233
Radbruch, Gustav   108, 198
Rădescu, Nicolae   120, 121
Raeder, Erich   104
Rahman, Judge Abdul (Rauf Rashid
   Abdul Rahman)   245, 247
Rajk, László   151–2
Rákosi, Mátyás   144, 151
Rallis, Dimitrios   60
Rallis, George   60, 160
Rallis, George (the younger)   60
Rallis, Ioannis   60, 160
Rambouillet agreement   222
Rangell, Johan Wilhelm   157, 159
Rašla, Anton   136, 141
Ražnatović, Željko (Arkan)   233
Reagan, Ronald   244
Rebel, The (Camus)   35
rebellion against the monarch   35
Red Army   133, 134, 144–5, 153, 154,
   160
Red Cross   51
regime change, Iraq   237ff
regime trials   251–3, 254
   Nuremberg trials as   103
   political component   252–3
   and transfer of immunity   255
   as 'trials of rupture'   252
   violence as background to   255
Reichskristallnacht   186
Reichstag Fire, Germany   154
religion and politics   21–2
Renthe-Fink, Cecile von   77
'republic of laws'   35

Revolutionary Committee, Athens
    65
Reynaud, Paul   68, 69, 70, 81
    and Pétain trial   81, 85, 86
Reyntjens, Professor Filip   211–2
Rhineland, German reoccupation of,
    1936   73
Ribbentrop, Joachim von   92, 95,
    104, 105, 136, 138, 158
Ribet, Maurice   72–3, 76
Richard II of England   25
Ries, István   147
Riom trial (1942, France)   60, 63–76,
    77, 78, 82, 86, 87, 88, 147, 155, 181, 182
    charges made   71
Robespierre, Maximilien   38, 41,
    42–3, 48–9
rogue states   15, 42
Röling, Bert   97, 169, 170, 173, 179
Roman, Petre   191
Romania   119ff, 143, 144, 149, 153, 155,
    158
    German WWII intervention in
        120, 121, 122, 124
    1940 annexations from   119
    reign of terror in   125
    trial of Ceauşescus   185ff
    trial of war criminals   122–3
    and Soviet Union   122ff
    war with Soviet Union   124, 126
    wartime activities in   124
Romashkin, P. S.   115
Rommel, Erwin   238
Roosevelt, Eleanor   75
Roosevelt, Franklin Delano   109, 110
Rosenberg, Alfred   95, 104
Rosenmark report   129
Rousseau, Jean-Jacques   51
Rowse, A.L.   24
RSHA (*Reichssicherheitshauptamt*)
    93–4
Rudenko, General   122
Ruge, Otto   100
Rump Parliament, England   23–4
Rumsfeld, Donald   241, 244
Russia   236

Ruthenia   148
Rwanda Patriotic Front (RPF)   207,
    208, 209, 211–12, 215–6, 219
Rwanda   13, 185, 207ff
    genocide in   209ff
    language   215–16
Ryti, Risto   157, 158–9

Saddam Hussein (Saddam Hussein
    Al-Majid)   15, 192, 237ff
    trial of   245–9
    charges against   246
    compared to Milošević trial   244
    culpability inferred by court   247
    legality of trial   242–3
    death sentence   248–9
Sadr, Moqtadr al-   249
Saint-Just, Louis Antoine Léon de
    41, 42, 48–9
Salamon, Mgr Louis Sifferin de   40
Sanson, Charles-Henri   50
Săracu, Dumitru   123
Sauckel, Fritz   104, 106
Sayre, Francis B.   168
scapegoat, concept of   31, 255
Scavenius, Eric   97
Schacht, Hjalmar   104, 105
Scheers, Johan   217–18
Scheffer, David   223, 224
Schirach, Baldur von   104
Schmitt, Carl   35, 257
Scudder, Henry   32
secularism, rise of   21, 31
Securitate, Romania   192
self-determination, right to   227
Serbia   151, 223, 226, 228
    'Greater Serbia' concept   136, 230,
        231, 234, 253
Šešelj, Vojislav   229, 234
Seyss-Inquart, Arthur   104
Shawcross, Sir Hartley   117
Shea, Jamie   224–5
Shigemitsu, Mamoru   164
Sierra Leone, Special Court in (est
    1996)   13, 210, 244
Simeon, Tsar of Bulgaria   153

Sions Memento, and God's Alarum
(Cheynell) 33
Slánský, Rudolf 141
Slovakia (1939–45) 129, 135, 145
  Slovak National Council 131, 135,
    140
  Slovak National Uprising 136
  Slovak nationalism 134, 137–8,
    138–9
  Slovak People's Party 134, 135, 138
  WWII declaration of
    independence 134, 135, 138
  see also Czechoslovakia, Mgr Tiso
Slovak-Yugoslav Friendship Society
  141
Slovenia 232
Small Retribution Decree,
  Czechoslovakia 130
Smallholders' Party, Hungary 151
Smid, Martin 186–7, 188
Smith, F.E. 55
social contract 28
Socialist Unity Party (East Germany)
  195, 203
societies, pre-modern 35, 41
  modern 35
Solem, Judge Erik 98, 99
Son Sen 17
Souldiers Catechisme, The 23, 32
sovereign immunity 180, sovereigns
  and the law 26–8
sovereignty 64
  and international law 196
  nature of 27
  sovereignty of courts 28
  theory of 27
Soviet Union 58, 83, 91, 92, 109, 112,
  113–14, 131, 136, 187, 188
  Bolshevik revolution 191
  staged trials, 1930s 58
  Nazi-Soviet Pact 80
  German invasion 113
  attacks on Eastern European states
    in WWII 116
  Katyn 116, 117

  invasion of Poland, WWII 116,
    149
  invasion of Romania 119, 121ff,
    124, 125
  and Nuremberg trials 104, 111,
    112, 113
  and Eastern Europe post WWII
    129
  influence in Czechoslovakia 129,
    132
  and events of 1989 186, 188, 189,
    190
  collapse of 195
  and Bulgaria 153, 155
  and Czechoslovakia 132
  and East Germany 202, 205
  and Finland 116, 157, 158–9
  and Greece 159
  and Hungary 149
  and Japan 165–6, 167
  and Romania 120, 121, 124, 153,
    189
  post-WWII intervention in Eastern
    Europe 119ff, 129ff
  reform rule in 188, 195
  Tokyo trials 165–6, 173
  trial of Germany for war crimes
    113–14
Spain 13, 38, 86, 199
  civil war 92
special tribunals and sovereigns 17
Speer, Albert 104, 106
Spoel, Tjarda Eduard van der 218
Srebrenica massacre, Bosnia 229
Stalin, Joseph 92, 101, 112, 113, 114,
  116, 120, 129, 154
  Stalinism 59, 123, 125, 131
Stanculescu, General Victor 191
Stang, Emil 101
Stasi 196
states:
  criminalising acts of state 113
  extent of legal jurisdiction 14, 15
  and law on conspiracy 254
  modern states 28

overriding of national sovereignty
14–15, 27
and regime trials   251–3, 255
and religious authority   21–2
social contract   16
state power   28
Stimson, Henry L.   110
Stoican, Vasile   124
Stoph, Willi   196, 198
Stratigos, General Xenophon   59
Stratos, Nikolaios   59, 61
Strauss, Franz-Josef   202
Streicher, Julius   104, 105, 121
Streletz, General Fritz   196, 203–4,
205
Stülpnagel, Major Otto von   57
Stürmer, Der   105
Sudan   15
Sudetenland   129, 133
supra-national institutions   13
jurisdiction   14
Supreme Court of Justice, France
(1940)   65–6, 67, 68, 69, 70
Svoboda, Ludvík   140
Sweden   158
Szálasi, Ferenc   144, 148, 150, 151, 152
Sztójay, General Döme   143, 148,
150–1

Tadić, Duško   229
Takayanagi, Kenzo   166
Talabani, Jalal   243
Tanaka, Giichi   168
Tanić, Ratomir   231
Tanjug   187, 188
Tanner, Väinö   157
Tanzania   209
Tass   188
Taylor, Charles   13, 210
Taylor, Telford   106, 117
Tennis Court Oath (French
Revolution)   37
Terboven, Josef   93, 94, 99
Thaci, Hashim   224
theology and politics   35, 225–6

theory of criminal liability   229, 230,
246
Theotokis, Nikolaios   59, 61
Thionville, Merlin de   42
Third International   92, 101
Thirty Years' War, Germany   21
Thorez, Maurice   80
Tikriti, Barzan al-   248
Timişoara, events of 1989 in   187, 188,
189, 192
Tirpitz, Admiral Alfred von   57
Tiso, Monsignor Jozef   129, 131, 134ff,
172
charges against   136ff
and Germany   137–8, 139
nationalism of   137–8
and Nazism   138–9
political beliefs   138–9
Tissier, Pierre   67
Tito, Josip   151, 153
campaign against Titoism   125,
141, 151
Ţiulescu, Constantin   123
Togliatti, Palmiro   120
Tojo, Hideki   163–4, 165
Tökes, László   187
Tokyo Charter   164
Tokyo Trials (International Military
Tribunal for the Far East)   97,
163ff, 214, 253
compared to Nuremberg Trials
163, 164
historical background to trials
168, 169]
innovations of   115, 167–8
states participating   165
as victors' justice   170, 171
Tomlinson, Colonel   24
Tomov, Judge Plamen   156
torture   13, 14
Trainin, Aron Naumovich   112, 113,
114
Transitional Justice Group (US)
241, 242
'transitional justice'   65, 131, 147, 175
in South America   180–4

Transylvania   119
treason   16, 18, 19, 256
  Bokassa and   178, 180
  Charles I and   25, 27, 29
  France   67, 77, 78, 79, 81, 83, 85,
    87, 88
  heads of state and   27, 77, 180
  Erich Honecker   195
  Greece   176, 177
  Hungary   152
  in Norway   91, 95, 96–7, 98, 101
  Romania   123
  Slovakia   136, 139, 140, 150
  post-World War I   60
  see also Quisling
Treaties of Westphalia (1648)   21,
  108, 237
Treaty of Eternal Friendship with
  Yugoslavia (Hungary)   148
Treaty of Lausanne (1923)   53
Treaty of Sèvres   53
Treaty of Trianon   151
Treaty of Versailles   55, 143, 151, 166,
  167
  war guilt clause   43, 108
Trial of God, The (Wiesel)   226
Trial of the Six (Greece, 1922)
  59–61, 63
trials in absentia   17–18, 53, 235
trials in The Bible   18
Tronchet, François-Denis   46
Tronchu, Charles   86
Trotsky, Leon   25, 58, 92, 101, 112
Tsolakoglou, Giorgios   160
Tuka, Vojtech   136, 139
Turkey   52–3, Ottoman   52–3
  Greek intervention post WWI   53
  nationalism in   53
Tutsis   207ff
tyrants   16

Uganda   208
Ulbricht, Walter   195, 205
Ullmann, Vilhelm   100
United Kingdom   56, 91, 92, 109, 110,
  158, 171

attack on French fleet (1940)   111
  and Iraq war   237, 238
  and Nuremberg trials   104
  planned occupation of Norway
    98, 99, 111
United Nations   109, 121, 210
  banning use of force in
    international relations   237
  Charter   239
  Convention on Genocide (1948)
    212, 216
  Human Rights Commission/
    Committee   182, 184, 248
  resolutions on Iraq   238–9
  and Rwanda   207, 209, 218
United Nations Covenant on Civil
  and Political Rights   210
United Nations Security Council
  14, 15, 200, 210, 225, 237, 238, 256
United Nations War Crimes
  Commission   113
United States   14, 56, 57, 108, 109, 110,
  165, 177, 208, 210, 237
  and Cold War   167
  and foreign policy   109, 110
  and Iraq war   237, 238ff
  and Japan   167, 172–3
  and Nuremberg trials   104, 108
  and Treaty of Versailles   108
  and Yugoslavia   225, 226
Universal Declaration of Human
  Rights   108
universalism, concept of   51
Universism   102

Vaclavnik, General Milan   186
Vance, Cyrus   226
Vance-Owen peace plan   226
Vasiliu, Constantin   124, 127
Vasiljević, Alexander   232
Vasiljković, Captain Dragan   233
Vatican   139
Veesenmayer, Edmund   150–1
Venizelos, Eleftherios   59, 60
Vergniaud, Pierre   38

victor's justice   17, 19, 55, 103, 117, 118,
    133, 149, 170, 171, 211, 212, 244
Videla, Lt-General Jorge   181, 182,
    183, 184
Viet Minh   172
Vietnam War   203
Viola, Lt-General Roberto   181, 183,
    183, 184
violence, collective acts of   31
Voiculescu, Gelu Voican   191
Voitinovici, Alexandru   123
Vyshinskii, Andrei Yanuarevich   113,
    114, 115–16, 117, 120–1, 124

*Wahrheit über die deutschen
    Kriegsverbrechen, Die*   57
Wall Street Crash (1929)   71
War Crimes Chamber of the Court of
    Bosnia and Herzegovina   244
war   47, 51, 170, 237, 243, 253
    aggressive war, concept of   97,
        107, 118, 165, 166, 170, 171, 211, 239
    and accountability   253–4
    concept of iustus hostis   51
    conventions on conduct of war
        52
    crime of declaring war   55, 66, 73,
        75, 88, 108, 109, 243
    criminalization of war   52, 109, 173
    definition of war   110
    distinction between private
        criminal acts and public acts of
        war   253, 254
    just war concept   33, 108, 226
    legality of war   109, unjustifiable
        war   107, 108
    nature of war   52, 254–5
    Nuremberg trial and   107ff
    political trials and war   252
    propaganda   52, 223
    public nature of war   253
    reasons for war   14, 15, 239–40
    religious wars, 17th century   21, 23
    right to wage war   54–5
    starting wars, responsibility for
        55

UN and use of force   237, 239
war crimes   23, 29, 54, 55, 57, 108,
    114, 115, 122, 123, 126, 146, 154, 157,
    163, 164, 165, 172, 196, 214, 230,
    242, 254, 256
war crimes trials   19, 52, 53, 59, 63,
    77, 96, 97, 107ff, 125, 148ff, 153ff,
    198, 252
war criminals   57, 144, 145, 146,
    153, 157, 167, 207, 221, 227, 232
war guilt concept   43, 51, 54, 72, 75
    see also Cold War, laws of war,
        Nuremberg Trials, Riom
        Trial, Tokyo Trials, Treaty of
        Westphalia, Trial of the Six,
        World War I, World War II
war on terror   15, 181, 190, 249
Warsaw Pact   186, 187, 188, 196, 201
weapons of mass destruction (WMD)
    225, 237–8, 240
Webb, Sir William   165, 167, 169
Wesel, Uwe   198
Wehrmacht   104
Wentworth, Thomas, Earl of Strafford
    23
Weygand, Maxime   81, 84, 86–7
Why We Fight (Capra)   168
Wiesel, Elie   225–6
Wilde, Oscar   19
Wilhelm II, Kaiser of Germany   52,
    53, 54–5, 56, 57, 107, 108, 166, 172,
    186, 203, 214
Williams, Bernard   182
Wilson, President Woodrow   54, 55,
    57–8
Winkelmann, Otto   150
Winter War, Finland-Soviet Union
    158
witnesses, anonymous, use of   215,
    232, 233, 248
World War I   43, 52, 64, 133, 172
    German activities against British
        53–4
    German armistice   87
    and changing nature of laws of
        war   52

World War II   16, 18, 27, 63, 143, 198
  post-WWII trials   18, 103ff, 163ff,
    175ff, 175, 221
  see also Nuremberg Trials, Tokyo
  Trials
  post WWII international system
    237
  see also United Nations

Yalta Conference (1945)   114, 165
Yamashita, General Tomoyuki   167,
  182
Yeltsin, Boris   195
Yugoslav National Army   228, 231
Yugoslavia   13, 15, 136, 148, 149, 155,
  210, 221ff
  anti-Yugoslav campaign   151

war of dissolution   228
regime change in   227
conspiracy theories   231
see also ICTY, Slobodan
  Milošević, NATO

Žabkay, Ernest   136, 141
Zaire   see Congo, Democratic
  Republic of
Zervas, Napoleon   160
Zhdanov, Andrei Alexandrovich   157,
  159
Zhivkov, Todor   186
Zinoviev, Grigori   111
Zoitakis, George   176, 177
Zubaidi, Adil Mohammad Abbas
  246